School Days, Rule Days

School Days, Rule Days

The Legalization and Regulation of Education

Edited by
DAVID L. KIRP
and
DONALD N. JENSEN

The Falmer Press
(A member of the Taylor & Francis Group)
Philadelphia and London

UK The Falmer Press, Falmer House, Barcombe, Lewes, East Sussex, BN8 5DL

USA The Falmer Press, Taylor & Francis Inc., 242 Cherry Street, Philadelphia, PA 19106-1906

First published 1986

Library of Congress Cataloging in Publication Data

Main entry under title:

School days, rule days.

Includes bibliographies and index.
1. Educational law and legislation—United States—Addresses, essays, lectures. 2. Education and state—United States—Addresses, essays, lectures. I. Kirp, David L.
KF4119.A2S29 1985 344.73′071 85-1537
ISBN 1-85000-017-4 347.30471
ISBN 1-85000-018-2 (pbk.)

Jacket design by Caroline Archer

Typeset in 10/12 Caledonia by
Imago Publishing Ltd, Thame, Oxon.

Printed in Great Britain by Taylor & Francis (Printers) Ltd, Basingstoke

Contents

Introduction: The Fourth R: Reading, Writing, 'Rithmetic — and Rules

David L. Kirp
University of California, Berkeley

I

During the past quarter of a century, the governance of American schools has been remade, even transformed. Local control of policy was the historic watchword — the 'Battle Hymn of the Republic,' as a state school administrator put it[1] — and that control was essentially political and professional, not legal, in character. Within local communities, dominance over decision-making was uneasily shared by lay boards of education and educational professionals. Tussles over the distinction between questions of policy (the province of the governing board) and questions of practice (properly the terrain of the educators) were frequent events.[2] State departments of education generally did little more than distribute aid according to a legislatively specified formula and provide modest technical assistance. The federal impress on education was almost undetectable. As late as 1960, the national education budget amounted to just half a billion dollars, administered by an Office of Education lacking both the taste and the talent for leadership. Neither the state nor the federal courts played a significant part in shaping school affairs. Judges confined their attention to issues of liability for mishaps in the chemistry laboratory and to matters of form in school contracts. The more momentous decisions were for others to reach.[3]

Centralization and legalization mark the two most noteworthy changes in this system of governance, and it is to these interrelated developments that the essays in this volume speak. The Supreme Court's 1954 decision in *Brown v. Board of Education*[4] underlies both changes. Most obviously, *Brown* put the courts centrally in the education policy business. Racial inequalities stemming from legally imposed segregation of students lay at the heart of the Court's concern, but the justices' opinion reached beyond race, potentially enveloping within the judicial net all questions of equity in public schooling. The Court in *Brown* spoke of the provision of education as the most critical function of state and local government, and wondered aloud whether any child deprived of adequate schooling could hope to succeed in life. This judicial language opened the door to a host of other rights-seekers. The handicapped, the non-English speaking, those living in poor school districts, and female students all saw in *Brown* the opportunity to convert the unfairness they suffered at the hands of politically-dominated and localist school systems into constitutional wrongs. They took advantage of that opportunity by flooding the courts with lawsuits.[5]

The elaboration of substantive rights embodies one element of legalization. The development of procedural protections — the right to formal review of official decisions — provides the other. Although English courts had insisted as early as the eighteenth century that a university student receive a hearing before being dismissed, that idea never took root in the United States, where protections accorded to students subject to school discipline compared unfavorably with those provided to pickpockets.[6] Like other government services, schooling was regarded as a privilege, not a right, and so could be denied at the discretion of responsible public officials. But in a series of 1960s decisions concerning welfare and public employment, the Supreme Court thoroughly savaged the distinction between rights and privileges. The extension of procedural protection to education was an obvious next step, taken by lower courts in the 1960s and subsequently affirmed by the Supreme Court in *Goss v. Lopez.*[7] Procedures originally developed in the context of criminal justice (concerning the right to notice, a statement of charges, an impartial hearing officer, and the like) were adapted to the setting of the school. And although proceduralism was originally regarded as the remedy for abuses of official sanctioning authority, it also became part of the arsenal of those seeking substantive rights. The handicapped in particular were able to obtain procedural protections of their entitlement to an 'appropriate' education, first from the federal courts and subsequently from Congress. Legalization thus became not just a judicial norm but also part of the regulatory regime.[8]

As this last example suggests, legalization and centralization proceeded apace and sometimes in tandem. One reason why Washington asserted greater authority over schooling was to turn the aspirations of the *Brown* decision into a functioning reality, since on its own the judiciary could not impose its understanding of racial justice on recalcitrant Southern school districts.[9] Beginning with the passage of the Civil Rights Act in 1964, the extent of federal intervention into the racial practices of Southern school districts was so substantial as to constitute a second Reconstruction.[10] Nor could questions about race be hived off from broader issues of education, since racial concerns insinuate themselves into seemingly every aspect of a school system, from teacher recruitment to the system of elections for school board members, from extra-curricular activities to ability grouping. Regulation in the name of racial justice thus leads to regulation more generally.

While race mattered greatly, Washington did not assume increased responsibility for education primarily to rid public schools of the taint of racism. A national government strongly committed to education as 'the answer to all our national problems,'[11] particularly those problems having to do with the educational failure of poor children, sought a significant role in molding educational policy.[12] Beginning in the mid-1960s, the poor and educationally disadvantaged, the handicapped, the limited-English-speaking, and other traditional have-not groups became a national interest. From less than half a billion dollars in 1960, the federal primary and secondary education budget grew to more than nine billion dollars in two decades.[13]

Centralization begat regulation. Washington did not merely raise and distribute funds, but instead sought to use scarce dollars to influence the course of educational policy, relying heavily on regulation to achieve its ends.[14] Money came with strings attached; and sometimes, as with bilingual education, requirements were laid on even when no funds were made available. The federal program rules fairly bristle with do's and don'ts: a thousand pages of regulations in 1977, as compared with just twelve pages a dozen years earlier, tells the tale. The federal strategy stressed compliance with federal standards which, as with compensatory education, were designed to assure that expenditures satisfy federal bookkeeping requirements,[15] or more ambitiously, as with bilingual education aid, that the substance of local programs matches Washington's expectations.

The new regulations were rooted in distrust of the motives and the capacity of local and school officials: 'We treated every state as if it were Mississippi,' Congressman Albert Quie remarked. Early scandals concerning expenditures of compensatory education funds for such implausible items as carpeting and air-conditioning a superintendent's office and even a fire engine fueled this suspicion.[16] Regulation came increasingly to entail control, and supervision displaced the encouragement and assistance that had formed part of the initial federal strategy. At the state level, parallel bureaucracies sprung up to administer the federal programs as well as new state initiatives. Over time, these state officials grew to share Washington's belief in the necessity for stressing compliance, as distinguished from assistance.[17] Regulation thus grew apace, at both the federal and state levels.

II

This volume both looks back over this recent governance history and points ahead to future policy courses. It appears at an apt moment in history. Just as the quarter-century since *Brown* marked a revolution in modes of education governance, the 1980s have witnessed the beginnings of a counterrevolution in full swing. The Reagan administration, eager to return responsibility for education to the state and local levels, has condemned the recent federal presence as officious intermeddling. Because Washington lacks both the competence to set requirements and the capacity to carry them out, the argument runs, it should only provide education support (at levels markedly lower than those previously fixed), leaving decision making to those with a more nuanced understanding of the issues.

The increase in legalization has also slowed perceptibly if less dramatically. The Supreme Court has not extended the reach of *Brown* to recognize a new generation of would-be holders of rights, but instead has sought to rein in the scope of that opinion. In *San Antonio Independent School District v. Rodriguez*,[18] the Court upheld against constitutional attack a state school financing system which resulted in wide inequities among districts; in *Milliken v. Bradley*,[19] the justices severely constrained the possibility of yoking city and suburban districts to overcome segregation; and in *Halderman v. Pennhurst State School and Hospital*,[20] the Court narrowly construed the Education for All Handicapped Children Act, preserving the authority of states to institutionalize handicapped youngsters. Although federal district courts have continued to recast school district policies in an attempt to undo the deep-rooted impress of segregation, Congress has sporadically mounted challenges to the judiciary's authority in this realm.

In the schools as well as in the courts, unhappiness with the idea of legalization is often heard. Imposing procedural requirements on student discipline practice potentially undermines the fragile authority of those who teach and administer in the school, some argue.[21] The due process entitlements of handicapped youngsters are scored as too expensive, subject to abuse by well-off parents seeking a private education at public expense, and a source of tension between parents and teachers who instead should work in tandem on behalf of the child.[22]

All issues of policy, aside from those left to the market, may be defined in one of four ways: as suitably left to professional expertise, as properly the province of bureaucratic norms, as fit for resolution in the political arena, or as giving rise to legal rights.[23] This four-wheeled cart of policy is inherently subject to wobble and strain, since these different modes of definition press for different forms of policy resolution. That tension may best be regarded not as a cause for concern but as a measure of a healthy governance system. Trouble arises when one of these contending understandings becomes too dominant. Legalization and bureaucratic control (understood here as centralized authority) clearly counted for too little in the educational policy calculus prior to *Brown*, and the claims of have-nots consequently got short shrift. Public education was at risk of failing in its nineteenth-century promise to establish a 'single educational ladder'[24] that all might equally climb.

The critics of legalization and regulation present a different and disquieting concern. Have rights-mindedness and rule-mindedness gone too far? Has the public school system been impaired by the loss of legitimacy that attends denial of authority to the policy and denial of respect to professional judgment? We need more fully to comprehend the working of legalization and regulation in order to sort through these criticisms.

III

Almost a century and a half ago, Alexis de Tocqueville noted the penchant of Americans for converting political issues into questions of law.[25] Like so many of Tocqueville's observations, this one has grown truer with time. The 'legalization revolution' has been much remarked, variously to describe,[26] to celebrate,[27] or to condemn[28] the phenomenon. We are even said to suffer from 'hyperlexis' — the disease of 'too much law' that has 'overloaded' all 'legal circuits.'[29]

There is a certain ahistorical quality to these comments. Henry Maine, writing of the displacement, several millenia ago, of status by contract as the basis of public relationships, was speaking of a legalization 'revolution,' even if he was not given to such rhetorical flourishes.[30] Pushing the clock back even further, one wonders how Hammurabi's Babylonian subjects responded to that first great codification of rights and responsibilities, eighteen centuries before the Christian era.

If legalization is not new, though, reliance on the courts and on court-like mechanisms to secure rights, in a system of decision committed to offering reasons for its conclusions, has become sufficiently important to be fairly described as a master trend of modern social change. Proposed explanations of this trend abound: the impoverishment of politics; the growth of bureaucratic organizations which deprive individuals of an active stake in decisions shaping their own lives; distrust — or more globally, delegitimation — of traditional sources of authority; a growing lack of consensus concerning societal norms; the attenuation of community; the emergence of a sizable public law bar eager to litigate broad policy concerns; and the willingness of judges to hear complaints that earlier would have been dismissed as not fit for judicial review (or as just silly). Legalization turns out to be a classically overdetermined enterprise, whose root causes are as hard to specify as are those of modernization itself.[31]

The appeal of legalization in the context of education is easy to understand. Education has historically been treated as a 'national religion,'[32] the promised panacea for all our social ills. Blacks, the poor, and immigrants have been particularly faithful parishioners, for education is seen as representing the royal road to economic security and inclusion in the political order. Yet the repeated failure of education to make good on this promise breeds frustration; persisting inequality grows less and less acceptable. The institutions of schooling are themselves both visible (and hence handy targets) and vulnerable. The technology of education is weak, the boundaries of educational organizations are loose and poorly defended, and the system of school governance is fractious and fragile. Seeking vindication through law thus seems terribly important and readily accomplishable.

The promise of legalization is great. Reliance on rules betokens a principled enterprise in which economic or political power counts for far less than in other arenas.[33] Normative judgments of the good society embodied in the Fourteenth Amendment's commands to equal protection and procedural fairness become governing standards. The idea of rights gives pride of place to the fundamental claims of persons to equal concern and respect in the design of political institutions, counterbalancing the utilitarian tendency to balance political interests and preferences.[34] That legal institutions rely on reasons supplied by the parties in public colloquy offers both a means to participate in decisions that affect one's life and a basis for review of decisions, hence a check on arbitrary official action.[35]

At a time when critics of legalization are more vociferous than defenders — a balance that the papers included in this volume reflect — it bears remarking that the promise of legalization has been greatly fulfilled. The history of America generally and of the public schools in particular may be told as a tale of progressive inclusion in the polity, and in that telling the forms and values of law have a central place.[36] The pathologies of legalization reflect the darker side of the aspiration. From means, rules may become ends in themselves, cut loose from the principled considerations that were their initial impetus. When this occurs, legalization degenerates into legalism.[37] To put the matter somewhat differently, the language of rights camouflages what are better phrased as political claims. The very idea of rights is diminished in stature when the mantle of law protects those whose injuries are slight or speculative, or affords too much protection for those whose most ambitious hopes should be tested in the political and economic markets. Legal reasoning sometimes fails to shed light on the task of organizational redesign, an essential element of suits involving institutional reform. Hearings themselves may merely harden antagonisms without reaching useful resolution.

In any area subject to legalization, such as education, both the strengths and the debilities of the phenomenon are evident. How might things be otherwise, given what we know about the inherently problematic nature of changing the ways public institutions do business? The useful policy question is not whether legalization is perfect but whether it represents a relative good, one which on balance promotes openness of process and fairness and efficiency in outcome. That question invites a contingent response, for instance, diminishes the possibility of arbitrary action but may also undermine the very best decisions, for these inevitably rest on discretion. Whether the benefits of these procedures outweigh the costs turns on the frequency and the systemic consequences of exceptional and arbitrary decisions, factors which will vary both with the institution and the substantive concern. To take a somewhat different example: creating legal rights for those, such as the handicapped, who have been excluded from the educational system usefully jolts the enterprise but may also spark inefficiencies and resentments. Such prods, though needed from time to time, cannot be constantly applied without doing institutional damage. Perhaps political judgments and professional expertise should hold sway once basic rights (an admittedly fuzzy notion) have been assured.

Efforts to implement the norms of law offer an instructive reminder that the dream of a centralized and rationally governed society managed by the contemporary equivalent of Plato's philosopher-king, which some political theorists and some lawyers fondly contemplate, is doomed to failure. The most interesting question is whether, over time, the values that inform the law can become suffused with the routine behavior of schools and other large organizations in the society, genuinely part of the ongoing official culture.

IV

Government regulation and legalization, its related development, is old news. Attempts by higher reaches of American government to influence the behavior of lower levels, whether through sanction or inducement — the working definition of regulation in education — form an indispensable part of a federal system of government. Yet, to an even greater extent than with legalization, regulation has assumed new and more noteworthy forms over time. Particularly since the 1960s, new (or newly-perceived) mischiefs have spawned innovations in the forms of government control. Although these undertakings extend well beyond education, they have influenced the mode of regulation in that domain, and so deserve attention.[38]

The newer approach to regulation differs from earlier efforts both in the substance of the rules and in the role of the state and local authorities in the design and enforcement of those rules. The entry and pricing policies of particular segments of the economy had been subject to public review since the establishment of the Interstate Commerce Commission in 1887. But with a few exceptions — the Food and Drug Administration's efforts, for instance — non-market activities of firms were disciplined by the market and private litigation, not regulated by government. This system began to break down as firms' behavior came to appear at once more prone to hazard and less susceptible to the conventional mechanisms of control. Prompted by blatant and visible mishaps, ranging from outbreaks of botulism to Three Mile Island and Love Canal, Washington has increasingly subjected worker safety, environmental hazard, hiring policies, and product fitness to official rule. It is widely argued that the public 'must have its own eyes and ears, an early warning system, and a corps of protectors free from the flaws of greed, miscalculation, and ignorance that made the market and private liability laws less than perfect deterrents.'[39]

The old regulatory regime had emphasized cooperation, both between the federal regulatory agencies and regulated industries and between Washington and those state agencies with similar mandates. But cooperation, the critics of that system declared, led not to a safer, cleaner, fairer world.[40] The enterprise of regulation was merely a symbolic activity of government, designed to keep citizens quiescent.[41] Discretion prompted only abuses of official power. This stance is consequently more adversarial in nature. Regulation entails the strict enforcement of rules by a corps of inspectors. Discovery of a violation automatically means sanctions, not solicitation of promises to do better in the future.

Because Washington could not (or at least would not) protect the populace from the hazards of toxic wastes and unsafe workplaces on its own, many of the regulatory initiatives of the past two decades have conscripted state and local government support: by one count, thirty federal laws adopted between 1964 and 1978 reached out to involve lower levels of government.[42] In the past, federal and state agencies worked in tandem on matters of shared interest, the federal government respecting state and local priorities and political concerns. But this, too, has changed with the press for more effective regulation. Statutes ranging from the Occupational Safety and Health Act and the National Environmental Protection Act to the Wholesome Poultry Products Act effectively hand the states their marching orders, turning them into 'little more than reluctant minions mandated to do the dirty work — to implement federal directives often distasteful at the local level.'[43] A variety of sanctions may be imposed on resistant states, including direct legal orders, fund cutoffs in one program for noncompliance with the demands of another (the Highway Beautification Act, for instance, denied highway construction money to states that failed to remove billboards), requirements spanning a range of federal programs (as with rules concerning racial discrimination and environmental protection), and federal preemption of responsibilities long assumed by the states (policing workplace safety, for example). This approach to regulation dramatically alters the pattern of relationships between levels of government. It challenges 'the very essence of federalism as a noncentralized system of separate legal jurisdictions, and instead relies upon a unitary vision involving hierarchically related central and peripheral units.'[44] The new regulation thus pushes federalism perilously close to federalization.

As even a cursory glance through the volumes of the Code of Federal Regulations reveals, rules spawn more rules. External pressures provide part of the explanation. Newly-galvanized interest groups and their allies in Congress, prone to characterize social harms 'as violations of moral Rights, automatically to be converted into protectable legal rights,'[45] have sought to impose government authority on previously uncharted private domains. The effect of this, as James Q. Wilson points out, is to give 'formal bureaucratic recognition to the emergence of distinctive interests in a diversifying economy'[46] and, one might add, a diversifying society. The process of regulation itself encourages the tendency to plug loopholes, apparent evasions of existing rules, with new rules. And boundaries are hard to set when the substance of rules is as evanescent and open-ended as with civil rights concerns. The rule-making organizations play an active part in this expansion too, whether from an imperialist tendency to search out new worlds to conquer or, conversely, from a desire to minimize the risk of public embarrassment by covering their flanks.[47] As with the increasing use of the forms and instruments of law, government regulation seems an inevitable and essential element of a structurally complex society.

Yet if regulation in some forms seems here to stay, the particulars of regulation have caused no end of consternation. A decade or so ago, the widespread concern was to make regulation more effective by broadening its reach and deepening its impress. If the latest generation of critics is right, that campaign succeeded all too well, for it is the excesses of regulation that now arouse most concern. *The New York Times*, that bellwether of centrist sentiment, observes that:

> Local governments are feeling put upon by Washington. Each new day seems to bring some new directive from Congress, the courts or the bureaucrats: cities must make public buildings accessible to the handicapped, states must extend unemployment compensation to municipal and county workers, and on and on. The mandates are piling up so fast that liberal governors and mayors are enrolling in a cause once pressed only by archconservatives.[48]

Some of this unhappiness has merely to do with 'the strains of propinquity,'[49] but other concerns are more serious. One worry speaks to the impact of regulation on political choices. The growth of regulation removes issues from democratic control, turning them over to bureaucrats who are only remotely and directly subject to outside check, thus producing 'a government of cartels and clients.'[50] Other objections have to do with how regulation works in practice. The new rules are held to be just too expensive: the 1983 Clean Water Act standards, for instance, may cost $120 billion to implement. Regulations are also scored as inflexible. Why, for instance, should Washington dictate the particulars of bilingual education?[51]

The regulations are further said to be inattentive to the calculus of efficiency, ignoring nice calibrations of costs and benefits; inconsistent in interpretation across agencies; too intrusive in specifying not only what goals localities must reach but exactly how they must behave; and ultimately ineffective. 'The mounting paperwork and red tape, the mandated expenditures, the federal intrusions into local decision making (have not) reaped commensurate benefits in the quality of human life,' their critics say.[52] Some alternate strategy — either less regulation or a very different strategy of regulation — is deemed in order.[53]

The regulatory history in education has been less dramatic in other fields. Although the federal government has supported education since the Northwest Ordinance of 1784, which made federally-held lands available for local schools, that aid was supposed to come without strings. The 1931 report of the Advisory Committee on Education urged that this tradition be maintained. It was fine for Washington to support schools, the report declared, so long as the law 'does not delegate to the Federal Government any control of the social purpose and specific processes of education.'[54] Although the New Deal set up numerous education programs, these left the state and local education establishments unthreatened. The federal effort was work- and welfare-oriented, a nominal spin-off of relief activities which did not compete with the mission of the schools. The very absence of a bureaucracy committed to pursuing an educational reform agenda assured that this undertaking would leave no immediate legacy.[55]

As already noted, the education initiatives of the 1960s were accompanied by a far more activist federal presence. But when compared with federal activities in, say, occupational safety, Washington's role has been more modest. Although the degree of discretion available to local school officials varies with the particulars of the program, educators have far more room to maneuver than their counterparts in private industry. There is a greater tendency to rely on school systems to generate their own processes of decision, rather than imposing a single approach. Punishments for violations of federal rules are less severe in character and less frequently meted out.

There are, however, parallels to be drawn between social regulation generally and regulation in education.[56] In education as elsewhere, critics charge, rulemakers have often ignored the cost consequences of their requirements. New burdens have been placed on states and localities, paying little heed to either the financial implications or the cost-effectiveness of these rules: standards concerning the handicapped and the limited-English-speaking are singled out as prime offenders in this regard. The tendency to inflexibility is evident in Washington's habit of imposing national norms, rather than allowing states to adopt more nuanced approaches to a particular issue: in drafting procedures for resolving disputes over the appropriate education of the handicapped, for example, existing state laws with the same aim were disregarded. Although education regulations more typically mandate procedures than outcomes, the possibility that the costs of those procedures (measured both in out-of-pocket expenditures and lost time) may be unreasonable has received little official notice, at least until recently. Most important, the critics assert, this system of regulation has generated a climate of mutual distrust, contributing to the demoralization of America's public schools.

These criticisms have provoked demands for a massive deregulation of education, as if schooling and trucking were indistinguishable activities in terms of government's proper role.[57] Yet for a number of critical reasons, that approach may misfire. For one thing, to the extent that regulation represents a response to the increasing complexity of managing education in this country, at all levels, deregulation won't help. Reducing the number and specificity of rules won't keep organized interests from pressing their views on government, nor will it simplify decision making. Indeed, fewer and more general regulations will increase ambiguity and heighten tensions. The problem of complexity, which rules are intended to address, won't disappear but will just emerge someplace else, as school officials struggle to adjust to a newly uncertain world.

For another thing, the critique oversimplifies the historical record. It ignores a critical distinction between rules advanced in the service of redistributive programs, aimed at getting federal dollars to the have-nots, and rules accompanying grants designed to encourage school system development, as with aid to the gifted, vocational education, or impact aid. In terms of regulatory detail, differences between these types of programs are modest, but objections to rules governing the redistributive programs are really just a politically palatable way of questioning whether the have-nots deserve priority treatment. If Washington is to interest itself in the plight of the educationally least well off, some prescriptive imposition may well be necessary.

The case for elaborate federal policing, even on behalf of the have-nots, may no longer be so compelling, however, because of how Washington and lower-level officials have learned to manage their relationships. For its part, even before President Reagan took office, Washington had become more inclined to use the standards of law as a lever to negotiate and less habituated to imposing its will on lower reaches than was popularly supposed.[58] For their part, state and local administrators have increasingly identified the federal initiatives with their own priorities. As a result, there is much less tension between school officials and Washington bureaucrats than the demand for deregulation presupposes.[59] This historical learning offers yet another reason to temper the critique of education regulation: deregulation is, in this respect, a 1980s solution to a 1970s problem.

As with legalization, policy toward regulation concerns itself with the '"right" balance, or mix, between order and spontaneity, between rationality and impulsiveness.'[60] The point is not that regulation in education poses no cause for concern, but rather that concern should be properly focused on the particulars of regulation. Washington while not abdicating the field, should be less rule-minded and more subtle, supple, and flexible in its dealings with state and local officials, concerned more with aiding them as they adapt federal norms to local exigencies. This approach differs from much of present official policy and past practice. If it prevails, regulation would have less to do with rule enforcement and more to do with strengthening the capacity of others to educate effectively.

Rule enforcement has its place, particularly in safeguarding the stake of the have-nots; but even here, it may be that past federal initiatives have afforded these claimants sufficient clout within school organizations to make continuing federal enforcement less vital. Concerning other types of educational policy, what is called for is the elaboration of a shift in the federal role from sanctioner to supporter that, informally, has already begun. Washington can properly speak to the public purposes of education, specifying educational ends and not just processes. If it does so with clarity, it may help restore the legitimacy of a national role called into question by the Reagan Administration.[61] By stressing cooperative problem solving, rather than the command and control mode of regulation, the national government may also be able to 'repersonalize responsibility with the regulated organization,'[62] enabling school personnel to embrace the obligation to treat the interests of the young as if they were identical to their own, rather than acting from fear of criticism or sanction. Much regulation becomes self-regulation in such a world, with Washington offering information, aid and direction. Modesty, not policy abdication, is what is wanted.

V

Except to the ideologue or the willful oversimplifier, the choice between more or fewer rules, more or less law, is necessarily a matter of degree. Such 'how much' questions know no nice calibration. And the extent to which reliance on regulation or legalization is sensible will vary with the circumstances. One wants to know how the claimants have fared under the existing policy regime; whether the suggested alternative will really improve their lot — and with what adverse consequences; and whether the capacity to coerce through law or regulation, a scarce resource, should be husbanded or expended in this instance. The right mix of policy strategies will differ for vocational education, racial discrimination, and the education of the handicapped. Moreover, the fact that the education system changes in response to policy ministration implies that strategies of external intervention, whether through regulation or law, do become outmoded. For that reason, it is unsurprising that the contributors to this volume reach different conclusions concerning the value of legalization and regulation in particular instances. It is these particulars that are crucial.

This volume addresses issues of *regulation*, which concern efforts of one level of government to control the behavior of another level, and issues of *legalization*, related to regulation, which entail establishing a system of decision committed to rules, trafficking in rights rather than preferences or interests, and justifying outcomes with reasons. These are terms of art, of course, and the essays stick to no single, hard-and-fast definitions. And although the volume separates regulation from legalization — maintaining a familiar line and making the sequence of papers a little more coherent — these are related concepts, as this Introduction suggests. Both, for instance, presume a degree of centralization and both customarily emphasize adherence to rules.

These papers grew out of a faculty seminar on Law, Governance and Schooling, sponsored by the Program on Law of the Institute for Research on Educational Finance and Governance at Stanford University that met from 1980 to 1982. That seminar did not completely bridge the differences in background and disciplines represented by the participants — students of law, politics, history, sociology, economics, and education were involved — but it did leave its imprint in terms of shared influences and common ideas. There are times when one wishes for a social science equivalent to Esperanto. Meanwhile, though, these efforts at finding common ground may be the best that can realistically be expected in multi-disciplinary ventures.

The volume begins with an effort to put regulation in historical perspective, with Paula Fass assessing why the federal government did not take on a significant responsibility for education in the New Deal. That paper notes the essential elements of a significant federal role — notably, the institutionalization of a national commitment to education and a willingness to confront the issue of racial equity — that speak not only to the New Deal but to the New Federalism as well. A paper by Paul Berman places issues of regulatory policy in theoretical context, contrasting a compliance orientation with a learning-centered approach. He considers those factors — organizational willingness and competence — that determine the impact of rules.

In a series of perspectives on the subject, Robert Kagan looks at regulation in a comparative fashion, shedding new light on regulation in the nominally different contexts of education and business. Ann Swidler and William Muir consider — in quite different ways — the cultural context of regulation: Swidler's interest is in the ways educators make sense of regulatory regimes. Muir's interest lies in the impact of regulation on teachers in the classroom. Eugene Bardach notes one unintended consequence of regulation, the creation of excessive paperwork which diverts administrators from the job of managing schools and school systems. Guy Benveniste's essay illustrates the pathologies of regulation, particularly the emphasis on rule-mindedness, in a paper that focuses on the education of the handicapped. Richard Elmore looks to the problem, William Clune to the strengths of the federal regulatory role in suggesting future policy directions.

The discussion of legalization also begins in an historical vein, with an essay by David Tyack that relates the changing role of law in governing schools over the past century-and-a-quarter. Lawrence Friedman zeroes in on part of that history, the law of student rights. John Meyer, whose paper really fuses legalization and regulation, fixes an organizational context for the role of law and rules in education. Deborah Rhode looks inside judicial decision-making, suggesting the relationship between issues of rights, on the one side, political and organizational concerns on the other.

Three case studies consider aspects of legalization in particular settings. Doris Fine examines the roles of a court and a special commission in shaping the policies of one city; Donald Jensen and Thomas Griffin look at the impact of legal rules on the way a state board of education functions. David Kirp and David Neal take up the education of the handicapped, looking not so much at rule-mindedness (Benveniste's concern), as at the impress of law-like norms and forms.[63]

In a concluding, future-oriented paper, David Kirp and Donald Jensen speculate about the continuing interrelationship between political preferences and legal rights, even under the New Federalism approach to educational policy: entitlements, they suggest, may clash with the political aspiration to reduce the federal role in education.

Most of these papers emphasize the defects of present arrangements. Yet they also recognize that regulation may sometimes be a good and needed thing — in securing financial accountability, for instance, or bringing about desegregation; that the present regulatory regime may be preferable to the politically likely alternatives; and that, as with paperwork or outsider participation in policy decisions, a course reform is sounder than policy abdication at the national level. They propose strategies for mixing and matching regulatory approaches to suit the circumstances of the case, strategic intervention by central government, greater participation by constituents in bending the rules to their will, more collegial and less adversarial relationships, and greater delegation of responsibility to lower levels of government.

These essays identify tensions in the system of governance, not panaceas. What is wanted turns out to be nothing less than a mode of decision-making responsive at once to national concerns and local variability; attentive to professional perceptions and political preferences; sensitive to the rights of the worst-off, yet resistant to the rigidities that accompany the degeneration of legality into legalism; and able to foster both compliance to rule and organizational adaptiveness. Each of these sets of wants embodies a tension, a balance hard to maintain. The policy puzzle is compounded further by the fact that these wants *all* must be maintained in equipoise, for pathologies in one realm — too much or not enough responsiveness to local wish, for instance — threaten the others.

Changes in how schools are governed sometimes matter in and of themselves, for we regard fidelity to law or attentiveness to popular preferences as ends as well as means of policy. Yet as John Dewey warned at the beginning of this century: 'It is easy to fall into the habit of regarding the mechanics of school organization and administration [and politics] as something comparatively external and indifferent to educational ideals.'[64] When how schools are run becomes an end in itself, policies get disconnected from outcomes, means from ends, and rules and structures from life in classrooms.

Governance reform also has a substantive aspiration: strengthening the schools' capacity to equip the young with those habits of mind needed to make sense of the contemporary world and to instill a commitment to the larger community, thus sustaining the public household. The nexus between the structure of education and the lives of children, taken up in a number of the papers,[65] seems at once plausible to intuit, devilishly difficult to grasp, and ultimately of deepest concern in framing proposals for reform. It stands as the next critical puzzle in assessing the impact of regulation and legalization on education.

Notes

1 Quoted in Murphy, J. (1973) 'The education bureaucracies implement novel policy: The politics of title 1 of ESEA 1965–72' in Sindler, A. (Ed.) *Politics and Policy in America*, 160 Boston, Little, Brown.

2 Martin, R. (1962) *Government and the Suburban School* 89, Syracuse, Syracuse University Press.

3 Compare Tyack, D. 'Toward a social history of law and public education,' in this volume.

4 347 U.S. 483 (1954).

5 See Kirp, D. (1977) 'Law, politics, and equal educational opportunity: The limits of judicial involvement,' 47 *Harvard Educational Review* p. 117. See generally Kirp, D. and Yudof, M. (Eds) (1982) *Educational Policy and the Law*, Chapters 5–7, Berkeley McCutchan.

6 See Seavey, W. (1957) 'Dismissal of students: "Due Process,"' 70 *Harvard Law*

Review 1406, 1407; FRIEDMAN, L. 'Limited monarchy: The rise and fall of student rights,' in this volume.

7 419 U.S. 565 (1975). See generally KIRP, D. (1976) 'Proceduralism and bureaucracy: Due process in the school setting,' 28 *Stanford Law Review* 841.

8 See NEAL, D. and KIRP, D. 'The legalization of special education,' in this volume.

9 See KIRP, D. (1982) *Just Schools: The Idea of Racial Equality in American Education*, Chapter 4, Berkeley, University of California Press.

10 See ORFIELD, G. (1969) *The Reconstruction of Southern Education*, New York, John Wiley; RADIN, B. (1977) *Implementation change and the Federal Bureaucracy: School Desegregation Policy in HEW, 1964–1968*. New York, Teachers College Press.

11 Quoted in PERKINSON, H. (1968) *The Imperfect Panacea: American Faith in Education, 1865–1965* at i, New York, Random House.

12 Compare FASS, P. 'The New Deal: Anticipating a federal education policy,' in this volume.

13 KIRST, M. (1981) 'Loss of support for public secondary schools: Some causes and solutions,' 110 *Daedalus* p. 45; see KIRP, D.L. (1982) 'Education: Can the Democrats offer both equity and excellence?', *The New Republic*, 31 March.

14 See BERMAN, P. 'From compliance to learning: Implementing federal education reform,' in this volume.

15 KIRST, M. and JUNG, R. (1980) 'The utility of a longitudinal approach in assessing implementation: A thirteen year view of title I, ESEA,' *Education Evaluation and Policy Analysis*, 5, September, pp. 17–34.

16 See, for example, NAACP Legal Defense and Education Fund, Inc., (1969) *Title I ESEA: Is It Helping Poor Children?*, Washington, DC, NAACP Legal Defense and Education Fund.

17 MURPHY, J. (1981) 'The paradox of state government reform,' 64 *Public Interest* 124, Summer; ELMORE, R. and MCLAUGHLIN, M. (1982) 'Strategy choice in federal education policy: The compliance-assistance tradeoff,' in LIEBERMAN, A. and MCLAUGHLIN, M. (Eds), *Policy Making in Education, 81st Yearbook of the National Society for Study of Education* Chicago, University of Chicago Press.

18 411 U.S. 1, 98 (1973).

19 418 U.S. 717 (1974).

20 101 S. Ct. 82 (1981).

21 See MUIR, W.K. Jr., 'Teachers' regulation of the classroom,' in this volume.

22 See, e.g. WEATHERLY, R. (1979) *Reforming Special Education: Policy Implementation from State Level to Street Level* Cambridge, MIT Press; HASSELL, C. (1981) *A Study of the Consequences of Excessive Legal Intervention on the Local Implementation of PL94–142* unpublished Ph.D. dissertation, University of California, Berkeley, and San Francisco State University.

23 See KIRP, D.L. (1982) 'Professionalization as a policy choice: British special education in comparative perspective,' 34 *World Politics* 137.

24 BARNARD, H. (1931) in BRUBACHER, J.S. (Ed.) *Henry Barnard on Education* 96, New York, McGraw Hill, quoted in BESTOR, A. (1953) *Educational Wastelands: The Retreat from Learning in our Public Schools* 26, Urbana, University of Illinois Press.

25 This section draws heavily on a presentation by Philip Selznick to the Berkeley-Stanford Faculty Seminar on Law, Governance, and Education, October 1980.

26 See, e.g., GROSSMAN, J. and SARAT, A. (1975) 'Litigation in the federal courts: A comparative perspective,' 9 *Law and Society Review* 321; FRIEDMAN, L. (1980) 'The six million dollar man: litigation and rights consciousness in modern America,' 39 *Maryland Law Review* 661.

27 See, e.g., JOHNSON, E. (1974) *Justice and Reform* New York, Russell Sage Foundation; CAHN, E.S. and CAHN, J. 'The way on poverty: A civilian perspective,' 73 *Yale Law Journal* 1317.

28 See, e.g., ROSENBERG, M. (1972) 'Let's everybody litigate?,' 50 *Texas Law Review* 1349; FRIENDLY, H. (1979) 'Should we be turning back the law flood,' *Legal Times of Washington*, 8 October at 7.
29 MANNING, B. (1977) 'Hyperlexis: Our national disease,' 71 *Northwestern University Law Review* 767.
30 MAINE, SIR H.S. (1864) *Ancient Law* New York, Scribner.
31 For a useful discussion of the roots of legalization, see ABEL, R. (1980) 'Redirecting social studies of law,' 14 *Law and Society Review* 305.
32 COMMAGER, H.S. (1950) *The American Mind* 10, New Haven, Yale University Press. See also WIEBE, R. (1969) 'The social functions of public education,' 21 *American Quarterly* 147.
33 See, e.g., DWORKIN, R. (1976) *Taking Rights Seriously*, Cambridge, Harvard University Press.
34 See, e.g., KARST, K. (1977) 'Foreword: Equal citizenship under the fourteenth amendment,' 91 *Harvard Law Review* 1.
35 See, e.g., FISS, O. (1979) 'Foreword: The forms of justice,' 93 *Harvard Law Review* 1, pp. 56–7.
36 See generally KIRP (1982) *op. cit.*
37 See SHKLAR, J. (1964) *Legalism*, Cambridge, Harvard University Press.
38 See generally WILSON, J.Q. (Ed.) (1980) *The Politics of Regulation* New York, Basic Books; RABIN, R. (Ed.) (1979) *Perspective on the Administrative Process*, Boston, Little, Brown.
39 BARDACH, E. and KAGAN, R. (1982) *Going by the Book: The Problem of Regulatory Unreasonableness* 11, Philadelphia, Temple University Press.
40 See, e.g., BERNSTEIN, M. (1955) *Regulating Business by Independent Commission* Princeton, N.J., Princeton University Press.
41 See, e.g., EDELMAN, M. (1972) *The Symbolic Uses of Politics* Urbana, III., University of Illinois Press.
42 BEAM, D. (1981) 'Regulation — the other face of the new federalism,' unpublished paper.
43 KRIER, J. and URSIN, E. (1981) *Pollution and Policy* 297, Berkeley, University of California Press.
44 DUBNICK, M. and GITELSON, A. (1981) 'Nationalizing state policies,' in HANUS, J. (Ed.), *The Nationalization of State Government* 52, 56, Lexington, Kentucky, D.C. Heath. See generally THOMPSON, F. (1981) *Health Politics and the Bureaucracy* Cambridge, MIT Press; MENDELOFF, J. (1979) *Regulating Safety* Cambridge, MIT Press; KOCH, E. (1980) 'The mandate millstone,' 61 *Public Interest* 42, Fall.
45 BARDACH and KAGAN, (1982) *op. cit.*
46 WILSON, J.Q. (1975) 'The rise of the bureaucratic state,' 41 *Public Interest* 77, Fall.
47 Compare DOWNS, A. (1967) *Inside Bureaucracy*, Boston, Little, Brown and Co. and NISKANEN, W. (1971) *Bureaucracy and Representative Government*. Chicago, Aldine Press; with WILSON, J.Q. (1980) 'The politics of regulation,' 359 in WILSON, (1980) *op. cit.*
48 'Fighting federal mandates,' *New York Times*, 16 August 1980, p. 20.
49 GRODZIN, M. (1966) *The American System* 121, Chicago, Rand McNally.
50 LOWI, T. (1969) *The End of Liberalism* New York, W.W. Norton. Compare BEER, S. (1978) 'Federalism, nationalism, and democracy in America,' 72 *American Political Science Review* 9.
51 See, e.g., STANFIELD, R. (1980) 'Are the federal bilingual rules a foot in the schoolhouse door?', *National Journal*, 18, October p. 1736. That issue was debated again in the 1984 Congressional renewal of bilingual education aid.
52 BEAM, (1981) *op. cit.*
53 See, e.g., ELMORE, R. (1982) 'Backward mapping: Implementation research and

policy decisions,' in WILLIAMS, W. *et al.*, *Studying Implementation* 18, Chatham, NJ, Chatham House.

54 United States National Advisory Committee on Education, (1931) *Federal Relations to Education, Report of the National Advisory Committee on Education, Part I: Committee Findings and Recommendations* 30, Washington, DC, Government Printing Office.

55 See generally FASS, P. 'The New Deal: Anticipating a federal education policy,' in this volume.

56 See generally KAGAN, R. 'Regulating business, regulating schools: The problem of regulatory unreasonableness,' in this volume.

57 On trucking deregulation, see ROBYN, D. (1982) *Braking the Special Interests: The Political Battle for Trucking Deregulation*, (unpublished PhD dissertation, School of Public Policy, University of California, Berkeley).

58 See, e.g., HILL, P. (1979) 'Enforcement and informal pressure in the management of federal categorical programs in education', Santa Monica, California, Rand Corporation.

59 See, e.g., RABE, B. and PETERSON, P. (1983) 'Educational policy implementation: Are block grant proposals based on out of date research?' *Issues in Education*, Spring, pp. 1–29.

60 BARDACH, E. and KAGAN, R. (1982) 'Conclusion: Responsibility and accountability,' in BARDACH, E. and KAGAN, R. (Eds) *Social Regulation* 343, 357, San Francisco, Institute of Contemporary Studies.

61 See SWIDLER, A. 'The culture of policy: Aggregate versus individualist thinking about regulation of education,' in this volume.

62 BARDACH, E. and KAGAN, R. (1982) *op. cit.*

63 Compare KIRP, D.L. (1982) *op. cit.* (note 23), who notes how little the British rely on legalization in resolving the problems of the handicapped. A similar contrast, between the United States and Britain, in the racial setting is advanced in KIRP, D.L. (1979) *Doing Good by Doing Little: Race and Schooling in Britain*, Berkeley, University of California Press.

64 DEWEY, J. (1902) *The Educational Situation* 22, Chicago, University of Chicago Press.

65 See, *eg.* MUIR, W.K. 'Teachers' regulation of the classroom,' and ELMORE, R. 'Differential treatment of states in federal education regulation' in this volume.

Part One
Regulation and Education

1 Historical Context

Before Legalism: The New Deal and American Education

Paula S. Fass
University of California, Berkeley

I

Since the 1954 Supreme Court decision in *Brown v. Board of Education*, and especially since the 1960s, Americans have become accustomed to active federal participation in education. We often assume that the recent past emerged from a kind of *tabula rasa*, a long prehistory of federal quiescence in which educational matters rested exclusively and naturally in the domain of the states and local school districts, where the silence of the Constitution seemed to leave the matter. In fact, American history is dotted with instances of federal activity affecting education.[1] Usually, however, these were simple legislative acts which, as in the cases of the Morrill Act (1862) and the Smith-Hughes Act (1917), provided federal assistance for special educational projects like the land grant universities or subsidies to encourage vocational education. Rarely did the federal government actively design a set of programs or policies which reached broadly and deeply into the realm of education.

The one important exception was the New Deal. The reform activities initiated by Franklin Roosevelt in the 1930s to cope with the devastations of the Depression were unprecedented in many ways. Not the least of these was the significant educational dimension of federal intervention which was carved out of the jigsaw pattern of economic relief. This federal activity was not only fundamentally new but had significant implications for defining a new federal responsibility in educational matters which anticipated our more recent experiences. In telling the story of the New Deal's educational activities, I will concentrate on three areas which I believe are most instructive in providing historical antecedents to and contrasts with current educational policy at the federal level: (i) how the New Deal helped to redefine the legitimate and necessary responsibility of the federal government for education; (ii) the effect of federal intervention on the education of blacks and other educationally deprived groups; and (iii) the nature of federal administration and its consequences. The New Deal provided important precedents which fundamentally altered beliefs about the role of the federal government in the area of education and raised, without completely defining, a new ideal of education as an entitlement. Just as significantly, the New Deal made it clear that the education of blacks was integral to any new responsibility that the federal government might assume. At the same time, the Roosevelt administration failed to anchor these changes in a lasting way because of the manner in which its educational programs were administered and because its educational innovations were not the result of a defined set of policies and goals concerning education, but were practical and temporary expedients. In this sense, the New Deal anticipated the educational developments of the post-1960s period but had few direct links with it either in institutions or programs.

To understand the nature and scope of New Deal innovations, it would be useful to begin with a brief examination of a classic document in American educational history, the 1931 Report of the National Advisory Committee on Education.[2] Appearing before Roosevelt took office, the Report serves as a convenient frame against which to define the changes introduced by the New Deal. The Report is often remembered for its innovative recommendation calling for federal financial assistance for education, but this is deceptive. In fact, the Report highlights and confirms traditional restrictions on the role of the federal government, and illustrates the dilemma of the Committee, which at once urged financial assistance and denied the federal government any active supervisory role. Although the Committee, appointed by President Hoover in 1929, was composed of a varied group of educators, public officials, and leaders of citizens' organizations and private industry, it was overwhelmingly dominated by professional educators. The makeup of the group represented, if not a cross section of public thought on education, certainly a good sample of those who were thinking more seriously about American education at the time. And the Committee, as well as its report, most nearly approximated the dominant views of the educational community.

The Committee took pains to discuss at length, and often with sentimental flourishes, the traditional roots of American localism in education and its fundamental contribution to democracy and citizenship. And even as it pointed to the precedents for federal aid to education, it carefully differentiated the earlier forms of federal aid, like land grants, which supported local autonomy, from the later more intrusive forms like the Morrill and Smith-Hughes Acts, which the Committee rejected as unwarranted attempts by the federal government to make policy. Noting the 'conflict between our traditional policy of State and local autonomy and this growing trend toward federal centralization,'[3] the 1931 report repeatedly reasserted the primacy of local control and left no doubt about the dangers implicit in innovation.

The report was not trying to build up an historical notebook of cases to support increased federal participation. Rather, it hoped to confine and severely delimit the proper realm of what it called federal 'cooperation.' This seemed especially necessary in the light of the Committee's recommendations for direct federal financial aid. The Committee reluctantly supported federal aid because of its recognition of the indisputable economic and social changes which had taken place as rapid industrialization transformed a formerly rural society and as a newly nationalized economy exposed and aggravated the glaring inequities in provisions for education by local communities.

The Committee's recommendations can be summarized as follows:

1 Control of education must remain exclusively with the states.
2 The federal government should assist the states through a general education fund, to be provided to the states with no strings attached, and to be distributed according to need.
3 There should be no federal aid for special education projects, which by their nature result in federal direction and an exercise of controls. Along with this, the Committee urged the elimination of all federal matching fund requirements in existing legislation (for example, vocational education).
4 A major purpose of federal cooperation in education is the collection and dissemination of information. Therefore, the federal government should actively pursue, encourage, and sponsor research activities.
5 The only legitimate federal requirement for administered aid is audits to ensure the proper expenditure of funds.
6 The federal government should establish a Department of Education with a Cabinet-level Secretary.

The first five points represent a fair summary of traditional values modified by the Committee's reluctant acceptance of the need for federal aid. The last recommendation seems incompatible with the others. If the federal government was to dispense funds with no controls and was to restrict itself to simple audits and the encouragement of research, why introduce a demand for a bureaucratic structure? Or, as a minority report written by two Catholic clergymen aptly put it:

> A Federal Department of Education will inevitably bring about centralization and federal control ... of education.... A Federal Department, headed by a Secretary in the President's Cabinet, is of its nature an administrative institution and nothing that could be written into any act setting up such a Department could prevent it from taking on administrative and directional functions in the course of time....[4]

The last recommendation is, in fact, only comprehensible in the context of the rest of the report, for only the last provision could ensure the delicate balance required by the others. Such a national center could provide the legitimacy and stature which an increasingly self-conscious profession demanded, while assuring it the leverage, through access to the President and Congress, for the continuous flow of unrestricted funds. The report wanted it both ways: money and the recognition of education as a national concern, and no federal controls over education, which technically rested with the states and localities but was in fact increasingly, if not explicitly, lodged in a self-confident profession. Only a department which educators could confidently hope to control would protect the schools from independent federal action.

The other minority report reminds us of issues which the majority simply ignored as beyond the scope of federal concern. This report, issued by three presidents of Negro institutions of higher education, presented the most fundamental challenge to the report as a whole. While the presidents proclaimed their general agreement with the report, they asked the federal government to assume the 'moral obligation which binds a central government to exercise special solicitude for disadvantaged minorities.' Presidents John W. Davis, Mordecai W. Johnson, and R.R. Moton declared that historical experience of the limitations of state action and the deplorable state of education for blacks made intervention on their behalf through supplemental grants for black education a necessity and an obligation. These grants, they added, should be administered just as the general fund was administered, 'in full accord with the principles of state autonomy.' Davis, Johnson, and Moton demanded only 'some definite increase in the per capita amounts and in the percentages of State support made available for Negro education.' They based their demands on the requirements of fairness and equity alone, and did not propose any restructuring of traditional federal-state relationships in education.

This plea, carefully worded to uphold and respect local autonomy and not to insult the Southern states, had no resonance whatever in the majority report. The majority raised the issue of black education only to dismiss it as one of the 'perplexing problems' whose solution 'might appear to be hastened by the Federal Government.' Instead, the majority noted steady improvement in Negro education and the 'impressive advance made by colored people,' which the Committee believed would continue to result from private charity. 'It seems clear that the actual limitations which still operate to handicap Negroes are primarily due to *imperfections* in the political, economic, physical and social conditions often surrounding them.'[5] Significantly, the statement also suggested that the role of education was limited, that education was only one of many social forces, and that equal opportunity in education could not substitute for or produce social equality. By 1938, a new Advisory Committee, appointed by Roosevelt and deeply affected by New Deal experience, would adopt a more imperial view of education and with it a different perspective on the role of education in society and on the government's obligations toward all the nation's children.

II

As the National Advisory Committee was deliberating and preparing its findings, the American economy had collapsed. The Depression, the coming of Roosevelt, and the incipient destruction of the financial foundation of thousands of school systems across the nation would profoundly affect educational experience in the decade of the thirties. But these changes did not immediately revise traditional beliefs about the role and responsibility of the federal government in educational matters. Nor were the implications of the innovations introduced by the New Deal immediately apparent. Indeed, what is striking about the initial development of federal educational activities in the thirties is how the federal government managed to assume a good part of the burden and responsibility for education without seeming to alter traditional relationships between the federal government and the schools. In this, the New Deal's actions concerning education were like its effects on other segments of the economy and society. Neither Roosevelt nor his administration questioned the legitimacy or normal functioning of basic American institutions.

The New Deal accomplished this legerdemain by erecting parallel structures to traditional educational institutions, structures which were federally administered and highly centralized but which did not technically interfere with or challenge traditional local and state control. New Deal structures were often vitally concerned with education, had an implicit educational philosophy and purpose, and were critical to the maintenance of educational stability, but were organized and legitimated under the rubric of relief. That they could do this effectively suggests how important education had become as a unit of the economy. It also suggests how crucially committed the New Deal was to federal intervention as a temporary expedient, not to be confused with basic revision of traditional institutions. The New Deal never overtly questioned the local basis of educational policy or the autonomy of the states in decisions about schooling. Roosevelt never even suggested or offered federal assistance to the schools on a regular and continuing basis; he was on record as opposing such aid. Nevertheless, the actions of the New Deal focused attention as never before on the federal government as an active participant in all phases of social life, accustomed American educators to federal action without necessarily alleviating their fears, and directed attention to basic inequities, inefficiencies, and 'paradoxes' that had been dormant or taboo subjects. In the end, the Roosevelt administration injected the federal government into the educational arena in such a way that it not only exposed educational failures but defined their redress as a federal responsibility.

By the time Franklin Roosevelt took office, the schools, like other segments of the economy, had taken a severe beating. After expanding enormously in the twenties in capital plant, services, program offerings, and population (especially in secondary schools), American schools were financially wounded and also under siege from those who sought to impose economies in this so-called social luxury.[6] Some schools, mostly in rural areas, were forced to close entirely, and almost all school districts reduced their budgets, often by as much as one-third, cutting deeply into teacher staffing and salaries.[7] The National Educational Association, as we shall see, responded with an urgent plea for immediate federal aid and with a long-term program of federal supports for education. Roosevelt and the relief administrators most immediately involved, Harry Hopkins and Harold Ickes, also responded. But aside from a one-time money grant amounting to something under $20 million in 1934–35 to keep some schools from imminent collapse,[8] they responded by assisting not the schools as organizations, but school people and plants. They did so through a mixed bag of work-relief programs, public works construction and repair project, work-study schemes, and supplementary social work enterprises. The educational import of these relief activities would subsequently become clear and was described and evaluated by Roosevelt's own Advisory Committee Reports issued at the end of the decade. But their immediate orientation and administration fell within the much broader scope of general federal relief activities, organized by and subordinated to FDR's alphabet-soup agencies, the Public Works Administration (PWA), the Works Progress Administration (WPA), the Civilian Conservation Corps (CCC), the Federal Emergency Relief Administration (FERA), and the National Youth Administration (NYA). These separately-run agencies, relying heavily on discretionary administrative policies whose purpose was to provide maximum individual relief, were coordinated with a variety of federal departments, but were almost never responsible to the Office of Education.

Thus, to speak of the New Deal's education activities is both to describe a massive program of school construction and repair, teacher employment, courses in literacy and naturalization, vocational rehabilitation, nursery schools, correspondence courses, educational radio programs, and subventions to high-school and college students, and to describe no educational policy at all. In most cases (the NYA was in part an exception to this), education was a by-product of work relief, and the educational content and purpose were defined in the course of the agencies' activities by the need to find appropriate employment for teachers, carpenters, masons, students, nurses, and unskilled laborers. Because of the way in which these programs were administered, it is difficult, probably impossible, to estimate even how much money was expended by the New Deal on educationally relevant programs. The WPA spent over $213 million on school construction and repair and loaned an additional $85 million for this purpose. The most clearly school-based agency, the NYA, spent $53 million on scholarship-like student work programs in the two years between 1935 and 1937, and lesser amounts in subsequent periods.[9] But how is it possible to determine what portion of the CCC budget was directed to education, or which of the many WPA programs were educational?

Since many of its educational endeavors were unfocused, the New Deal often discovered its educational commitments in the process of program administration. When the CCC, the most popular of the New Deal work projects, got under way, its aim was to provide out-of-work youth from relief families with immediate employment in conservation work. This would give them something useful to do and learn while a portion of their salaries was sent home to aid their needy families. It soon became clear that explicit instruction — not only in the technical aspects of conservation, but often in basic literacy — was urgently needed. Additionally, as the CCC sought ways in which to occupy and stimulate camp enrollees in their non-working hours, it turned to education in subjects like Latin, mathematics, and history, as well as in vocational skills and literacy.[10] At first, these activities were entirely voluntary, but the moral pressure on enrollees to occupy their time usefully made the educational supplements almost as basic to CCC activities as the work regime. By 1938–39, more than 90 per cent of the Corps members were enrolled in some instruction, averaging four hours per week. Two-thirds of these enrollees were in job-related classes, but one-third were in strictly academic classes.[11] An educational adviser had early been attached to each CCC camp, and it is clear that the camps, by utilizing various local educational resources, helped to educate thousands of young men, providing many with basic literacy and remedial instruction, and some with welcome advanced education. When Congress extended the life of the CCC in 1937, it formalized its educational activities by providing each camp with a school building and increasing specifically educational appropriations. By 1941, credit for educational work completed in CCC camps was provided by 47 states and the District of Columbia.[12] The CCC had certainly become the center of a federally administered educational enterprise, but the camps were run by the War Department, with personnel and responsibilities shared with the Departments of Agriculture and Interior and, to only a limited degree, the Office of Education[13].

The ambiguities which marked the administration of the CCC and its policies pervaded New Deal educational activities. The National Youth Administration, superficially more focused in its goals, was even more administratively fragmented. Established in 1935 as an autonomous division of the WPA, the NYA had a clear objective: to permit students in secondary schools and colleges to continue their education by providing them with part-time, often on-campus, jobs as clerks, janitors, and research assistants, or in construction projects, playgrounds, and nursery schools. The NYA also provided work relief with a prevocational goal to unemployed out-of-school youths of school age. During 1936–37, at the height of its activities, the NYA provided almost half a million students with this kind of assistance.[14] Some of this work had already been done under the auspices of the FERA on an ad hoc basis.[15] Organizationally autonomous, though nominally under the WPA, the NYA 'has in principle worked in close cooperation with local, State, and other Federal governmental agencies and numerous non-governmental agencies,' the 1938 Advisory Committee Staff Report concluded.[16] As we shall see, this close cooperation was strongly disputed by some educators, who felt that they had, in fact, been ignored in both the organization and administration of the NYA. More significantly, the Office of Education had no major role in its organization or operations.[17]

In reality, the coordination of the NYA was often an administrative nightmare, with cooperation between student aid officers, work project administrators, state departments of education, and school officials necessary to establish school quotas, to determine who qualified scholastically and financially, and to define which jobs were necessary or desirable.[18] The students receiving aid sometimes changed from month to month, depending on any number of factors: their continued need, their academic status, the determination of the most appropriate work, whether quotas had been filled, etc. At each step, a host of variables (with responsibilities in different federal, state, and school agencies) had to be coordinated. Nevertheless, the NYA worked — from the perspective of the student who was able to stay in school; of the public, with whom it was popular; and in terms of New Deal policies, whose principal objective was to keep youth off the labor market. Similarly, despite the resentment of educators, the NYA in no way affected the content of education, which was the main basis of the stated fears of the educational establishment. Educators like Lotus Coffman, President of the University of Minnesota, proposed that innovations like this provided 'an easy step . . . to a situation where the materials of instruction were suggested and then required from Washington.'[19] In fact, educators, as well as the NEA and the Office of Education, disliked and were suspicious of the NYA, more because they were irked over having been ignored by Roosevelt in instituting and administering the program — and because it was 'divorced from the existing educational agencies' — than because they were seriously worried about centrally imposed curricula.[20] By 1938, the Office of Education was actively seeking to undermine the NYA, and in 1941 the Educational Policies Committee of the NEA called for the abolition of the NYA and the CCC.[21] Thus, the NYA both succeeded and failed. It succeeded in instituting a truly radical new program of student assistance and in initiating a wholly new sense of federal responsibility for education. And it failed, not because it was difficult to administer, but because it did not muster the support of that educational establishment without whose support the NYA's innovations could only be short-lived and temporary.

In addition to the CCC and NYA, which were the only exclusively youth-oriented programs, the New Deal also provided a variety of other educational programs, many run by the WPA. These included worker education, nursery schools, vocational retraining, and parent education.[22] In all these programs, the federal government saw its role as simply providing funds. It selected personnel on the basis of relief needs, but left program content to various professional groups and state departments of education. According to one of the Staff Reports: 'Under the Works Progress Administration the emergency education program is conducted on a State basis. This practice derives from the principle of operation underlying all Works Progress Administration policies, which assumes that the determination of the nature and content of the program is essentially a State and local government responsibility.'[23] A glance at the WPA projects makes clear that the programs were careful to provide educational offerings that did not conspicuously compete with traditional school programs, or compensated for cuts made necessary by the emergency. In fact, however, this was a less than candid assessment of the impact and consequences, if not the intent, of New Deal educational endeavors. In the first place, the New Deal programs were making statements about American education and direction. The programs were all work-coordinated. As a result the relief projects became actively involved in underwriting a practical vocationalism and helped to define this as a deeply educational issue and responsibility. In so doing, they helped to emphasize the value of education in job terms and as essential to economic opportunity in America. Roosevelt's Advisory Committee would confirm this relationship between education and economic opportunity.

Secondly, the experience of education as a by-product of relief helped to legitimate a broader, more welfare-oriented view of education, which included a variety of school-centered services like health, vocational guidance, and pre-school and adult education, and would culminate in a policy that eventually placed education in a broadly defined Department of Health, Education, and Welfare.

Thirdly, the Roosevelt programs avoided the Office of Education. Thus, at a time when federal involvement in education was growing and might have invested the Office with vastly more power, FDR chose not to do so. This choice was probably crucial to the subsequent dismemberment of the New Deal educational programs, which remained fragments of a temporary set of relief expedients. In not wishing to deal with, compromise with, or contend with the educational establishment, Roosevelt at once made certain that his programs would be tentative and preordained that educators would evolve their own set of principles or demands about federal aid. The NEA, as we shall see, did just that.

Fourthly, the educational programs of the New Deal were aimed at the poor. As the Advisory Committee Staff Report on the WPA explained: 'Here, perhaps, lies its greatest contribution and its strength. An educational offering of major significance has been made available to the poor and the needy. . . .' The people can learn; the people want to learn; the people intend to learn. What the regular educational agencies have failed to provide, the people have found — in a relief program.'[24] Education for all was a possibility and an imperative. Only the inattention of traditional educational institutions had failed to awaken or to feed the legitimate educational needs of all the people. The New Deal programs were at once an implicit criticism of established educational offerings and a demonstration of the fact that the federal government could do what established agencies had failed to do.

The criticism implied by an educational agenda for the poor meant more than an extension of education to those previously ignored. The New Deal programs encouraged an awareness of how poverty often underlay inequalities in educational attainment. Before the 1930s, equal educational opportunity was more often a catchphrase for providing people with only as much education as they could use than it was a platform for eliminating inequalities in access to education. But New Deal programs, and especially the NYA subsidies, provided a profound challenge to this perspective. As Harry Hopkins made clear in an informal address to NYA state administrators in 1935:

> Well, I think we have started something. It seems to me that what we are starting is this: that anyone who has capacities should be in college and should get a higher education, and that he is going to get it

> irrespective of his economic status. That is the crux of the thing, to decide once and for all that this business of getting an education and going to law school and medical school and dental school and going to college is not to be confined to the people who have an economic status at home that permits them to do it.[25]

Hopkins changed fundamentally the meaning of equal educational opportunity and proposed that the federal government 'should meet the problem of equal educational opportunity head on . . . We propose to give anybody in the United States a chance to go to college if he wants to.'[26] Whether the source of this radical understanding was a consequence of the lessons of long economic depression or whether the Depression and the Roosevelt administration provided a haven for the expression of radical ideas that could not have been voiced in such high places before, the New Deal provided a context in which a new view emerged of the role the federal government could and should play in making education available to all. By exposing not only educational deficiencies, but the social conditions which explained them, the federal government became responsible for education as part of its new obligation to eliminate gross inequalities and social deprivations of all kinds.

Finally, the New Deal's educational programs both exposed and were attentive to the educational needs of black Americans in a wholly unprecedented way. Much of this attention was the result simply of the discovery of black poverty — a poverty long borne, but also deeply exacerbated by the Depression. It is fairly clear from the most recent study of the New Deal's relationship to blacks that Roosevelt initially had no plans or policies to deal with the special needs of black Americans.[27] Nevertheless, by the mid-thirties, Roosevelt — often through the intercession of his wife Eleanor, and in response to aggressive actions of individuals like Mary McLeod Bethune, President of the National Council of Negro Women, his Secretary of the Interior, Harold Ickes, and the activist head of the NYA, Aubrey Williams — began to make provision for the needs of blacks. Where blacks had received far less than their fair share of relief in the early phases of the New Deal, they began to be employed in larger numbers in construction projects and other relief programs by mid-decade. More significantly for our purposes, black schools and colleges received significant federal appropriations, some of them specifically targeted for Negro colleges in the South.[28] The response of blacks to New Deal offerings was enthusiastic. Turning eagerly to the many opportunities for instruction offered through the WPA, blacks benefited especially from the skilled manpower programs and literacy classes. Their response revealed the extent of black educational deprivation and provided blacks with instruction that had simply not been available to them before. The experience of blacks with the NYA and the CCC reveals something of the manner in which New Deal programs operated and the potential of federally sponsored programs. At the NYA, Executive Director Aubrey Williams, attacked as 'a nigger lover,' saw 'progress in the Negro's educational and economic status as one of his top priorities.'[29]

The NYA regulations specifically forbade discrimination in student selection and paid black students exactly what was paid to whites for their jobs. The agency included in the student aid program almost all of the nation's 120 Negro colleges. The NYA also had a special fund to aid 'eligible [black] graduate students who cannot be cared for within the quota for graduate aid of a particular institution, after it has made a just allocation for Negro graduates from its regular quota.'[30] This fund, set aside for use by blacks only, was specifically aimed at answering the sad lack of opportunities for professional education for blacks.[31]

At the CCC camps, blacks, who had been initially short-changed in their 10 per cent quota, were by mid-decade enrolled up to that proportion.[32] At the same time, the CCC program, useful as it was for individuals, had less to recommend it as an advance for black equality, since blacks were sequestered in segregated camps where educational advisers but not other supervisory personnel were black.[33] Black CCC units constantly provoked local opposition, and according to one student of the camps, 'in response to any slight pressure CCC camps for Negro enrollees were cancelled or moved.'[34] This paradox — an apparently aggressive program to provide blacks with their due and a program which continued traditional social policies — was thoroughly in line with the New Deal's record in other areas, and has as much to do with the fragmented way in which the New Deal programs were organized and run as with Democratic Party politics. New Deal agencies provided a wide berth for discretion, making positive leadership as well as standpat policies possible. The CCC, run by a War Department accustomed to segregated units, found it difficult to give blacks even their due; the NYA, run by Williams and Ickes, sought to do more.

But the paradox is more far-reaching, for New Deal policies, despite the benefits rendered blacks, can be summed up in the term 'separate and equal.' This sounds incongruous to our post-1954 ears, but had meaning in the context of the manifestly deprived condition in which black schools were kept in segregated states by state appropriations — a condition shockingly revealed by New Deal investigations.[35] The retention of segregated schools in the context of a developing ideology of equality meant that New Deal activities were both ultimately limited and fundamentally distinguishable from the issues which define equal opportunity today. The New Deal experience, especially at the NYA, with its special fund for additional graduate instruction and its clear anti-discriminatory policies, suggests that in the case of the education of blacks, experimentation by the federal government, and indeed administrative discretion, could and did open up new possibilities for blacks, providing many with literacy, others with skills, building classrooms, and permitting thousands to remain at school. As significantly, the New Deal experience demonstrated the potential efficacy of federal intervention. As Aubrey Williams noted in a statement to the Chicago Urban League in 1936: 'It is only by having a *national* administration . . . that it has been possible to break down and overcome . . . attitudes and provide a program in which all men are treated as equals . . . their need and not their birth nor their color the only criterion for their treatment.'[36] The New Deal thus provided a significant precedent for federal intervention in efforts aimed at producing racial equality.

At the same time, the Roosevelt administration had established neither a policy of equality nor goals for black education which could institutionalize the advances achieved and ensure the continued responsibility of the federal government for black educational advancement. In this sense, the experience of blacks in the New Deal highlights the failures as well as the successes of the New Deal in the field of education generally. Clearly, the federal government could intercede effectively and beneficially on behalf of a 'disadvantaged minority.' But it did so in the way charity is dispensed — through the good graces and caprice of the benefactor. Like charity, too, the actions made the need for help apparent and raised the issues to consciousness at least for some. By acting without an accompanying statement of the legal rights of the recipient or the moral obligation of the benefactor, the New Deal failed to establish a new *pattern* of government intervention on behalf of blacks that could bind its successors.

III

The manner in which the New Deal went about its educational business — through a package of relief expedients, without educationally specific goals, with each program separately run and all of them largely independent of the Office of Education — meant that the New Deal was not burdened by the views of the traditional educational establishment or confined by a central administrative agency which defined policies across the board. But this independence had its costs. Roosevelt did not enlist the assistance of that establishment in his efforts, nor develop their stake in the enlarged vision which was gradually emerging from New Deal experiences. Instead of cooperating, the New Deal and the educational establishment, at least insofar as the latter was represented by the National Education Association, went their separate ways. Throughout the twenties and thirties, the NEA had hoped that the federal government would provide the profession with more authority through a new Department of Education. At the very least, they expected that educational programs of the New Deal would be directed by and channeled through the Office of Education, where the NEA's views and assistance would be sought. As we have seen, Roosevelt acted differently, usually ignoring and bypassing the Office in the administration of his programs. He acted apart from both the profession and its closest government bureau. As a result, professional educators found themselves slighted at just the time when education was becoming a federal concern. A look at the attitudes of the NEA, the most articulate, well-organized, and powerful of the professional educational organizations, demonstrates the degree to which the administration increasingly diverged from the profession's more traditional views about the legitimate role of the federal government in education. It also helps to define the actual limits of New Deal activities.

Beginning in 1932, the NEA began a series of efforts in the form of special emergency investigatory committees, educational coalitions, and legislative lobbying groups to alert teachers, the Congress, and the public to the danger that threatened American education.[37] Initially, the NEA hoped that Roosevelt would welcome its participation in efforts to meet the emergency situation and sought to find ways to 'bring the nation's schools . . . within the beneficent sphere of the New Deal.'[38] Roosevelt, however, ignored the organization. In that context, the NEA developed its own comprehensive program for long-term federal aid to education as well as demands for immediate relief. The overwhelming consensus of NEA policies was that the time had arrived for some kind of federal assistance to education, but that it should be assistance in line with traditional federal-state relations. Thus, Willard Givens, Secretary of the Association, introduced the organization's recommendations bluntly: 'Federal participation in the support of education is inevitable. . . . The Federal Government has an inescapable interest in the maintenance of public education, and must bear with the states the financial burden . . .'.[39] Distress in local school districts had now become dramatically clear, and the educational establishment had to act quickly, on its own, before, as many feared, they were presented with a *fait accompli.* This conclusion was partly based on exaggerated fears about the increasing power of the federal government in all spheres, and partly a justifiable recognition that the Roosevelt Administration was in fact developing educational programs which increasingly threatened traditional federal-state relations.

In 1934, the NEA's Educational Policies Commission was organized in light of 'present trends to establish new educational agencies to serve large numbers of youth and then to remove them from the custody of the organized agencies of public education and new practices in such fields as pre-school and adult education, and even deep into secondary and college levels.'[40] We should note the word *custody* used here. As the thirties progressed, the NEA repeatedly made clear that it, together with the traditional local and state educational boards, had a proprietary interest in the nation's children and that the federal government threatened that interest. Thus, Lotus Coffman noted in a statement that undoubtedly touched many sore wounds: 'Every school superintendent knows that during the last three years there have been at times as many as three, and sometimes more, federal officers seeking jurisdiction over some of the youth of *his* community. Each educator knows, too, that there have been established in each state a federal officer in charge of adult education and another in charge of the education of unemployed youth; and that these officers were appointed in many instances without the knowledge or consent of the state superintendents, and that they may operate entirely independently of them.'[41] Note how easily Coffman moved from claiming jurisdiction over the youth of *his* community to claiming jurisdiction by the states over adults and unemployed persons who were manifestly not within the domain of state superintendents.

The NEA was so eager to protect its turf that its views and policies tended to rigidify in response to New Deal activities. Throughout the thirties, the NEA sought federal aid and repeatedly reaffirmed traditional educational values. Thus, while John Sexson, of the Educational Policies Commission, noted that 'much discussion has gone on thruout [*sic*] America during the period of the emergency as to whether the federal government has by grants and subsidies sufficiently stimulated education . . . ,' he went on to declare that 'public schools should grow up as local units; they should be administered by local boards of education, elected by a vote of the people. This, however, should not be interpreted to mean that the Federal Government should not render financial assistance to the states in carrying on services or institutions of government which are under the control and management of the states.'[42] Paul R. Mort, who spent much of his time during the thirties devising mathematical formulas for federal aid to the states,[43] reflected the NEA's determined posture most succinctly:

> Our social and economic welfare demands a more adequate educational program than the poor states can provide. . . . There would seem to be no question but that all people, rich or poor, are vitally concerned with the establishment of a minimum of educational opportunity at least sufficiently high to safeguard ourselves against danger. . . . This result cannot be attained without federal aid.[44]

In its programs, the NEA proposed that both interim aid[45] and more long-term comprehensive federal assistance to education be distributed to the states directly according to a predetermined formula (so as to leave no room for administrative discretion), and 'the manner in which the funds received shall be used for the maintenance of a program of public education [should be] left wholly to the respective states.'[46] In the various versions of their legislative programs, the NEA agreed to a limited set of conditions upon which federal funds would be contingent: that each state set a minimum school term of 160 days; that the states spend at least the amount per school-age population that they had spent at some earlier time (variously 1936 and 1933); and that the states, in distributing aid, take 'into consideration the total population and each population group for which schools are specifically maintained.'[47] This last proviso was meant to assure equal distribution to black schools in segregated states. In fact, the first contingent would have little effect on the quality of education received by deprived groups unless the states also raised their minimum days requirements in compulsory school attendance laws; the second was playing with Depression-shrunken budgets; and the third could in no way prevent the siphoning off of state and local appropriations from black schools, which would be replaced, not supplemented, by federal funds. The NEA permitted the federal government just enough control to save face, but not enough to affect education.

In its programs, the NEA consistently upheld local autonomy and general school fund appropriations. It opposed special appropriations, which were viewed as a form of federal control over the content and direction of education. It decried federal interference in all essential matters. Indeed, NEA's agenda profoundly resembled the proposals of the 1931 Advisory Committee. The NEA stood pat with its hand out.

The NEA's position on local control was at once traditional and defensive. For the NEA, the Depression and the New Deal confirmed the wisdom of conservative policies. In this sense, Roosevelt was justified in acting apart from the organization, since it seemed wholly unable to support federal experimentation, but he also helped to strengthen the organization's intransigent posture. In acting separately from the recognized organs of the profession and not including them actively in the formation or administration of his policies, Roosevelt not only alienated a group which remained constantly suspicious of federal encroachment on sacred turf, but one whose active assistance would have been necessary to any continuing federal program and in the formulation of effective long-term policies. Roosevelt appears to have been interested in preventing just such a development. He never proposed that education become a continuing part of federal activity, nor did he envision a larger, more aggressive role for the Office of Education, and he certainly saw no place for a Department of Education in Washington. Roosevelt repeatedly ignored the NEA, not from neglect, but with conscious intent. And for political reasons and because of his personal beliefs, Roosevelt opposed continuous federal aid for education, which the NEA had adopted as part of its platform for educational revitalization. As a result, the profession had no reason to see the federal government as anything other than an antagonist. While the New Deal had injected the federal government into the educational arena, and while some individuals like Hopkins and Williams had begun to envision a new federal leadership in education, the New Deal had neither developed a long-term program for directed federal aid nor enlisted the aid of educational professionals and rank-and-file educators with a commitment to and stake in the innovations implied in the new federal participation.

IV

The NEA's experience of the Depression and the New Deal's growing awareness of the requirements of American education were radically different. For the educational establishment, the Depression had emphasized the basic need for federal assistance to shore up an antiquated and inadequate financial structure which underlay what they believed to be a sound locally-rooted educational enterprise. The New Deal programs had responded to human miseries and needs, primarily for bread, but eventually for literacy, skills, and other forms of learning. The relief efforts uncovered vast inequities not only in local abilities to fund education, but in Americans' ability to afford to be educated and in their access to the education they needed. This was agonizingly clear in the case of blacks, but was also obvious from the experience of students aided by the NYA, laborers in WPA projects, and nursery-school children.

The Depression thus generated two quite distinct and irreconcilable sets of perceptions. On the one hand, it sharpened the views already contained in the 1931 National Advisory Committee Report and reaffirmed by the NEA which called for federal aid with no active, independent federal participation in education. On the other, it produced a keen understanding of inequities which only federal activism could remedy, and which for some New Dealers, like Williams and Hopkins, resulted in a new vision of an aggressive federal leadership in a new educational democracy.

Just as the 1931 National Advisory Committee Report provides a convenient statement of pre-New Deal views, its successor, published just seven years later, allows us an unusually effective perspective on the possibilities and limits of federal participation opened up by the New Deal. Although the Committee's Report was never adopted by either Roosevelt or his immediate successors, it articulated a new vision of federal responsibility for education and a new ideology of equal educational opportunity which incorporated the ad hoc experiences of the New Deal. The composition of the 1938 Committee was very different from Hoover's. Significantly, educators were now in the minority, their places taken by a kind of Rooseveltian coalition of labor, government, agriculture, and industry.[48] This makeup anticipated the new, more comprehensive conception of education as a necessary part of a functioning society that the report would adopt. The Committee's report and its twenty-one Staff Studies were based on an exhaustive set of investigations of various aspects of American education, as well as investigations geared to defining the legal precedents for federal aid and possible financial aid formulas. These were conducted by a staff of ninety-nine researchers and advisers. A number of the staff reports summarized the educational results and implications of several New Deal relief agencies, thus at once evaluating and legitimating these new educational endeavors.

From the outset, the Committee Report adopted a broad perspective on education, noting that the schools had become the most important educational agency in modern society. According to the report, children needed, and the schools must provide, new social and welfare services which would assume the burden of socialization once carried by a closely integrated network of family and community agencies. Educators had said this often enough before, but the report must be compared not with the usual rhetoric of educators, but with the modesty and local community orientation of the 1931 report, which described schools as part of, and not a substitute for, the richly democratic life of small communities. Where the earlier report emphasized how the schools were an extension and product of that local democracy, the new report proposed that the schools provide a means for bringing democracy about. The report noted that many of these new social services had been provided through various agencies of the New Deal, and concluded that the time had arrived for continuing national commitment to 'improved educational services for all children. All of the children of this country, regardless of economic status, race, or place of residence are entitled to an equitable opportunity to obtain a suitable education. . . .' The benefits of localism as the primary context of democratic schooling had given way to a new imperative for national goals for the education of all of America's children, and we can already hear the early strains of 'entitlement' arguments with which the 1960s and 1970s have made us familiar. Finally, the report noted that 'the Committee is convinced that the Federal Government must continue and expand its efforts to improve and enlarge the social services, including education, and that it must exercise a large measure of constructive national leadership, because in no other agency can representative national leadership be vested.'[49] The federal government thus had the obligation to provide for and protect the legitimate rights of its citizens in various areas, including education, and the document is in fact dotted with forceful statements to that effect.[50] The Report not only raised the principle of entitlement, but described education as a force which can and should be used as an instrument to encourage social equality.

At the same time, the report showed the strains of the mixed New Deal experience, whose innovations were at once radical and limited. Those limitations were the result of the New Deal's failure to develop a long-term program for federal action or to challenge the traditional local basis of school control and administration. Roosevelt hoped his programs would serve their purpose and evaporate. In fact, however, they generated new ideals and possibilities. At the same time, they produced neither effective policies of a strictly educational kind, nor a new professional education leadership, nor machinery for turning the principles which were implicitly emerging from New Deal experience into policy. This tension is reflected in the report, which ineffectively knits together new ideals with old procedures: enlarged federal responsibilities with an almost exclusive dependence on local school administration and state distribution formulas. Those limitations make the report a less than completely convincing document of the possibilities of federal leadership in education. In the end, the report short-circuits its radical new vision by concluding, not that the schools had been inadequate, but that their financial structures were inefficient:

> The major reason for the great inequalities in educational opportunity is the manner in which financial support is provided for the public schools. . . . If every locality were equally provided with taxable resources in education, there would be little need for Federal participation in the financial support of education.[51]

In fact, this conclusion flew in the face of some of the evidence, especially that provided by Doxey Wilkerson in a detailed study of the state of black education in segregated school systems. The inequalities in facilities, the disparities in funding and teachers' salaries, and the blatant discrimination against blacks and black schools in segregated states could not be defined as good faith inefficiently underwritten. The New Deal programs had, as we have seen, uncovered the special need of blacks in ways that could not be ignored if the federal government was to exercise real leadership. The response of the Committee, however, was not to call for special aid for black education, or for new federally administered programs, but to make each of the elements of the federal funding program (divided by goals like teacher education, adult education, vocational education, apprenticeship training, etc.) contingent on 'an equitable distribution of the Federal funds between facilities for the two races.'[52] This proviso was repeated throughout the recommendations made by the Committee, which, by prohibiting a reduction in state and local funding when federal funds were received, further protected Negro schools. The recommendations of the Committee were much more far-reaching and much more specific than those of the 1931 report, defining a host of target areas for appropriations in addition to the general fund, and making each of these contingent on equitable allocation to black schools, and on other provisos to which I will return. And it is in the context of this much expanded view of federal obligations that the statements about equal opportunity for blacks must be placed. Blacks were to get their fair share of each of the allocated funds, but the report did not call for equal education for blacks (which was obvious from its acceptance of segregated schools), and not even for equal though separate facilities. The demand was restricted to equal distribution of federal funds and a maintenance of contemporary levels of state and local appropriations.

The New Deal's mixed legacy for blacks is nowhere clearer than in this report, which was so much a product of New Deal experience. The Roosevelt administration raised the issue of inequality to national consciousness and made it central to any federal aid to education, but never fundamentally challenged the traditional institutional matrix within which this inequality functioned. The New Deal had not questioned segregated schools, as it had not challenged segregated CCC units. Certainly, this was based in part on political considerations, since Roosevelt always had to act with a careful eye to the support of Southern Democrats. But it also resulted from the pragmatic manner in which New Deal perspectives had evolved and from the fact that the New Deal experience had generated principles without policies and goals without implementing procedures. Its goals for education as part of an enlarged commitment to social welfare were large, but its procedures were ultimately limited to small measures such as an 'equitable allocation' of federal funds.

This was, in fact, the limitation of the entire report, and it illustrates both the strength and the weakness of New Deal educational activities. The New Deal projected the federal government into a new education orbit, but its measures were meant to be temporary, so that after the Depression the nation could return to 'normal' operations. The precedents set by the New Deal were thus self-limiting. The New Deal had created no permanent federal agencies with a continuing educational outlook and policies that were intended to outlive the emergency. Moreover, as we have seen, the New Deal had done nothing to assuage the profession's fears about the dangers of federally sponsored education programs. Little wonder that the Advisory Committee fell back on local administration. The one exception to this was the Committee's recommendation that the CCC and NYA be retained, and newly coordinated in a National Youth Services Administration, to be run as a separate agency under the auspices of 'a department including public health, education and welfare, if such a department should be established.'[53] Here the New Deal agencies provided a direct precedent for a new program and an alternate means of administration.

The report thus tried to bridge the old and the new, and in order to effect the larger educational purposes to which it committed the federal government, it provided the government with considerable muscle. The federal government could withhold money if certain conditions for funds were not met. These terms included not only the already noted 'equitable distribution' clauses for black institutions, but also the provision that certain kinds of aid — schoolbooks, transportation, and scholarships — be made available to children in private (including parochial) as well as public schools. This, too, was a notable departure, based on the principle that the federal government issued these funds to individuals, not to schools — a view heavily influenced by New Deal experience. Another recommendation permitted the federal government to withhold funds for school buildings if rural districts did not proceed with consolidation projects; and yet another required that the state establish special departments through which funds would be channeled and which would be responsible for overseeing proper expenditure and reporting. The Committee thus took seriously its belief that the federal government had an obligation to assist in the education of all its citizens and that it also had a responsibility to see that the funds were actually used for that purpose.

In the end, despite its limitations, the report of the Advisory Committee provides a striking contrast to its predecessor. For the 1938 Committee, education had become a national responsibility not only because many local school districts were poor, but because the education they provided was weak, limited, and unequal. The federal government's role was therefore to provide financial assistance not simply to remedy the districts' poverty, as the 1931 Committee had proposed, but in order to rectify this situation. In contrast to the recommendations of the 1931 Committee, which rejected special education grants, the 1938 Committee sought to use money for very specific purposes: to improve vocational training, to improve teacher training, to make textbooks free and available to all, to provide transportation, to permit college students to continue their education despite family poverty, to consolidate and enrich rural schools, and to strengthen black schools. Although Roosevelt had hoped to return the nation to a situation that existed in education in pre-Depression days, the Committee he appointed incorporated the experience of his emergency administration to propose a profound alteration in the federal government's relation to education. For the Committee, the Depression had brought the federal government face to face with the underlying defects of American schools and made it clear that the federal government could do something about these.

V

While the Depression thus changed the relationship of the federal government to education, it did so in ironic and problematic ways. The New Deal had operated without a sense of the future. Its discoveries about education and the goals it pursued came in the course of experience. At no time did Roosevelt seek to anchor his educational programs in long-term commitments or in a central bureaucracy with clear aims and enforcement procedures. Roosevelt never intended to challenge the traditional principle of local control. He never even supported federal aid to education. The National Education Association never revised its views about the role of the federal government in education and continued to seek general assistance without federal supervision. The way the New Deal operated, by providing temporary alternative channels of educational opportunity, without the active assistance of the educational establishment and without developing a vested central educational bureaucracy, meant that it failed to institutionalize its new perceptions about federal obligations for education, or to produce a vested educational interest in innovative approaches.

The New Deal thus had a profound effect on principles but left no immediate instrumental legacy. Its greatest strengths -- experimentalism, freedom from rigid central directives, the ability to innovate by allowing agencies wide discretion, as at the NYA, and the ability to create programs as it went along to suit the needs of its clients, as at the CCC — were also its weaknesses. The New Deal could be innovative because it was unencumbered by a bureaucracy which would have enforced regularity and most likely have been dominated by a generally conservative profession. As a result, however, the New Deal was unable to leave to the future any continuing programs, personnel, or agencies. The experiments in education were effectively over when, one by one between 1939 and 1942, the WPA, CCC, and NYA were reduced and disbanded. The war, the accompanying renewal of prosperity, an increasingly conservative Congress, and the strengthening opposition of the NEA and the Office of Education to educational programs operating outside of 'normal' channels together turned the New Deal programs into temporary experiments of an emerging welfare state. Although the New Deal programs were thus no more than an educational flash in the pan, the experience nevertheless changed the meaning and nature of all future discussions about the federal government and education. The New Deal changed perceptions of the nature of educational deprivation and the role of education for national prosperity and the welfare of the people. Above all, by redefining equal educational opportunity, the experience of the New Deal recast the nature of federal responsibility in terms of the rights Americans possessed in education. And the New Deal itself would serve as a precedent for and reservoir of ideas in the 1960s and beyond.

Notes

1 For a general introduction to pre-New Deal federal legislation, see ZEITLIN, H. (1958) 'Federal relations in American education, 1933–43: A study of New Deal efforts and innovations.' Doctoral dissertation, Teachers College, Columbia University, chap. 1; also U.S. Office of Education, (1938) 'Federal Aid for Education 1935–36 and 1936–37,' Leaflet No. 30, by Timon Covert, Washington, D.C. Zeitlin's study is also the best general introduction to New Deal educational activities.

2 United States National Advisory Committee on Education, (1931) *Federal Relations to Education: Report of the National Advisory Committee on Education, Part I, Committee Findings and Recommendations* Washington, D.C., hereinafter cited as 1931 Committee Report. Part II of the Committee Report, United States National Advisory Committee on Education, (1931) *Report of the National Advisory Committee on Education, Basic Facts* Washington, D.C., provides a detailed summary of the state of education in the United States.

3 1931 Committee Report, pp. 12–13.

4 *Ibid.*, p. 103.

5 *Ibid.*, pp. 108, 110, and 25 (my emphasis).

6 See, for example, the statement by STRAYER, G.D. (1933) 'Educational economy and frontier needs,' *Proceedings of the Seventy-first Annual Meeting of the National Education Association*, 71 pp 581–9. All the *Proceedings* of the Association will hereinafter be cited as *NEA Proceedings*. See also RIPPA, S.A. (1962) 'Retrenchment in a period of defensive opposition to the New Deal: the business community and the public schools, 1932–1934,' *History of Education Quarterly*, 2, June, pp. 76–82.

7 STETSON, P.C. (1933) 'A national outlook on education,' *NEA Proceedings*, p. 87; and (1934) 'Education, the foundation of enduring recovery.' *Journal of the National Education Association*, 23, February, p. 46.

8 See REEVES, F.W. (1937) 'Purpose and functions of the Advisory Committee on Education,' *NEA Proceedings*, p. 28; and ZOOK, G.F. (1934) 'Federal aid to education,' *NEA Proceedings*, p. 40.

9 REEVES, F.W. (1937) *op. cit.* p. 28; RAWICK, G.P., (1957) 'The New Deal and Youth: The Civilian Conservation Corps, The National Youth Administration and the American Youth Congress,' Doctoral dissertation, University of Wisconsin, p. 214. For a summary of expenditures on various programs and projects directed by the WPA, see CAMPBELL, D.S., BAIR, F.H. and HARVEY, O.L. (1939) *Educational Activities of the Works Progress Administration*, Staff Study Number 14, prepared for the Advisory Committee on Education, Washington, D.C., pp. 29–31 and 44. For a summary of the NYA's expenditures, see JOHNSON, P.O. and HARVEY, O.L. (1938) *The National Youth Administration*, Staff Study Number 13, prepared for the Advisory Committee on Education, Washington, D.C., pp. 28 and 44.

10 See, for example, MARSH, C.S. (1934) 'The educational program of the Civilian Conservation Corps,' *Bulletin of the Department of Secondary-School Principals of the National Educational Association*, 50, p. 222.

11 ZEITLIN, H. (1958) *op. cit.* p. 92; and American Council on Education, (1941) *The Civilian Conservation Corps: Recommendations of the American Youth Commission*

of the American Council on Education, Washington, D.C. p. 18.

12 Zeitlin, H. (1958) *op. cit.*, p. 95.

13 American Council on Education, (1941) *op. cit.* p. 20; and the Advisory Committee on Education, (1938) *Report of the Committee*, Washington, D.C., pp. 115–22, hereinafter cited as 1938 Committee Report.

14 See Johnson, P.O. and Harvey, O.L. (1938) *op. cit.* p. 7 and *passim*; and Reeves, F.W. (1937) *op. cit.* p. 28.

15 Zeitlin, H. (1958) *op. cit.* pp. 191–3.

16 Johnson, P.O. and Harvey, O.L. (1938) *op. cit.*, p. 12.

17 According to George Rawick, the Office of Education was actively hostile to the NYA and by 1938 was campaigning to destroy the agency. In 1940, the Office of Education was given some role in its vocational education program, and very soon thereafter the office absorbed large portions of its defense industry training program. By then, the NYA had been effectively destroyed as a New Deal agency; Rawick, G.P. (1957) *op. cit.* pp. 252–61.

18 For a chart of responsibilities in administration, see Johnson, P.O. and Harvey, O.L. (1938) *op. cit.* p. 10.

19 Coffman, L.D. (1936) 'Federal support and social responsibility for education,' *NEA Proceedings*, p. 417.

20 *Ibid.* See also Zeitlin, H. (1958) *op. cit.* pp. 295–8, for a discussion of the NEA's resentment of Roosevelt's handling of the NYA.

21 Rawick, G.P. (1957) *op. cit.* p. 266.

22 See Campbell, D.S. *et al.*, (1939) *op. cit.*, *passim.*

23 *Ibid.*, pp. 20–21.

24 *Ibid.*, p. 157.

25 Hopkins's statement is reprinted in Zeitlin, H. (1958) *op. cit.* pp. 348–52, the quotation appears on p. 349.

26 *Ibid.*

27 Sitkoff, H. *The New Deal for Blacks, the Emergence of Civil Rights as a National Issue: The Depression Decade*, New York, Oxford University Press, pp. 34–57.

28 *Ibid.*, p. 68.

29 *Ibid.*, p. 73.

30 Johnson, P.O. and Harvey, O.L. (1938) *op. cit.* pp. 27–8.

31 For the state of professional education for blacks in segregated systems, see Wilkerson, D.A. (1939) *Special Problems of Negro Education*, Staff Study No. 12, prepared for the Advisory Committee on Education, Washington, D.C., pp. 65–9.

32 Zeitlin, H. (1958) *op. cit.* p. 107.

33 American Council on Education, (1941) *op. cit.* p. 18.

34 Rawick, G.P. (1957) *op. cit.*, p. 148.

35 See Wilkerson, D.A. (1939) *op. cit. passim.*

36 Quoted in Zeitlin, H. (1958) *op. cit.* p. 205, note 36 (my emphasis).

37 According to a report by Norton, J.K. (1934) 'Work of the Joint Commission in the Emergency in Education for 1935,' *NEA Proceedings*, p. 36: 'An investigation just completed for the Joint Commission on the Emergency in Education reveals that no less than four hundred educational committees and commissions have recently prepared reports or are now conducting investigations, which are pertinent in planning educational recovery and reconstruction.' Norton also reported that there was now available 'a Directory of National Deliberative Committees on Education.' Of course, not all of these were NEA organized or directed, but the numbers tell us something about the alarm within the educational community.

38 Rule, J.N. (1934) 'Report of the Federal Advisory Committee on Emergency Aid in Education,' *NEA Proceedings*, p. 47.

39 Givens, W. (1937) in 'Federal support for education: The issues and the facts,' *Research Bulletin of the National Education Association*, 15, September, p. 156.

40 SEXSON, J.A. (1936) 'The Educational Policies Commission,' *NEA Proceedings*, p. 465.
41 COFFMAN, L.D. (1936) *op. cit.* p. 417 (my emphasis).
42 SEXSON, J.A. (1936) 'Federal relations to public education,' *NEA Proceedings*, p. 55.
43 See, for example, his staff report: MORT, P.R., LAWLER, E.S. *et al.*, (1939) *Principles and Methods of Distributing Federal Aid for Education*, Staff Study No. 5, prepared for the Advisory Committee on Education, Washington, D.C.
44 MORT, P.R. (1936) 'Symposium on Federal Support of Public Education,' *NEA Proceedings*, pp. 401 and 402.
45 For the NEA's Six Point Program for emergency relief, see RULE, J.N. (1934) *op. cit.* pp. 43–7.
46 GIVENS, W. (1937) *op. cit.* p. 158.
47 *Ibid.*
48 REEVES, F.W. (1937) *op. cit.* p. 29.
49 1938 Committee Report, pp. 4–5.
50 *Ibid.*, pp. 38 and 33.
51 *Ibid.*, pp. 19 and 48.
52 *Ibid.*, p. 49.
53 *Ibid.*, pp. 209–10.

2 Theoretical Frame

From Compliance to Learning: Implementing Legally-Induced Reform

Paul Berman
Berman, Weiler Associates

Legalization and reform. These words fit uncomfortably together. Yet, the past two decades have witnessed a marked increase in law-like mechanisms to change how, and to whom, schools, hospitals, prisons, mental health facilities, local and state governmental agencies, nursing homes, and other local institutions deliver social services. No public service area has escaped the entanglement of comprehensive legislation, massive federal and state regulation, and endless litigation prior to, and following, complex court decisions. These legal interventions in local operations have generally failed to secure the dramatic results their proponents expected. And the cost to federal, state, and local institutions, and ultimately to the public, has been high. Nonetheless, legalization continues.

The present legalistic web has been spun not by central design, but by uncoordinated drift. Time and time again, in situation after situation, courts, legislators, and regulators have promulgated policy without paying attention to how local deliverers of social service could comply. Despite some success, the following frustrating cycle of implementation often has unfolded: legislation, regulations, or court decisions are met at the local level by confusion, resistance, or painfully slow and half-hearted compliance; judges, agencies, and regulators eventually respond by tightening rules and toughening enforcement; and local institutions ultimately 'comply' by adhering narrowly and legalistically to the letter of the law, which has become by then exceedingly intricate.

This legal tangle creates numerous problems: extensive and costly delays in implementation, energy-sapping social conflict and frustration, and, most importantly, disappointing outcomes for the law's intended beneficiaries. Students, women, handicapped children, prisoners, mental health patients, and other legally empowered groups often realize much less in practice than they should according to the law. Similarly, economically disadvantaged groups, the presumed target of many legally induced reform efforts, often seem to experience a much smaller gain in their conditions than expected.

Thus, on the one hand, local institutions have become enmeshed step-by-step in overlapping, often conflicting, rules, procedures, and paperwork; on the other hand, they often fail to fulfil the law's demands. Moreover, the creeping legalization engulfing local institutions may have advanced so far that the basic delivery of service has eroded: limited local resources — time, energy, creativity, as well as money — become diverted to cope with non-delivery issues.

Why has social policy become excessively legalistic? What can be done to change it without rescinding the rights and guarantees that federal and state laws seek to establish and protect?

This chapter argues that the answer to the first question rests largely on how central authorities think about the law's implementation. The argument follows a simple outline: (i) central authorities assume that local institutions can comply with the law; but, (ii) local institutions often cannot comply because some laws unintentionally imply a process of change that amounts to a basic institutional reform of a type that local systems may not be capable of achieving; (iii) local institutions instead resist or comply symbolically, which brings forth the legalistic enforcement cycle sketched above; and (iv) the misperception of institutional local realities is so pervasive that it appears to reflect an ideology of compliance held by many central authorities in this country, regardless of the authority's position (legislator, regulator, or judge) or the law's substance.[1]

If the problem of legalization thus lies in deeply held, yet inaccurate, perceptions of how law-like mechanisms can induce local institutional reform, the solution first of all requires a change in consciousness. Public policy officials need to examine their basic assumptions. They need to think strategically, and ask whether the intended law can be implemented, and, if so, at what cost. Or, alternatively, they need to consider how an intended law can best be implemented in light of local institutional realities.

Thinking strategically does not mean that the coercive force of law — to guarantee individual rights, for example — should be abandoned. On the contrary, this essay argues that a balance between coercion and other forms of influence needs to be struck on a case-by-case basis. Accordingly, later sections explore how central authorities might conceive of the problem of local implementation of law as one of developing a balance of incentives and disincentives that is appropriate to different local settings.

A plea for strategic thinking may strike those trained in legal disciplines as counter to the law's main functions in society. It seems to place such cornerstones as the rule of principle, uniform application of the law, and non-negotiable rights to the side for short-term considerations of effectiveness. If lawmakers and enforcers are so lax, won't the rule of law in society itself be eroded with unforeseeable long-term consequences? Perhaps. Yet good policy, whether or not it embodies law-like mechanisms, must first of all be implementable. No implementation, no effect. When ineffectual law is further compounded by increased legislation, then the law's legitimacy will also erode. Society thus seems to be left with the choice of backing away from the reform efforts of the past or learning to do them better. This essay explores the latter alternative.

The Macro-Policy Context in Education

This paper examines the issues raised above in the context of educational policy, though the theoretical arguments advanced here apply equally well to other policy areas. A brief sketch of the educational context shows that the use of law for policy-making takes many different forms, so that legalization arises not from one source — e.g., the courts — but from various sources operating separately and taken together.

One form of central intervention in local affairs is legislative action followed by executive agency enforcement, e.g., state-level accountability laws followed by State Department of Education enforcement[2]. Or, at the federal level, Title I of the Elementary and Secondary Education Act provides funds for economically disadvantaged students, and federal administrative agencies establish myriad regulations to make sure the money is spent for the intended purposes[3].

Another form of central intervention arises from court action, desegregation being a prime example. The mechanisms for enforcement in this case are quite different from legislative action and agency enforcement. For example, the courts are administratively more decentralized and often exercise more latitude in their legal rulings than do centralized agencies of state and federal governments[4].

In addition to these separate activities by different branches of federal or state government, the last five or ten years have seen a marked increase in central intervention that involves complex interactions among legislation, regulation, and judicial proceedings. These interactions constitute a macro-policy in education, despite their often diffuse, and at times contradictory, character. One example is federal activity intended to guarantee civil rights for handicapped students. Section 504 of the Rehabilitation Act of 1973 and PL 94-142, the Education for All Handicapped Children Act, establish regulations that local school districts must meet, including the establishment of due process grievance procedures[5]. The Office of Civil Rights (formerly in HEW, now in the Department of Education) is charged with obtaining compliance with these regulations. Most importantly, these laws establish the right for parents of handicapped children to take civil action in state or federal district courts to challenge the way school districts discharge their responsibility.

Bilingual education presents an even more complex interplay between court decisions, legislation, and government enforcement efforts. In 1968, the Congress amended the Elementary and Secondary Education Act to include a Bilingual Education Act (Title VII) which provided funding for local bilingual programs. (A number of states have similar and, in some cases, stronger legislation.) But the main action — and controversy — stems from a 1974 Supreme Court decision, *Lau v. Nichols*, which held that 'Linguistic minority students have a statutory right to effective bilingual instruction'[6]. Subsequent cases adjudicated by lower courts had mixed rulings, perhaps because the *Lau* opinion did not establish how school districts could satisfy the right to effective bilingual instruction[7]. After the *Lau* decision, HEW issued the '*Lau* remedies,' which enumerated educational approaches school districts could take to be in compliance with the affirmative requirement to provide equal educational opportunity for non-English-speaking or limited-English-speaking students. The Office of Civil Rights is charged with enforcing the federal regulations embodied in the *Lau* remedies, though its efforts have not been very effective. In addition to OCR's lack of resources to investigate possible violations and initiate judicial proceedings against 'violators', supporters of bilingual education, as well as administrative officials, have argued that the *Lau* remedies are too ambiguous and hence create serious enforcement problems. To clarify the legal ambiguities, the Department of Education announced its intention to publish new and more specific regulations (*Federal Register*, 1970) — an enterprise subsequently abandoned.[8] Of course, all these federal, state, and local legislative, administrative, and judicial activities engender, and occur in the midst of, political and pedagogical controversy over the legitimacy and appropriateness of bilingual education in general and the effectiveness of federal policies in particular.[9]

And so the tugging and pulling goes. The evolving policy and its implementation — in bilingual as well as the other educational areas mentioned earlier — consist of interactions among legislative, judicial, and administrative activities designed to secure the compliance of school districts with regulations that call for far-reaching changes in how school districts operate (a point to be elaborated on subsequently). Though most of the policies discussed above have made modest progress, none have realized their expectations. School people argue that they are overregulated, government officials often call for more specific regulations and/or better enforcement, and the public's many voices seem to agree only that public education is not doing its job.

The root of the problem, I believe, is twofold. On the one hand, the American educational system is being asked — no, required — to accomplish goals that are extremely difficult to achieve and that may require institutional reform. On the other hand, the law-like mechanisms used to influence school districts to accomplish these goals and reform themselves may be ineffectual and, in some cases, cause more harm than good. The remainder of this paper examines both sides of the problem, starting with how regulators traditionally seek to implement the law.

The Simple Theory of Compliance

This paper cavalierly speaks of various law-like mechanisms — legislation, regulation, and adjudication — as if they were variations on a single theme. There are, of course, many significant differences among these forms of central policymaking. Yet, they are united by a common motif: a concern with compliance.

The predominant and traditional orientation toward how statutory legislation, regulation, and judicial decisions should be implemented is compliance. The implicit theory of compliance is simple enough. Laws, regulations, and decisions are to be obeyed. If not, a sanction is applied. The hope is that most people or organizations will obey either because they are law-abiding, or because they wish to avoid the sanction. To make the threat real, enforcement systems must identify violators or non-compliers and place the accused before a judicial process that rules on their guilt.

Underlying the simple theory of compliance are three assumptions that bear critical examination:

1 The 'offending organization' (e.g., a school district) *can* comply with the law, regulation, or decision,
2 Compliance is a *discrete, definable act* bounded in time and substance,
3 The law, regulation, or decision used as a standard to assess compliance or non-compliance *should be applied uniformly*.

Though these assumptions, and the theory of compliance implied by them, may be appropriate for many cases of law, regulation, or adjudication, they may be faulty premises on which to base many social policies. I shall examine each assumption in turn and, by so doing, offer a more complex view of compliance.

Willingness and Capacity

The notion that potential or actual offending school districts can in fact 'obey' demands for compliance 'if they only wanted to' is at the very heart of law-like mechanisms. Indeed, the raison d'être of the law, regulation, or judicial decision in this policy arena is to compel local organizations to do what they would not do voluntarily. But what happens when the organization is willing to comply *and* does not have the capacity to do so?

This question is not meant to be rhetorical. The search for an answer raises profound issues for the implementation of law in social service delivery areas. To illustrate the meaning of this question, I shall briefly explore the problem in bilingual education.

The general aim of national bilingual policy (defined by court decisions, national legislation, and administrative actions) has been to ensure that schools provide an 'equal educational opportunity' for limited-English-speaking and non-English-speaking students. This broad goal has usually been translated into a more specific objective, which is that students who speak little English should be able to learn basic subjects in their primary language while they are learning English. Such training, it is argued, would improve the academic achievement of these students, lower their drop-out rate, and raise their self-concept.[10] But these objectives — even in their narrowest interpretation

— are hard to achieve. The plain truth, bluntly put, is that most school districts currently lack the needed institutional capacity to operate an effective bilingual program[11].

The Los Angeles Unified School District provides an illustration of the problem. In the 1979–80 school year, about 20 per cent of Los Angeles students were classified as limited-English-speaking or non-English-speaking (*Los Angeles Times*, 1980). The total, which represents approximately 100,000 pupils, includes over 87,000 children whose native language is Spanish; the other language-deficient pupils represent eighty foreign languages! According to California bilingual legislation, which in many ways is stricter than the *Lau* remedies or the new proposed federal regulations, the district must provide bilingual classes whenever there are ten or more non-English-speaking or limited-English-speaking pupils at the same grade level in the same school.[12] In 1980, Los Angeles offered bilingual classes in six languages (Spanish, Armenian, Chinese, Korean, Tagalog, and Vietnamese). For each of the other students — speaking at least seventy-five non-English languages — the district is required to develop individual learning plans, though how these plans are to be implemented is anyone's guess.

Los Angeles has a serious shortage of qualified — or even semi-qualified — bilingual teachers in languages other than Spanish, and far fewer bilingual Spanish-speaking teachers than are required. To cope with this supply problem, the district can take two steps. First, it can hire more bilingual teachers from its local or regional market. Unfortunately, that source of supply has been largely tapped, even when credential requirements are eased (as the California legislation allows). Were supply plentiful, however, the teachers' union would object strenuously to district policies that replaced tenured or credentialed teachers already employed by the district.

Secondly, the district can develop — and in fact Los Angeles has developed — an internal program for training existing staff members. This staff development activity truly requires organizational innovation. Teachers must learn a culture other than their own well enough to teach basic skills to pupils from that culture in a way that 'maintains' the cultural heritage. But neither an agreed-on pedagogic approach nor even standard curriculum material exists for either teaching the teachers or teaching the students. Moreover, many standard operating procedures of the district have to be changed or replaced by new organizational inventions in order to accommodate the teaching of the staff, who necessarily have continuing teaching responsibilities. Some changes might include new role definitions for the teachers of teachers, new incentive structures for the staff, release and substitute time arrangements, sharing of classes, and agreements with teacher unions and administrator associations. In short, Los Angeles needs to reform its organizational operation in order to implement a bilingual program as fully as the law implies. To execute this reform — and hence truly be in compliance — Los Angeles must engage in a complex and difficult organizational learning process.[13]

Los Angeles may be unique in the size and scope of its bilingual problem.

Yet, each school district has its peculiar problems and, as importantly, its unique institutional capacity for learning to respond to central mandates. Many school districts do not fully possess this institutional capacity to learn, though some do to some extent for some programs.[14] How much capacity a given district has probably depends on (i) its managerial competence (e.g., leadership, development of differentiated support structures, and high organizational integration); (ii) the supportiveness of its organizational culture (e.g., a high degree of trust and the presence of an innovative climate); and (iii) the difficulty of the problems facing the district. In any event, it seems evident that school districts vary enormously in their capacity to implement legally-induced reforms.

The discussion has thus far focused on the institutional capacity of school districts, because this side of the local policy situation is often neglected or misunderstood. Instead, the willingness — or lack of willingness — of districts to comply with the law receives most public attention. Some school districts indeed have been "unwilling" to comply with some laws at least some of the time, and these cases have been widely publicized. Nevertheless, districts differ widely in how willing they are to comply. Willingness is not eagerness, of course, and school people typically comply with the *letter*, not necessarily the spirit, of law, regulation, or judicial decision, because, as one district official told me, 'The law is the law'. On controversial issues, forces other than the routine law-abidingness of school administrators come into play. Willingness — or the lack of it — results in these cases from an idiosyncratic political process among competing local actors and interest groups, not from an individual superintendent's personal belief about the correctness or incorrectness of national policy.

In summary, the assumption that all, or even most, school districts can comply if they only wanted to is frequently faulty. So is the assumption that all, or even most, districts are unwilling to comply most of the time. Instead, districts differ in *both* their capacity and willingness, as Table 1 indicates.

Table 1 Variation in school district context

		District willingness to comply	
		Low	High
District capacity to comply	Low	a	b
	High	c	d

This diagram, of course, simplifies the relationship between capacity and willingness by assuming that they vary independently. It may be argued, on the contrary, that districts with a low willingness to comply usually have a low capacity (or at least present that face to judges and regulators). However, I know of no empirical study that has attended to this relationship; nor have many researchers attempted to define and measure the concepts here called willingness and capacity. Consequently, rather than define these concepts precisely and worry about their interrelationships, it seems more profitable at present to use them to provoke thought about the importance of variations in local institutional contexts. The remainder of the paper accordingly makes the simplifying assumption that local capacity and willingness vary independently. Hence, both matter for the law's implementation.

Act Versus Process

The simple theory of compliance also assumes that compliance is an act, rather than a process. Acts of compliance for many types of laws, regulations, or judicial decisions in non-social service delivery areas consist of installing devices, paying fines, filling out and submitting reporting forms, etc.[15]. These acts are discrete and bounded in substance. Most importantly, once a device is installed, a fine paid, or a form submitted, only routine inspection and monitoring may be necessary to ensure continuing compliance. In other words, implementation of the law in non-social service delivery areas often consists of a discrete act of compliance, followed — and sometimes not even followed — by routinized and delineated inspection.

But a direct and simple implementation is typically not possible for the kinds of social situations this paper has discussed. Though the submission of a plan or program in desegregation, bilingual education, or aid to handicapped children, for example, may satisfy formal compliance requirements, this is little more than a step in a direction whose path and ultimate destination are unavoidably uncertain.

I have argued elsewhere[16] that insofar as these local plans (in compliance with law, regulation, or judicial decision) imply a broad scope of change in the routinized behavior of organizational members (e.g., teachers teaching teachers, as in staff development for bilingual education) and are based on undeveloped theories of pedagogy or organizational change, then local implementation should be *adaptive*. This means that plans have to be modified, revised, and often redrawn as evidence of problems as well as successes becomes available. Effective implementation looks, in short, like an organizational learning process. The result is that effectively implemented local programs rarely resemble the plan they began with, the one which may have been the basis for the act of compliance.

Let me reiterate this point by referring to Table 1. High capacity, high willingness districts are the most likely to implement effective reform in accordance with the *spirit* of the law, regulation, or judicial decision. But, in doing so, they may violate the *letter* of compliance. For example, I have seen effective Title I, ESEA programs that covertly violate regulations about comingling of funds.[17] Or, in the bilingual area, some districts have produced innovative programs by targeting their own resources along with funds from Title VII, ESEA on carefully selected schools that have high concentrations of limited-English-speaking or non-English-speaking students; yet, several of these districts have been cited by OCR for violating the *Lau* standards, which stress comprehensiveness of coverage, not intensity — or effectiveness — of programs[18].

In contrast, districts that try to maintain fidelity to initial compliance plans are likely to have either (i) programs that break down and cause conflict, turmoil, and disillusionment (I hypothesize that such districts will have a high willingness and a low capacity) or (ii) programs that are implemented symbolically (I hypothesize that such districts will have a low willingness). The important point is that symbolic implementation, by its fidelity to initial plans, satisfies the letter, not the spirit, of compliance. For instance, some critics suggest that the Individual Education Program for each handicapped child (mandated under PL 94-42) is often pro forma[19]. Also, I have seen schools meet the California state requirement that bilingual classes have one-third English-speaking students by employing a permissable ruse. They place low achieving minority students (usually blacks) in these classes. Unfortunately, these native English-speaking students have difficulties learning basic skills, and their difficulties are often exacerbated by the bilingual classroom context. Furthermore, the limited-English-speaking students suffer also, and so do their teachers. In these instances, the programs comply and nonetheless fail to achieve the federal or state goals which they were presumably pursuing.

In summary, the effective implementation of law in social service delivery areas often consists of a local learning process that has inherently uncertain results. In this context, an initial act or plan for compliance is only a first step. Local organizations that try to maintain fidelity to their plans — and thus be in compliance with the letter of the law — may very well produce programs that are ineffective.

Uniform Versus Differentiated Strategies

The simple theory of compliance also holds that legislation, regulation, and adjudication should establish uniform standards that should be uniformly enforced in all affected organizations (e.g., school districts). Without uniform standards, there is no equity, it is argued, and clear precedents cannot be established. Moreover, unless enforcement is uniform, corruption or undue political influence might result in lax and inequitable enforcement.

The preceding sections suggest major difficulties with these views. Local delivery organizations in general, and school districts in particular, vary both in their willingness to comply and in their institutional capacity to comply, as

Table 1 illustrates. A uniform approach makes the most sense if *all* affected organizations have a high capacity and a low willingness to comply. In this case, non-compliance could be attributed to resistant local attitudes. Many federal, and state, and some court, policies seem to be premised on this perception. But districts differ in their willingness and capacity to comply. The cost of uniform enforcement to local organizations (in terms of money, extra administrative time, paperwork, demoralization, etc.) may very well be *unreasonable*, as Bardach and Kagan (1982) have put it, for those organizations that have a high capacity and a high willingness.[20] In other words, if enforcement were based on the assumption of uniformly low willingness, then local organizations (e.g., school districts) that have high willingness (for the same level of capacity) would be unduly taxed. Moreover, it seems unreasonable to apply to a low capacity organization a *standard* based on the belief that all local organizations have a high capacity.

Furthermore, the preceding section argued that compliance should often be thought of as a *process*. A given local organization's effectiveness in formulating and implementing its plans will depend on where it is in the process. Thus, standards and/or enforcement procedures might be more effective (and realistic) if they, too, varied according to the stage of development of implementation.

In short, legally induced reform might be more effectively implemented at the micro-level if critical variations in local context were taken into account, either during macro-policy formation or during the design of macro-implementation strategies for enforcement.[21]

Put in other terms, different local organizations should be treated differently by lawmakers and enforcers. But such a differentiated strategy raises practical and theoretical questions, not the least important of which is the fear that enforcers might apply uniform standards inequitably. There are thus two apparently conflicting desiderata: (i) different districts should be treated differently, so that unreasonableness is minimized; and (ii) the same district should be treated in the same way by different enforcers, so that inequities are minimized. Table 2 illustrates various possibilities.

Table 2 Enforcement trade-offs

		Different districts treated	
		Same	Differently
Same district treated	Differently	Compounded Errors	Type II Error
	Same	Type I Error	Ideal Balance

The ideal situation occurs when government inspectors, enforcers, monitors, and the like are so well selected, trained, and imbued with a common purpose that they can *reliably* adapt centrally determined laws, regulations, or judicial doctrines to variations in local situations. Reliability here means that different insepctors would apply similar enforcement procedures and come to similar conclusions about compliance for similar districts. Herbert Kaufman's (1960) analysis of the U.S. Forestry Service offers an example of how the socialization of professionals can produce an effective yet decentralized and flexible execution of centrally determined policy.[22] The courts, thought of as enforcers (or decentralized macro-implementers) of Supreme Court doctrinal decisions, have sometimes been both reliable enforcers and adaptive in dealing with the local situation[23].

The ideal balance has, however, been rarely achieved during the course of the last twenty-five years of extensive federal and state involvement in local affairs. Instead, there have been shifts — perhaps even cycles — between what Table 2 labels as two types of errors: Type I errors, in which different districts are treated in the same way despite their differences; and Type II errors, in which different inspectors treat the same district differently. I will explore this issue somewhat more closely by examining the sources of differences among districts, as previously depicted in Table 1.

That table assumed that districts vary both in their willingness and their capacity to comply. The obvious implication is that the policies used to deal with these different situations should be different, and Table 3 takes the light-hearted next step by suggesting different types of policies that might be used to influence district behavior in the desired direction. A policy for a high capacity district with low willingness (cell (c)) might be tough standards and tough enforcement, which for short I will refer to as the 'give 'em the sticks' strategy. The high willingness, low capacity case (cell (b)) might be better approached with 'carrots,' for the issue here is to help these districts learn how to implement the innovation in order to comply with the law's intent; money, technical assistance, and relaxation of standards and enforcement procedures (particularly permitting more time) are appropriate policy instruments. Districts in cell (a) should have doses of both sticks and carrots; those in cell (d) require neither, but instead should be basically left alone.

Now let us return to the issue of the dangers of making errors in a system of lawmaking and enforcing that allows for differences among local organizations. The following cases are those in which high willingness districts would be treated as if they were low willingness (see Tables 1 or 3):

(b) treated as (c)
(b) treated as (a)
(d) treated as (c)
(d) treated as (a)

In each of these situations, sticks would be used, though either carrots or nothing at all would have been appropriate. A wrong diagnosis would lead to a prescription that is clearly unreasonable and, worse yet, ultimately ineffectual

Table 3 Matching strategies to the situation

		District willingness to comply	
		Low	High
District capacity to comply	Low	Sticks and Carrots (a)	Carrots (b)
	High	Sticks (c)	Leave Alone (d)

(at least for the top two cases): symbolic implementation, resistance, or extensive delays and breakdowns could be expected.

An example drawn from PL 94-142 (the legislation advancing rights for handicapped students) might illustrate the perverse implementation that can arise when 'sticks' are relied on inappropriately and excessively. The law specifies (among other requirements) that school districts follow a prescribed procedure in diagnosing each handicapped student and developing an individualized education program (IEP) for the student. This procedure and the IEP require meetings and consultations among teachers, parents, administrators, and other district specialists who should be particularly sensitive to the special education needs of handicapped children. For the IEP process to work effectively, schools and districts typically have to train and/or hire specialists, sensitize and reeducate teachers (some of whom may not agree with the 'mainstreaming' philosophy of PL 94-142), change and develop new lines of communication among the staff and with parents, reorganize the times and schedules of the staff, and alter authority relations within the school. These steps require complex organizational learning. Many districts currently lack the institutional capacity to learn in ways that implement the spirit of the law. Yet, the law uniformly applies to all districts, so 'sticks' are necessarily used in many situations where additional 'carrots' might be more efficacious. Hassell (1981), for example, examined two districts that had the required capacity and two that did not.[24] Her findings illustrate the perverse effects in districts without the needed capacity:

> Where high degrees of legal intervention existed, school districts focused more on rules and legal procedures rather than on children and their educational needs. The total amount of time and attention devoted to defensive strategies (by the district) was great enough to significantly lessen the time, priority, and resources devoted to the handicapped and their special education (Abstract, p. 2.).

Let us now turn to another possible situation suggested by Table 3. The following cases are low capacity districts treated as if they were high capacity districts:

(a) treated as (c)
(b) treated as (d)

The faulty diagnosis here also would result in ineffectual policy — that is, local behavior that does not implement the law at all or in the ways intended. In these instances, the districts would not be beaten over the head unnecessarily, but neither would they receive the help they would need to implement the law.

The remaining possibilities shown by Table 3 involve laxity, not unreasonableness. The following cases would needlessly give resources, provide assistance, or relax standards and enforcement procedures:

(d) treated as (b)
(c) treated as (a)

Laxity in these cases does not seem so serious, because the law might be implemented anyway (at least for (d) treated as (b)). The real problems for non-compliance would come from:

(a) treated as (b)
(a) treated as (d)
(c) treated as (d)
(c) treated as (b)

These situations require sticks — tough, firm standards and enforcement procedures — but would not receive them.

Thus far, various kinds of possible problems have been catalogued. The potential for these implementation problems arises in the first instance because of natural variability among school districts. They become real problems when the implementation strategies chosen to achieve compliance do not match the underlying local variation. This mismatch can occur in two ways. The first, which I have called Type I error, is the result of a uniform policy of standards and enforcement. Regardless of whether that policy is (a), (b), (c), or (d) as indicated in Table 3, its uniformity implies that it will be *systematically* inaccurate — and thus likely to be ineffective — for all local situations other than the one on which it is premised.

The second type of error, Type II, is the product of unreliability among inspectors (enforcers, local courts, regulators, etc), and one might expect the distribution of implementation problems to be random or at least uncoupled from the policy itself.

For example, the Office of Civil Rights has regional offices with the equivalent of regional inspectors. These regional offices seem to differ in how they enforce the legal standards in bilingual education, so that the New York regional office may follow different strategies from those followed by the Western or Southwestern offices. Moreover, 'inspectors' within a regional office may differ in their approach because of differences in competence, dedication, knowledge of local districts, workload, or belief in the regulations themselves.

There is a trade-off between Type I and Type II errors: (i) by establishing a uniform policy, Type II error would decrease, but Type I error would increase; (ii) by following a differentiated policy that allows local adaptations, Type I error would decrease at the expense of more Type II error. To put the matter succinctly, differentiated implementation strategies could help to reduce some problems (systematic unreasonableness, ineffectualness, and inefficiency), but could create others (unreliability of inspectors, local courts, and enforcers).

In light of this analysis, what is the best strategy? Should law, regulation, and judicial decisions be implemented in a uniform or differentiated way?

Whatever else the analysis does, it suggests that the above questions have no pat answers. Policymakers should choose implementation strategies that match the local policy context and do not simply reflect the habitual behavior of federal bureaucracies and courts. The law and its enforcement might be relatively uniform under several conditions: (i) when all local institutions have approximately the same willingness and capacity relative to a given policy; (ii) when the implementation 'costs' (excessive legalization, misspent local time and energy, etc.) of Type I error — treating different districts as if they were the same — are deemed to be worth the benefits; and (iii) when the application of a uniform policy is a long-term strategy to force districts to develop their capacity.

Let me close this section by elaborating on the third condition. It might be argued that the uniform application of the law to low capacity organizations will *force* them over time to develop the capacity to implement the law. Title I of ESEA has been cited as an example of this type of forced improvement strategy[25]. Federal officials required districts to spend Title I funds exclusively on eligible disadvantaged students, despite evidence that most schools did not know how to improve instruction for these students. Some analysts maintain that such enforced accountability will ultimately force districts to improve their capacity. The results after a decade of Title I seemed mixed. Some districts seem to have responded in positive ways and have developed an organizational infrastructure (e.g., compensatory education specialists and administrators) that has improved education for the disadvantaged. Many other districts have not. In these cases, symbolic implementation, bureaucratization, and legalization abound, all to the detriment of students. These mixed results cause me to wonder whether schooling could have been improved with a more differentiated strategy, perhaps one in which schools were held accountable for uniform minima but were given differentiated incentives beyond those minima.[26]

Conclusion

The simple theory of compliance is too simple for the complex reality of social service delivery systems. The implementation of legislation, regulations, and court orders often requires local systems to change their standard operations.

But such change can imply a complex, difficult, and uncertain organizational learning process. Local organizations differ dramatically in their institutional capacity, as well as in their willingness to accomplish this learning. For a wide range of policies during the past twenty years, local systems could not or would not learn adequately. At best, they complied with the letter of the law, but often with scant positive benefit for the law's intended targets.

The problem for central authorities also involves learning. The legalization of the past decades ironically reflects a type of aberrant learning in which central authorities have often tried to improve the law's effectiveness simply by tightening enforcement, increasing accountability, or clarifying guidelines. A more sophisticated type of learning is needed, however: the assumptions underlying the theory of compliance must be reexamined. Hard questions need to be asked: How can central authorities (legislators, regulators, judges) develop ways of distinguishing different local conditions? How can coercion to guarantee individual rights be balanced with assistance to help local systems learn how to realize the law's intent? How can the law be applied uniformly so as to establish legitimate norms and ensure minimum compliance, yet be enforced differentially so as to be more effective?

The value of these questions lies in the asking, for they can have no fixed or final answers other than those provided by trial and error during implementation. Taken together, however, they point to the major mistake of the recent period of federal intervention: *local systems cannot be reformed unless central systems are correspondingly changed.* Legislators, agencies, and courts must thus evolve new forms. Just as local systems need to learn for reform to work, so do central authorities. And, moreover, local and central levels need to learn interactively. Learning to learn together, rather than abandoning needed social reform, is the challenge of the Eighties.[27]

Notes

1 This chapter need not review the constitutional constraints that inhibit federal and state actions in this country. The federal system, which guarantees considerable autonomy for local actions, forms the legal context of the issues discussed above.

2 Wise, A.E. (1979) *Legislated Learning: The Bureaucratization of the American Classroom* Berkeley, University of California Press.

3 Goettel, R. (1978) 'Federal assistance to National Target Groups: The ESEA Title I experience,' in Timpane, M. (Ed.) *The Federal Interest in Financing Schooling* Cambridge, Mass., Ballinger.

4 Kirp, D.L. and Babcock, G. (1981) 'Judge and company: Court-appointed masters, school desegregation and institutional reform,' *Alabama Law Review*, 33, 313.

5 Stearns, M. *et al.* (1980) *Local Implementation of PL 94-142* Menlo Park, CA.: Education Research Center, SRI International, December.

6 Congress followed the *Lau* decision with legislation (the Equal Educational Opportunity Act of 1974) that extended the right to effective bilingual instruction to students in all public schools, whether or not the districts accepted federal funds. Various states also followed with legislation mandating bilingual instruction. See

PLASTINO, A.J. (1978–79) 'The legal status of bilingual education in America's public schools: Testing ground for a statutory and constitutional interpretation of equal protection,' *Duquesne Law Review*, 17: 2 (1978–79), 473–505.

7 The *Lau* opinion was based on Title VI of the Civil Rights Act of 1964 and on a subsequent HEW memorandum (1970) that informed districts that they must take steps to rectify English-language deficiencies. TEITELBAUM, H. and HILLER, R.J. (1977) 'Bilingual education: The legal mandate,' *Harvard Educational Review*, 47: 2, (May), 138–170. For a discussion of Congress' role in bilingual education, see THERNSTROM, A.M. (1980) 'E Pluribus Plura — Congress and bilingual education,' *The Public Interest.*

8 The Reagan Administration has recently withdrawn the draft regulations. To date, the status of federal efforts and intentions in the bilingual area is highly uncertain. However, bilingual education still provides an interesting case history of creeping legalization.

9 For a flavor of the debate, see CARDENAS, J. (1975) 'Bilingual education, segregation, and a third alternative,' *Inequality in Education*, 19; US. Commission on Civil Rights Clearinghouse, (1975) *A Better Chance to Learn: Bilingual Bicultural Education* Washington, DC., THERNSTROM (1980), *op. cit.*; and 'Teacher's fluency a key: Instruction methods vary in the bilingual classroom,' *Los Angeles Times*, September 6, 1980.

10 The Supreme Court's 1974 *Lau v. Nichols* decision said only that limited-speaking students have a right to special language services. Both the *Lau* remedies and the proposed bilingual regulations under the Carter Administration required districts to develop a program with the objective of enabling students to learn reading, writing and arithmetic in their native language while they were also learning English, as outlined above.

11 BERMAN, P. and MCLAUGHLIN, M.W. (1977) *Federal Programs Supporting Educational Change, Vol. VII: Factors Affecting Implementation and Continuation* R-1589/7-HEW Santa Monica, CA, The Rand Corporation.

12 The California law also requires that, when possible, one-third of the students in each bilingual class can be fluent in English.

13 The text above provides an example, drawn from bilingual education, of the need for local learning in order for school districts to be fully in compliance. BENVENISTE, G. (1981) *Covert Purposes in Federal-State-Local Linkages: The Case of Bilingual Education*, School of Education, University of California, Berkeley, September; and BENVENISTE, G. 'Implementation and intervention strategies: The case of PL 94-142,' in this volume, offer an excellent analysis of the learning needed to implement PL 94-142, the Education for All Handicapped Children Act, and in billingual education. Also see HARGROVE, E.C., GRAHAM, S.G., WARD, L.E., ABERNATHY, V., CUNNINGHAM, J. and VAUGHN, W.K. (1980) *School Systems and Regulatory Mandates: A Case Study of the Implementation of the Education for All Children Act*, Institute for Public Policy Studies, Vanderbilt University, for further details on PL 94-142. Case material presented by KIRP and BABCOCK, *op. cit.*, illustrates the learning process involved in desegregation cases in which there are court-appointed trustees.

14 I believe that improvement of the implementation of macro-policy awaits an understanding by policymakers that no policy in the social service delivery arena works all the time in all places, but that some policies work sometimes in some places. This theme is developed more fully in BERMAN, P. 'Toward an implementation paradigm of educational change,' in LEHMING, R.L. and CAIN, M. (Eds.) (1981), *Improving Schools Using What We Know*, Beverly Hills, CA, Sage Publications; and BERMAN P. *Some Things Work Some Times: Learning to Do Social Policy* (forthcoming book).

15 KAGAN, R.A. 'Regulating business, regulating schools: The problem of regulatory

unreasonableness,' in this volume.

16 BERMAN, P. (1980) 'Thinking about programmed and adaptive implementation: Matching strategies to situations,' in INGRAM, H. and MANN, D. (Eds.), *Why Policies Succeed or Fail*, Beverly Hills, CA, Sage Publications.

17 Indeed, my impression is that such 'violations' are very common among those programs that *improve* schooling for the targeted children.

18 SUMNER, J. and ZELLMAN, G. (1977) *Federal Programs Supporting Educational Change, Vol. VI: Bilingual Education.* R-1589/6-HEW Santa Monica, CA, The Rand Corporation.

19 BENVENISTE, G. (in this volume), *op. cit.*; WEATHERLY, R. and LIPSKY, M. (1978) 'Street level bureaucrats and institutional reform: Implementing special education reform,' *Harvard Educational Review*, 47: 2.

20 BARDACH, E. and KAGAN, R.A. (1982) *Going by the Book: The Problem of Regulatory Unreasonableness.* A Twentieth Century Fund report. Philadelphia: Temple University Press.

21 The above proposition is an instance of a more general formulation of the implementation theory, which states that implementation strategies should match the policy situation (see BERMAN, P. (1980) *op. cit.*). The terms *macro-* and *micro-implementation* are discussed more fully in BERMAN, P. (1978) 'The study of macro and micro-implementation,' *Public Policy*, 26: 12 (Spring). Simply put, macro refers to a central authority that attempts to influence relatively autonomous organizations or organizational units, each of which has its own implementation problems that are called micro problems.

22 KAUFMAN, H. (1960) *The Forest Ranger: A Study in Administrative Behavior*, Baltimore, Johns Hopkins University Press.

23 RODGERS, H.R. and BULLOCK, C.S. (1978) *Coercion to Compliance*, Lexington, Mass., D.C. Heath.

24 HASSELL, C. actually classified districts into legal/regulatory or professional types. I have taken the liberty of calling the first type low capacity, which seems consistent with her description. See HASSELL, C. (1981) *A Study of the Consequences of Excessive legal Intervention on the Local Implementation of PL 94–142*, School of Education, Berkeley, University of California.

25 KIRST, M. and JUNG, R. (1980) *The Utility of a Longitudinal Approach in Assessing Implementation: A Thirteen Year View of Title I, ESEA 2 Education Evaluation and Policy Analysis No. 5*, Institute for Research on Educational Finance and Governance, Stanford University, September.

26 This strategy was suggested to me by DAVID KIRP (see KIRP, D.L. (1980) *The Bounded Politics of School Desegregation Litigation*, Graduate School of Public Policy, Berkeley, University of California). It also might make strategic sense for central policymakers to begin implementation by focusing on local unwillingness to comply and then later *switching* to strategies aimed at enhancing local organizations' capacity (BERMAN, P. (1980) *op. cit.*).

27 The discussion implicitly suggested three levels of learning: (1) correcting errors so as to improve performance within a fixed set of assumptions about local reality; (2) correcting assumptions about local reality; (3) learning to learn so as to allow assumptions to evolve. These levels are based on BATESON, G. (1975) *Steps to an Ecology of Mind*, New York, Ballantine. See BERMAN, P. (forthcoming) *op. cit.* for a fuller analysis.

3 Perspectives

Regulating Business, Regulating Schools: The Problem of Regulatory Unreasonableness

Robert A. Kagan
University of California, Berkeley

In recent years, educators have expressed dismay about the 'over-regulation' and 'legalization' of school administration and of the educational process itself. Law and education are seen as conflicting ideals. Of course, schools have long been subject to a dense web of legal controls, such as the state statutes that dictate periods of attendance, establish credentials and tenure rules for teachers, and prescribe some curricular elements. But these laws generally are legitimated by tradition or consent; rarely do they lead to major disputes between levels and institutions of government. Today's outcry relates to a more recent and controversial outpouring of judicial rulings and statutes that often are experienced by local educators as excessive impositions on their discretion and authority.

The source of legal constraints central to this essay are the numerous federal and state statutes concerned with social equality in the schools. These include laws and categorical grant programs designed to induce or compel local districts to provide a better education for racial minorities, the economically disadvantaged, non-English-speaking students, and mentally and physically handicapped students, as well as equality between the sexes in curricular and extracurricular offerings and facilities. Many of these laws impose extensive reporting requirements on school districts and demand regular student testing in order to ensure that federal and state funds are spent lawfully, fairly, and effectively. Such provisions usually are enforced by federal or state 'auditors'; and in some cases, because they are couched in terms of substantive and procedural rights for members of the beneficiary groups, they also can be enforced by private lawsuits.

Most critics of regulation do not question the ends sought by programs to benefit disadvantaged students. They complain of the pursuit of those ends through detailed mandatory regulations, bureaucratic monitoring, and litigation over legal rights. They claim that school administrators and teachers, anxious to avoid trouble with 'the law,' are forced to devote too much time to formalistic compliance, paperwork, and ultimately meaningless legal procedures. Priorities, it is said, are distorted. Money is wasted. Fear of legal action engenders a defensive, legalistic attitude by educators that further drains the schools' already depleted reservoirs of trust and authority.

One may be tempted to dismiss such complaints as self-serving rhetoric by local administrators who simply want to be let alone, or as an overreaction to conflicts that inevitably accompany the first few years of any governmental program that seeks far-reaching social and organizational change. Laws requiring educational programs for the disadvantaged are redistributive in effect. They require the redirection of a certain amount of educational attention and financial resources away from the mass of middle-class and upper-working-class students who traditionally have been at the center of educators' concern (and whose parents have been the core of educators' political support). Given such redistributive goals, detailed legal prescriptions and monitoring clearly are needed, and a considerable amount of legal coercion should be expected. Indeed, notwithstanding complaints of 'legalization,' it is not difficult to document a substantial incidence of non-compliance on the part of local school districts, or instances of inadequate, rather than over-aggressive, enforcement. From this perspective, there is perhaps not enough regulation; and if enforcement entails costly or annoying adherence to bureaucratic reports and legal processes, that is simply the small price that must be paid for effective and important social change. The problem, in this view, is not in the rules but in the attitudes of educators.

There is a good deal of power in this argument. To think that redistributive measures could be accomplished without legal rules and pressures, on the basis of exhortation and 'trust' of local educators alone, surely is utopian. But it is also a mistake to dismiss complaints about regulation as unfounded or unimportant. Instead, both defenders and critics might benefit from recognizing a recurrent paradox in the way rules tend to operate: those who point to non-compliance and inadequacies in the control system and others who point to overly controlling rules *both* may be correct. They simply are pointing to different slices of reality.

Among any population of regulated individuals or organizations, there always will be some 'bad apples' who deliberately disregard or evade applicable social goals and legal norms; with respect to these, the applicable rules and enforcement procedures will not seem strict enough. But in the same population, there will be others — 'good apples,' we might call them — who generally act in accordance with the general thrust of the law, and yet who have entirely valid complaints about the way certain specific requirements (designed primarily to cope with the bad apples) work out in their particular case. Every legal system must confront the problem of 'unreasonableness' vis-à-vis the 'good apples' as well as the problem of 'effectiveness' vis-à-vis the 'bad apples,' for to disregard the complaints of excessive legal control by the more responsible citizens — who usually comprise a majority of the population to be controlled — ultimately may erode the legitimacy of the law itself.

This recurrent problem leads to fundamental questions of legal philosophy that are quite relevant to the issue of regulation in schools. Is the experience of excessive legalization and regulation an inevitable feature of the attempt to make law effective? Or, is it, at least in part, a product of a particular set of legal concepts and strategies that currently are prevalent? Is it possible to implement a system of controls that would impose lesser constraints on 'good apples' than on 'bad apples,' that would advance equity in education and at the same time minimize the regulatory inefficiencies imposed on well-intentioned schools?

This chapter will not attempt to provide any definitive solutions to these problems. Its more modest goal is to offer some insight into the causes of, and possible cures for, 'over-regulation' in the educational context by comparing the 'regulation' of schools with the regulation of business enterprises, a field with a long and varied history and in which problems of 'over-regulation' have received a good deal of attention.[1] The first half of this chapter will explain why many well-intentioned protective regulatory programs produce 'unreasonable' and indeed counter-productive results in large numbers of individual cases, describe strategies of 'flexible regulation' that tend to curtail regulatory unreasonableness, and discuss obstacles to the implementation of flexible regulation. The second half of the essay will point out parallels between these aspects of business regulation and the implementation of legal controls in public schools.

Regulating Business

The Rise of Legalistic Regulation

Regulatory programs designed to protect the health and safety of consumers, workers, and the general public are by no means a recent phenomenon. Starting in the late nineteenth century, American legislatures established safety regulations and inspection programs for factories, mines, meat-packing plants, boilers, railroads, ships, water suppliers, dairies, and building construction. But the relevant regulations and statutes were often laced with such words as 'reasonable' and '*to the extent possible*', allowing enforcement officials room for flexibility. Enforcement officials relied heavily on persuasion, warnings, and informal negotiation to prod violators toward compliance, espousing the goal of cooperation rather than legal coercion.[2]

To many observers, this traditional regulatory approach often was too lax, too prone to negotiate compromises that unduly sacrificed public protection. In response, many safety and environmental-protection statutes enacted in the late 1960s and early 1970s, especially at the federal level, were designed to promote a 'tougher,' more legalistic enforcement style. The goal was to establish regulatory systems based on deterrence rather than conciliation and cooperation. Strict rule enforcement and formal sanctions were to replace negotiated settlements. Statutes began to articulate regulatory standards in absolute terms, omitting open-ended phrases that would make regulators vulnerable to the arguments of regulated interests and their attorneys. To facilitate uniform enforcement, statutes and regulations often prescribed highly specific safety or pollution-control technologies, 'good manufacturing practices,' sanitation devices, testing procedures, and so on.

To increase deterrence, many regulatory statutes of the late 1960s and early 1970s sought to make penalties tougher and easier to impose. Criminal penalties were authorized for individual corporate officials. Corporate violations also were made punishable by 'civil penalties' of up to $25,000 per day, in order to reduce incentive for firms to drag out disputes in litigation. Some agencies were empowered to impose sanctions themselves, rather than prosecuting violators in court. In agencies inspectors were instructed to issue formal citations for all violations they saw — and fines for all 'serious' violations were made mandatory.

Statutory schemes also strengthened the ability of citizen complainants and advocacy organizations to push agencies toward strict enforcement. Under the Clean Air Act, civil rights acts, and other statutes, complainants and advocacy organizations were authorized to sue alleged violators or the agency itself, if regulatory officials failed to enforce the law as written.

Finally, to facilitate enforcement, the burden of proof was often shifted from regulators to regulated enterprises. Business were instructed to assemble detailed records documenting their compliance-related activities, ranging from efforts to hire minority construction workers to the frequency of inspection of cranes and hoists. By law, manufacturers must promptly report to the relevant agency reported incidents of injuries associated with the use of their products, 'fugitive emissions' stemming from breakdowns of pollution-control equipment, and so on. Under new licensing schemes, enterprises had to provide prior documentation of compliance with regulatory standards and obtain a permit in order to continue to operate each piece of polluting equipment before building new factories, and before marketing an ever-broadening range of new products.

Legalistic Enforcement and Regulatory Unreasonableness

The shift toward legalistic enforcement has not been universal. Some older state agencies have been relatively unchanged, and even the most legalistic agencies retain some areas of discretion. Nevertheless, the shift in the form of regulation has had tangible effects. In the 1970s enforcement officials and regulated enterprises both reported an increase in strict rule-application, formal citations, and penalties, and a decline in bargaining at the inspectorial level. Business investment in pollution control and in worker protection equipment soared. There was a striking increase in the numbers, salaries, organizational status, and intra-organizational powers of corporate safety engineers, toxicologists and other specialists hired to 'keep the company out of trouble' with enforcement agencies.

If legalistic enforcement increased regulatory effectiveness, it also led to an increased incidence of regulatory unreasonableness. Strict application of regulations can be characterized as unreasonable if compliance does not yield the intended benefits; if compliance would produce incremental improvements but only at enormous costs, diverting capital and human energy; or if regulation-prescribed facilities or procedures are more expensive than less-costly alternatives that are of comparable effectiveness.

Unreasonableness stems primarily from the difficulty of devising a single regulatory standard that will make sense in scores of different copper smelters, nursing homes, and food processing plants, each of which employs a somewhat different technology, a somewhat different staff of workers and supervisors, and a somewhat different quality-control system. The ultimate goal in many regulatory programs is to induce an attitude of social responsibility, whereby plant managers or nursing home administrators are continually alert to all of the diverse harmful acts that may result from their technologies and their employees' activities. But a regulation cannot simply enjoin nursing home aides to 'be caring, sympathetic, and alert to sources of discomfort,' or instruct a plant manager to 'be alert to previously unrecognized sources of danger to employees and instill in employees a positive attitude toward safety.' Such a regulation would clearly be unenforceable, and probably violative of due process norms as well. Regulations, therefore, focus on the things that the enforcement official can *see* on his intermittent visits to the site: enduring physical features (such as machine guards or sulfur dioxide scrubbers), fixed inputs (such as maintenance of a specified patient-staff ratio in a nursing home), and permanent records (such as mandatory charts kept by nurses or quality-control engineers, documenting their activities). But these specified facilities, ratios, and signatures are only rough proxies for the underlying attitudes of carefulness, attentiveness, and cleanliness that we actually care about; given the diversity of the world, the degree of risk posed by any particular regulatory violation will often be rather slight.

The 'badness of fit' between general regulations and the diverse hazards that lurk in particular establishments is exacerbated by the politics of much contemporary social regulation.[3] Legislatures and regulatory rulemakers often overreact to particularly dramatic accidents or egregious instances of corporate misbehavior by promulgating prophylactic rules for all enterprises in an industry, even those that previously had been induced by market pressures, liability law, or existing regulations to adopt generally adequate controls.

The unreasonableness inherent in over-inclusive regulations would evaporate if enforcement officials consistently overlooked violations that are not in fact serious under the particular circumstances, or accepted reasonable substitutes for prescribed protective measures and reports. But such exercises of inspectorial discretion are precisely what the newer legalistic enforcement style sought to prohibit. Agencies and individual inspectors whose citation rates fall below the statistical norm can be called on the carpet to explain why. The individual inspector thus comes to conceive of his or her job as finding and eliminating violations of the rules, not as drawing representatives of the regulated enterprise into discussions of regulatory goals and the problems in that enterprise that must be solved to attain them.

Not surprisingly, compliance specialists in regulated enterprises persistently complain of the legalism and unreasonableness of much regulatory enforcement. One study, drawing on interviews with businessmen, labor union officers, and municipal officials in Janesville, a city of 50,000 people in southern Wisconsin with more than sixty-five manufacturing concerns, concluded:

> A specific criticism levelled against regulation by supporters and detractors alike is that the people who administer and enforce regulations . . . are too rigid and unyielding. . . . What the people in Janesville say they want is a spirit of accommodation in which the two parties, the regulated and the regulator, try to work out a mutually acceptable solution to a common problem. What they get, they say, is an adversary relationship in which the regulators more often than not try to force something down their throats because it is written down in a manual, not because it is supposed to be a better solution.[4]

This is not to say that all or even most regulatory rules or individual enforcement actions are unreasonable. The point merely is that legalistic enforcement makes the incidence of unreasonable requirements much higher than it might be, and that the sum total of orders or requirements that are unreasonable under particular circumstances is inevitably very substantial.

Regulatory Unreasonableness and Ineffectiveness

Although legalistic enforcement does produce some gains in effectiveness, it also prevents regulatory programs from reaching their maximum potential effectiveness. In a diverse and dynamic economy, regulatory rules that focus on enforceable requirements such as physical facilities and record-keeping inevitably capture only a small proportion of the harms that the program is designed to prevent. For example, studies indicate that even if employers adhered to Occupational Safety and Health Administration (OSHA) regulations perfectly and continuously, workplace injuries could be reduced by only about 10-15 per cent.[5] Post-mortems of major accidents, from Three Mile Island to DC-10 crashes to scaffold collapses, typically point to causes other than noncompliance with regulations.[6] At bottom, socially responsible conduct requires the continuous vigilance, imagination and motivation of workers and supervisors. A focus on rule violations diverts regulators and the regulated alike from such fundamentals. Moreover, when enforcement is dominated by official checklists, inspectors are blinded to novel hazards and organizational weaknesses.

For these reasons legalistic enforcement stimulates resentment. When enterprises are penalized for violations that they justifiably believe are not serious, or when they are ordered to spend money on precautions that seem unnecessary, they denigrate inspectors as ignorant and arrogant nitpickers who provide no help in solving 'real problems.' When regulatory enforcement officials cite and punish all violations as if they stemmed from willful evasion and amoral penny-pinching — even though a majority of violations probably derive from breakdowns in basically well-intentioned compliance programs or from principled disagreement with regulatory requirements that seem unreasonable in a particular site — managers of regulated enterprises are doubly resentful. They complain that they are 'treated like criminals,' that their good-faith efforts are never taken into account, and that legalistic enforcement officials mistrust them and ignore their arguments.

One of the bitter fruits of resentment is a higher level of legal contestation and political conflict. Employers have spent thousands of dollars appealing OSHA fines and abatement orders that would cost them far less to absorb without protest. Rates of appeal to administrative hearing officers and the courts have increased dramatically in agencies that have switched to legalistic enforcement practices. The agencies, in turn, become more legalistic. 'Now every inspection must be treated as a potential court case,' enforcement officials say, and inspectors spend correspondingly more time recording, documenting, and photographing rule violations, but less time on the factory floor talking to workers and managers.

Another consequence of resentment is destruction of vitally-needed cooperation. If regulated enterprises resent and mistrust enforcement officials, they are less likely to be forthcoming about their problems or about any information that they feel will be misinterpreted and converted into a citation. Inspectors, in turn, must focus even more on visible and obvious violations, and are less likely to discover the more serious sources of harm that might be discovered through extensive and frank discussions with corporate compliance specialists.

Reform Strategies: Flexible Enforcement

The logically appropriate cure for excessively legalistic enforcement, in most cases, is a more flexible mode of regulatory enforcement, a compromise between indiscriminately coercive legalistic enforcement and the wholly conciliatory approach it was designed to supplant. Stringent rules may well be necessary to provide guidance to regulated enterprises and to give enforcement officials 'backbone' and authority. Summary enforcement powers and heavy penalties *are* needed to deal with the 'bad apples' in the regulated industry, and the threat of aggressive enforcement is needed to keep even moderately 'good apples' on their toes. The notion of flexible enforcement, however, suggests *selective* application of formal sanctions — reserving them for cases in which the violation is in fact serious or the offender is probably lacking in good faith. Enforcement officials would suspend strict enforcement or accept compromise solutions when violations are unusually difficult to abate, when they stem from technically grounded disagreement, or arise from inadvertent failures. Moreover, flexible enforcement, recognizing the limited capacity of regulations to capture diverse and constantly emerging sources of harm, would make *eliciting cooperation* a primary goal of enforcement.[7]

Strong enforcement powers, if used selectively, can actually enhance cooperation. By suspending enforcement long enough to listen to the arguments of the regulated enterprise, the inspector gains a reputation for reasonableness, which in turn helps him push for qualitatively important compliance efforts. Like the plea-bargaining prosecutor, a flexible enforcement official can trade non-enforcement of less important violations for prompt action on more serious ones, or even for reforms that go beyond the letter of the law. When this occurs, the inspector acts as a consultant, analyzing organizational weaknesses in the regulated firm and serving as a catalyst to stimulate self-analysis. This approach capitalizes on the fact that corporate industrial hygienists and quality-control, safety, and environmental engineers have more detailed knowledge of their company than outside regulators can hope to acquire. What those specialists may lack is intra-corporate power. Flexible enforcement would concentrate on stimulating in-house experts to rethink their priorities while directing the coercive power of government to problems those specialists perceive as most serious and solvable.

Reform Strategies: Building Self-Regulatory Capacities

Some regulatory programs have begun to draw back from strict enforcement of detailed industry-wide rules in favor of explicitly compelling businesses to establish strengthened self-regulatory systems tailored to risks posed by the particular firm's operations. The details of regulation, in effect, are delegated to the firm. For example, CAL-OSHA agreed to drop routine inspection and enforcement of general regulations at a giant construction site in return for an agreement whereby the general contractor and the unions formed a joint safety committee with powers to plan and implement safety standards. CAL-OSHA inspectors in turn periodically monitor the effectiveness of the self-regulatory system. And the Department of Agriculture recently adopted a plan to cut back intensive governmental inspection and detailed standards for meat-packing plants where companies demonstrate they have established highly sophisticated quality-assurance programs.

A parallel strategy is to compel companies to designate specific officers to be responsible for in-house regulatory efforts, to specify their responsibilities in writing, and to report compliance measures to the regulatory agency. For instance, the Securities and Exchange Commission has required some corporations to establish audit committees, comprised in part of outside directors, to police corporate compliance with anti-fraud regulations, and it requires independent accountants to certify that the corporation has an effective system to prevent violations of the Foreign Corrupt Practices Act. Christopher Stone has suggested that key personnel, such as safety engineers or researchers in charge of tests on new drugs, should be licensed and subject to 'disbarment' for failure to discharge their responsibilities or for 'caving in' to pressures from 'production.'[8] Food and Drug Administration (FDA) regulations for intravenous fluid manufacturers require them to grant quality-assurance units absolute authority to reject raw materials, prevent shipments, and stop processes that they believe unsafe or that violate company-prescribed quality-control rules (which must be approved by the FDA).

Limits of Reform

Governmentally-mandated self-regulatory systems, even though they appear to delegate discretion to the regulated enterprises themselves, can easily lead to almost the same kind of unreasonable results as direct regulation, particularly in the area of reporting and paperwork burdens. Enforcement officials, after all, remain responsible for discovering *abuses* of the 'delegated discretion.' Hence, they demand documentation of how decisions are made, whether they are having positive effects, and so on. For the purpose of bureaucratic routine, moreover, regulators insist that documentation of steps that companies take to prevent harm must be set forth in uniform reporting categories. Each time an abuse of discretion is discovered or a serious accident slips through the precautions of a self-regulatory system — and this *will* occur, even in systems as sophisticated and well-motivated as commercial airline maintenance — the regulators respond by adding another layer of mandatory self-inspections or reports, a new series of double-checks and signatures and so on. Thus, many corporate personnel officers and charge nurses in nursing homes come to be preoccupied as much with documenting and justifying their deeds in writing as with doing them. The tendency to cumulate self-regulation requirements was revealed when the Federal Railroad Administration announced during the Carter Administration that, upon review, it could safely eliminate certain mandatory self-inspection steps that would save the railroad industry $100 million a year.

Agency officials often feel compelled to enforce both substantive and procedural (reporting) regulations strictly and uniformly because they lack the expertise to enforce them flexibly. Enforcement officials often find it difficult to judge precisely how great a risk would be posed by failure to adhere to a particular requirement, whether it be a guard on a machine or a signature on a batch-release form. Faced with this uncertainty, the enforcement official also risks making two kinds of errors: being unnecessarily strict or being unduly lenient.

Being too strict and legalistic imposes unnecessary costs on the regulated enterprise, and the inspector may be accused by the firm's representatives of being unreasonable. Being unduly lenient, however, typically entails a much larger set of risks for the official. Even if leniency is justified, an inspector's failure to insist on literal compliance can lead a disgruntled complainant to call the inspector's superior or make the complaint public, with intimations that the inspector may have been corrupted. Most importantly, should the inspector's discretionary judgement be mistaken, should the violation turn out to be really dangerous, it might lead to a serious accident. In the ensuing investigation, any sign of an unpunished violation will quickly be interpreted by the news media (and some politicians) as proof that the agency is to blame.

Just as threatening as the possibility of physical catastrophe is the fear of scandal. Any regulatory official inclined to grant front-line enforcers discretion to suspend enforcement where appropriate and work for cooperation takes the risk that sooner or later, however competent and dedicated his staff, some inspectors will turn out to be foolish or corrupt. In the event of catastrophe or scandal, the best defense for an agency is that it has done everything possible to enforce the regulations as they are written, as uniformly and strictly as possible.

Not surprisingly, therefore, bureaucratic and political superiors tend to chastise enforcement officials more severely for being too lenient than for being too strict. Sticking to the rules is the safer, easier, and most predictable course.

Regulating Schools

There are obvious parallels between the evolution of protective regulation and the growth of legal controls over public schools. In both fields, there has been remarkable growth in the sheer number of rules and regulations, partly because local entities — schools or factories — have been seen as insufficiently attentive to their broader social responsibilities and as unresponsive to less legalistic modes of control. 'Dumping' children who pose discipline problems into special education classes is treated as analogous to the dumping of industrial wastes into the environment. Ignoring the special needs of non-English-speaking or economically disadvantaged students is like an employer's indifference to the need of the inexperienced factory workers for more protective equipment than the experienced workers might require.

The standards promulgated by the government to control school districts are in some cases stated as conditions on grants-in-aid; but given the financial pressures on most urban school districts, they are just as mandatory, in effect, as EPA regulations. Like environmental and safety rules, educational regulations require investments in new kinds of teaching personnel and administrators, and they shift responsibility for resolving conflicting claims on scarce resources away from local administrators to government officials in Washington or state capitals. Therein lies the potential for unreasonableness. Like the world of business, school systems are surprisingly diverse, and centrally formulated regulations that strike an appropriate definition of responsible behavior in one district may be unnecessary in others.

The 'Unreasonableness' Problem: Some Apparent Differences

Before pursuing the parallels further, however, we should consider certain differences between legal controls on schools and legal controls on business that might lead one to expect a weaker propensity toward legalism and unreasonableness in regulating the former.

Education law standards grant more discretion to the regulated. Business regulators, perhaps more confident in their technical judgments about how to produce certain effects (safety, pollution abatement, etc.), or more confident that business could afford or invent the necessary control techniques if really forced to, have often prescribed very specific performance standards, facilities, machines, and procedures. Lawmakers in the educational field, on the other hand, have more often left substantive standards vague or open-ended. The Education for All Handicapped Children Act (PL 94-142) requires an 'appropriate education' for all children. Chapter I of the Elementary and Secondary Education Act provides funds for meeting the educational needs of economically and educationally deprived children but does not precisely define those needs or dictate the content of the courses or prescribe the levels of educational attainment that the students must reach. Federal laws require expanded programs for non-English-speaking students, much as the Clean Air Act requires greater industrial expenditures on air pollution control. But bilingual education standards, at least as originally articulated in *Lau v. Nichols* and the 1974 Equal Educational Opportunity Act, do not prescribe any particular 'technology' for assisting those students (unlike the EPA, which prescribes the best available technologies for specific processes) and do not prescribe any particular educational outcomes (again unlike the EPA, which prescribes measurable maximum emissions per day or per pound of processed material).

Instead, like some of the more recent 'reforms' in business regulation, the federal laws concerning educational equity have sought to mandate effective self-regulatory systems. They have required local school districts to devise their own plans and programs, to appoint special education compliance specialists, to establish local program committees with parent representation, to conduct assessments of each child's needs, and so on. Thus, the regulations appear to be primarily procedural or structural rather than substantively specific. To use Paul Berman's terminology, they appear to opt for 'adaptive' rather than 'programed' implementation.[9]

Legal sanctions for violations are more limited, less automatic. The educational laws have not vested in federal officials the same kinds of strong and automatic legal sanctions that business regulators have acquired. Individual school officials, unlike corporate officers, are not subject to personal criminal prosecution for violations of regulations. The major sanctions provided by law are a cut-off of federal funding or suits for reimbursement. These remedies, however, are extremely difficult to apply because of their severity and their counterproductive effects (fund cut-offs would *further* limit educational offerings for disadvantaged students), and because such actions often generate strong political pressures against federal officials by local legislators. Federal auditors have no legal authority to impose less drastic (and more acceptable) sanctions on non-complying school districts, such as immediate fines or remedial orders. Although parents can sue school districts for violating federal education law, the paucity of specific substantive standards in those laws would seem to allow the courts more discretion than a court confronted with a suit by a labor union complaining of a corporation's violation of an OSHA regulation that requires certain machine guards or maximum noise levels.

Regulatory 'failures' are less dramatic. One of the reasons for the cumulation of over-inclusive business regulations and legalistic enforcement is that new regulations are often passed in reaction to horrifying catastrophes or dramatic scientific discoveries: a railroad tank car full of toxic chemicals crashes, hundreds of cattle die from pesticides in their feed, or the ozone layer is shown to be depleting. For the enforcement officials and rulemakers, it seems better to err on the side of more safety, wider margins of error, and so on.

For educational regulatory officials, on the other hand, a district's failure to file program evaluation reports, or retest mentally handicapped students, or give extra help to those who speak English poorly, might ultimately have serious consequences for the life-chances of particular children, but these consequences are hardly as dramatic and irreversible as sudden death or cancer. There is more likely to be an understanding on the part of education policymakers, moreover, that educational 'technology' is uncertain and choices arguable than among lawmakers dealing with controls on manufacturing or transportation technology. Finally, while business regulators at times seem to believe that corporations can easily finance compliance costs out of profits or pass them on to thousands of consumers via price increases, educational lawmakers appear more cognizant of the fiscal problems of local school districts. Major education laws, unlike business regulations, often include funding provisions: the dispensation of federal tax monies to help the regulated school systems comply.

Nevertheless, the regulation of schools seems to have been affected by some of the same tendency toward legalism and unreasonableness noted in the discussion of business regulation.

Open-Ended Standards and Regulatory Unreasonableness

Although substantively vague educational statutes might have been expected to promote a more informal, non-legalistic approach to disputes about the laws' requirements, the result has been, at least arguably, a great deal of legalism and regulatory unreasonableness.

The traditional critique of open-ended statutory standards in business regulation — such as the requirement of 'just and reasonable' rates or 'feasible' safety measures — was that such standards would be interpreted so as to favor the interests of the regulated industry. That critique rests on the assumptions that pro-regulation interests usually are disorganized and weakly represented in the administrative process, and hence that regulatory officials will be overwhelmed by regulated firms' constant presence, control of information, or political influence. That configuration of interest groups, however, does not necessarily describe regulatory programs initiated in the 1960s and 1970s. Thus, in major educational regulatory programs, the 'regulated' are represented in the administrative process, to be sure, by associations of school superintendents and on some issues by the National Education Association, but their presence has been balanced and sometimes outweighed by well-organized advocacy groups for racial and ethnic minorities and for handicapped students. Members of such advocacy groups have often been placed directly on regulatory staffs.[10] Civil rights organizations and parents' groups have been empowered to take federal and state agencies or school districts to court for failing to take seriously the statutory goals of full equality. In this context, the lack of substantive specificity of educational statutes, which seems to give local districts discretion, in fact provides more discretion for ideologically-minded enforcement officials and judges to read their own substantive views into the law, even to the point of unreasonableness.

Several major laws invite such a result. Statutory goals such as 'appropriate education' for each child or 'equal educational opportunity' (like the goals of 'health' and 'safety' in the 1970 Clean Air Act and the Occupational Safety and Health Act) represent enormously ambitious aspirations, perhaps never fully attainable in a world of limited resources. Yet, the statutes do not obligate enforcement officials or judges to weigh the incremental costs of each additional mandatory step toward full equality and educational achievement. The result is that administrators and judges, pressured by advocacy groups invoking the unqualified statutory language, often have been induced to require compliance measures whose educational benefits probably are exceeded by costs or which simply exceed the resources of local school systems.

One example is provided by the cumulation of regulatory requirements under the Equal Educational Opportunity Act of 1974, which calls for states to 'take appropriate action to overcome language barriers that impede equal participation by the students.' HEW regulations pursuant to the law called on all states to conduct assessments and prepare plans tailored to each child's linguistic needs and to train bilingual teachers. Then some courts, at the urging of concerned parent groups and with the backing of certain educational theorists, extended these procedural steps into substantive requirements, interpreting the law to require schools to provide bicultural as well as bilingual education, and in one notorious case in Ann Arbor, Michigan, to require special instructional programs for black students who speak non-standard 'black English.'[11] Such judicial decisions become precedents for administrative action: the Office of Civil Rights in HEW demanded that 334 school districts must begin bilingual-bicultural instruction or lose federal school aid. The open-ended statutory language provides no 'stopping point' at which bilingual goals should be balanced against other educational goals.

Open-ended standards in business regulatory statutes, such as 'clean' water or 'safe' workplaces, may also be susceptible to overly expansive interpretations. But safety and pollution control laws are also more amenable to rational economic analysis and scientific measurement, more easily reduced to regulations requiring 'testable' abatement measures than the essentially moral and emotional issues of social justice raised by laws designed to promote educational equality.[12] If an OSHA enforcement official pushes a manufacturer to adopt a controversial safety device or fume-reduction scheme, the detailed standards in the regulations, or studies by engineers or epidemiologists, provide the manufacturer with grounds on which to appeal and also give the courts a relatively objective handle on the question. Not so with vague educational statute criteria, such as the 'appropriate education' called for by the Education for All Handicapped Children Act. When a parent claims that publicly-subsidized placement in a specialized private school is the most 'appropriate' education for his or her child, there are no fixed standards or engineering traditions against which to test the claim. Hence judges differ, results are unpredictable, and litigation is encouraged. The underlying issue, 'Should the public schools be paying for very expensive private placements?' is treated as the 'legal' issue of which educational service is 'appropriate' — or as it seems to be interpreted, '*most* appropriate' — for the handicapped child.[13]

Accountability, Enforceability, and Mistrust

As suggested by the earlier discussion of mandatory self-inspection rules for railroads and other business, the fact that educational laws tend to dictate mandatory procedures and reports rather than substantive teaching techniques or substantive outcomes does not exempt them from the possibility that they may prove to be unreasonably costly to comply with in relation to the benefits produced. The time and effort involved in arranging conferences with experts and parents of handicapped children for the preparation of individual plans under PL 94-142 has been well documented.[14]

The propensity of procedural requirements to become more and more elaborate is illustrated by the federal programs for bilingual and vocational education. Under administrative interpretations of bilingual education statues and regulations promulgated under President Carter, school districts were compelled to conduct annual surveys to ascertain the number of limited-English-speaking students, each child's first-acquired language, and the language most often spoken in the home, and then to classify the student's level of English proficiency and assign that student to an appropriate program. Under the 1976 amendments to the 1963 Vocational Education Act, local agencies must file plans that show how vocational courses are coordinated with the offerings of other agencies in their area and how they fit in with the state vocational education plan. The state plan must provide statistics on labor demand and supply to justify the occupational skills selected for training, describe how special efforts will be made to provide 'adequate training to economically and academically disadvantaged persons, for handicapped persons, for the bilingual,' and set forth procedures 'to reduce sexual stereotyping in occupations.' In addition:

> Each local agency is to count each student enrolled in an occupational program to the detail of a six-digit occupation code . . . identifying the student by race and sex. The local agency is also required to show enrollments of disadvantaged, handicapped, and bilingual students, . . . how many students complete specific types of vocational programs and what happened to them later, i.e., . . . got a job, . . . got a job in a line of work for which they had been trained, etc.[15]

These requirements are rational, in terms of program goals, but they clearly require an enormous amount of time and effort.

One burdensome and annoying feature of many procedural requirements is that the school district not only must comply with substantive programatic requirements, but also must continually prove that the requirements have been met, as in the case of some business regulations discussed earlier. To prove that it has not been arbitrary, the district must articulate in writing its goals and objectives for each program (or in the case of handicapped students, for each child). Decisions must rest on reviewable written rules and hard evidence (tests, surveys, statistics), not on intuition or 'professional judgment.'[16] Consultations with parents and psychologists, when required by law, must be carefully formalized and documented. Under PL 94–142, not only must schools prepare an individualized educational plan (IEP) for each student, but parents must also sign it, presumably to provide compliance with notice and consent objectives.[17]

This formalism stems from the emphasis on accountability that pervades the process of delegating discretionary decision-making (or, more accurately, allowing discretion to stay where it originally was) in a regulatory system. Accountability satisfies certain needs of enforcement officials — especially their need to demonstrate to their political superiors, to advocacy groups, and perhaps to themselves, that they are doing *something* to ensure that the law is being complied with. Because auditors (like inspectors) come only infrequently, they cannot easily and reliably observe basic processes such as how children are taught, how thoughtfully classification decisions are made, and so on. Just as business regulations often specify particular facilities and equipment because inspectors can only observe that which endures, educational regulations must prescribe the preparation of enduring documents that auditors can review. And, just as equipment specifications are only rough proxies for real risks, the completion of (or failure to complete) required forms and reports will often correlate poorly with the real issue: teaching quality or thoughtful classification.

The elaboration of formal accountability devices and requirements for rational documentation would not necessarily lead to unreasonableness if they were not required of all districts and all cases. Enforcers of criminal law require regular reports only from those on probation and parole, not from all citizens. In educational regulation, however, as in business regulation, when new reporting, testing, and other procedural rules are generated to correct gross abuses perpetrated by 'bad apples' (districts wholly indifferent or antipathetic to the statutory goals), those requirements are imposed on *all* districts, including the reasonably 'good apples.' Thus, Jeremy Rabkin has written of the Office of Civil Rights in HEW, 'It was one thing to charge particular Texas school districts with discrimination ("on the basis of national origin") because they had left otherwise capable Chicano children to vegetate in classes for the mentally retarded simply because of their difficulties with the English language,' but quite another for HEW to go on to require all school districts in the nation to remedy language deficiencies of 'national origin-minority group students' by undertaking special surveys and diagnoses of all students from non-English-speaking homes.[18]

In business regulation, strict uniformity of treatment is the prevalent legal norm because government does not want to appear to aid Firm A by regulating it less stringently than its competitors, even if Firm A is more socially responsible. Similarly, in educational regulation, the government must avoid charges that it has not provided equal treatment to political sub-units. Thus, it could be politically dangerous for HEW to have imposed bilingual instruction requirements on the offending Texas schools and not on other school districts.

In business regulation, another reason for uniform treatment is the belief that businesses are *all* intrinsically profit-hungry bad apples. None can be trusted; they all must be 'on probation.' Some education laws, too, seem to be based on the comparable assumption that local school boards are congenitally resistant to legally mandated affirmative action for racial and ethnic minorities, as evidenced by past failures to provide equal education. From this perspective, strict and detailed accountability rules, uniformly enforced, seem essential.

Perhaps more important than this 'offensive' justification for detailed accountability rules — the desire for more control — is a 'defensive' one: the desire of politicians and enforcement officials to protect themselves from charges of waste and ineptitude. Most education regulations are tied to funding programs, and the *bête noire* of all funding agencies is misapplication of funds by their clients. To funding agencies, a scandal involving waste or misuse of funds is the analogue of a death-dealing physical catastrophe for safety-regulating agencies: it is the type of error that they can be most severely blamed and punished for. Early Title I (aid for economically disadvantaged students) reviews turned up an embarrassingly large number of instances in which financially pinched school districts illegally used federal funds to meet normal budgetary needs. Education enforcement laws and regulations enacted since then are all the more inclined to treat all districts as potential offenders, elaborating fund-allocating and accountability rules in ever-tightening detail.[19]

Yet another ingredient in the proliferation of formal legal controls is mistrust by pro-regulation advocates and lawmakers of the enforcement bureaucracy itself. The theory, of course, is that regulators will be captured by the regulated, especially if they share a common professional training, as in the case of educators. As with business regulation, the presumed antidote is to empower beneficiary groups to sue both regulators and the regulated for failure to implement statutes and regulations strictly.[20] Once in court, the spirit of legalism — the judgment of human behavior wholly in terms of written rules and regulations — flourishes, at least in the hands of many judges. Enforcement officials have lost cases — and hence lost face — for failure to require strict adherence to regulatory provisions, regardless of their educational importance.[21] Each court case, moreover, acquires the status of a precedent, requiring administrators to apply the same definitions and compliance steps in their dealings with all school districts.

Literal Compliance and Its Consequences

The proliferation of detailed accountability rules might not be problematic if the regulations were only sporadically enforced or enforced in a selective, flexible manner. The few studies that exist, however, indicate that enforcement of education laws, whatever its weaknesses, is sufficient to produce a considerable amount of literal compliance and a considerable amount of unreasonableness. The precise amount, to be sure, is hard to estimate, but it is the dynamics of the enforcement process that leads to unreasonableness which concerns us here.

Despite the understaffing of enforcement agencies and the absence in major education laws of graduated and easily employed legal sanctions such as fines or summary corrective orders, federal enforcement officials are not toothless. Their visits, even if not frequent, are not entirely predictable and are viewed by local school administrators with some concern. Like enforcement officials in many business regulatory programs, federal auditors have found that their chief sanctions are not formal but informal: the ability to harass non-complying entities with more intensive scrutiny, or the capacity to subject them to adverse publicity. Burnes reports, for example, that local districts worry about showing a good compliance record to federal auditors primarily because of the 'tedious, time-consuming and expensive' experience of being subjected to 'audit exceptions.' School superintendents and board members also worry about the political embarrassment of having such exceptions reported in the press as failures to comply with federal laws designed to help the disadvantaged, raising the possibility of losing federal aid.[22] In consequence, there are real incentives for local school administrators — never known for their boldness — to stick to the regulations as literally as they can in order to minimize risk and uncertainty.[23]

Of course, some districts are 'bad apples' which flagrantly violate applicable regulations or even evade court orders; and many districts, like business firms, will invest considerable energy in resisting regulatory requirements that they think unreasonable or counterproductive. But few districts can afford to be bad apples on most issues, with the attendant risk of bad publicity and expensive lawsuits. Enforcement officials in most business regulatory agencies acknowledge that their programs would collapse without the general commitment of most firms to 'voluntary compliance' with most regulations once they are on the books.[24] Even more than business executives, one would expect school administrators to be committed to compliance with law and bureaucratic regularity. Thus, Stearns *et al.* found generally widespread compliance with the forms and procedures required by PL 94-142, despite complaints about their unreasonableness,[25] and more recent studies show a reasonably high level of compliance with the complicated reporting and aid-targeting regulations under Title I programs for disadvantaged students.[26]

It is not clear to what extent federal (or state) enforcement officials interpret and enforce the detailed education regulations in a literal, legalistic manner. Some officials undoubtedly adopt a somewhat flexible enforcement style with respect to some regulations.[27] But there are also indications that many do not; and given the powerful incentives for enforcement officials to protect themselves against charges of ineptitude, it would be surprising if legalistic enforcement were not widespread, even when conservative, 'anti-regulation' officials man the highest positions in Washington. As in the case of many business regulatory agencies, strict enforcement is a safer posture for regional and state level career enforcement officials. Consider, for example, the comments of an official in the California regional office of the Office of Civil Rights (OCR) responsible for enforcing laws preventing discrimination against the handicapped. Asked if regulatory requirements ever were adjusted to different conditions, capabilities, or attributes of different schools or districts, he replied: 'There better not be. If I find out about it, those EOSs (Equal Opportunity Specialists) will hear from me.' And again: 'We're here to enforce the laws.... If you're guilty, you're guilty. There are no extenuating circumstances.' While this might appear to be defensive hyperbole, special education teachers and administrators from Berkeley, California (a district with an active and committed special education program) view Office of Civil Rights enforcement officials in terms remarkably similar to the way businessmen in Janesville, Wisconsin, talk about inspectors from other agencies. One complained that OCR officials *could*, but don't 'act as colleagues with the districts in implementing the legislation. I don't mean that they should be soft, but they could *help* us to implement.' Another said: 'From my experience, they are a police agency. . . . They don't appear to deal with the real issue — the child. Not one has asked about where the child is today. They deal only from the . . . bureaucratic point of view.'

Of course, if one believes that the school district is a 'bad apple,' then OCR's stance may be justified. But failure to make such distinctions, or even to try, is the essence of legalism.

As in business regulation, legalistic enforcement of detailed accountability schemes or school administrators' belief in the necessity for strict compliance leads to a considerable amount of non-productive effort, diverting those local educators who are in fact dedicated to the statutory goals from important tasks to low-priority compliance activities. A 1977 National Institute of Education study, based on a survey of state Title I directors, concluded that the extensive regulations dealing with the planning and delivery of educational services 'establish a complex process of instructional planning that is not demonstrably connected to . . . the quality of instructional services.'[28]

One consequence of such overinclusive requirements is the demoralizing experience of wasted time and effort. Compliance with procedural requirements can displace activities that teachers and other service providers regard as more important or educationally valid,[29] just as industrial safety engineers complain about the way in which OSHA inspections divert them from higher-priority safety goals. School districts spend more effort negotiating with highly educated parents over whether the public school should pay for specialized private services than on the proper classification of the disadvantaged children who presumably were to be the primary beneficiaries of a more finely individualized and participatory pupil-assignment process.[30]

When a school district's efforts are diverted toward proving it is in compliance with regulatory procedural requirements, it may even have to forego more imaginative, but harder to document, instruction techniques. With respect to enforcement of Title I compensatory education regulations, Burnes states:

> Because many local districts have historically found it easier to document that services are supplementary (to regular non-Title I programs) when the children are in a 'pulled out' class, most districts . . . do pull children out of the regular classroom to receive Title I services, even though few research data suggest this is a more effective teaching strategy.[31]

Arthur Wise argues that pervasive requirements of evaluation by testing induce some educators to focus on those educational goals that can be easily measured.[32] For teachers who see their role as broader — stimulating creativity, transmitting a cultural heritage and modes of thought, teaching oral skills, etc. — a focus on meeting testable objectives seems in no small degree to trivialize education and divert them from more important objectives.

Legalistic procedures can also lead to 'over-compliance,' that is, to measures by school districts that are required neither by the letter nor the spirit of the law, but that will help keep the district out of legal trouble with auditors, parents, and advocacy groups. In a study of the implementation of PL 94-142, some school districts were found to have 'given in' to questionable demands by aggressive parents of handicapped children for special services because the administrators wished to avoid due process hearings and appeals; those legal proceedings, administrators noted, often draw media attention and make both the administrators and the district 'look bad.'[33] Conversely, fears of legalistic enforcement can lead to defensiveness in relationships with parents.

School districts do not seem to have resorted to the increased legal contestation and appeals that have marked the business response to legalistic regulation. But there certainly has been enough resentment to stimulate a significant political counterattack, as reflected in the Reagan Administration's proposal to eliminate regulation of schools by consolidating all categorical grant programs into unrestricted block grants to the states. As in the case of business regulation, the bitterest fruit of legalistic regulation has been an undiscriminating deregulation movement that threatens to undermine the positive contributions of the programs.

Possibilities and Limits of Flexible Enforcement

With respect to business regulation, it was suggested that a strategy of flexible enforcement could be not only more reasonable than legalistic enforcement, but also more effective, in that it could lead to more cooperation and more imaginative approaches to the achievement of regulatory goals. The assumptions that underlie that suggestion would also seem to be applicable to the enforcement of school regulations.

One assumption, for example, is that while explicit legal mandates and some threat of enforcement is necessary, most regulated entities are responsive to informal regulatory instructions, or at least those that appear reasonable under the circumstances, without having to be hit with severe and automatic sanctions for all violations. When such attitudes exist in the schools, literal and inflexible enforcement of detailed regulations may do more harm than good.

Perhaps the most important achievement of tougher business regulation has been stimulating corporations to hire in-house professionally trained technical experts who share with enforcement officials the general values and goals of the regulatory program, who manage shadow inspectorates inside corporations, and who become advocates for regulatory goals in internal struggles over resources. Similarly, Paul Hill points out that local school officials appointed as 'compliance officers' and told to master the detailed federal regulations on expenditure of special education grants remain local employees, 'but their special expertise — and thus their professional standing is based on the . . . programs they manage. These officials constitute a special interest group within the ... education agencies that employ them. Within some limits, the federal government can rely on them to take autonomous action on behalf of compliance with the intent of federal programs'.[34]

The threat of enforcement, of course, has been crucial in creating the in-house compliance staff and in giving them a measure of 'clout.' Moreover, the existence of some specific regulations is important in this regard, because the categorical nature of federal regulations helps local specialists mobilize support for their programs vis-à-vis other budget items,[35] just as quality-control engineers in food processing plants cite FDA regulations when dunning management for funds for projects the engineers think important. For this reason, replacing categorical grant regulations with unrestricted block grants might severely undermine the position of specialists at the local level. Flexible regulation, on the other hand, would suggest retention of the legal power provided by categorical regulations, but would use it selectively or sparingly. The idea of flexible regulation calls upon enforcement officials to regard local specialists as allies and expert informants, to omit punishment or adverse publicity for formal violations that local officials can show are not serious,[36] and to direct governmental pressure toward problems the local specialists regard as important.

Flexible enforcement also would require enforcement officials to be alert to the reasons for a school district's failure to comply with regulations. If some Title I violations represent wholly unjustifiable attempts to divert federal funds for general educational purposes, other violations represent not attempts to evade the general purposes of the law, but attempts to achieve them in ways that local educators believe to be fair and appropriate — even if not in accordance with the regulations drafted in Washington. Moreover, as the business regulation experience indicates, when officials criticize or penalize all departures from the regulations, without acknowledging that the good faith judgments of professionals in the particular setting might be more important than the steps required by the rulebook, they incur resentment and run a serious risk of destroying the cooperative impulse so necessary to the achievement of statutory goals.

Many corporate regulatory violations, as suggested earlier, are due not to calculated evasion but to some sort of 'organizational' failure — weaknesses in supervising safety and maintenance routines, failures to follow up on known problems — often in contravention of official corporate policy. This suggested regulatory strategies aimed primarily at building regulated firms' capacity to comply. Similarly, the main reason most local districts fail to meet Title I objectives is not calculated evasion but a sort of organizational incompetence.[37] This might include indecision about what will work, getting overwhelmed by regulatory deadlines and administrative difficulties, and letting planning demands slide in the face of the many other problems, pressures, and crises faced by urban schools. From this standpoint, as Richard Elmore argues, enforcement officials would be better advised to conceive of their jobs in terms of consultation or 'helping' — providing information, organizational analysis, and instructional advice, rather than enforcing rules.[38] The US Department of Education does now send management teams to the states not only to address compliance issues, but also to 'concern themselves with the management capacity' of the state agencies 'to promote more effective programs.' But assistance from both federal and state officials 'seems to be addressed primarily to showing (local district) officials how to run compliant programs,' not 'to helping . . . (them) provide more effective programs.'[39]

In business regulation, as discussed earlier, movement toward flexible enforcement, however desirable, is politically and bureaucratically difficult. The inevitable recurrence of catastrophic accidents, combined with the difficulty of assessing the seriousness of violations, makes it hard for enforcers to be sure it is safe to substitute its own control method for the one specified in the rules. Informal negotiation with business over legal obligations carries the risk of criticism for 'selling out.' Legalistic enforcement is safer.

In some ways, the conditions for flexible enforcement are more hopeful in the educational area. The business regulation agencies that have moved toward flexible regulation tend to specialize in a particular industry or a limited set of technologies — for example, truck safety regulators and some specialized FDA units. At the other extreme, OSHA inspectors who go from industry to industry are less capable of making subtle distinctions, analyzing weaknesses, seeing through weak excuses, or offering constructive suggestions. On that continuum, education law enforcement officials are relatively specialized. With proper training and indoctrination in a less legalistic conception of enforcement, they could learn to be more selective in enforcement and more helpful to local schools.

On the other hand, school regulators deal with an uncertain technology. Since no one knows for sure what would be a good compensatory or bilingual education strategy, it may be hard for the Office of Civil Rights official to decide whether a deviation from a program-related regulation is serious or not, or whether a failure to adequately document a referral of a handicapped child covers up a failure to think about the case carefully. Here, too, an insistence on following the rules is a far simpler choice for the bureaucrat.

Similarly, it is hard for enforcement officials to make the value judgments implicit in many decisions concerning nonliteral compliance. Many controversies arising under PL 94-142, as noted earlier, while legally about the 'appropriate education' due a handicapped student, are also about whether the school must pay for privately provided special education services, and hence are about redistributing scarce educational resources to a special few. A school's refusal to make the referral may be based at bottom on an implicit cost-benefit argument: the added benefits for the special student (especially because they set a precedent) are not worth the costs this and similar decisions will impose on other students by diverting resources from 'regular' education. Lacking conceptual tools or hard data to 'test' such a cost-benefit analysis, and lacking any statutory guidance concerning the maximum a community's education system should be compelled to sacrifice in order to assist the most unfortunate, it is obviously very hard for an enforcement official or a judge to evaluate the school's argument. Moreover, the characterization of the choice in terms of violating or respecting the legal rights of the handicapped child makes any consideration of the issue in cost-benefit or compromise terms legally unorthodox and, in the views of some advocacy groups, highly illegitimate. And such advocacy groups, it must be remembered, are empowered to take the school district to court, or appeal the decision of an enforcement agency or a trial judge who seems to be 'watering down' the unqualified rights established by statute.[40] Uniform and literal application of the regulations is thus a legally and politically safer course for enforcement officials and judges.

Similarly, there is always the danger that flexible enforcement officials will err, that an independent investigation will reveal serious misallocation of funds or a highly publicized violation of some children's rights, thus embarrassing the enforcement agency's leadership. These scandals can occur even in a strict regime, of course, but a record of stringent insistence on accountability requirements at least provides the agency with some defenses: it can place the blame on insufficient appropriations for enforcement.

In the business regulation sphere, regulators have been provided with legal authority to think in trade-off terms at the rule-making level by recent statutes and presidential orders that require agencies to analyze the relative costs and benefits of alternative proposed regulations. President Carter's Regulatory Analysis Review Group and a similar panel established by President Reagan were authorized to review rules proposed by Executive Branch regulatory agencies and to issue public criticism of those that the governmental economists did not think cost-efficient. It might be useful to subject proposed educational regulations to similar prior analyses, or to review existing accountability regulations with an eye to reducing the most extensive reporting and testing requirements, especially with respect to those districts that do not have a demonstrated record of bad faith in the implementation of statutory goals. At the enforcement level, to prevent 'individual case unreasonableness' stemming from legalistic application of generally reasonable but inevitably overinclusive regulations, flexibility would be bolstered by a legal mandate authorizing enforcement officials and judges to consider exceptions, modifications, and variances, and without an unreasonably heavy burden of paper justification.

Constructing criteria for such non-uniform treatment and developing a legally-defensible rationale for a flexible mode of implementing regulations are important, hard to meet goals for the regulation of schools and of business alike. The alternative may be continuing political backlash and wholesale deregulation that throws out the baby of progress along with the bathwater of regulatory unreasonableness.

Notes

1 BARDACH, E. and KAGAN, R.A. (1982) *Going By the Book: The Problem of Regulatory Unreasonableness* Philadelphia, Temple University Press, (A Twentieth Century Fund Report). The research on which the study was based entailed interviews of field inspectors and higher enforcement officials of the Federal Food and Drug Administration, the Occupational Safety and Health Administration, the Louisiana Air Pollution Control Administration, and the following California state agencies: the Division of Occupational Safety and Health, the Food and Drug Division of the Nursing Home Division in the Department of Health, the Bureau of Motor Carrier Safety, the Milk and Dairy Section of the Department of Agriculture, and the Bay Area Air Pollution Control District. In addition, we interviewed numerous managers and engineers in companies regulated by the above agencies, concentrating on a limited number of firms in certain industries: iron and steel foundries (4), aluminum manufacturers (2), automobile assembly plants (2), blood banks and blood products manufacturers (2), petroleum refineries (3), trucking firms and trucking departments (3), nursing homes (2), and dairy products manufacturers (2). We also interviewed labor union officers in four of the above companies and safety experts from two insurance firms. The research was conducted during the 1977–80 period.

2 Similar patterns can be found in contemporary studies of regulatory enforcement in Great Britain and in Sweden. See, for example, CARSON, W.G. (1970) 'White collar crime and enforcement of the factory acts,' *British Journal of Criminology*, October, p. 394; HAWKINS, K., (1984) *Environment and Enforcement*, London, OUP and KELMAN, S., (1981) *Regulating America, Regulating Sweden: A Comparative Study of Occupational Safety and Health Regulation in the United States and Sweden* Cambridge, MIT Press.

3 See WILSON, J.Q. (1974) 'The politics of regulation', in MCKIE, J. (Ed) *Corporate Responsibility and Business Predicament*, Washington, D.C., Brookings Institute, pp. 135–168; LEVIN, M. (1979) 'Politics and polarity: The limits of OSHA reform,' *Regulation*, November/December, pp. 33 and 36; and ACKERMAN, B. and HASSLER, W. (1981) *Clean Coal/Dirty Air*, New Haven, Yale University Press.

4 DANACEAU, P. (1980) *Regulation: The View from Janesville, Wisconsin, and a Regulator's Perspective*, Washington, D.C., U.S. Regulatory Council, March, p. 10.

5 See studies reported in MENDELOFF, J. (1974) *Regulating Safety: A Political and Economic Analysis of the Federal Occupational Safety and Health Program*, Cambridge, MIT Press; and BACON, L.S. (1980) *Bargaining for Job Safety and Health*, Cambridge, MIT Press.

6 See SILLS, D.L. *et al.* (1981) *The Accident at Three Mile Island: The Human Dimension*, Boulder, Westview Press; and (1979) 'Behind the crash: FAA inquiry charges many errors in manufacturing and maintenance of DC-10 airliners,' *Wall Street Journal*, 17 July, pp. 1 and 25.

7 See also MUIR, W.K. Jr's portrait of the 'professional' police officer in his (1977) *Police: Streetcorner Politicians*, Chicago, University of Chicago Press.

8 STONE, C. (1979) *Where the Law Ends: Social Control of Corporate Behavior*, New York, Harper Colophon.

9 BERMAN, P., (1980) 'Thinking about programmed and adaptive implementation: matching strategies to situations,' in INGRAM, H. and MASON, D. (Eds)., *Why Policies Succeed and Fail*, Beverly Hills, Sage Publications.

10 Among the advocacy organizations involved in Washington lobbying in the administration of Title I, for example, are the National Advisory Council for the Education of Disadvantaged Children, the National Welfare Rights Organization, the Legal Standards and Education Project of the NAACP, the Lawyers Committee for Civil

Rights Under Law, and the NAACP Legal Defense and Educational Fund. Paul Peterson, in his forthcoming book on federal education policy, reports several instances in which 'exposés' or detailed recommendations issued by such organizations resulted in tighter and more detailed regulations and increases in the Office of Education's enforcement staff. PETERSON, P. *Federal Policy and American Education* (A Twentieth Century Fund study), Chapter 4.

11 See *Martin Luther King Jr. Elementary School Children v. Michigan Board of Education*, 473 F. Supp. 1372 (E.D. Mich. 1979); and GLAZER, N. (1981) 'Black English and reluctant judges,' *The Public Interest*, Winter, p. 40. See generally EPSTEIN N., (1977) *Language, Ethnicity, and the Schools: Policy Alternatives for Bilingual-Bicultural Education*, Washington, D.C., Institute for Educational Leadership, George Washington University.

12 See, for example, *Industrial Union Department, AFL-CIO v. American Petroleum Inst.*, 448 U.S. 607 (1980).

13 See KIRST, M. and BERTKEN, K. (1981) 'How fair fair hearings,' a summary of their research findings in *IFG Policy Notes*, Vol. 2, No. 1, Winter, Institute for Research on Educational Finance and Governance, Stanford University; and STERNS, M. GREENE, D. and DAVID, J.L. (1979) *Local Implementation of PL 94-142* Menlo Park, Educational Research Center, SRI International, December.

14 STERNS, M. *et al.* (1979) *op. cit*, p. 91.

15 BENSON, C.S. (1980) 'Centralization and legalization in vocational education,' paper presented to a Stanford-U.C. Berkeley seminar on law and governance, Institute for Research on Educational Finance and Governance, Stanford University.

16 See *Lora v. Board of Education of New York*, 456 F. Supp. 1211 (E.D. N.Y. 1978).

17 STEARNS, M. *et al*, (1979) *op. cit*, pp. 89–90. It should be added that the requirement to submit detailed written proposals concerning the use of funds, and to provide for objective measurement of educational results, was also required for Title I (aid to low-income students) and many other federal categorical grant programs. The 1978 Title I amendments (partly because self-evaluations by many school districts were castigated as insufficiently scientific and objective) provide that the evaluations must be prepared by 'independent' evaluators, pursuant to standards prescribed by federal officials.

18 RABKIN, J. (1980) 'Office for Civil Rights,' in WILSON, J.Q. (Ed.) *The Politics of Regulation* New York, Basic Books, pp. 325–32.

19 See Lawyers' Committee for Civil Rights Under Law, (1977) *An Analysis of the Legal Framework for State Administration of Title I of the Elementary and Secondary Education Act of 1965*, Washington, D.C.; and TIMPANE M. (Ed.), (1978) *The Federal Interest in Financing Schooling*, Cambridge, Ballinger.

20 Indeed, under federal law providing aid to retarded and other developmentally disabled students, recipient states must establish independent advocacy organizations empowered to sue service providers for non-compliance with applicable laws and regulations. Federal civil rights statutes encourage lawsuits to correct violations by school districts and inaction by law enforcement officials by allowing winning parties to collect their counsel fees from the defendant agency. The Office of Civil Rights in HEW was, in fact, the object of repeated successful suits by minority group organizations concerning inadequate enforcement, and was subjected to court orders requiring more prompt and thorough response to complaints.

21 The 'comparability' concept stems from Title I provisions designed to ensure that federal monies are used only 'to supplement, not supplant' preexisting services and that students in the program are receiving educational services comparable to those being offered students in better-off districts. (It is not hard to imagine the complexity of the effort that would be required to demonstrate such 'comparability' if the standard were taken truly seriously.) For example, in *Nicholson v. Pittenger*, 364 F. Supp. 669 (E.D. Pa. 1973), Pennsylvania state school administrators were held to

have violated federal regulations requiring full 'comparability' in educational services between schools that receive Title I aid and the 'richer' schools that do not. The court's opinion does not discuss the extent of disparities, the problems of preventing them, or their importance in educational terms (perhaps because nobody knows their importance). The court-ordered remedy, moreover, was to call for more documentation and formal rationalization.

22 BURNES, D. (1978) 'A case study of federal involvement in education,' *Proceedings of the American Academy of Political Science*, 33, p. 87.

23 Similarly, commenting on studies of the implementation of PL 94-142, Christine Hassell observed that deviating from federal or state regulations 'are a source of fear and uncertainty to those at the local level who are working in new roles and areas of responsibility.... Under these conditions, even professionals ... will adhere to rules rather than following their own discretion.' HASSELL, C. (1981) 'Learning vs. the Law,' Institute for Research on Educational Finance and Governance, Stanford University, *IFG Policy Notes*, Winter.

24 Of course, even if most managers have this attitude with respect to most regulations, that still leaves room for a large number — in absolute terms — of willful corporate regulatory violations. To recognize those violations, however, does not undercut the general point about the high proportion of law-abidingness with respect to most regulations.

25 STEARNS, M. GREENE, D. and DAVID, J.L. (1979) *Local Implementation of PL 94-142*, Menlo Park, CA., Education Research Center, SRI International, December.

26 See KIRST, M. and JUNG, R. (1980) *The Utility of a Longitudinal Approach in Assessing Implementation: A Thirteen-Year View of Title I, ESEA*, Stanford, Institute for Research on Educational Finance and Governance, June; and GOETTEL, R. (1978) 'Federal assistance to National Target Groups: The ESEA Title I experience,' in TIMPANE, M. (Ed.,) *op. cit.*

27 During the early 1970s, for example, Office of Education officials were reluctant to enforce Title I requirements that federal funds be used to 'supplement, not supplant' local spending. See US National Institute of Education, (1977) *Administration of Compensatory Education*, Washington, D.C., Department of Health, Education, and Welfare, pp. 40–44.

28 HILL, P. (1974) *Enforcement and Informal Pressure in the Management of Federal Categorical Programs in Education*, Santa Monica, CA. The Rand Corporation. discussing the National Institute of Education's (1977) *The Administration of Compensatory Education*, Washington, DC.

29 WEATHERLY, R. and LIPSKY, M. (1977) 'Street level bureaucrats and institutional innovation: Implementing special education reform,' *Harvard Education Review* 47, p. 171. Weatherly and Lipsky studied the implementation of a Massachusetts law that, like PL 94-142, requires schools to prepare an individualized plan for each student, including mandatory conferences, meetings with parents, and written justifications, in every case. Special education teachers and administrators seemed to take the purposes of the law very seriously, said Weatherly and Lipsky, despite weak monitoring efforts by the state. But they regarded the legally prescribed steps as a substantively meaningless 'bureaucratic hurdle to be gotten over as quickly as possible' in a majority of cases.

30 STEARNS, M. *et al*, (1979) *op. cit.*

31 BURNES, D. (1978) *op. cit.*

32 WISE, A. (1979) *Legislated Learning: The Bureaucratization of the American Classroom*, Berkeley, University of California Press.

33 *Ibid.*, p. 103.

34 HILL, P. (1974) *op. cit.*

35 BERMAN, P. and MCLAUGHLIN, M.W. (1978), 'Federal support for improved educa-

tional practice,' in TIMPANE, M. (Ed.), *op. cit.*

36 Non-compliance with Title I regulations, for example, is undoubtedly of varying degrees of seriousness. It is wholly indefensible to spend compensatory funds on audiovisual aids for the auditorium, on salaries for football coaches, or on band uniforms. It is less reprehensible, however, when funds are spent on new educational programs that are perfectly targeted toward only the *most* disadvantaged students as required by the dictates of federal 'concentration' regulations. And it is still less serious when funds are spent on plausible compensatory education classes, but without meeting regulations stipulating clear articulation of objectives and frequent and 'scientific' evaluation of results.

37 BERMAN, P. and MCLAUGHLIN, M.W. (1978) *op. cit.*

38 ELMORE, R. (1979) *Complexity and Control: What Legislators and Administrators Can Do About Implementation*, Seattle, Institute of Governmental Research, University of Washington.

39 GOETTEL, R. (1978) 'Federal assistance to National Target Groups: The ESEA Title I experience,' in TIMPANE, M. (Ed.), *op. cit.* The capacity-building strategy was illustrated by Judge Weinstein's decision in *Lora v. Board of Education of New York* (456 F. Supp. 1211 E.D. N.Y. 1978). The judge found that the city had violated the Civil Rights Act and federal education regulations by referring disproportionate numbers of minority children to special schools for emotionally disturbed and disruptive students. But he recognized that the 'racial imbalance' problem was a difficult one, largely because white parents tended to send their children to private schools when the district sought to refer them to special schools. And, he recognized that the city had not been violating the law deliberately or acting in bad faith, having set up certain due process mechanisms. The judge thus rejected the plaintiffs' demands for more explicit rules to govern classification and referral of students, saying: 'Courts are not in a position to lead the most advanced of the educators . . . in enforcing non-existent standards.' And the remedies Judge Weinstein called for were essentially *educational*; for example, he ordered school administrators to inform all teachers in the system of the court's concern about possible bias in decision making, to give relevant referral committees special training in avoiding racial or cultural bias in evaluation, to provide clearer (and fewer) notice forms for parents and provide an advocate for children considered for referral, and to increase minority representation on decision-making staffs. One could imagine regulatory enforcement officials, too, using their legal power with respect to violations to strike 'plea bargains' whereby the district agrees to undertake 'capacity-building' reforms (as opposed to more faithful and detailed adherence to the testing and documentation regulations).

40 See RABKIN, J. (1980) *op. cit.*

The Culture of Policy: Aggregate versus Individualist Thinking about the Regulation of Education

Ann Swidler
Stanford University

This chapter is concerned with an issue that normally lies just beyond the horizon of debates over policy and governance in education: that is, the cultural understandings that shape and constrain the legitimate ends of public policy. Problems of governance in education arise in part from the distinctive technical and institutional features of the educational enterprise. But the difficulties of educational governance are also rooted in deeper American dilemmas, particularly those concerning the relationship between private claims and public purposes.[1]

Americans are, bit by bit, assembling the elements of a centralized welfare state. Whether prompted by judicial or legislative action, much of what we have called legalization in education involves expanding the sphere of public responsibility, making the claims of individuals on the public sphere more extensive and more uniform, and integrating local, state, and federal levels of responsibility. The problem is that both politically and culturally Americans do not like centralized planning and administration. Their vocabulary of moral and political debate rests almost entirely on conceptions of society as made up of autonomous, freely choosing individuals who should, at least ideally, be responsible for their own welfare.[2] American ideology conceives the role of government narrowly, justifying it not as planning or providing for the welfare of society as a whole, but as overcoming problems of coordination, conflict, or corruption arising out of the actions of individuals. We increasingly have a welfare state, but we remain unable to generate culturally legitimate commitments to public purposes which might guide its actions.

Thus, as federal and state involvement in education grows, there is an increased sense of crisis. One way to describe this is as a loss of a sense of mission and purpose in education. But the other way to understand the frustration and dissatisfaction of those involved in educational governance is to recognize that what we have done is to expand the sphere of government regulation and centralized controls over education while failing to tie these to a set of mandates or positive educational purposes government is supposed to pursue. New controls seem necessary to achieve particular ends, but without a sense of legitimate collective purposes, public power in America is bound to remain illegitimate, frustrating and demeaning those subject to its authority, demoralizing those who exercise it.

I wish to suggest, then, that a proper focus of thinking and research for those who wish to understand the crisis of educational governance is the set of cultural images and understandings that provide the basis for policy debate.[3] The approach I have pursued here is a set of exploratory interviews with officials involved in formulating, implementing, and overseeing educational policy in California. I have been particularly interested in finding out how understandings of the public purposes education might serve are formulated and justified by those who deal with the nitty-gritty of educational governance on a day-to-day basis.

Many scholars have noted that public education in America lacks any single, clear public mandate. While scholars can point out rich, and continually evolving, public purposes which have emerged over the course of American educational history[4], both state and federal educational regulation has steadfastly avoided formulating a set of educational purposes that might guide public policy. John Meyer has noted that the states, where legal responsibility for education is lodged, do set minimal standards for the provision of education by professionally qualified personnel, and that they sometimes specify the general outlines of such matters as curriculum and textbook selection.[5] However states, like the federal government, lack clear, overall educational policies, even where they are extensively responsible for providing or administering educational funding. States have taken responsibility for administering federal monies, but without comprehensive policy guidance. As Berke and Kirst[6] observe:

> An overarching problem of state administration in general, but particularly in education, is the norm of 'localism.' The respect and deference to local control, strongest in New England, maintains a firm foothold in all states. In education, 'the religion of localism' is a shorthand expression of a sociological norm which says that the local communities should be the dominant partners in the American governmental mix of federal, state, and local entities. This means that the LEA should have the major voice in determining policies, directions and operations of schools. Localism helps to restrict the prerogatives, scope, and style of SEA [State Education Agency] operations.

Despite the growing concentration of fiscal and administrative control at federal, and especially state levels, there is an enduring reluctance or ambivalence about formulating educational purposes that might guide (and restrain) the uses of this growing power. This uncertainty about purpose, the public culture from which it derives, and the creative improvisations that education administrators with centralized public responsibility necessarily make are the focus of this essay. They describe contrasting approaches to educational governance: on the one hand, rigid and frequently ineffective strategies based on enforcing compliance with fixed rules or standards, versus, on the other, more flexible strategies oriented toward encouraging voluntary cooperation, solving problems, and rewarding substantive progress toward public goals. If, then, compliance-based strategies have so many disadvantages, and strategies that permit learning and negotiation have many advantages, why have the objectives of educational reform so often been attempted on the basis of the assumptions built into the compliance model?

There are, of course, institutional reasons why much of recent educational reform has come from courts enforcing rights, rather than legislatures articulating comprehensive public policy. But I would like to argue that one fundamental ingredient of the problem is cultural, resting on the essential individualism, moralism, and localism of American conceptions of the public good.

Historically, of course, public education in America has rested on a richly elaborated set of public purposes — in essence the creation of productive and democratic citizens, a kind of nation-building through the creation of virtuous individuals.[7] But these public purposes are irreducibly individualist in their basic assumptions. The public good can be realized only by and through the moral and construction or reconstruction of individuals.

This fusion of individualism and moralism pervades American public life, emerging particularly strongly in relation to education, which is the quintessential technique for pursuing public goals by attempting to shape particular kinds of individuals. When Americans wish, for example, to reform society, they do so by attempting the moral reformation of individuals.[8] This individualist principle, in turn, makes group life dependent on the moral agreement, and thus the character and will, of individuals, creating strong pressure for both consensus and conformity within groups.

Individualism and moralism emerge with great clarity in other arenas of American public policy. Constance Perin, for example, has analyzed the public images that lie behind local decisions about housing and land use in American cities — images of such fundamentally individualist matters as the moral differences between homeowners and renters or the moral dangers of urban life itself.[9] Similarly, Judith de Neufville has examined the symbols and myths invoked in land-use planning, particularly the myths of private property and small-scale ownership which developed around the 'Jeffersonian image of the yeoman farmer'[10]. Finally, Joseph Gusfield has done an extensive study of the symbolic definitions surroundings drinking-driving as a public issue.[11] The problem of automobile deaths in accidents involving drunken drivers has been defined entirely as a matter of persuading (or forcing) individuals not to mix drinking and driving. Other kinds of public policies, involving such matters as the design of automobiles or highways, for example, have historically been ignored in pursuit of the highly dramatized image of the 'killer-drunk.' Even more telling, perhaps, for our purposes, is Gusfield's claim that during the 1960s, when the focus of public action began to shift toward such issues as safety in the design and manufacture of automobiles, the individualist and moralist aspect of public policy remained. '[T]he new consciousness ... replaces the motorist, drunk or sober, by the automobile industry as the bête noire of safety advocates'[12]

Unlike traffic safety, land-use planning, or health-care regulation, educational policy does not conflict directly with ideals of private property and the inhibition against interfering with private economic and market choices. What replaces the sanctity of private property in the educational arena is the tradition of local control of schools. Education is legitimately a public function to the extent that it embodies and perpetuates the values and choices of a local community.

There are thus two fundamental dimensions to the cultural dilemmas faced by those who would govern education at the state and federal levels. First, educational purposes are conceived in largely individualist and moralist terms which make it difficult to formulate public policies to govern the kinds of aggregate or collective outcomes with which most policy makers deal. Second, as federal and state responsibility for funding public education grows, the tradition of local control still means that there is no legitimate state or federal responsibility for education as a whole. Both these aspects of the American political culture have, paradoxically, fed the tendency of state and federal regulators to stress compliance over problem-solving and assistance.

If education is fundamentally neither a federal nor state responsibility, national and state intervention in education can be justified only as a defense of individual rights against neglect or malice on the part of local school authorities. Federal funding for education, for example, has been defined as responding to special and narrowly delimited educational crises — failure of schools to teach disadvantaged children, the extra burden on local school districts of educating children of federal employees who do not pay local taxes, a crisis in national defense preparedness, or the special educational needs of handicapped children. Although in actual practice each of these federal programs is rapidly expanded to allow broader and more geographically dispersed funding than its original mandate implied,[13] there is still no overall federal interest in education beyond correcting specific failures and abuses.

Major federal interventions in education have been undertaken to ensure the 'rights' of disadvantaged groups of children and parents — economically disadvantaged children, handicapped children, and limited-English speaking children. The appeal to rights seems to legitimate federal intervention even in autonomous local arenas like schools. However, the language of 'rights' implies precisely the kinds of absolute but limited claims that preclude more adaptive and flexible educational governance. In theory, at least, negotiation, compromise, adaptation to local capacities and circumstances, and continual learning from experience are inappropriate when applied to matters of rights.

If federal and state roles in education are limited to enforcing individual rights and correcting serious flaws in the coverage or implementation of locally organized educational programs, then it is little wonder that federal and state educational administrators so often rely on the compliance mode in their attempts to influence schools. Even when what the courts or federal and state administrators impose are in fact demands for institutional innovation, for improved services, or for novel programs to serve formerly neglected groups, such innovative programs must be defined as correcting flaws or inequities in current programs, not as developing a positive educational program.

In America, then, the suspicion of public power and an inability to formulate clear public purposes leads paradoxically to a stress on compliance by public officials who have a stronger mandate to protect individual rights and curb local abuses than to pursue active public ends. These tendencies in turn interact in peculiar ways with the individualism and moralism of American civic culture. On the one hand, a stress on the virtues of voluntarism and local initiative serves as a brake on state and federal intervention, sometimes, for example, leading to the provision of federal monies with no clear provision for effective monitoring or oversight.[14] On the other hand, individualism and moralism give educational governance a punitive cast. Federal and state administrators are not implementing new social policy; they are enforcing law against the recalcitrance of bad, law-violating schools and school districts. Americans are embarrassed about articulating common purposes, and they prefer sheriffs to either politicians or planners.

Varieties of Public Purpose

The distinction I have drawn above between righting particular wrongs and constructing more comprehensive public policy is of course considerably muted in practice. While legislation and regulation may be framed in terms of rights, political bargaining and negotiation enter at every stage of the process.

The problem for effective governance in education is not that there is no legitimate public language of policy debate, but that the dominant language enshrines individualistic images of the values that should guide policy. The parents and students who are the consumers of educational services are presumed to be autonomous, freely-choosing actors who know what educational services they want and how much they are willing to pay for schooling. Teachers are supposed to know what the content of a good education should be; and good, dedicated teachers are thought to be at the heart of the educational enterprise. Parents want 'the best' education for their children at a reasonable cost, and the community has a diffuse interest in the creation of competent citizens, capable employees, and so forth. Choices about what other values the schools should promote are thought best left to representatives of local community values — school boards, PTAs, and parents and teachers themselves. The role of state government has been to facilitate adequate provision of these services (through licensing laws, certification requirements, compulsory attendance laws, school building codes, and so forth), while the federal government has intervened primarily to ensure equity in access to educational goods, however defined.

This fundamentally individualistic and voluntarist imagery has provided justification for substantial federal and state involvement in education, under a patchwork of programs targeted to specific groups. But it provides little guidance to those directly involved in formulating and administering educational policy. By its very nature, the work of these legislators and administrators implicitly, and sometimes explicitly, raises questions about aggregate planning and public purpose. The difficulty they face is to link the work they do and the choices they must make to a meaningful moral and political vocabulary.*

Individualistic language is in part enforced by political realities. Because those involved in the politics and administration of education are often trying to win funds for schooling from potentially reluctant legislators and voters, they tend to stay close to the public language of 'quality education' or the 'right' of each child to an education. On the other hand, it may be most difficult for those directly involved in educational politics or administration to develop any comprehensive view of educational policy. A local school official, with long experience dealing with federal and state legislators and administrators, claimed that it was difficult for anyone to think comprehensively about educational policy because the world of educational policymakers was 'so hectic.' Legislators just want to know 'what works,' and few administrators have a mandate to think comprehensively about education. Most are simply trying to administer particular legislatively mandated programs. State legislators, who legally have the authority to determine the shape and quality of public education, may be least likely to formulate overall educational policy. A senior staff member of an education committee of the California legislature, when asked about educational policy, said the legislature had no educational policy. 'Policy is ideological; that's close to God. Policy isn't a series of bills.'

State versus local control, the legislative staff member argued, is the consuming issue of educational governance. But the state has taken a contradictory position. In 1968 the legislature began passing bills to give the locals more power, and by 1973 had a 'permissive bill,' leaving most matters to local control. But at the same time, they have kept adding categorical programs and building up the State Department of Education. While the legislature doesn't govern education, its members have little faith that any other public body can either. The State's Department of Education ought to provide leadership in education, but it doesn't. It sees its role as advocating all educational programs,

* The section that follows is based on interviews with California legislative staff and state Department of Education administrators, except where indicated. I both quote and paraphrase my interviewees, from notes taken during each interview. Interviews were conducted in 1981 and 1982.

rather than choosing among them, and it has been successful in getting money from the legislature, but that is all.

If legislatures are largely unwilling or unable to think comprehensively about educational policy, we might nonetheless expect to find some capacity for overall planning at the point where competing educational demands meet — in budget decisions, for example. And indeed, a staff member of the Legislative Analyst's Office, responsible for analyzing and making recommendations about all items in the California governor's budget and analyzing the fiscal impact of all legislation, spoke with great intensity about the need for a comprehensive educational policy against which the success or failure of particular programs could be judged. In his view, the State completely fails to do this. At least since 1970, the legislature has removed all specific curriculum requirements and requirements for the time students must spend on specific courses. This was intended to eliminate the 'seat-time straitjacket,' giving local districts more flexibility and affirming that 'Sacramento wasn't all-knowing.' The effect is that while there are 'program goals' there are no 'output goals.' There are lots of 'little, special programs,' like bilingual education or compensatory education, but there are no general goals. 'What if one of these programs succeeds? What about a bilingual student who learns English? Then there are no goals for his education.' The state requires that certain courses be taught, but there are no requirements in terms of the time spent on particular courses or course content. It is hard, in his view, for the legislature to address issues of educational goals, in part because of the ideology of local control and in part because of a lack of consensus. The legislature delegates the selection of priorities to the local level. This means that local people are never told what the state expects them to do with the funds it provides.

Despite his commitment to the ideal of coherent educational policy goals, and his acute awareness of the trade-offs that must necessarily be made between one educational goal and another, this budget analyst is himself uncertain about the ends education should serve, and even more unsure about how to link up his professional concerns as a budget specialist with his personal sense of what public education could or should accomplish. In his professional role, he says, the goal is 'all kids should learn up to their maximum ability in the most efficient possible system,' but that doesn't give much realistic guidance. His job is to evaluate programs against 'analytic goals,' which must be concrete and measurable, to find out whether a particular program has the effects claimed.

Aside from the search for clear output goals against which to measure program success, budget analysts have few independent criteria for thinking about educational policy. In general they look for 'inefficient' programs which can be cut to reduce costs, and they don't look for areas in which to increase example of the state's Program Review policy, designed in part to encourage measure come under particular scrutiny. The legislative analyst offered the example of the state's Program Review policy, designed in part to encourage schools to evaluate their own operations and to develop capacities to plan on their own. In his view, although the Program Review unit claimed to carry out 'quality reviews,' it 'lacked sufficient objective measures of quality.' 'The claim that "good things happen and people feel better" isn't enough. Couldn't that be achieved without spending a million dollars? If reviews are such a good thing, wouldn't people review themselves?' He was proud that his office stuck to an 'analytic basis' for evaluating programs, even if it was 'mechanistic,' and 'frequently didn't make common sense.'

Budget recommendations are also made on the basis of equity considerations, asking why some particular subgroup of children or families should receive funding, rather than having funding available to all potential recipients in the same category. The Legislative Analyst's office has recommended, for example, that state funds for reimbursement of costs of bilingual education mandated by courts and the federal government instead be reallocated to all school districts with limited-English-proficient students. Similarly, the Legislative Analyst's office had recommended that a special program for gifted migrant children in one California county be discontinued in favor of using the money to identify more migrant children for the state's regular programs for gifted children. There was no rationale for funding a program which was too expensive to be made available to more than a small number of migrant children.

Responsibility for statewide budgetary planning then forces the budget examiner to think comprehensively about education. More than other state officials, he needs a comprehensive, clear educational policy in order to do his own job effectively. He thinks the state should have clear educational goals, uniformly applied. He also naturally thinks in terms of trade-offs between one program and another, and is thus particularly sensitive to the need to set priorities 'in a world of limited resources.' Finally, he, virtually alone among state officials, actively welcomes centralization of governance, both over program content and administration. He would, for example, have a statewide salary schedule for teachers. 'Teachers' salaries shouldn't be related to the money local districts can spend, if in fact it's a statewide system. Especially since Proposition 13,' he argues, 'all money effectively comes from the state in the sense that the legislature allocates property tax dollars. All local property taxes are now limited in amount by law, and local property taxes are counted in the state's formula as an offset to state aid.' The 'locus of decision making' for local schools has made a radical shift to the legislature and the Governor, but they in turn provide resources without taking responsibility for saying what they should be used for.

For all his emphasis on the state's responsibility for educational governance, however, the legislative analyst is surprisingly diffident about the substantive goals educational policy should pursue. However intensely he speaks of technical matters within his professional domain — equalizing salaries among school districts, or evaluating programs according to clear output goals — his professional perspective offers him little guidance about the substantive purposes education should serve. When pressed about educational priorities, he refers first to the 'questions I have at a personal level.' And these questions are primarily matters of resources insufficient to meet competing goals. 'Are we funding schools at a level sufficient to accomplish our goals? Are students spending enough time in school? Is a five-period day sufficient to achieve higher levels of competence?' Managing education well means facing squarely the need for trade-offs. 'If admission standards to the University of California go up, is this going to exclude certain kids? If you have to provide vocational education, and so forth, maybe you can't give enough students Physics or whatever to meet the University's requirements.'

The budget analyst is, thus, more likely than other state officials to think in aggregate terms about educational policy, looking for comprehensive policies that produce measurable outcomes, rather than thinking purely in terms of the rights or well-being of particular children or groups of children, or of the competence or effort of teachers, parents, or local administrators. There is little of traditional American moralism in his political rhetoric. Yet, at the same time, his view of policy as a matter of measurable relationships between outputs and inputs cuts him off from a wider vocabulary in which he might think or talk about educational purpose. When pressed on the question of purpose, he must jump tracks, stepping out of his professional role with its concerns about comprehensive policies with clear goals and uniform administration, to speak again in terms of an educational purpose that would replicate in other students what he personally has learned and found most valuable. Here public values like good citizenship, skills that enable one to deal with the modern world, and capacities that would make one a productive worker again enter the picture. But they are cast outside the frame of public responsibility as matters of somewhat idiosyncratic personal preference. A professional responsibility for thinking in aggregate terms enforces a narrow technocratic view of policy objectives, which has difficulty incorporating or legitimating wider concerns about educational purpose.[15]

Creative Pragmatism — Centralizing Policy Through an Ideology of Voluntarism

Despite the growing state role in educational administration, no broad, innovative conception of all overall purposes of education has emerged, at least among the administrators and policymakers I have interviewed. However, in at least some parts of California's Department of Education, new conceptions of an active state role in education have begun to develop. What is most striking about these ideas is that they find a mandate for central policy initiative precisely in an ideology of voluntarism.

The administrators I interviewed in California's Department of Education were surprisingly hostile to ideas of monitoring and compliance, particularly given that monitoring compliance with federal and state legislation is one of their primary responsibilities. These administrators stressed that California's current Superintendent of Public Instruction, Wilson Riles, insisted that state administrators were 'not here to govern, but to offer leadership.'[16] A staff person in special education, like other administrators I interviewed, said the Department sought ways to emphasize quality, not just compliance; to give assistance to local school districts in achieving educational objectives, rather than simply monitoring their compliance with state and federal laws. A member of the Program Review unit, close to Riles' inner circle, described himself and those close to Riles as even more hostile to compliance. Under Riles, he said, the Department of Education has tried to strongly deemphasize compliance in favor of positive encouragement to local districts to think about improving educational quality. The first impulse of the state bureaucracy, he said, was of course to try to enforce compliance, but they had learned not to 'create a system designed for the bad guy and lay it on everyone. . . . The bad guys will keep getting away with bad things and will make a business out of dealing with the regulators. Good people will get frustrated, driven out.' People need help understanding programs and putting them in place. Compliance instead produces 'manipulation of symbols' and doesn't penetrate to classrooms.

What then takes the place of 'compliance' for these California education adminitrators, who in fact see themselves as still battling the dominant tendency in their own Department? They have attempted to develop an alternative approach, in which direct monitoring is replaced by indirect pressure, and in which the stress is on assistance to districts and schools to carry out programs they themselves initiate and shape.

The attempt to transform compliance pressures into assistance can be illustrated by the way the office of Program Evaluation and Research of the State Department of Education handled the demands created by the state law (AB 3408) requiring that students pass proficiency examinations in order to graduate from high school. A high-level administrator of Program Evaluation and Research pointed out first that unlike most state programs the requirement for proficiency exams allowed each school district to set its own standards and assigned no compliance role to the State Department of Education. Instead they were to provide 'technical assistance.' Key to this approach is the notion that local administrators and teachers are kept from meeting the goals of state programs in large part by not knowing what it is they are supposed to do or how to do it. It was thought important to assure a wide distribution of the skills school districts needed in order to prepare their own proficiency tests. The state office of Program Evaluation and Research trained people from local districts in how to construct tests on condition that those people would in turn be loaned to other districts to train other local school personnel. Thus the state 'did training of a network of trainers,' putting skills in the hands of local school personnel.

Even more central to the ideal of assistance over compliance enforcement was the way the program evaluation and research administrators dealt with problems or potential problems in the proficiency test requirement itself.

Many districts, for example, feared lawsuits from parents of students who failed the examinations. Rather than mandating specific standards for tests designed to make them lawsuit-proof, the state officials hired an outside legal consultant to advise districts on the general sorts of steps they might take to develop a 'reasonable' program — steps such as giving students sufficient advanced warning, soliciting community input during the development of the test, and so forth. On a more troublesome issue — that of testing children of migrant workers, who might be tested in schools with standards quite different from the school in which they had actually been educated — the preference for practical solutions over legalistic enforcement was even more in evidence. As the program evaluation administrator put it, from a compliance point of view, 'it's insoluble, because it's a problem of practice, not policy.' Instead of trying to solve the hypothetical tangle of responsibility this situation might create, his office first did research on the actual school enrollment patterns of migrant workers' children and discovered that the vast majority move among only a few districts. Then his office asked 'how could local districts be helped to solve this problem.' They then assembled the proficiency standards of the districts that enroll ninety per cent of migrant workers' children and had each district compare its own standards with those of the other districts. Then each district knew that it 'had the responsibility to teach for the standard of the district where the kid will be.' Insoluble as a matter of abstract principle, the problem of giving fair proficiency tests to the children of migrant workers could be solved only by helping local districts with additional information and encouraging them to make changes in their teaching practices which would in turn make their testing programs reasonable.

These state administrators claim that a compliance orientation directs energy away from real educational goals. As an example of 'mindless, knee-jerk compliance,' the program evaluation administrator described demands by some legislators for state review of all proficiency tests to make sure they did not discriminate against minority students. His office instead stressed to concerned legislators that detailed review of all local district tests would be enormously expensive and would take needed resources away from the more crucial objective, making sure students learn more. His office instead tried to make sure local districts understood how to develop a good proficiency test and then 'tried to get people to do a detailed review of their own tests.' He acknowledged that there had been relatively 'few takers' for this proposal because districts feel too pressed and busy, but his emphasis remained one of stressing voluntarism and self-help. Key here is his view of how the state can influence educational policy, and what are the necessary limits of its powers. His office tries to elicit willing cooperation, it seeks out the best people in local districts and appeals to them, and assigns the 'top-flight' people at the state level to provide technical assistance.

This educational administrator proposes no single unified vision of educational policy, but he strongly advocates a general kind of state approach to particular problems — pragmatic, voluntarist, and based on gathering and disseminating information more than on enforcing regulations and rules. One important priority in his view is helping teachers 'teach basic skills better.' There is a 'lot of assistance available,' but most of it has never been translated into practical forms that teachers can use. There is a second new wave of proposals to mandate how many years of various subjects high school students must take. 'The effect of such legislation is likely to be marginal. The real issue is what kids are taught, not what it's called, and we don't know anything about course content.'

The best interventions are those that stimulate voluntary or spontaneous change, and are often indirect. 'The most powerful intervention you could do would be just to change the state code to make school superintendents publish every year a whole lot of data about their schools. Test scores are sent out every year, and they get a lot of newspaper attention. Parents want their local schools to improve students' scores.' It would, he argued, have an important effect if schools also had to release data on dropouts, retention rates, the numbers of periods a day of instruction students actually received, and the numbers of students who took different kinds of classes. 'Do a "passive intervention." Don't tell schools to do things, but create pressures. If nobody cares even after the information is made public, then what would you have done with trying to enforce compliance?' One should, in his view, 'try to inspire people to do the best they can do, rather than meet your minimal expectations — or what it's easiest for you to check on.'

Two other programs of the California State Department of Education embody even more fully the strategy of centralization through voluntarism which seems to be emerging in California's educational administration. These are the School Improvement Program, a state sponsored program offering supplemental funding to selected schools, and Program Review, the state's particular version of the task of monitoring compliance with federal education regulations. Both programs, according to state education administrators, attempt to define 'compliance' as narrowly and clearly as possible, making it a 'vestigial' matter, so that they can devote their best energies to improving 'school quality.'

The School Improvement Program supplements the budgets of almost half California's schools, with participation in the program concentrated especially in the lower grades. Although the supplement it offers is relatively small, School Improvement monies are important as one of the only supplemental sources of funding schools can seek that is not tied to a specific program or student population. The School Improvement Program was designed in part to encourage community participation in school governance. Participation in the program requires the creation at each school of a School Site Council (SSC) made up of parents, teachers, and (at secondary schools) students. The SSC submits a plan to the state for overall improvement of school programs, based on a comprehensive school plan. Schools then compete for School Improvement funds based on the quality of their plans, the success of other School Improvement schools in the district (as measured by Program Reviews, discussed below, and by a school's success in raising its students' test scores compared to scores of students with comparable background characteristics), and the apparent commitment of school leadership to making planned improvements.[17]

According to a high level administrator in the Program Review unit, the plans submitted by the School Site Councils are only partially successful. Developing the plan gives the councils 'something to do,' but 'we haven't figured out how to get the schools to *own* the plan.' The difficulty is that they still regard it as 'an application or a contract,' rather than as a way to develop internal capacities to plan and coordinate their school's educational activities.[18] Thus the School Improvement Program seeks to improve the 'quality' of education, not by mandating specific educational changes, but by stimulating a school and its community to galvanize local resources on behalf of educational improvement. This faith in a process of activity and involvement, rather than a specific set of educational innovations, is characteristic of the state effort to reconcile local voluntarism with centralized policy initiative.[19]

Program Review is the state program that most fully embodies the California State Department of Education's regulatory philosophy. The central idea behind Program Review is planning, but not comprehensive planning at the state level. Indeed, according to a top administrator of the program, at the state level the realities are 'too complex and ambiguous' for planning. The critical problem is 'how rational planning relates to ethical choices,' and 'the people who really make decision' don't use plans except for 'symbolic cover.' Program Review instead attempts to stimulate individual schools to plan for realizing their own educational objectives. This kind of planning, it is hoped, can stimulate a profound process of self-examination and generate a renewed sense of shared purpose in local schools.

Program Review grew from the State's responsibility for monitoring compliance with federal laws. During the 1970s, state education administrators became disillusioned with the compliance strategy and began to try to look directly into classrooms to judge the components of effective teaching. According to the program's current administrators, this form of evaluating schools also proved frustrating. Instead of processing forms and 'punishing people when the forms weren't right,' state administrators found themselves demanding that teachers have measurable objectives, a time schedule that showed they were meeting their objectives, and so forth. Thus, attempts at more realistic regulation, more in touch with the realities of classroom life, began to generate more and more heavy-handed and formulaic regulation.

Out of this frustration grew Program Review, carried out as part of the compliance-monitoring mandate of the State Department of Education. All funds that the state administers are monitored through the Consolidated Application Program, so that each school district submits only one application for all the federal and state programs for which it is eligible. But the stress of this program is now on periodic reviews of individual schools, carried out by teams of three to six people sent into local schools for an intensive three-day review of a school's activities and programs. Program Reviews stress improving school quality, rather than monitoring compliance with the demands of specific state and federal programs.

Program Review is supposed to be 'child-centered,' focusing on the 'received program,' the program as children actually exprience it, rather than on the program provided by adults. The administrators' hope is that the experience of going through the review process will itself change the consciousness of members of the local school community about how the school actually operates. This change in consciousness is considered the essential prerequisite to school improvement.

Program Review administrators freely use moral terms in their description of how the program works. They insist that unlike the stress on compliance, which gives 'bad people' in the schools additional power, Program Review depends on finding 'good people' in the school who want improvement. 'The review is designed to be catalytic in the context of the school's own change process. . . . It's not designed for data gathering, but for the school itself. You need someone in the school who wants leverage, wants change. It creates a three-day thunderstorm, but someone had to dam up the water.' One way to create such change agents in the school is to get them involved in the review process by having them serve on review teams at other schools. Hence program review relies primarily on volunteers, usually parents and teachers, who come to Sacramento for an intensive training program before going out as members of review teams to other schools. This process frequently produces 'converts' who are then enthusiastic about applying the program-review approach in their own schools.

What then are the purposes this approach to improving educational quality is supposed to serve? Here the ideology of program staff and administrators is well worked out: on the one hand, 'the idea of quality will emerge out of the process,' and on the other, 'what makes a school good is obvious but unspoken. Our purpose is to make the obvious spoken, then get out of town and hope someone does something.' School quality is at one level a natural, shared value. But it cannot be imposed by the state, because the specifics vary from school to school. 'The chief failures of schools are not in instructional technology, but in how well they are implementing the one they have.' Quality depends on the will or capacity of people in local schools to put resources to work, rather than on the resources themselves. Yet at the same time, quality is objective, and evaluators from a wide variety of perspectives can recognize it (after they have been through the State's training program, which trains from 2500 to 3000 people a year). However, quality is not just a matter of morale; 'there is no point in feeling good about bad performance.' Rather, quality depends on an internal willingness of people in the school to take responsibility for the way the program actually affects children. Program Review can arouse that sense of responsibility by involving members of the school community in a process of self-evaluation prior to the actual review, and by making the criteria of bad performance 'vivid,' so that people have to face it. But Program Review can't assure quality.

The Program Review unit of the California State Department of Education is a somewhat odd place to look for clues about how aggregate policy planners come to terms with the traditional American language of political and moral debate. Program Review seems to have found a conception of its public mandate precisely in an extreme emphasis on individual and community voluntarism. It seeks to create good education in part by finding and mobilizing 'good people,' and converting others to an active commitment to quality education. Like other American social movements, it seeks renewed public order through something akin to religious revival, with the difference that this time the revival is to be sparked by state regulators and administrators.

Aggregate versus Individualist Thinking about Regulation

It should be clear by now that there is no necessary incompatibility between individualist thinking and conceptions of collective purpose. Indeed, in American public life, the classic form of public purpose has been the desire to recreate or transform individuals. The public order exists, at some level, for the moral fulfillment and personal happiness of individuals. I have argued, nonetheless, that traditional American public language leaves something of a vacuum when it confronts problems of policy formation and regulation in an increasingly, if always haphazardly, centralized modern state. Here, where problems of policy and regulation often pose themselves as issues about aggregate welfare, or about public purpose that cannot be directly translated into matters of the well-being of individuals, policymakers and regulators are left without guidance from American political traditions. The challenge of aggregate policymaking and regulation is particularly great in a political system which has relied so strongly on an individualist, moralist, and voluntarist language of public policy debate. In an arena like educational policy, the strain between traditional definitions of the public good education is supposed to realize and the approach to which aggregate policy planners are driven is particularly severe. I believe this cultural gap accounts in part for the crisis in educational governance, which is at least in part caused by an inability to formulate legitimate public purposes which would allow federal and state administrators to play an active, constructive role in shaping the educational system which, in spite of themselves, they increasingly control, both fiscally and legally.

When policymakers with responsibility for administering programs that implicitly raise questions about aggregate planning and collective purpose have difficulty linking the work they do to a traditional moral and political vocabulary, it seems to me that there are three possibilities for how they may shape their work. First, policymakers and administrators who deal with aggregate policy matters may operate to some degree in a moral and political vacuum, cut off from a public language that might provide links between technical decision-making and wider conceptions of purpose. In this vacuum, they may rely on their own technical training (the norms of welfare economics or the principles of budgetary analysis) or they may accommodate a technical view of the planning enterprise to a relatively cynical view of the realities of politics, pressure groups, and interest conflicts. These responses are approximately those I found in the Legislative Analyst who insisted on the primacy of technical analysis of whether programs produced measurable outputs which justified their expense, and of the legislative committee staff member who insisted that policy was impossible in the face of fragmented political realities. Both these policy experts held strong personal views on what constituted a good educational system and on what needed to be done about education in California. But they had difficulty integrating their personal views with their public roles, and they relied, and insisted that others relied, on traditional individualistic imagery about what made a good teacher or a good school or what constituted a good education.

A second possibility for administrators and policymakers who deal with aggregate policy issues is to try to create links between the policy choices they make and the traditional moral and political vocabulary. And the third possibility is that those who deal with aggregate policy concerns may begin to develop new conceptions of collective purpose. The various regulatory programs of the California State Department of Education — the response of the office of Program Evaluation and Research to the task of supervising high-school proficiency examinations; the School Improvement Program; and the approach of the Program Review unit to the task of monitoring compliance with federal legislation — seem to me to embody a mix of the latter two alternatives. In some ways these three programs invoke the most traditional aspects of an individualist, moralist, and voluntarist approach to public policy. They rely on local participation, on identifying or converting good people at the local level to support educational change and on the notion that parents, teachers, and administrators in local schools can identify for themselves what kind of quality education they want for their children. At the same time, these state programs legitimate a strong role for central educational authorities in stimulating and facilitating the discovery of purpose and the capacity for planning at the local level. They draw traditional conceptions of quality education, while they embody and teach a notion that only self-conscious, clearly articulated, shared purposes can be adequate guides to educational excellence.

There may even be great significance to the fact that these three state programs seem, each in a slightly different way, to have drawn on some of the language and imagery of the counter-culture of the 1960s and 1970s to develop a form of public policy based on faith in group process and the perpetual quest for self-discovery and self-realization. While the belief in self-actualization seems, from one point of view, the ultimate expression of an individualist voluntarism, it also represents a weakening of classical utilitarian notions of the autonomous individual, with fixed needs and wants, who pursues a clearly-defined self interest. Selves (and organizations) that are always ready to transform themselves, that have open and fluid rather than fixed identities, may be a product of the growing importance of bureaucratic regulation in a public world supplanting market coordination of purely private motives and interests. For at least this one segment of California education administrators, creation of public policy based on creative voluntarism means asking individuals to engage in a continually changing public arena within which purposes and values are continually transformed.

There are many policy arenas in which aggregate and individualist modes of thinking may come into conflict. Furthermore, the tension between American individualism and the modern state's drive toward public regulation is likely to be a permanent one. But we can address neither the specific problems of governance in education nor the more general issues of planning, politics, and administration in a welfare state unless we recognize that a system of public governance that operates in isolation from an evolving sense of public purpose, and therefore of restraint by such purposes, is indeed the greatest danger to democracy.

Notes

1 The perspective on public purpose I employ here derives at least in part from the work of PHILIP SELZNICK and PHILIPPE NONET. For a recent summary see NONET, P. and SELZNICK, P. (1978) *Law and Society in Transition: Toward Responsive Law*, New York, Harper and Row. The work of BELLAH, R.N. (1967) 'Civil religion in America,' *Daedalus*, 96, Winter, pp. 1–19; and *The Broken Covenant: American Civil Religion in a Time of Trial*, New York, Seabury Press, 1975 has also strongly influenced my thinking.

2 PHILIP SELZNICK has pointed to the centrality of privitism and voluntarism in the American legal tradition. See SELZNICK, P. (1976) 'The ethos of American law,' pp. 211–236 in KRISTOL, I. and WEAVER, P. (Eds.), *The Americans: 1976*, Lexington, Mass., D.C. Health.

3 As DAVID KIRP has shown, courts have in fact been extremely flexible and willing to adapt to local political realities, even when dealing with matters of rights. MILBREY MCLAUGHLIN argues, nonetheless, that courts are ill-equipped to provide effective governance in education. It is also possible that federal and state administrative agencies implementing rights may tend to be more rigidly compliance-oriented than are the courts that mandate rights in the first place, both because the administrative agencies are subject to a different, and potentially more threatening, kind of public scrutiny, and because they necessarily deal with compliance in the aggregate, rather than, as courts do, with individual cases for which individualized remedies may be sought. See KIRP, D.L. (1980) *Legalism and Politics in School Desegregation*. Unpublished paper, School of Public Policy, University of California, Berkeley; MCLAUGHLIN, M. (1981) *The Courts and Social Change*. Unpublished paper, Santa Monica, CA., The Rand Corporation, March.

4 CREMIN, L. (1961) *The Transformation of the School*, New York, Random House; CREMIN, L. (1977) *Traditions of American Education*, New York, Basic Books; TYACK, D.B. (1974) *The One Best System: A History of American Urban Education*, Cambridge, Harvard University Press.

5 MEYER, J.W. (1979) 'The impact of the centralization of educational funding and control on state and local organizational governance.' Program Report No. 79-B20, Institute for Research on Educational Finance and Governance, School of Education, Stanford University, August.

6 BERKE, J.S. and KIRST, M.W. (1972) 'Intergovernmental relations: Conclusions and recommendations,' in BERKE, J.S. and KIRST, M.W. (Eds.), *Federal Aid to Education: Who Benefits? Who Governs?*, Lexington, Mass., D.C. Heath, p. 389.

7 MEYER, J.W., TYACK, D., NAGEL, J. and GORDON, A. (1979) 'Public education as nation-building in America: Enrollments and bureaucratization in the American states, 1870–1930,' *American Journal of Sociology*, 85, November, pp. 591–613; MEAD, M. (1951) *The School in American Culture*, Cambridge, Harvard University Press; CREMIN, L. (1977), *op. cit.*
8 BOYER, P. (1978) *Urban Masses and Moral Order in America*, Cambridge, Harvard University Press.
9 PERIN, C. (1977) *Everything in Its Place: Social Order and Land Use in America*, Princeton, N.J., Princeton University Press.
10 DE NEUFVILLE, J.I. (1981) 'Symbol and myth in public choice: The case of land policy in the United States.' Working Paper 359, Institute of Urban and Regional Development, University of California, Berkeley, July.
11 GUSFIELD, J.R. (1981) *The Culture of Public Problems: Drinking-Driving and the Symbolic Order*, Chicago, University of Chicago Press.
12 *Ibid*, p. 47.
13 PETERSON, P.E. (1981) 'Federal policy and American education.' Paper prepared for the Twentieth Century Fund, Spring.
14 BERKE, S. and KIRST, M.W. (1972), *op. cit.*
15 ROBERT BELL, in an important study of the ways purposes are formulated and applied in federal policy-making, notes that the logic of welfare economics comes to dominate much of the debate over policy options between the Office of Management and Budget and executive agencies because it provides one of the only tools available for thinking about policy in aggregate terms. At the same time, Bell notes, welfare economics offers a narrow, technical conception of purpose, cut off from wider political or moral language. See BELL, R.K. (1980) *Constructing the Public Interest: A Sociological Analysis of Administrative Deliberation and the Interpretation of Federal Subsidized Housing Policy*. Unpublished dissertation, Department of Sociology, University of California, Berkeley.
16 One should, of course, take such statements as symbolic rather than as necessarily realistic descriptions of the working of state bureaucracy. Some legislative staff members, for example, complained that 'leadership' was precisely what Riles failed to offer. He had, they claimed, offended the legislature by refusing to make comparative evaluations of educational programs competing for state funds, and he had rarely suggested new legislative initiatives. The State Department of Education, because of its stress on the ideology of voluntarism, might in fact be unlikely to formulate policy of the sort that would be easily translatable into a legislative program.
17 This paragraph is based on an interview with a Program Review administrator and on California State Department of Education, (1981a) *School Improvement: Making California Education Better*, pamphlet, Sacramento, CA, California State Department of Education.
18 Outside evaluators give the School Improvement Program mixed reviews. According to BERMAN, P. *et al*, some schools use the program for leverage for educational change, but many others see it simply as a supplemental funding source. More problematic still is the evaluators' argument that the schools most likely to make good use of the School Improvement Program are those which are already functioning well, while the program is of least help to schools which are functioning poorly. See BERMAN, P., WELLER, D., CZESAK, K., GJELTEN, T. and IZU, J. (1981) 'Improving school improvement. Seminar I. How schools view and use the school improvement program: Preliminary hypothesis.' Berkeley, CA, Manifest International, October.
19 SELZNICK, P. analyzes the tradition in American law of stressing procedure over substantive policy and points up some of its weaknesses for developing conceptions of public purpose. See SELZNICK, P. (1979) *op. cit.*, p. 228.

Teachers' Regulation of the Classroom

William K. Muir, Jr.
University of California, Berkeley

I

Discussions of the regulation of schooling usually focus on the behavior of educators under the commands of non-educators and address the issue, under what circumstances do teachers (and their professional supervisors) submit to the regulation of outsiders like courts, agencies, and legislatures, and when do they not?

Teachers are subjected to outside commands because in their classrooms they command others. At least at the elementary and secondary school levels, teachers are authorized to control in detail the lives of their students.

I want to explore the nature of the teacher's control in the classroom for two reasons. First, an appreciation of the nature of power in the schoolhouse will help the reader to understand the tension created when non-educators superimpose their rules on the regime of teachers at work. Regulations conceived in statehouses and courthouses are intended to affect what goes on in the classroom, but they presuppose teachers' continued control there. If external regulations assume the maintenance of classroom order, yet upset the authority of teachers on which order depends, then outside interference may lead to unhappy and unintended results.

Second, there is a theoretical reason for exploring the regime of teachers. In the microcosm of the schoolroom, we may learn something of a general nature about the antagonism between regulators and those they regulate. Specifically, by analyzing the reaction of pupils to the regime of their teachers, we may come to understand the reaction of teachers to the regime of their state. Furthermore, from the successes (and failures) of teachers with their pupils, we may learn something about ways by which public officials may successfully regulate teachers.

II

If by regulation we mean the prohibition of activity except when officials expressly permit it, then the most heavily regulated party in the educational system is the student. If regulatory intrusiveness is measured by the specificity with which officials may define the ways in which an activity must be carried out by the subjects of the regulation, then among the most intrusive regulators in the free world is the schoolteacher.

The keystone of the public school system is the compulsory attendance law, which places every American youth under the thumb of schoolteachers seven hours a day, five days per week, thirty-five weeks per year, eleven years a lifetime — 13,000 hours of pervasive regulation. Schoolteachers have the authority to diminish the free choices of students radically. They frustrate and intermeddle in the immediate interests of the children. They regulate where pupils may sit, with whom they may converse, what topics they may discuss, what they may do, and how they may do it.

During school hours a teacher is authorized to subject youngsters to regulation of the minutest details. A schoolteacher's control approaches total power. Unless students comply, unless they show up at a particular school, attend a particular class, behave in particular ways, complete particular tasks, and reach a particular level of skill at doing them, then teachers may reduce their grades, humiliate them, extend their school day, withhold their diplomas, and, in the last resort, initiate criminal proceedings against them and their parents for attempting to flee the schoolhouse. Even though students are no longer subject to whippings, for practical purposes the formal powers of punishment enjoyed by teachers are dire. Students live under the threats of teachers, and teachers are authorized to bring those threats to bear on any wayward defiance of their regime.

Part of the justification for extending such regulatory power to schoolteachers is that schools are expected to shape the character of students.[1] Civilized society expects educational institutions to help transform each young pupil, willy-nilly, into an adult capable of self-government in an active and free society. Therefore, it authorizes teachers to drill students in 'good' behavior. The students often resist such efforts at character-shaping: learning the particular skills and moral orientations of adulthood is arduous, uncomfortable, and, for some, pointless. To preempt disruptive resistance, teachers are given still more regulatory power. They can, for example, dictate when children may go to the bathroom, hang up their coats, or sharpen their pencils.

Despite these expansive regulatory powers, however, in day-to-day reality teachers often feel out of control. Even if they can prevent students from acting disruptively, they are at a loss to elicit the personal improvement which justifies the severe classroom regime in the first place. The shortcoming in the teachers' regulatory power is that it depends upon coercion. At least in the last resort, if a teacher lacks sufficient resourcefulness or authority to enlist students' willingness to submit, a teacher must induce order by coercion, and coercion is a highly problematic form of control. Let me momentarily digress on the general nature of coercion and then return to the practice of coercion in the classroom.

III

Coercion — the use of power and force as a means — depends on intimidation. As a consequence, parties in a coercive relationship to one another are almost invariably antagonistic. At least the victimized party generally feels the urge to terminate or avenge matters.[2]

Coercion involves the gaining of a ransom by threatening harm to a hostage. The victimizer commits himself to injure something of value to the victim (the hostage) unless the latter turns over something else of lesser value (the ransom). 'Your money or your life,' whether announced by the mugger or the tax collector, is the classic utterance in the coercive relationship. From the victim's viewpoint, it makes little difference if the victimizer is a criminal or an official. The means are the same. Extortionists and regulators alike exercise control by presenting dilemmas: their victims must either accept the loss of a substantial degree of freedom or lose all their freedom.

Coercion is likely to become a mutually antagonistic relationship. Victims tend to want to retaliate as soon as they have the chance to do so. Victimizers, therefore, must always be preoccupied with the task of self-defense. Those who have recourse to coercion are caught up in a vicious circle, threatening and at the same time suffering counterthreats.

The ironic feature of coercion is that some persons, by virtue of having nothing to lose, are virtually 'threat-proof.' Lacking possessions, they neither expose hostages nor have ransoms of much value. For example, childless couples are invulnerable to kidnapers, because they have no kids to lose; impoverished couples are likewise rarely bothered, because they have no ransoms to pay. Moreover, the dispossessed are ideal practitioners of coercion on others, because their victims have nothing to retaliate against. Watch a jalopy and a Cadillac vie for priority at an intersection, and usually the paradox of dispossession will be played out. The driver of the jalopy almost always wins the deference of the possessor of the Cadillac, because jalopy drivers have much less to lose from a collision.

There are exceptions, even to the intersection case. There are Cadillac owners who are so heavily insured that they can afford to be indifferent to the threat of damage. If they can communicate their financial indifference in a convincing way, the jalopy driver may see that his threat to injure is not much of a threat at all. Generally speaking, in coercion, a detached person, one who is indifferent about the destruction of his possessions, is in as strong a coercive position as one who has no possessions. For that reason, the king who disdains his daughter is not likely to be compelled to deplete his treasury to recover the princess from her kidnaper. A dramatized indifference is frequently a useful defense against coercive aggressors.

Coercion is basically psychological. People who make threats do not want to execute them. Practitioners of coercion seek a ransom, and threatening hostages is a means of securing it. Carrying out threats means failure, at least in the short run. One ends up with neither the ransom nor the hostage. The union leader does not want to call his followers off the job and require them to pick up their pickets. For one thing, the rank-and-file members stop being paid, and that hurts. For another, the employer may be forced out of business; the workers then lose their jobs — and their hostage. The union leaders want the employer to take the possibility of a strike seriously and capitulate in anticipation of the workers' walkout. Thus, whether a strike threat will succeed hinges on whether the employer credits the workers' sincerity. It is vital that he believes that the workers really mean what they are threatening — that they will gladly destroy their paymaster unless they get additional pay. To make that threat convincing, a union leader's appearance of vindictiveness may convince the employers that the workers are mean and intend to be so. In coercion, 'face,' a reputation for ill will and brutishness, plays a critical part. Whether one is a union leader, parent, or lawyer, the nastier the reputation of one who resorts to coercion, the less nasty one may have to be. The more savage the threatener appears to be, the less likely the victim is going to call his bluff. If one's threats are given credence and the victim capitulates, then there is no need to behave savagely toward the hostage of the victim.

One final observation: even in the face of the direst threat, there is a defense. If the intended victim cannot comprehend that threat and the threatener knows it, the latter will give up and no coercion will occur. It is fruitless to practice a threat over the telephone on a deaf person or one who does not speak the same language. The obvious crazy who does not see the peril implicit in another's threat may have successfully defended against it if the threatener detects the incomprehension. Sometimes fools can safely tread where angels ought not to go.

To sum up, then, coercion is a form of control in which a favorable balance of power is enjoyed by the dispossessed, the detached, the remorseless, and the irrational. They are invulnerable, while those who are productive, caring, kind, or reasonable are exposed and susceptible.

The problematic aspect of coercion is that it turns civilized values upside down and reverses the civilized pattern of incentives. Where coercion rules, there are no rewards for developing one's talents, empathy, trust and intelligence. In coercion, personal assets are transformed into liabilities. The goods one produces attract thieves; the things one cares about expose more hostages; forgiveness implies weakness; and being alert to dangers amplifies the threats of others. In coercion, motives run in a contrary direction. In short, as a potential target of threats, a person is moved to dwarf his self, his hopes, and his cache of things cared about; and as a potential practitioner of threats, he is motivated to cultivate his brutish side.

IV

What happens when coercion is exercised in the classroom? In a purely coercive confrontation between teacher and student, no one should doubt the outcome. Despite having all the formal instruments of coercion, the typical teacher is going to lose control. The students, the subjects of regulation, are not going to submit. For one thing, they expose virtually no hostages; the teacher offers plenty. Compared to teachers, youths are more dispossessed, less empathetic, and more likely to be senseless about the 'long-run' consequences of their actions. Teachers, on the other hand, have careers to lose, hopes to be dashed, prior sacrifices to be made vain, and the perspective to see what is at stake. In contrast to them, pupils are the perfect dwarfed target — dispossessed, indifferent, and unseeing.

For a second thing, students lack the remorse which hobbles teachers as practitioners of coercion. The capacity of students — under certain circumstances, at least — to be defiant, insolent, inattentive, and insubordinate is unlimited. Recall an incident in Willard Waller's classic, *The Sociology of Teaching*. The incident Waller describes occurred in the 1920s, when the tools of school discipline still included corporal punishment, and courts had not yet prescribed limits to teachers' disciplinary discretion. The story illustrates the potential savagery of even the best-mannered children. Waller quotes a teacher's account of the last day of a five-day ordeal in study hall supervision:

> The fifth and last day of my torture came. It was pandemonium. That day from the first bell on, I was perfectly helpless, and saw nothing to do but stand up and take my punishment. The inkwells were flying faster than ever. I tried to make a plea, but it was unheard. I couldn't make my voice carry above the din. I smiled grimly and settled down to hold on for the forty-five minutes. There were signs that the more timid boys were genuinely concerned about the danger they ran. One boy was hit and had to go out of the room with a slight cut over his eye. An inkwell came very close to my head. Midway in the hour a boy got up, looked at me indignantly, and cried out, 'I'm not going to stay in here any longer.' Then he fled from the room. A dozen others rose and started to follow him. I stood in front of the door as if to bar their exit. Then the whole assembly room arose, and rushed angrily out of the room, whooping and stamping their feet. I did not try to stop them. I was glad it was over.[3]

Why was the teacher 'perfectly helpless'? While the teacher had the formal authority to pacify, he was constrained by scruples from applying it savagely. On the other hand, the things he cared about were sitting targets for the coercive practices of the students: his identification with the 'more timid' and vulnerable boys, his hopes for an orderly and productive study period, and his job (which could be made intolerable by supervisors who wanted him to keep things quiet and above scandal, no matter what the means).

Conversely, some of the students were indifferent, at least on that day, to any legitimate sanctions available to the teacher: a reduction in grades, reports to the principal, and expulsion.

In schools, the balance of power will be tilted even more adversely against the teacher in hopeless classrooms. In coercive confrontations with lower-tracked students (particularly those who are handicapped by societal prejudices and feel they will fail no matter what their efforts to get a good job and succeed at it), a teacher virtually has nothing to withhold by way of punishment. If a teacher threatens students, they will call the bluff, and then the teacher will have to escalate the stakes to a level of savagery which the law prohibits.

If a teacher has the formal responsibility to regulate but has neither the capacity nor the will to prevail in a coercive confrontation, he or she has few choices. One thing which might be done, as just noted, is to decide to become unacceptably punitive, even violent. By setting aside all scruples regarding brutal insults, biting sarcasm, and physical browbeating, classroom instructors may gain control. They will find themselves, however, slipping into cynicism. Cynicism supports insupportable punishments by dehumanizing the students. By placing blame on students and holding them all hopeless, harsh teachers seek to escape the guilt they feel about their vehemence.

A second option for a teacher is to abdicate. A Boston schoolteacher, interviewed by her colleague Sara Freedman, describes an instructor who has just adjusted her expectations downward to the point where she has become perpetually indifferent to her professional responsibilities:

> There's one teacher in our school who should not be teaching. She doesn't get up from her desk and move around the class, really, and she does a lot of absent-minded things, and she really doesn't do anything creative with the kids. She's had it. Parents will say to me, 'My child had Miss H. last year', as if I will understand.[4]

A third response is to quit, and nearly every teacher has thought seriously about this option. For example, another Boston schoolteacher interviewed by Freedman uttered this *cri de coeur*:

> I was just thinking of one other thing that I didn't like about having a bunch of tough kids in my class and what it did to me. And that is, I felt I yelled a lot. I didn't yell a lot, but I yelled. I didn't like that, and I also physically managed those kids, by the arm, take them over, and I can remember huffing and puffing after doing that. And thinking, 'What the hell am I doing? Isn't there another way?'[5]

Coercion is not always doomed to such bleak outcomes as escalation, irresponsibility, or resignation. Sometimes pure intimidation may succeed in gaining passive submission to the regulatory order, but what will be lost is student morale: the pupils' willingness to do more than passively suffer their defeats.

Teachers, therefore, who want to gain productive compliance with the classroom regime must rely on means other than coercion. But the teachers' arsenal, like that of other regulators, is limited to two alternatives: exchange and authority.

V

The first means of control is exchange. Teachers may attempt to purchase submission to their regulatory claims. The question is, what price must they pay to get student compliance? By and large, teachers have little of value to offer as their end of the bargain. In part, unless the students' immediate wants are academic (the one need which teachers are professionally trained to satisfy), teachers may not be competitive with suppliers of the things students really want. Friendship, prestige, physical security, solace, money, self-respect — these are the resources which students desire, and anyone who can supply their wants more cheaply and abundantly will compete with the teacher and subvert the educational enterprise.[6] Alternatively, if a teacher has personal and non-academic resources which the students want (such as the ability and time to teach the skills of dressmaking or flyball-catching), those resources must be dispensed prudently and selectively. Teachers who use their personal resources to buy compliance from a class face a dilemma. One horn of that dilemma is universalism: assisting one student heightens the expectations of classmates, who believe they are entitled to equal assistance. The other horn is depletion: if every good deed is universalized, the teacher will invariably exhaust her time and energy, especially since non-academic obligations are in addition to academic duties. Non-academic benefits tend to take time. Being a Boy Scout leader, showing up at weekend socials, counseling individuals and coaching teams lay heavy claims to hours outside of the classroom job. They are rarely nickle-and-dime benefits; hence, they deplete the providers of them.

The other service which a teacher may trade for student compliance is relaxation of the regulatory regime in the classroom. Leniency — ignoring infractions, reducing standards, forgiving sins — is not necessarily a bad thing in classrooms, but it has its problems. First, it often leads to inequity: the worst-behaved students get the greatest forgiveness, while their victims and peers, who have done nothing to be forgiven, receive nothing for their good behavior. Second, leniency may corrupt the regime in the classroom: the rules and standards may suffer ridicule and lose their connection to moral obligation. Third, leniency is subject to diminishing returns, rising expectations, and blackmail: a teacher may have to surrender increasingly and pay an even larger premium to keep matters quiet and out of public earshot.

I do not want to make exchange appear as an irrelevant basis for regulatory control. It is not. As the perceptive sociologist, Mary Metz, points out, a teacher 'may build up obligations of exchange through many kinds of indirect, even self-conscious interchange . . . Such obligations may even be enforced by (students) who are aware of, or share in, favors done.'[7] But the limits of exchange are real, the provision of legitimate benefits exhausting, and the long-run dangers of leniency as an exchangeable resource very great.

VI

If coercion heightens antagonism to a regulatory regime in the classroom and exchange tends to corrupt it, only one recourse is left. Regulation must be moralized: to adopt Rousseau's memorable phrase, teachers must transform their might into right, and obedience into duty.[8] I shall give the name authority to such moralized means of control.

A model of an authoritative relationship consists of a program or script (sometimes loosely called a subculture) which consists of a variety of roles.[9] Each role comprises a generally understood set of rights and duties, and defines what actions are permitted, obligatory, and forbidden to an occupant of that role. So long as one wants to work within the particular community governed by an authoritative script, one adopts a role, thereby linking oneself up with the other role-players or actors.

Why do individuals enter into authoritatively defined roles and willingly accept external dominion over their actions? One answer is that roles contain more than definitions of right and wrong. They contain valuable causal and philosophical theories as well.

On the one hand, roles provide explanations and illuminate matters otherwise shrouded in doubt. In that sense, they have a hunch content, so to speak. A script containing many roles coordinates the actions of many actors and enables some predictions about the future. An individual can come to depend on persons and actions subject to their common script. Moreover, each role-player can make things happen within the script, because he learns the cues which evoke others to respond dutifully.

If, in fact, the script works, if reality is orderly and confirms the actors' predictions and desires — harm is fended off and benefits are secured — then allegiance to the script is gradually strengthened. Each role becomes more heartfelt, and the various players channel their energies with greater gusto into their parts. We say that their characters come to be shaped to their roles. Their behavior becomes moralized in two senses: individual conscience is engaged (guilt), and fellow actors encourage one another to conform to the dictates of their roles (shame). Conversely, if things do not happen as predicted and confusion results from adhering to a script, belief in it is undermined. Allegiance to the moral community weakens; ambiguity and equivocation erode the certainty with which individuals had played their parts. Faith in the enterprise is shaken, and demoralization sets in.

Roles also have a philosophical content. They are purposeful, investing work with meaning and immortality and inviting personal commitment. The story goes that three men were asked what they were doing. The first said, 'I am laying stones.' The second answered, 'I am building a wall.' And, the third replied, 'I am building a cathedral.' Roles permit the individual to connect up one's small contributions to the greater enterprise and take credit for it.

Thus, the reason why individuals accept authority willingly is that it relieves technical and existential uncertainty. Authority relationships permit individuals who don roles to get on with matters without paralyzing self-doubt. In David Kirp's splendid phrase, authority enables us to 'suspend disbelief' and to leave what is unknown or unknowable to others, to those 'in authority.'[10] The cost of this dispensation from doubt is to accept the regulation written into the roles constituting the social script.

Much more needs to be said about this classic notion of authority. For one thing, each individual plays a part in many scripts, and the various roles of any one individual may conflict and be internally contradictory. Secondly, one function of leadership is to rewrite the scripts of life from time-to-time — sometimes marginally, sometimes radically — and the changes can often have unsettling consequences. And thirdly, within an accepted role the individual actor is required to classify particular situations so as to bring them within the more abstract notions of right and wrong defined by the role. All of these phenomena — role-conflict, role-redefinition, and situational classification — affect the stability and reliability of authoritative regimes.

Nonetheless, authority does stabilize our situations. We let 'authorities' govern our lives and enlighten our self-interest to such an extent that more often than not we want to do what those in authority expect of us, despite the lack of any immediate reward or sanction.

Sensitive observers of public schools have emphasized the vital importance of the teacher's authority in the classroom. The sociologist, Mary Metz, in her insightful research on two junior high schools during the turbulent 1960s, was struck by the fact that the bulk of the teachers and students played their parts in the 'service of a moral order to which both (teachers and students alike) owe(d) allegiance.'[11] That is, despite the breakdown of confidence at large, the meagerness of teachers' resources, the limits of their punitive powers, and the universal questioning of contemporary values, 'in fact most classes . . . were conducted with a civility and some semblance of concentration.'[12]

While teachers and students had their conflicts, their struggles were fought in principled terms, within the notions of right and wrong morally legislated into their roles as teachers and students.

Here we must wonder why students were willing to 'suspend disbelief,' why they did not radically defy the duties of studenthood. This is a puzzling question, especially since, as the organizational theorist Charles Bidwell points out, school systems are distinguishable from the typical moral orders in society. Most organizations are voluntary. The phone company or a political party distribute roles on the basis of achievement to persons who want to enter them. In contrast, schools are organizations where only the teachers have voluntarily hunted out their roles, while students have been assigned theirs, with little regard to their immediate interests. Students are involuntarily captives of their roles.[13]

One reason why students accept the role assigned to them is that they are very young when they enter school and relatively ignorant of alternative definitions of what they might be doing. It is easy to get first-graders to accept their part because they do not know they have a choice. (In the 'old days,' what is recalled is students' enduring ignorance of competing notions of their place.)

Yet, there was something other than ignorance inclining students to accept the classroom authority in the schools studied by Metz. There was, even in the hearts of the most skeptical adolescents, a yearning for assurance in the face of their own technical and existential uncertainty. By accepting the particular responsibilities of the student role, they evaded the crushing burden of adult responsibility for the larger society, about which they knew too little and which they were not ready to accept or renounce. In one of many insightful passages, Metz discusses why accepting the role of pupil relieved students, even the worst treated ones, of having to make a 'premature' decision about their later lives.

> At the same time that the black children in the lower tracks might find the school's curriculum both irrelevant and useless to them, they recognized perfectly clearly that the school is the agent of the larger society and must represent its values. If what the school teaches is irrelevant to their lives, then their lives are irrelevant to the larger society. It is, therefore, usual for such children not simply to reject the curriculum but to have a highly ambivalent attitude toward it. It is in this context that one can understand the importance in these students' eyes of a teacher's genuine efforts to teach. Teachers who do not continue to try despite the students' resistance are telling them they cannot learn what the society calls important. They are offering an insult. One teacher who consistently yelled at children and occasionally hit at them was universally chosen by her students as their least-liked teacher. But the reason given was less often her angry attacks than her disinclination to explain the work or to help children who were having difficulty with it.[14]

The adolescents in Metz's study were unwilling to discard all chance of attaining the meaning which the larger society could offer their later lives, and they resented as 'an insult' a teacher who denied them the right to play the student role, with its privilege to delay existential choices.

VII

Authority does not mean perfect uniformity. Teachers and students are different; they instruct and learn differently and hold to a broad variety of notions about their schools. Moreover, teachers in America may play their pedagogical role in many acceptable ways, such as by resembling parents, bureaucrats, scholars, therapists, or facilitators. Authority does not deny a degree of individuality to its subjects.

While allowing for some variety, however, authority approaches its limits when fundamental questions are raised and left unanswered. 'In the beginning was the Word,' counsels St. John. The beginning — and essence — of authority is the 'word,' the vital tradition conceded by all those who play their roles in the social script. In individual schools, authority depends on the existence among the faculty and students of a single broad consensus on educational philosophy. The consensus deals with 'core' questions of purpose, such as the relationship of individual achievement to collective order, the commitment to excellence or equality, the relative importance of knowledge and creativity, the kind of teaching style preferred, and whether the goal is to teach the child or the subject. Choices always have to be made among alternative purposes. Authority is strengthened over time. The longer the same priorities are maintained, the deeper grow the habits and attitudes which support a particular tradition. Teachers who agree with the traditional choices are galvanized into activity; those who do not agree fall back quiescent. Students and outsiders are encouraged or discouraged to speak up by the apparent agreement among those 'in authority.'

Any apparent consensus is strengthened when there is no strong authoritative and competing view. When the consensus is broken, however, when officials speak at odds, then the definition of what is happening in the schools — the 'word' — becomes incomprehensible. The center of authority no longer holds; things fall apart; and confusion reigns.

David Kirp, a lawyer and educator, provides an illustration of how subversive a judicial opinion may be of classroom authority relationships. In an article entitled 'Proceduralism and Bureaucracy: Due Process in the School Setting,' he analyzes the implications of *Goss v. Lopez*,[15] in which the United States Supreme Court ruled on the minimal due process requirements for student discipline and short-term suspensions from school. Kirp writes:

> The court ... voices its understanding of the proper relationship between the student and his school. '(I)t would be a strange disciplinary system in an educational institution,' writes Justice White, 'if no communication was sought by the disciplinarian with the student in an effort to inform him of his dereliction and to let him tell his side of the story in order to make sure that an injustice is not done.' That observation presumes a particular kind of relationship between adults and children in school. It implies the desirability of colloquy and exchange of information, rather than one-way communication of policies. It indicates that there may be valid perceptions of injustice to be gleaned from students. Most importantly, it treats the educational value of interchange between students and disciplinarians as of greater moment than allegiance to hierarchy.

In short, the *Goss* majority elevates to constitutional status a particular view of how public school officials should relate to their students.[16] The point Kirp makes is that two authoritative sources — the local school administration and the external authority of the Supreme Court — may speak contradictory 'words,' with one educational philosophy emphasizing traditional ideas of 'hierarchy' and the other urging a modern notion of mutuality between teachers and students. Moreover, Kirp points out that the Court's opinion in *Goss v. Lopez* makes no effort to reconcile the competing ideas of worthiness: the clash between tradition and modernity is left unresolved.

Outside official sources, such as the courts, have an effect on school authority because they vindicate groups previously quiescent; that is, persons who share the views of the outside officials are made self-conscious and are encouraged into activity.[17] They may be lawyers, slightly unhappy parents, or even members of the school board. Once encouraged by the support of someone in authority, they are likely to become assertive carriers of these non-traditional views in the locality in which they live. At the same time, outside officials may stagger those who have been 'in authority.' The criticism, explicit or implicit in their discordant regulations, may undermine confidence among the traditionalists.

When that happens, the moral basis of local classroom authority may be threatened. With each official notion that implies conflicting values and prescribes mutually contradictory roles for students and teachers to play, the older social script no longer provides the sanctuary in which disbelief can be suspended. Even so well-intentioned an external regulation as one concerning the teaching of limited-English-speaking children may have unsettling effects. Students who were once certain they wanted to make the honor roll find themselves thinking that the regulation may imply they are gullible or their efforts unworthy. When the teacher of English is derogated by some governmental agency for being inadequately solicitous of non-English-speaking populations, she is shaken in her faith that getting students to understand Shakespeare is worth the effort. When authorities collide, suddenly no one is as willing to 'suspend disbelief' as formerly. Everything of importance is at issue.

All the fundamental questioning which results may be useful, even necessary, but it undermines the regime of authority on which student submission has depended. Even though students once derived confidence from moral order which let them pursue adolescent goals, why should they continue to submit when that order begins to speak equivocally and destroys self-confidence? When students lose their faith, however, when they begin to doubt the word of their teachers, order in the classroom becomes hard to achieve. Effortlessness is lost. As Metz stresses: 'There are enormous savings in time and in psychic and intellectual energy if a class will take the word of adults that some of these subjects which are not inherently appealing will in fact be of use to them.'[18] When 'the word of adults' is thrown into doubt, the teacher must reach down for personal resources, or, lacking them, resort to coercion. The possibility of increased coercion in the classroom points to an important lesson.

The lesson is this: when external regulators are convinced that major changes must be made in school systems — and sometimes they must, as many essays in this volume make clear — the moral fabric of schools is bound to be fiercely tested and sometimes badly rent. It is crucial that those who seek to regulate schools from the outside craft their regulations with respect for those internal traditions. It may sound timid to suggest that change for change's sake is unwise and that elephants are best eaten in small bites, but reducing the necessity to use coercion in the classroom (and reducing the cynicism which develops in the hearts of those who exercise it) is worth it.

VIII

All this discussion tends to overstate the case. In fact, authoritative regimes, including classrooms and school systems, are more resilient than analysis of them makes appear possible. Ignored and even buffeted, authority still maintains some governance over our behavior without our knowing it — which is, of course, the secret of its success. It penetrates our hearts and minds, and we willingly reject competing allegiances.

Yet, we have learned in the past several decades, when institutions like schools and universities were under attack and partially collapsed as a result, that authority may be mortal. Institutions of moral 'attachment,'[19] as Metz calls complex organizations of every stripe, fell apart into rampant and uncommitted individualism. To prevent further chaos, the frightened and the strong turned to force, hoping to recover the peace which once seemed a part of the natural order of things.

I think it fair to assert that external regulation played its part in demoralizing the school organizations it impinged upon. Some outside officials, with purposes quite extraneous to the traditional goals of those they regulated, negligently wreaked disastrous consequences. I use the word *negligently* advisedly, because they did not want to wreck the enterprises over which they shared governance. Judges who commanded school systems to change did not try to abdicate their responsibility for preventing educational collapse. If judges — or any officials — fell short of their good intentions, it was not for lack of them.

To succeed in the purpose of revitalizing the organizations they deign to regulate, however, outside officials must develop skills to nurture as well as nudge the authority on which organizations depend. One crucial skill is what Chester Barnard called the capacity for moral creativeness.[20] By that phrase, Barnard meant the prudence and eloquence to preserve traditional organizational purposes while imposing new demands. Successful reconciliation of what at first appear to be the cross-purposes of tradition and modernity requires unflagging effort to articulate and dramatize organizational continuity throughout the uncertain days of adjustment to change. Success depends on a sympathetic understanding of the habits and attitudes of the regulated industry. If official power lacks moral creativity, if it tampers recklessly with the careers and lives of those who make up the collective enterprise, if it is heedless of the miraculous way individuals coordinate themselves in a single purpose, if, in short, officials are morally blind to the subtlety of authority, then they will be abusive and corrupting. Worse, official power will soon find itself turning to increased use of coercion and justifying recourse to it with destructive hatred of the very enterprise it was supposed to serve.

It takes courage to play the regulator's part well. Regulators who observe their moral responsibilities sensitively will be accused of being taken in by the enterprises they are appointed to regulate. In fact, co-optation may result. By knowing the industry within their jurisdiction so well, by feeling so fully the responsibility for keeping operations going, regulators may not fulfill their public purpose to alter things. To avoid the two extremes — of destructiveness and innocuousness — regulators have to play their equivocal roles with a skillful integrity of considerable magnitude. There is no help for it. Regulation, whether by court, agency, or legislature, is not a job for unprepared or innocent pilgrims. If regulators do not understand the authoritative regimes with which they tamper, they will soon reap the wind.

That should surprise no one. For regulation is political in the sense that it depends on the arts of human control. Officials must win over by persuasion those of us who play their parts in the social script. If they fail to get a workable agreement, however, force lies at their disposal, a last resort to which events and supplicants may compel them. But, in using force, they may be turning away from the possibility of ever again cultivating a working agreement.

Regulators would do well to recall Max Weber's powerful warning in 'Politics as a Vocation':

> He who lets himself in for politics, for power and force as a means, contracts with diabolical powers and for his action it is not true that good can follow only from good and evil only from evil, but that often the opposite is true. Anyone who fails to see this is, indeed, a political infant.[21]

Regulators who take responsibility unaware of the subtlety of authority and the need to obtain agreement to it may find themselves fulfilling their contract with the devil. If evil then flows despite their good intentions, history may rightly denounce them as political infants. That would be a sad epitaph for those who began with such humane purposes.

Notes

1 Kirp, D.L. (1976) 'Proceduralism and bureaucracy: Due process in the school setting,' *Stanford Law Review*, 28, May, p. 841; and Bidwell, C.E. (1965) 'The school as a formal organization,' in March, J.G. (Ed.) *Handbook of Organizations*, Chicago, Rand McNally, pp. 997–1022.

2 Muir, W.K. Jnr (1977) *Police: Streetcorner Politicians*, Chicago, University of Chicago Press, Chapter 3.
3 Waller, W. (1932) *The Sociology of Teaching*, New York, Russell and Russell, p. 167.
4 Freedman, S., Jackson, J., Boles, K. and Rotblat-Walker, S. (Boston Women's Teachers Group), (1981) 'Teaching as an imperilled profession' (Unpublished paper) January, p. 7.
5 *Ibid.*, p. 30.
6 Bidwell, C.E. (1965) 'The school as a formal organization', in March, J.G. (Ed.) *op. cit*, p. 982.
7 Metz, M.H. (1978) *Classrooms and Corridors: The Crisis of Authority in Desegregated Secondary Schools*, Berkeley and Los Angeles, University of California Press, p. 99.
8 Rousseau, J.J. (1953) *The Social Contract*, (trans. and ed. Frederick Watkins) Edinburgh and New York, Thomas Nelson, vol. 1, Chapter 3, p. 6.
9 Barnard, C.I. (1938) *The Functions of the Executive*, Cambridge, Harvard University Press, pp. 163–74.
10 Kirp, D.L. (1976) *op. cit.* p. 855.
11 Metz, M.H. (1978) *op. cit*, p. 26.
12 *Ibid.*, p. 121.
13 Bidwell, C.E. (1965) 'The school as a formal organization', in March, J.G. (Ed.) *op. cit.* p. 973.
14 Metz, M.H. (1978) *op. cit.*, pp. 87–8.
15 419 U.S. 565 (1975).
16 Kirp, D.L. (1976) *op. cit.* p. 551.
17 Muir, W.K. Jr. (1974) *Law and Attitude Change*, Chicago, University of Chicago Press, pp. 108–10.
18 Metz, M.H. (1978) *op. cit*, p. 251.
19 *Ibid.*, p. 16, note 16.
20 Barnard, C.I. (1938) *op. cit*, p. 279.
21 Weber, M. (1946) 'Politics as a vocation,' in *From Max Weber: Essays in Sociology*, (trans, and ed. Gerth, H. and Wright Mills, C.) New York, Oxford University Press, p. 123.

Educational Paperwork

Eugene Bardach
University of California, Berkeley

Like nearly everyone else in the society, educators have been obliged over the last fifteen or twenty years to absorb a steadily growing burden of paperwork. In the six-month period between July and December 1981, for instance, California schools and school districts were obliged to submit to the State Department of Education seventy-eight different annual reports on one or another matter, such as the Special Education Master Plan, the Annual Report of Pupil Transportation Expense, the Preschool Incentive Grant Application, the School Immunization Survey, the Bilingual Teacher Waiver, and the Survey of Basic Skills: Grade 12. Each month during this same period, another five reports were due, including the Claim for Reimbursement: Child Care Food Program and the School-Age Parenting and Infant Development Program Report of Attendance, Income, and Expenditure. Twelve quarterly reports were due, such as the Declaration of In-Kind Contributions for Campus Children's Centers. And, up to sixty-nine reports, due 'as required,' could also have been called for, *e.g.*, the Application for One-Time Funds to Children with Special Needs and the Family Child Care Home Approval Survey.[1]

At the federal level, the U.S. Department of Education estimated that some 1.2 million hours per year would be spent in fiscal year 1981 by state and local agencies filling out federal reports and forms. This includes items like the lengthy annual reports on Title I expenditures (for the educationally disadvantaged), periodic surveys like that on participation of non-public schools in federal education programs, and special evaluation studies like one on Title VII in-service teacher training programs and another on the role of federal funding in facilitating desegregation.

Many of the reports required by the state, and alluded to above, really originate with the federal government, just as many reports required of local schools by the school districts originate in state regulations. Eventually, however, the burden of much of the information collection activity is passed along to school principals (and vice-principals) and ultimately to teachers. When the burden of filling out forms and the like falls to the lowest level of the educational hierarchy, the teachers, pure quantitative measures of the burden, such as the number of hours needed to do the work, will not suffice.

Professional demoralization and alienation must also be taken into account. Consider the testimony, for example, of one elementary-school teacher:

> In a typical day an elementary teacher deals with sign-in sheets, lunch counts, hall passes, absence slips, rollbooks, attendance cards, class count forms, parent communications, textbook and materials requests, lesson plans, student evaluations, documentation (and) paperwork relating directly to teaching students. Additionally, different levels of the bureaucracy frequently request distribution and collection of questionnaires, ethnic surveys, free lunch applications, permission slips, walking trip permits, emergency cards, class schedules, federal forms for Impact Aid, home language surveys, audio-visual surveys, needs assessments, nine-week objectives, yearly objectives, report cards, requests for special services, testing materials, program descriptions, time cards, field trip requests, and several profile cards for each student. (All this at a time when teachers are also being told there is not enough paper for lessons and art projects.)
>
> Much of the paperwork is related to monitoring, evaluating, regulating, and verifying the teacher's behavior. It results from mandates at the federal, state, district, and school levels. . . . Those teachers who do attempt to criticize the paper overload find that they cannot get to the source of it. It becomes simpler to do it pro forma than try to comprehend it. Teachers learn that their documentations are usually passed up the line without being read. Even when they are read, administrators have no time to verify the accuracy of the statements. Morale is lowered and paperwork becomes a meaningless exercise.[2]

The Uses of Paperwork

Paperwork has a bad name among educators as it does among many other people, and unquestionably this bad name is, in part, deserved. Yet, it is important to see the paperwork problem in perspective. Much paperwork does serve a purpose. Any notions as to how to reduce the paperwork problem — and this chapter will aim to furnish some — must take account of these purposes.[3]

In this section, I offer a qualitative listing of instrumental functions of paperwork. In doing so, I heed only the functions of paperwork that are pertinent to certain collective, or public, purposes, and ignore (for the time being) the uses of paperwork for private or narrowly self-interested ends.

1 *Substitute for Direct On-Site Inspection*

It is necessary to state the obvious: much paperwork aims to force people to reveal truths they might otherwise prefer to keep hidden, and in doing so, it forces people to shape their conduct so as to make the revelations acceptable to whichever parties might audit the paper and, thus, indirectly monitor the conduct itself. This sort of paperwork is directed, in a word, at *compliance*. It secures compliance, ultimately, by pressure and threat, and detects and punishes the deviant cases of non-compliance that occur when pressure and threat fail.

It is equally obvious that *self*-revelation via forms and reports is not the only way to monitor the regulated population. Direct on-site inspection is another method frequently used in many policy areas, ranging from occupational safety to restaurant sanitation. Yet, there are many advantages to self-revelation as opposed to revelation by outsiders, especially from the enforcement agency's point of view. For a given expenditure of agency funds, paperwork can greatly extend and deepen the reach of regulatory surveillance compared with what could be done with inspectors. Inspectors must be paid by the agency, but paperwork imposes a burden of self-inspection and self-certification on the regulated parties themselves. Secondly, the time and transportation costs of site visits are much larger than the costs of sending reports and other documents through the mails. True, the agency must incur costs for printing, collecting, storing, and auditing the paper flow that it has mandated, and these can be substantial. Yet, in many cases the cost advantage still lies decisively with enforcement through paperwork. To take a homey example, it is a lot less costly to have parents and teachers produce and transmit the information about the eligibility status of potential student recipients of Title I aid than to have auditors dispatched by the federal government visiting in every school and classroom. The federal auditors in this field (like income tax auditors) can best be deployed monitoring the suspect cases and generally acting as a deterrent to dishonest eligibility reporting.

It may also be noted that paperwork and site visits can usefully be combined. Nursing homes in California, for example, are required to maintain extensive records on patient care and financial practices that are regularly audited by inspectors on their occasional visits to the facilities. And California state-sponsored school-site evaluation teams typically prepare themselves for their visits by reviewing the paperwork files of the schools they are to visit.

Another advantage of enforcement via paperwork over direct inspection is that the latter method simply cannot monitor any of the things that the former can — at least at a reasonable cost to those who must comply. Direct inspection is best suited to enforcing rules that bear on the physical environment — *e.g.*, machine guards on dangerous equipment, but it is much less suited to enforcing rules that govern less tangible yet no less real features of the social world, such as decision processes, motives, intentions, understandings, and so on. This is true in regard to attempts by the U.S. Department of Agriculture, say, to monitor the internal corporate quality-control system of food processors; and the point is even more relevant to a field like education, where so much of the service technique as well as the management method is intangible.

2 *Pseudo-Contracts*

Compliance with regulations is frequently a process rather than a one-time affair: next year's plans almost always include reports on last year's activities. In many social programs, plans and reports are a staple feature. They can figure in the ongoing compliance process primarily if they become elements in a continuing negotiation process between an applicant and a funding source. The applicant points to past accomplishments, while the funding source points to past discrepancies between promise and performance. The applicant points to promises to do better next time; the funding source asks for better assurance that the promises will be kept this next time. And so forth. Of course, inspectors can negotiate in the same way; but plans and reports have the added advantage of creating a documentary record of negotiations, mimicking the legal and moral symbols of private-party contracting, and intensifying personal responsibility by fixing individual signatures to paper promises.

Probably this process does not occur as much in education as it does in certain other program areas. To the extent that it does occur, the relevant negotiators may be local 'advocates' for compliance rather than donor-agency officials and auditors. For instance, Paul Hill describes a 'sex equity action plan' adopted by a school board subsequent to a self-evaluation report that had revealed certain discriminatory practices. Hill reports that the plan 'then became a valuable accountability device in the hands of the district's "advocate" compliance coordinator and the public advisory council whose actions he orchestrated.'[4]

Another example of paperwork as 'contracting' is even more explicit: the individualized education program (IEP) that is required under California law for students who are handicapped in some way (physically, emotionally, or intellectually) and are receiving services under the Master Plan for Special Education and the federal Education for All Handicapped Children Act. The IEP documents at some length the student's present performance levels, the goals and objectives for the student during the next instructional period, and the resources needed to achieve the goals and objectives. An IEP report can easily run five or six single-spaced pages. It must be reviewed by the student's parent and a number of consulting specialists and school officials. In spirit as well as in form, it frequently has the character of a contract, and in fact does sometimes become a key document in formal administrative hearings or even litigation following parental complaints.

3 *Due Process and Participation*

Paperwork requirements may have an especially useful attention-focusing role when the joint action of many semi-autonomous parties is at stake. I mentioned above 'plans' that made promises about future action. If the plan is to be produced and executed by only one party, the promises made in the plan perhaps have some chance of being carried out. The more parties involved in the plan, however, the less likely it is to be meaningful — at least under most conditions. Each separate interest describes what it is doing and what it proposes to do in the future, but there is usually no social or political mechanism for reconciling divergent submissions or for imposing some priority order on the several projects. As one person familiar with EPA-mandated local 'transportation control plans' (aimed at reducing auto usage and therefore smog) has said, 'The main instrument of planning here is a staple gun.'

Nevertheless, there may sometimes be value in having divergent or even opposed interests, which might otherwise not have a forum, participate in the 'planning' process. For example, privately sponsored social service and mental health agencies in California have often used the forum provided by the annual process of state-mandated county plan preparation to seek larger allocations at the expense of public agency service providers who normally dominate the expenditure of state and county mental health funds. The Health Systems Agencies (HSAs) set up by the 1974 National Health Planning and Resources Development Act were to incorporate a 'consumer' majority on each board. The framers of the act assumed that physician interests and those of other professional or institutional providers dominated health planning, and they wanted to give more of a say to consumers who were 'broadly representative of the social, economic, linguistic, and racial populations of the area.' The structures created to accomplish this purpose were in fact effective in this limited respect, but the overall effect on policy outcomes was insignificant, since the HSAs had only advisory power and could be overridden by state bodies.[5]

In education, probably the outstanding example of paperwork intended to serve this function is the process of developing an IEP for a handicapped student. The process is now relatively formalized, with each of its steps marked by not insubstantial piles of paperwork. Because the designers of the law were attempting to reform a pattern of abuse and neglect, they designed a set of procedures that were intended to focus attention on the genuine educational needs of every handicapped student and to protect students who were not genuinely handicapped from being stigmatized as such and deprived of opportunities available to the non-handicapped. Extensive student assessment procedures are required, including consultation with number of professionals and specialists. Parents must be brought into the discussion; and if they are unwilling or unavailable, then the professionals in charge of the student's disposition must document their own failed attempts to induce parental participation.

School-site parent advisory committees are invoked as a way of involving parents both as potential supporters and as potential critics of certain programs. More broadly, these committees are forums for the airing of views and the resolution of controversy; and in some important cases, they are also genuine power-holders, *i.e.*, when they must approve school program plans for the expenditure of special state- or federally-funded assistance. In California, the annual school-site application for the full range of state and federal assistance must be approved not only by the principal, but also by at least four parents and one teacher as well. The parent who chairs the 'school-site council' must approve the plan to expend funds under the state's 'school improvement program,' and three parents must approve the plan to spend Title I funds, including a parent who chairs the bilingual education subcommittee and a parent who chairs the preschool advisory subcommittee. Of course, not all of these committees function very actively, and in many schools the signatures are obtained merely pro forma. However, there are also many schools in which parental participation is broad and intense.

4 *Consciousness-raising*

As we have said, much educational paperwork aims to induce compliance. Yet, in an important sense, 'compliance' and its close relative, 'deterrence,' are much too narrow definitions of the objectives of the paperwork regime. The idea behind the reporting and documentation requirements typically is not merely to banish misbehavior, but to encourage higher levels of performance, greater commitments to acting 'responsibly' and even 'creatively.' We do not want a special education teacher merely to avoid doing harm to a student, but to accomplish something positive as well, a 'something' which is hard to specify in law and regulation or to enforce through any conceivable set of paperwork requirements. A principal, or district-level administrator, should not merely throw a Spanish-speaking teacher and twenty-five Spanish-speaking students together in a classroom for a few hours and consider his or her duty discharged. Legally, it may be, but the periodic reporting requirements ideally should serve as reminders that the state and federal governments *care* about the problem of limited-English-speaking (or non-English-speaking) students and that the principal should care as well.

In this respect, as in many others, the regulation of education is similar to most health and safety regulation. The problems in these areas are continuous and often pop up with novel features. Hence, only a diffuse attitude of concern and responsibility is suited to dealing with them. We do not want a manufacturer merely to install proper machine guards and issue a safety manual to foremen. We want 'safety consciousness' on the part of all personnel, from the lowest wage earner to the highest manager.

Probably paperwork is less suited to consciousness-raising than is direct inspection, which can multiply face-to-face contacts that potentially (if not commonly, in practice) are better able to inspire and educate than are contacts mediated by paper flows. Nevertheless, the steady, day-to-day obligations of some sorts of paperwork might have certain advantages. Just as inspectors can serve a reminding function, so too can the continuing obligation to fill out certain forms and documents.

Indeed, so too can the continuing obligation to *read* certain forms, documents, and other written communications. Perhaps the most interesting and surprising discovery I made in the course of my fieldwork was that educators count as part of 'the paperwork problem' the *reading* of memoranda, circulars, notices, and so forth. In fact, the three principals and vice-principals I interviewed all responded to the open-ended question, 'What sort of paperwork do you find the most burdensome?' with immediate and fulsome accounts of what they had to read. They had to be prodded into mentioning the kinds of paperwork that required them to *write* reports or fill out surveys or complete documents. Most of the writing requirements that came their way, they said, were passed along to either teachers or clerical help. Not that they felt free of the paperwork burden. Quite the contrary. They felt 'deluged' and 'swamped,' but by the obligation to read rather than to write.

Yet, whichever aspect of the paperwork phenomenon one considers paramount, both might play the same role in 'consciousness-raising.' The psychological and social processes at work are subtle, and I do not pretend to understand them. But to the extent that I have been able to catch a glimpse of them, I should say that paperwork of both the reading and the writing varieties has some of the qualities of *ritual* for educators.[6] It is perhaps not so much the content of the documents read or written as it is the sheer mass of words devoted to one or another topic that makes an impression. The amount of attention given to matters of ethnic identification, the poverty (and non-poverty) status of children, and financial accountability in the flow of documents throughout any large urban school district is a constant reminder that these are matters one is supposed to care about. As David Tyack pointed out in a seminar discussion, in the late nineteenth century teachers were supposed to care a lot about tardiness and truancy — and so computed periodic attendance rates to three decimal places! A second ritual aspect of paperwork is that it creates a separate fictional world, reflective of this real one, but only somewhat so, that is in important respects more comforting and more manageable. Violent acts by students turn into 'incident reports,' and a band of tuned-out, sullen, and barely literate sixth-graders becomes a statistical cohort of 'educationally disadvantaged' students. To the extent that educators become involved in this parallel world, however, and take it seriously, involvement probably enhances feelings of solidarity and mutual support — partly because those who participate share a common language not fully appreciated by outsiders, and partly because they are all implicated in the continuing distortion of 'reality' in the interests of protecting the education community as a whole, and each of themselves individually, from a harsh reality. Finally, it should be noted that ritual is not merely an expression of group cohesiveness, but an instrument of power wielded by the majority or other dominant groups to keep deviants in line, or at least to communicate to the deviants what the correct line is. Those educators who really don't care at all about poverty students or ethnic sensibilities or financial integrity are constantly reminded that others do and that they *should* care. The fact that these reminders come in code, signaled by the volume of paperwork on certain topics rather than by a more manifest and explicit vehicle, may in fact heighten their persuasive power over the long run.

The Real World of Educational Paperwork

Despite these many actual and potential uses of educational paperwork, much paperwork in the real world is bound to be useless or worse. In part this occurs for the same reason that all regulatory paperwork — and indeed, regulation — is bound to be excessive: it imposes standardized prescriptions on highly varied problems, and this necessarily produces a large number of cases in which regulatory structures are too burdensome or are inappropriate to the true situation. Surely there are *some* cases in which the elaborate procedures surrounding the development of the IEP produce better results for the individual child, but in many cases these procedures are simply a waste of time and energy. It may be that the child's problems and needs are obvious, and the indicated course of action a foregone conclusion. Or, it may be that the school district has such limited resources that the development of an ideal IEP is simply a charade. Although certainly there are *some* districts, schools, and teachers that systematically dump troublesome students into special education classes that deliver little educational benefit to these or other students, there are many other districts, schools, and teachers that genuinely try to do the best they can for students, and for whom the procedures and associated paperwork are a terrible and demoralizing encumbrance.

Another similarity between educational paperwork and regulatory paperwork more generally is their sensitivity to demands and criticisms originating in the political environment, particularly the legislature. The essence of a 'compliance' regime, after all, is that some (perhaps many) people are assumed to be misbehaving unless they are constantly monitored and discouraged from doing so; and the political climate surrounding such a policy is bound to be one of suspicion, first of those who are being monitored, and secondly of those who are supposed to be doing the monitoring. Laxity, cooptation, and perhaps even corruption are the besetting enemies of all compliance programs. And so, of course, is the constant *suspicion* that these enemies may, secretly, be in the ascendant. Frequently, more reporting and documentation requirements are involved to banish such suspicion.

The dynamic is best illustrated in some areas outside that of education, where suspicions intermittently erupt in the wake of scandals or sudden catastrophes which bring in their wake more paperwork. Consider, for example, what happened when the *Washington Post* revealed in September 1979 that the U.S. Department of Agriculture (USDA) was daily shipping hundreds of dollars' worth of usable office furniture for burial in the District of Columbia's Lorton dump. Notwithstanding the promises from the U.S. General Accounting Office (GAO) to get a better grip on things, one month later a GAO auditor testified that he saw two thousand pieces of furniture stored in a USDA basement and $38,000 worth of new, largely unopened cartons of furniture in the agency's attic while the department continued to buy new furniture. The result was, first, a government-wide freeze on new furniture acquisitions, then a General Services Administration order (issued after prodding by Congress and the Office of Management and Budget) to every federal agency to draw up and submit an annual furniture requirements and expenditures budget. Exemptions from the freeze were virtually impossible to get, leading to the usual assortment of anomalies and inefficiencies, such as expensive electric typewriters remaining unused for want of typewriter tables. The annual furniture requirements and expenditures budget quickly became a bureaucratic laughingstock because it was irrelevant to the day-to-day practical wisdom that — to the skeptics, at any rate — ought to guide furniture acquisitions. It lasted only one year.

The paperwork governing the use of human subjects in university-sponsored scientific research is another case of overreaction leading to overgeneralization. Researchers must document their intended procedures and have them cleared by a central campus committee charged with protecting human subjects. Researchers must also provide the committee with detailed assurances of how they will inform subjects of their risks and their rights to withdraw from the research. In principle, this sort of regulation may be beneficial. In practice, however, it spread from biomedical research, where it was clearly appropriate, to areas where its value was dubious — *e.g.*, administering balance-beam walking tests to elementary-school children.

In the case of elementary and secondary education, we do not see the eruption of acute crises that produce demands for more accountability. Rather, the accountability crisis is chronic. There is no need here to dwell on the declining status of public-school teachers and administrators, the breakdown of public confidence in large portions of the school system, the mistrust by minority groups of the practices and intentions of school administrators and teachers from a more mainstream background, and the difficulty inherent in the educational enterprise of demonstrating in any technically rigorous way just how effective the schools may or may not be. These conditions add up to a powerful magnet for scrutiny and criticism and, of course, for a flood of reports and data. Persons whom I interviewed in the California State Department of Education insisted that most of their own demands for data and reports grew out of prior demands levied in the statutes and appropriations bills or out of anticipated demands that *might* arise in oversight hearings. These legislative demands covered a broad spectrum of issues, from simple statistical counts as to how much money is spent on how many Title I students in which school districts, to whether money spent on teacher in-service training is producing positive results. And, of course, the State Department of Education, in turn, must be suspicious of the truthfulness of reports from the district level. Especially in the current era with the bulk of school budgets supplied by the state treasury, the districts must respond to the state's increasing concern that all its monies will be spent responsibly and honestly. Since so much state money is tied, on a per student basis, to reported 'average daily attendance' (ADA), a lot more resources than previously are expended on collecting these data (appropriately broken down by assistance eligibility category) and to auditing the data that are collected and reported. It is only in recent years, for example, that the state has demanded audits of student absentee notes, so that invalid excuses or non-existent notes could be invoked as reasons to demand local reimbursement of state monies tied to the ADA figure.

The technical problems of designing 'good' paperwork are often formidable and can inspire administrators to try to compensate by imposing more and more documentation requirements. It is worth remembering that a central function of documentation is to force regulated parties to reveal truths that might otherwise have remained hidden. However, the correspondence between what documentation reveals and the underlying reality is likely to be rather weak. One reason is that devious people will attempt to hide infractions if they think they can get away with doing so. While control agencies naturally try to design paperwork systems that will permit auditors to detect evasion, this task is not necessarily simple. The Environmental Protection Agency, for example, for some time toyed with the idea of requiring extensive annual reports from all hazardous waste generators and hazardous waste disposal sites concerning what materials had been sent and received, respectively. By feeding these data into a computer and instructing the computer to match the alleged inflows and outflows, staff thought that they would be able to discern discrepancies and track down violators. On further analysis, however, it turned out that such a task would have been extremely costly, even with computer assistance, and well-nigh impossible were reporting firms to take even moderate pains to disguise the truth.

In the case of education, the problem of deception takes on a different and subtler character. In this area, the typical problem is to monitor the use of grant-in-aid funds, to ensure that they are being used for the purposes for which they were allocated by the funding source (usually the federal or the state government). Yet, the technical difficulties of doing this are often so great as to be insurmountable. As Stephen Barro has pointed out, trying to enforce donor priorities by tracking funds from their source to their final use is virtually hopeless unless the prescribed use and the tracks that lead to it are highly visible against the background of all the other tracks and destinations in the great thicket of state and local education programs.[7] The main problems here are that donor funds can often be used to substitute for funds that would otherwise have come from the recipient's own budget, and that it is necessarily obscure just when and to what degree this substitution might be taking place. Strict record-keeping and dedicated auditing can allow the thicket to be penetrated to some extent, but not completely. Even truthfulness and green-eyeshade commitment to accuracy are not enough to make documentation correspond adequately to the realities that underlie it. Frequently, there are immense technical difficulites in representing in words and numbers a reality that often is subtle, elusive, and obscure even to the most self-scrutinizing and honorable individual. Consider, for instance, the inherent limits of words and numbers as descriptors. While it may be possible to document that $500 in grant funds were indeed expended, and legitimately so, for three teachers to attend a conference on science education, say, it is not possible to document what they learned there, or indeed whether they paid any attention to the conference proceedings even while seated in their midst. Or, consider student 'ethnic identification': operationalizing this concept for documentation purposes leads quickly to such perplexing issues as 'genealogical purity,' cultural assimilation or distinctiveness, and the appropriateness of various methods of eliciting the information (such as self-reporting or visual inspection). Conceptual and moral questions aside, the purely technical aspects of the problem are quite problematic in themselves.

While this brief review of 'the real world of regulatory paperwork' has not surveyed all the reasons for its characteristic excessiveness, it has highlighted the more fundamental and probably remediable ones. In the following section, we shall examine some others in the context of exploring certain measures that might be taken to mitigate these excesses.

What Is To Be Done?

It is useful to distinguish between two sorts of 'excessive' paperwork: the sort that achieves some desired objective but at a cost (in time, money, or aggravation) that is considered too high; and the sort that, whatever its costs, is simply ineffective and therefore wasteful. The distinction is useful mainly because it reminds us that remedies to shrink or abolish excess sometimes need to be joined to policies that furnish some functional equivalent for whatever is lost in the process. In this connection, we may mention, without elaboration, the proposal to substitute a standards-of-service approach for a tracking-of-funds approach in federal grants management that Barrow advocates. Simply put, the idea is that grants could be conditioned on the recipient unit (a state or local education agency) meeting certain standards of effort or performance, e.g., spending no less than $400 per child on compensatory education, or spending on handicapped students no less than 1.5 times as much as is spent on regular students. All the paperwork that went into the (largely ineffective) tracking of federal funds could then be eliminated. To be sure, other sorts of paperwork would rise up to take its place — although they would probably be less onerous. The important point here, though, is that federal controls over local allocation decisions would not necessarily be weakened and might even be strengthened relative to those that exist now.

Most of the 'excessiveness' targets we could plausibly aim at, though, are of the type where the paperwork is nearly pure waste. They originate not so much in the substantive requirements of policy and programing as in the organizational and political pathologies that surround policies and programs. While it is true that excessive paperwork of this type might serve some *interest*, and the attack on such interests might be repelled and certainly would be resented, it may not be necessary or desirable to invent a substitute to satisfy the deprived and disappointed interests. With these preliminary observations, then, let us turn to some possible remedies for excessive educational paperwork.

1 *Central Clearance and Oversight*

One important reason that paperwork increases is that the people who impose it do not pay the full costs of doing so. To be sure, they may have to pay for the reproduction of forms, the mailing, and the processing and storage of information when the forms are returned; but they do not have to expend time and energy filling out the forms (or to read memos, in the case of paperwork that does not require a written response). Moreover, those who impose paperwork on others can usually be expected to hold an exaggerated idea of its benefits. If it is a request for data, let us say, normally the data will be thought to serve some purpose related to their agency's mission; and it would not be surprising if agency personnel had an inflated idea of the importance of this mission. Even more importantly, because it is very little recognized just how irrelevant most 'data' are to making important policy or managerial decisions, requests for data frequently arise out of sheer ignorance, albeit an ignorance allied to good intentions.[8]

One approach to this problem of distorted incentives and systematically mistaken beliefs is to institutionalize an organizational unit that will act as a counterpoise. The inappropriate beliefs and motivations may remain, but they will be checked and balanced by a force tending in the other direction. An example from outside education is the Office of Management and Budget (OMB), which, under the Paperwork Reduction Act of 1980, reviews almost all federal agency reporting forms and requests for information. In the California State Department of Education, an interesting and relatively successful unit of this type is the Data Acquisition and Review Committee, which came into being in 1977. It reviews almost every proposed new data collection effort for the department. It vetoes some, trims others, encourages the consolidation of still others, and facilitates access to existing data sources by users who otherwise might have initiated the collection of data afresh. Its function is similar to that of the Federal Education Data Acquisition Council, which came into being a year later.

Such bodies are essentially regulatory, although in the nature of the case the people they regulate are often themselves regulators. Like all regulators, the DARC and the FEDAC are not universally loved. Their review processes take time, their criticisms may wound egos, and their decisions and policies may even threaten jobs. Given the great volume of paperwork in education, a large number of people are employed doing it as their principal occupation; and to abolish the paperwork means to abolish their jobs and/or to diminish their status. Of course, it is easier to forestall proposed new data acquisition efforts than to abolish old ones, for the old ones have a constituency. One of the first targets of the DARC from among existing reports was the copy of student drivers' licenses that came to the State Department of Education. Tens or hundreds of thousands of these pieces of paper came to Sacramento annually and were subsequently thrown away. No one had any use for them. But when the DARC proposed to abolish the procedure, initially it ran into much resistance, especially from local driver education instructors and program administrators. The director of the DARC conjectured that 'it was just habit with them. They didn't want to change, and they didn't want to be told that what had been going on was useless, even if they knew it anyway.' The district people were supported by their professional driver education counterparts in Sacramento, whose inertia has permitted the wasteful practice in the past, and — we may suppose — who feared that too close a look at their practices more generally might lead to workload reductions and then to personnel reductions.

The apparent success of central clearance at the state and federal levels raises the possibility that a comparable institution could be made to work at the district level. Obviously, this would make sense only for large school districts that generated a lot of paperwork themselves. Since district officials like to blame the paperwork burden on the state and federal governments, it might prove embarrassing to admit implicitly that the district was indeed in a position to partly remedy the problem. However, the California State Department of Education, which likes to deflect blame as much as any other bureaucracy, did manage to overcome this political obstacle and establish the DARC; and a comparable argument can be made regarding the FEDAC.

A useful took to back up the staff of a central clearance office might be a 'sunset' policy that automatically terminates the life of any data request procedure after a certain time unless the procedure is explicitly reauthorized.

2 *Redistributing the Paperwork Burden*

It is not only the total burden of paperwork that is of concern, but its incidence as well. The social loss imposed by paperwork is greater if the incidence is on educational personnel who are playing especially productive roles in the system, *e.g.*, classroom teachers as opposed to front-office clerks. Although it is dangerous to generalize about which roles most deserve to be spared, we might speculate that: administrators should usually absorb the reporting requirements that might otherwise fall on teachers and parents; 'project coordinators' who oversee state and federal special grant money that requires financial and program accounting should absorb the burden that might otherwise fall on general-purpose administrators like principals; district-level 'research' and statistical specialists should lift the burden off school-site project coordinators or other administrators; and clerks should be given the paperwork jobs that otherwise fall to administrators and professionals in general. Best of all, certain routine data processing and reporting tasks should be given to a computer.

Just how far this sort of specialization can be carried depends on budgetary resources and on the magnitude of certain diseconomies associated with specialization. Budgetary resources in most school systems have been unusually hard-pressed for the last several years and are likely to remain so. This means that it may not be possible to invest in productivity-increasing but expensive computers, or to retain central office personnel whose duties had revolved mainly around decreasing other people's paperwork burdens. It may sometimes work out that there is a conflict between the goal of overall paperwork reduction and the goal of sparing the most productive personnel. Consider, for instance, the new CBEDS (California Basic Educational Data System) instrument, a computer-readable survey that is administered on a single day in October every year to every teacher, principal, and superintendent. The intention is to create a data base that will permit the State Department of Education to prepare a variety of statistical reports, including all those required by federal agencies and a good many requested on an ad hoc basis by curious legislators or others. In theory, CBEDS would displace many separate reporting efforts that previously fell to individual school sites and school districts, since it would make available a vast reservoir of highly disaggregated data from which one could draw almost any combination of frequency distributions and cross-tabulations for almost any reporting purpose. This looks like beneficial workload redistribution in the sense that it consolidates reporting on a single day and turns the processing job over to clerks and computers. But the price is an added burden on professionals' (teachers') time that had not previously existed. Of course, CBEDS may in the long run also manage to remove some burdens that had fallen on teachers; and this reduction, together with the reduction of the burden on specialized administrators, may in the end offset any new burdens. For the time being, however, teachers dislike CBEDS, and district-level administrators are divided on whether it is making their lives easier or harder.

3 *Reducing Excessive Standards of Accuracy and Comprehensiveness*

Whether intended primarily for the State Department of Education or for professional peers sometimes brought in to review it, the annual school-site plan is typically a bulky and unreadable document. It may obfuscate as much as it reveals, though not necessarily intentionally. However, one elementary-school principal decided to compress his entire statement into a few pages, and the result was passed around among his fellow principals as though it were a piece of the true cross.

Another principal told me of how, instead of responding to a statistical request with full deference to the level of accuracy required, she simply estimated the numbers. 'The staff person who knew the exact numbers was away on vacation,' she said, 'and I knew my estimates would be reliable enough for the purposes the district has in mind.'

A district official in charge of overseeing the implementation of PL 94-142 told me of how he made a special effort to reduce the level of detail required in the IEP write-up prepared for each student considered for special education. 'I just put a few headings on the form, like "Present Levels of Performance" and "Prioritized Annual Goals" that conform to what state and federal regulations indicate. But I don't go beyond this. I leave it to the professionals to put in whatever level of detail they think is needed in the particular case.'

4 *Filtering Junk Memos, Notices and Reports*

One principal I interviewed had an excellent reputation among his teaching staff for protecting them from paperwork. 'Look,' he said, 'here's a notice about a conference on a new approach to student discipline that the district wants me to send to the teachers in case they're interested. I'm throwing it away. The district just ran a large-scale, in-service training program four months ago in which we all got trained in a completely different approach. This just undermines what we did. So, why even bother the teachers with it?' Of course, he said, one has to be careful not to overdo it, but 'the teachers know that I filter these things and are grateful that I do it.'

If the junk memos and requests do get through to the teachers, or to other presumptive data providers, these persons can do their own filtering. That is, they can simply ignore the demands made on their time and energy by discarding the offending items without a response, or in some cases without even a glance. One can view this sort of conduct as insubordination or as intelligent time management, depending on one's sense of hierarchy and on one's sense of the substantive importance of the item at issue.

Outright refusal to fill out a form or answer a survey is probably quite uncommon, to be sure, especially since educators have learned to be docile in the face of such demands. Delay, however, is probably more acceptable, and hence more widely used. One principal told me of his Deputy Superintendent sending out a memo asking for some information that the principal thought was pointless; the principal decided not to respond until he was badgered once or twice by his superior. He added, 'There's some chance he'll come to see it's pointless, too, or anyway forget about it; and so I'll have avoided another piece of paperwork.'

5 *Demythologizing 'Data'*

Of what use are 'data'? Data are symbols that (purportedly) describe conditions in the real world. They are useful to the degree that they help people improve their understanding of how the world works and/or indicate courses of action that are likely to be superior, in some sense, to the courses of action that would probably have been selected otherwise. Useful data therefore become a form of 'evidence' supporting an interpretation of things, or possibly also an argument about what course of action to take. Such data are known as 'information.'

Converting mere data into genuine information normally requires the work of active intelligence. The data must be brought together with some pre-existing theory, and the theory must be modified (or reaffirmed) in the light of the data. This, at any rate, is what happens, in a general way, at the individual psychological level. Since organizations also collect data with the aim of converting at least some of them into information, it is also necessary to understand how this process works. Unfortunately, the social scientific understanding of such matters is still quite rudimentary. It is safe to say, though, that most large organizations — and especially public organizations — probably collect too much data. That is, given that collecting data is costly — to someone, if not always to members of the organizational unit collecting the data — the marginal costs of much data probably exceed their marginal value considered as potential 'information.' To put the matter more graphically, there are lots of unread reports taking up shelf space and gathering dust, and there are reams of computer output that few people can interpret at all, much less use to make a decision about anything.

Surely there are many reasons for this, but one that needs immediate emphasis is the fact that it is usually genuinely difficult to know whether any particular data are in fact informative, even when one has them in hand. And before one has them, it is literally *impossible* to know whether they might be useful. As the saying goes, 'We don't know what we don't know.' Hence, it is always possible to convince ourselves that if we knew just a few more facts ('data'), we might suddenly grow a great deal wiser (more 'informed'). Furthermore, it is impossible to *prove* to a person thus convinced that such a belief is mistaken and that the costs of further data collection are really not worthwhile. Add to this the fact that those who pay the costs are not usually those who conceive of the likely benefits, and multiply that by the tendency to underestimate the real costs involved in 'merely' filling out a statistical survey or documenting the reasons for a pupil assignment decision, say, and the dynamic towards more and more paperwork is obvious.

As one former district superintendent told me, 'people get bright ideas and just tack things on.' That is, they add questions to existing survey instruments. The same applies to more ad hoc requests for data: 'somebody decides it would be nice to know something, and before you know it, letters are being sent to a bunch of principals asking for information.'

Computers, moreover, with their apparent ability to search through massive data files and to correlate everything with everything else, support the illusion that all data are potentially informative. It is little noticed that the bureaucratic and human context in which computers are utilized often constrains their actual use within quite narrow limits. Consider, for instance, the case of the Environmental Protection Agency staff proposal, mentioned above, to require extensive annual reports from all hazardous waste generators and hazardous waste disposal sites concerning what materials had been sent and received, respectively. The designers of the proposed annual report requirement scarcely consulted with the computer operators in the EPA to see if the data they would have obtained could have been processed usefully. Not until many months had been invested in preparing the reporting forms did they go through the exercise of imagining what they would have done with these data if they could have been processed. Among the questions they needed to ask were the following:

- If we find an apparent discrepancy between wastes generated and wastes properly disposed of, how do we know this is not simply a case of incomplete or tardy reporting?
- How do we know we haven't lost the forms or punched the data into the wrong places?
- If we proceed with an investigation as though there were a potential violation, what backlash do we create if it turns out that there is no violation, but only a bureaucratic snafu?
- How can we tell if someone is lying? What sorts of additional computer runs and other inquiries will be necessary merely to establish probable cause for further investigation? Will we have the resources to do these tasks?
- If the regulated community discovers that it is difficult for us to process and utilize these data, do we risk our credibility as enforcers of more important requirements?

Although it took the EPA staff many months to get around to posing such questions, ultimately they did so; and as a result, they scrapped the annual report requirement.

In introductory courses to graduate-level social statistics, students first planning a survey are often urged to make up 'dummy tables' filled with imaginary data so as to put a check on the collection of data that will prove to be unintelligible, unreliable, unanalyzable, or unenlightening. It is a very instructive exercise, expressing a profound bit of wisdom. But even when students accept its wisdom, they find it hard to put the prescription into practice. It would be surprising if educational bureaucrats — for whom data collection often has the same ritual meanings as it does for social science students — were better able or more willing to go through the same sort of drill. The OMB and the GAO like to berate agencies for having failed to do pilot studies with data collection instruments before imposing new requirements. But a cheaper and even more effective procedure would be for agencies to simulate their decision and policy processes; that is, to do a bit of role-playing to see how they would (or would not) be affected by the data that might (or might not) come pouring in on any particular tide of paperwork.[9]

6 *Substituting More Efficient Rituals*

Although we have been assuming, to this point, that data-requesters *want* the data to be useful in some sense — that is, to be 'information' — data requests originate from many other motives as well. In some cases, there is a desire to appear 'rational,' modern, and up-to-date. In other cases, there is simply a desire to wield power, to show who's boss, by successfully imposing some sort of paperwork burden on others. Perhaps a softer version of this attitude is what prevails in the education field: the desire to communicate to another party that that party is *accountable* to the person or agency generating the data, *e.g.*, as regards Title I project reports or the results of standardized tests administered to certain classes of students.

But perhaps our softening of 'power' into 'accountability' does not go quite far enough, since the idea of 'accountability' itself, in the context of educational programing, is rather pale. Although educators talk a lot about the need for accountability and about the public's demands on them to be more accountable, in fact it is hard to hold them accountable for much. Even if their performance is poor, a combination of bureaucratic monopoly power, union rules, civil service regulations, and the 'lock-in effect' of grant-in-aid programs substantially insulates most of the individual and organizational participants in the educational system from the sort of accountability that is backed by sanctions.[10] Adverse publicity and moral suasion are the main tools invoked on behalf of 'accountability,' and these are not always very powerful (although sometimes they surely are). Perhaps we should speak instead of *responsiveness.* I said above that paperwork serves certain ritual functions, but one that I have not mentioned so far is its function as a vehicle for democratic participation. Practically everyone in the system except the classroom teachers is in a position to ask someone else to undertake some bit of paperwork, especially if by paperwork we include the reading of memoranda and other such items as well as writing. Again, except for teachers, almost everyone has a little bit of power to keep someone else responding to himself or herself in at least a small way. Most often the responsiveness ritual involves superiors obtaining expressions of deference (paperwork) from subordinates, but it can also involve peers relative to one another, which underlines the other side, the democratic side, of paperwork rituals.

To the extent that these speculations have any merit, it may be the case that reducing merely ritualistic paperwork cannot occur unless substitute rituals — presumably less wasteful ones — are instituted. Exactly what these might be is hard to say. Much depends on the particular relationship within which the responsiveness element is to be maintained and preserved. In some cases, face-to-face contact might substitute for paper communication with greater benefit and lower cost to all parties concerned. (One elementary-school principal told me that she eliminated vast quantities of paperwork by keeping an open door and encouraging teachers and parents to use it.) In other cases, such as the relationship between administrators and school board members, reciprocal 'stroking' could be worked out across a whole range of different issues over which they interact routinely.

Conclusion

The starting point of this essay was the observation that educators feel burdened by a lot of paperwork, that it has been increasing in recent years, that much of it is 'excessive' in some sense, and that many educators are demoralized by the phenomenon. From this starting point, we explored the legitimate purposes that paperwork was presumably invented to serve in the first place. We then reviewed the reasons why paperwork, even when directed to these purposes in general, might nevertheless be 'excessive' and burdensome in particular applications. Finally, we suggested a number of ways in which these excesses might be curbed.

Surely this essay has raised more questions than it has answered. By way of conclusion, therefore, I shall suggest some specific directions for future research. The most important of these concerns a more precise estimate of the magnitude of the paperwork burden in education, particularly its qualitative rather than its quantitative aspect. What exactly is involved in the 'demoralization' we referred to so loosely? Is it that paperwork is 'sterile' and therefore represents a direct assault on the professional person's self-image as dedicated and productive? Is it that by effectively reducing discretion, paperwork — or at least that portion aimed at 'compliance' — leads to policy choices that the professional regards as inappropriate or even perverse? Or is it that it is demoralizing only when those who bear the burden do not believe in the rationale for the paperwork in the first place, or do not believe that the originators of the demands for paperwork really understand what they are doing? In any event, whatever the subtle ways in which demoralization occurs, and whatever forms it takes, how extensive is it anyway? Only careful and extensive empirical work can throw light on these questions.

Assuming that paperwork does lead to some demoralization among educators on a scale great enough to be considered 'a problem,' we need a perspective on the larger problem, of which this may be a part. First, might it not be the case that all 'minor professionals' are vulnerable to the same demoralization as educators? The minor professions, such as elementary education, social work, law enforcement, correctional guidance, and nursing, cannot function without some degree of discretion and freedom from strict supervision. Yet, they do not have the prestige, nor perhaps the competence or trustworthiness, to deflect criticism for the occasional abuse of discretion that lawyers or doctors can invoke on behalf of their respective professions. Have any of these other professions discovered remedies for the problem that could be embraced in education?

Secondly, to what extent is the problem shared by all public-sector employees, whether educators or minor professionals or anything else? Demands for 'accountability' have been increased on all public-sector employees in recent years, with an accompanying increase in legislative oversight, media attention, and general citizen interest. Demands for evaluation and, hence, paperwork have grown apace. Furthermore, the vulnerability of these employees to criticism has almost certainly increased defensive 'cover your ass' behavior in the public service; and this development, too, has increased the reliance on documentation and thus 'paperwork.'

Finally, is 'paperwork' not simply a corollary of all forms of bureaucratic concentration of power and responsibility, whether in the public or the private sector, and whether or not the process touches professionals or non-professionals? Probably, if one interviewed employees in some sub-division of General Motors, one would hear that they, too, were overburdened by paperwork, that much of it was wasteful and foolish, and so on. Do educators sustain more of a paperwork burden than anyone else in a large organization (or constellation of organizations)? Perhaps they do. But how *much* bigger is the burden? In any case, are there paperwork reduction remedies available in the private sector that could be applied to the problems experienced by educators?

Excessive paperwork is not the most baneful problem of our time. Nor is it by any stretch of the imagination the most important cause of demoralization in the education profession. Yet, it might be one of the more remediable causes — up to some point — and further research in this area could prove to be not only intrinsically interesting, but somewhat useful as well.

Notes

1 California State Department of Education (1981) *Data Acquisition Calendar, July-December 1981*, Sacramento.
2 Peretti, D. (1980) 'Implementation problems in the standardized testing program' (seminar paper on file with the author) March.
3 On regulatory paperwork more generally, see Bardach, E. (1982) 'Self regulation and regulatory paperwork,' in Bardach, E. and Kagan, R.A. (Eds) *Social Regulation: Strategies for Reform*, San Francisco, Institute for Contemporary Studies, Chapter 14. See also Bardach, E. and Kagan, R.A. (1982) *Going by the Book: The Problem of Regulatory Unreasonableness* (a Twentieth Century fund report) Philadelphia Temple University Press, especially Chapter 3.
4 Hill, P.T. (1979) *A Study of Local Education Agency Response to Civil Rights Guarantees*, Santa Monica, The Rand Corporation, January, p. 16.
5 Morone, J.A. and Marmor, T.R. (1981) 'Representing consumer interests: The case of American health planning,' *Ethics*, 91, April, pp. 431–50.
6 Feldman, M.S. and March, J.G. (1981) 'Information in organization as signal and symbol,' *Administrative Science Quarterly*, June.
7 Barro, S.M. (1981) 'Federal education goals and policy instruments: An assessment of the "strings" attached to Categorical Grants in education,' Timpane, M. (Ed.) *The Federal Interest in Financing Schooling*, Cambridge, Ballinger.
8 Tenenbaumand, E. and Wildavsky, A. (1981) *The Politics of Mistrust*, Beverly Hills, Sage Publications; Malvey, M. (1981) *Simple Systems, Complex Environments*, Beverly Hills, Sage Publications; and Dery, D. (1981) *Computers in Welfare*, Beverly Hills, Sage Publications.
9 Unfortunately, this mental exercise is complicated by what might be thought of as the paradox of deterrence. If regulatory documents received by an agency were immediately to be shredded or burned without a glance at their contents, this fact would not necessarily prove that documentation was excessive. Indeed, it might

prove the reverse. A prime function of regulatory paperwork, after all, is deterrence; the best testimony to the system's deterrent effectiveness might therefore be a compliance level so high that there would be no point in the agency's auditing the paper flow in search of violators. The IRS, for instance, is alleged to routinely destroy the majority of employer-and taxpayer-submitted documents because the storage and search costs involved in auditing them would be too high relative to their yield, and because the taxpayers' fear that they *might* be audited induces sufficient compliance anyway.

10 On the 'lock-in effect,' whereby donors and recipients end up in a mutual financial or political dependency, see WILLIAMS, W. (1980) *The Implementation Perspective*, Berkeley, University of California Press.

4 Case Study

Implementation and Intervention Strategies: The Case of PL 94-142

Guy Benveniste
University of California, Berkeley

In this chapter we introduce the notion of intervention strategies to explain why and when certain change efforts are successful. For our purpose we have selected the Education For All Handicapped Children Act of 1975 (PL 94-142) to illustrate the unforeseen consequences of inappropriate intervention strategies. Since education, in general, and special education in particular, relies heavily on professional competence for delivery of service, our discussion of intervention strategies focuses on the peculiarities of institutions where professional knowledge is important. What we have to say about special education applies equally to public health, research, the running of universities or even to companies using complex technologies.

An intervention strategy is the choice of linkage between two or more organizations in a loosely coupled system. Education and many other social sectors can be thought of as loosely coupled systems[1] where many different organizations with different purposes, responsibilities and resources overlap and impinge on each other. If we think of the governance of American education, we think of a complex mosaic where legislatures, the courts, local bodies, state and federal agencies deal with teacher unions, parents' organizations, students and the general public, each involved in some partial aspect of education, each partially controlled or affected by other actors.

In a loosely coupled system transactions take place — for example, courts make decisions, legislative mandates are enacted, federal agencies set rules for implementation, districts accept monies and other inducements to initiate novel activities. Many of these transactions include a control element, *i.e.*, when a district accepts monies to initiate a new program, the monies come along with a control package dictated by the legislative mandate or regulations of the implementing agencies.

Controls between semi-independent organizations are necessary to protect the purposes of donors and to facilitate implementation. Considerable attention has been given in the literature on the nature of controls and the kinds of slippage or even mutations that take place at the time of implementation.[2]

In this paper we seek to better understand how and when different intervention strategies are well suited or poorly adapted to different situations. We focus on situations where the task does not always lend itself to routinization and where professional discretion is important.

We select control points as the relevant variable. By control point we simply mean whether implementation controls are mainly exercises on input, output, or process variables.

This chapter argues that the choice of control points and the selection of control linkages is determined by characteristics of the task in the implementing agency. Some tasks can be controlled at outputs, others at process or inputs. Some can be controlled simultaneously or at all three. But many implementation failures or distortions can be attributed to the selection of the wrong control point and the wrong linkage.

A Few Definitions

Intervention strategy	The choice of control points and linkages.
Control point	Is this intervention affecting input, process or output variables?
Choice of linkage	What kind of reporting and what kind of positive or negative inducements are used?
Input controls	Since all organizations require input resources to survive, control of inputs is probably the most effective way of controlling organizations.
Process controls	These are directed at internal behavior concerned with the way service or product are provided.
Output/outcome controls	Output interventions are focused on characteristics of the product and service performed. Outputs are usually defined in terms of immediate organizational consequences, *i.e.*, the output of a higher education institution may be a cohort of graduates with a diploma.

Implicit here is the notion of disclosure. Output controls necessarily involve the implementer in saying something about what has been done. One question therefore, is to whom to disclose? To clients? To professions? To sponsors? To the public at large? The relevant imagery here is: 'tell us what you have done so that we can decide whether to ask you to continue or do something else.' Outputs are often linked to input resources. For example, output information is used to generate input resources: 'you achieved the goal, therefore we continue to fund you.'

Output controls tend to be used in planning situations where there is concern that a large number of loosely connected organizations coordinates their efforts.

Output controls can either enlarge or reduce an implementer's discretion depending on the specificity of disclosure. They therefore fall either in the adaptive or the programmatic category.

Implementation and Rewards or Punishments

Linkages based on transactions imply that rewards or punishments take place: for example, when output controls are linked to inputs, we can describe a system of reward or punishments that is activated and brings about implementation; 'you are not doing what we expected, we do not fund your program unless you change your ways.'

If an intervention is to make a difference, if implementation is not trivial (it would take place in any case), social power has to be exercised. Power may emanate from very tangible threats (the enforcement model) or from positive inducements (reward model). Therefore, in any implementation situation we can describe a system of reward and punishment that helps explain why implementation takes place: 'they had to implement, the court ruling gave them no latitude,' or 'they knew it would be to their advantage to consent.'

The system of reward and punishment consists of several distinct elements: the actual rewards or punishments, the criteria for their application, the officials who apply them (inspectors, peer evaluators, etc.), the sampling or measures on which performance is evaluated.

Implementation failures can always be attributed to the system of reward and punishment. If people do not implement, it usually means that for some reason or other they find advantage in not implementing. To be sure, there are other explanations — they may be ignorant of expectations or incapable of performing as wanted. But for our purpose here, we will focus on the system of reward or punishment (R & P).

Two principal cases interest us: the first is when implementation fails because the intervention is not linked to R & P: there is no way to determine compliance or there are no inducements or punishments for complying. The second is when the R & P is activated but it distorts behavior within the target organization. The criteria or measures of performance may be inadequate or the system of R & P generates defensive strategies that corrupt the purpose of the intervention. For example, teachers who are evaluated on their student performance on standardized tests may focus their teaching on how to take tests or corrupt test results by manipulating test conditions.

These problems become particularly significant in task situations that include a learning element. If implementers are punished when they attempt to learn how to do things differently, the experimental adaptive behavior required for implementation will gradually be extinguished. In other words, the system of R & P can also be the direct cause of implementation failures.

This is why the choice of control point and linkage is relevant. There are task situations that can be controlled and the existence and activation of the system of R & P does not create significant distortions. But in certain cases — as we shall now see — controls have to be limited if they are not to undo in practice what they are to achieve in theory.

Learning and Uncertainty

Let us arbitrarily divide the world of implementation into four categories: either goals are specific and measurable or they are numerous and not easily measurable; either the task is routine or it requires a learning component (see *Table 1*).

Table 1

		Process	
		Routine	*Learning*
	Specific measurable	Electric generation	First men to moon
Goals	*Vague not measurable*	Post office	PL 94-142

These categories are not exhaustive but they capture the relevant types of implementers. We want to show that different control points and linkages are appropriate to each of these categories:

- First, we have implementers with specific goals and a routine process: for example, electric generation.
- Second, those with specific goals but the process includes a learning component: for example, sending the first men to the moon.
- Third, those with vague, not easily measurable goals and a process requiring learning bahvior: here we will include many aspects of the running of social sector institutions in health, education and welfare.

Implementers with specific goals and routine processes are amenable to input, output and process controls, *i.e.*, electric power plants are controlled by inputs, process rules and electric generation output measures. Implementers with specific goals but needing a learning process are amenable to input and output controls, *i.e.*, the scientists on the first men on the moon project respond directly to the successes and failures of successive attempts to take off. Implementers with vague goals and a routine process are amenable to input and process controls. The post office responds to selected attempts to rationalize process and to input controls. No one is really looking at unforeseen or undesirable consequences of bulk mail flood. Implementers with vague goals and a process requiring learning behavior are only amenable to input controls. Many tasks in health, education or welfare cannot be controlled through output or process controls. They have to be controlled through input controls: for example, budgets or the socialization of professional staffs.

This last point is central to our discussion. Too often the design of legislation disregards control points. It is assumed that process controls or output controls can be utilized when in fact these introduce undesirable distortions and can even be a principal factor in implementation failure. As we shall see in the case of PL 94–142, process controls were instituted in task situations where they were not always desirable. Some of the goals of the legislation might have been better served if input controls had been used. The evidence suggests that the impact of unsuitable controls on service delivery is not negligible.

To be sure, this does not mean that social sector implementers are only amenable to input controls. Quite obviously there are tasks or aspects of the implementation of programs that are amenable to output or process controls. For example, one can count students, patients, cases; one can establish criteria for admission, etc. But the point to be made is that many dimensions of task performance are not amenable to such controls and each time they are used, inevitable distortions and unforeseen consequences result.

The choice of linkage is also relevant. In general, individuals and organizations respond better to positive inducements than to negative sanctions. The latter always generate defensive strategies. These defensive strategies can become very expensive, time consuming, and actually make it that much more difficult to bring about change. Negative sanctions are best used in situations where (i) the goals to be achieved are precise, are easily measured and compliance can be determined; and (ii) it is known that implementers can implement. Positive sanctions are preferable in situations where goals are vague, not easily measurable, compliance can only be partially evaluated and the learning process is important.

Why are Undesirable Controls Used?

Why, one might ask, are undesirable controls used? The principal factors are:

1 The drafters of legislation or the drafters of federal and state regulations are often preoccupied with their own programs whose objective and success is paramount to them and their agencies. They disregard and often do not care about the context in which the activity is to take place, either because they are unfamiliar with it or because they distrust distant and unknown implementers. Therefore, they seek to invest foolproof controls.

2 If control is the objective, then obviously the combination of input, process and output controls is, in theory at least, the most foolproof.

There is therefore a natural tendency in designing controls to over-design and to assume that more control is always preferable.

3 Negative sanctions are easier to create than positive inducements simply because most negative sanctions cost less than most positive inducements. Also, there exist institutions to punish — namely, the courts, the prisons etc., but surprisingly in our society, there do not exist similar institutions to reward.
4 Since negative sanctions tend to be easier to use with process controls, it follows therefore that there exists another natural tendency to use process controls in preference to the others.
5 Input controls such as reliance on professional socialization are long-term controls. They cannot be instituted overnight. Therefore there is a tendency to underplay professional controls in favor of short-term expedients. But the fundamental error is that not enough attention is given to professional socialization at a historical time when professional socialization may be far more important to the running of complex technological societies than we realize.
6 In short, erroneous control strategies may well be an important source of the general malaise and ineffectiveness prevailing in many social sectors. Teacher burnout is not exclusively due to excessive and trivial paperwork but it is due to a large measure to the perceived arbitrary and inconsequential impact of control structures that do not fit the needs of clients, of those who deliver services and of the general public.

The Implementation of PL 94-142

PL 94-142 is in the input-process compliance mode. Budgetary inputs are tied to overall compliance with statutory provisions. The legislation culminated a decade of court and legislative interventions including seminal decisions in Pennsylvania, the District of Columbia, and in California. The act was passed in 1975 and implemented in 1978.[3]

The law, interestingly, has several distinct objectives reflecting the several major problems in special education which had led to earlier court interventions and previous legislation:

1 A first objective is to ensure that every child needing special education has access to an appropriate education. School districts can no longer deny a responsibility for severely handicapped children. These, in the past, were often left to the vagaries of other agencies or to whatever help their parents could obtain. Districts are to identify children in or out of school who have been excluded from special education. They are either to provide supplementary aids and services (i.e., speech pathology, audiology, therapy, counseling, transportation, etc.), or in those

instances when a district does not have facilities for a given disability, the district is obligated to reimburse parents for private services. Cooperation between districts is also encouraged.

2 A second objective of the legislation is to ensure that children are not arbitrarily assigned to special education. In the past, special education was sometimes used to stream certain minority children that were perceived, for one reason or another, to be a problem to conventional classroom teachers. Thus, certain districts had very high enrollments of minorities in special education. The statute provides for fair assessment procedures (parental consent, non-discriminating assessment of disability, many types of assessments, interpretation of results by licensed expert teams) and an individualized education program for each child, to ensure that children not be arbitrarily streamed in special education programs.

3 A third objective of the legislation is to reduce, as much as possible, the extent to which children are in special education. This is the notion of mainstreaming or least restrictive enrollment. In the past, once a child was assigned to special education, the child tended to remain there. Moreover, many children who might benefit from conventional classroom exposure were denied access. Special education classes were separate and tightly compartmentalized away from conventional classrooms. The statute provides that children's programs in special education are to be evaluated periodically and that each child in special education who can benefit from it, be mainstreamed, *i.e.*, attend conventional classes.

Compliance at local district level is to be achieved through two procedural guarantees: the mandated Individualized Education Program (or IEP) meeting and the existence of due process safeguards. The Individualized Education Program or IEP meeting involves administrators, teachers, parents, the child when appropriate, attorneys or advocates representing parents. The IEP document which is signed by parents and others attending, is to have a specific content: basic assessment information, long-range goals, specific services needed, description of extent child can be mainstreamed, date of placement in program, rationale for placement, list of individuals responsible for implementation of IEP, criteria which will be used to evaluate success of IEP. The IEP is to guarantee that all relevant parties, including parents, participate in the decision-making process and that their agreement be in writing. Each time a child is assigned in or out of special education, an IEP takes place.

In addition, due process safeguards are provided to the parents and child. These include formal written notices of actions, descriptions and explanations of actions taken, descriptions of assessment procedures used. These are to be provided to parents in their native language and the school is responsible to ensure that parents understand the communication when it is translated. They also include appeal procedures whereby parents have access to the child's record, have the right to ask for a panel of three impartial experts (one selected by the parents, one by the district, one by the experts themselves). The panel is to be informal but parents have the right to be accompanied by counsel and receive a verbatim record of the hearing and can compel the attendance of witnesses, introduce evidence and cross-examine witnesses. In California, subsequent appeals go to the State Superintendent of Public Instruction and ultimately to the courts.

Within districts, arrangements for handling these procedures differ depending on the organizational arrangements for special education. Generally large districts may have many different administrative units handling different disabilities: speech impaired, hard of hearing, visually impaired, emotionally disturbed, mildly mentally retarded, trainable mentally retarded, orthopaedically handicapped, deaf, blind and special learning disabilities. In smaller districts, fewer special services may be available. But in general the mandate to have students' referral and placement into or out of special education programs requires participation of administrators *i.e.*, principals, teachers, psychologists and other evaluators, counselors and experts in the disability area. Lawyers may be involved in the initial meeting but more often come into action when parents, for one reason or another, seek redress for what they consider unacceptable placement.

Implicit Assumptions of PL 94-142

The statute assumes that it is possible to pursue several different objectives simultaneously; it assumes that obliging districts to provide special education to children previously excluded can be pursued without detriment to the objective of assuring a fair assessment to all or to the objective of mainstreaming. This, as we shall see, can be a problem.

The statute deliberately focuses on parents to motivate implementation. It adopts the generally accepted notion that there need be someone to prod districts into implementation. In the absence of strong monitoring by state or federal agencies, parents are the logical agents of change. To be sure, the act's regulations include provisions for site visits, but these cannot deal with day-to-day implementation. Therefore the implementation design focuses on parents. The notification requirement, the procedures of the IEP, and the appeal process are all geared to allow parents a strong voice, strong enough to create the necessary impetus for implementation. The underlying assumption, of course, is that parents are motivated, capable and have the necessary resources to act as expected. This, again, may be an erroneous assumption.

The legislation assumes that districts can easily reach agreements with parents regarding the provision of necessary service. Since unavailable services are to be provided by having districts reimburse parents for private services, the opportunity for conflicts regarding district capability or child needs was probably underestimated.

The legislation also assumes that the goal of mainstreaming will be accepted by professionals in the districts. But in practice mainstreaming is acceptable and encouraged as long as the students involved are not too different from those in conventional classes, that is, as long as the handicapped competency fits within range of normal children. This kind of mainstreaming might be referred to as a 'redefinition of handicap' and is necessarily marginal. It may involve large numbers of students when wrong classifications have been used but otherwise is not too significant. Beyond redefinition, mainstreaming will be undertaken when and if close cooperation and *trust* can be maintained between regular classroom teachers and special education teachers and other professionals who will help the conventional teacher. The law assumes that close cooperation exists and that the law itself does nothing to deter such cooperation.

To summarize, this law uses process controls to pursue certain objectives. The law expects parents to exercise leverage on districts and tends to underplay the role of district professionals. While districts receive federal and state funding, strong negative sanctions can be exercised by parents who are able to complain and have ultimate access to the courts.

But the handling of handicapped children is clearly a learning process, where learning *how to do* is most significant. It is the kind of situation where experts would like to say things like: 'Well, we are not sure what might work best: in this case we would like to suggest that this or that might be tried.'

Some of the approaches that might be best for a child might be done in the school and some might be done out of school. The education of the handicapped is clearly an extreme case in education where cooperation between the family, the child, and the school is important. It also implies use of talent that may be out of the school. As we shall now see these assumptions about the potential role of parents, the nature of district/parent conflicts and the existence of internal professional cooperation were not realistic and many pitfalls were encountered in the implementation of the law.

Pitfalls

Are parents motivated, capable and active? Yes and no. Some parents are and some are not. Parent education, wealth, social class and mental health make a difference. Some parents are very involved with their handicapped children; some are not. The extent of handicap also makes a difference. Parents of near normal children are less aware and less involved in the child's deficiency than parents of children with a serious or crippling disability.

Are parents aware of the law and able to intervene? Again, important differences exist across parents and across districts. In some districts many parents are well-informed and well-organized, and legal talent is readily available. In other districts parents are less aware of the law, are not organized, and do not have ready access to legal or even other experts. Therefore, the interventions of parents are not consistent or sustained.

What kinds of legal conflicts are generated between parents and districts? One might assume that some parents might object to school classification or even dislike teachers but in practice, most of the legal conflicts between parents and districts center around the issue of reimbursement for private services. School administrators are quick to learn not to recommend specialized services the district cannot provide, since each time this happens the district can incur additional (and often high) expenditures. Some active parents, who have used or heard of private services, use the law to receive reimbursement for such services. When legal talent is readily available, these parents exercise leverage on the schools. In addition, third party interests are generated. Outside experts or private institutions handling handicapped children are not uninterested bystanders. In some instances, they have been providing services to parents who were affluent enough to obtain them. They can now supply services to those parents who were not able to afford to use them before. In any case, they have a stake in getting children labeled so that placement will be outside the schools. They can and do exercise pressure on parents.

In districts where parents of handicapped children are organized, where there has been a history of legal interventions and where districts already spend considerable sums for placement in private services, the system of R & P operates strongly against such referrals: unless there is an obvious danger or impossibility to do otherwise, school administrators, teachers, and experts will be careful to avoid recommendations that lead to such placement or services. Where we might assume that children in need of special services should have a right to them, we have a system of sanctions that tends to reduce the propensity of districts to make certain needed referrals. Furthermore, those parents who respond to external pressures and perceive the law as a means for placing their child in private schools at district expenses and who aggressively confront the district in the IEP and through appeals and court cases, are shifting the intent of the due process protection: so while the appeals procedure may have been conceived to protect the child from incorrect classification, they tend to be used to resolve allocative disputes regarding outside services.

What about cooperation between special educators and classroom teachers? Obviously we can expect to find differences between districts. But, in general, cooperation between special educators and conventional classroom teachers is not automatic. In most districts, there is a long tradition of bureaucratic separation whereby special education is a department quite separate and some distance from conventional classrooms. Cooperation between conventional classroom teachers and special educators traditionally takes place at the time of referral. Each maintains domain autonomy and independence. Therefore, mainstreaming is a major innovation. To do so when parents can exercise strong leverage complicates matters. We can easily understand that there will be less cooperation between regular classroom teachers and special education teachers and other experts in those districts where the threat of legal conflict is high. Since referrals and transfers in and out of special education programs imply additional burdens to some teachers and since legal conflicts are inevitably time-consuming and threatening, we can understand that such conflicts are bound to generate internal tensions, such that there might not exist necessary trust between the members of a potential team serving the child. Here we can expect to find that people are more concerned with protecting their position than in attempting to solve problems. Teachers may spend more time making sure that all the necessary forms are properly filled out than in addressing the special needs of children. These patterns carry over to experiments or any other endeavor which is perceived to be difficult and breaks with conventional ways of handling children. We can therefore expect to find more lip service being paid to mainstreaming than actual implementation.

We can also expect far less effective cooperation between school and parents in these same high conflict districts. Here, what should or could be a cooperative endeavor becomes open warfare. The fact that some parents can and do play a legal role, rapidly places most parents in a perceived adversary relationship. Even if belligerent parents are only a fraction of the total, the defensive strategies of the district affect all parents. Thus, in large urban districts where we can always expect to find a few aggressive parents and many others who are poorly educated, unaware of the law, etc., the adversary relationships generated by some parents means that these other parents are also treated cautiously and do not get much help. Where it was assumed that the rights of children should be protected through a procedure called in IEP, we have a procedure that can easily be converted into an adversary proceeding. Parents who understand little about the law and the procedure will not receive much help during these adversary meetings. They will be told to sign a form and we can even expect that many IEP reports will be routinely written in a legalistic language less designed to address the problems of the child than to defend the district against potential attack. Some parents will not even bother and will not respond to district attempts to attend the mere formality of an IEP.

To these implementation pitfalls we need add a different kind: PL 94-142 is not the only law on the books that affects special education. The actual implementation of some of the objectives of this statute may sometimes result from other statutes or even from school administrators' perceptions of the broader political context. For example, PL 94-142 is not the only statute designed to avoid arbitrary classification and minority streaming into special education. Some states have established permissible quotas, whereby the percentage of minority enrollments in special education cannot exceed by some figure total minority enrollment in districts without eliciting some official justification. Moreover, minority sensitivity to such streaming makes it a politically delicate issue. Districts are increasingly careful not to give the appearance of using special education to resolve ethnic problems. Therefore the fact that minority enrollment in special education does go down does not necessarily mean that PL 94-142 is successful. It simply means that other rules and regulations based on different control point strategies *do* have an impact.

Implementation Patterns

The implementation of PL 94-142 is particularly interesting because two distinct patterns of implementation are evolving and these two patterns permit us to observe directly how process controls can distort service delivery.

First, we have districts where there are already considerable legal conflicts. These will tend to be districts in urban or close suburban areas where some parents of handicapped children are informed and organized, many legal firms are interested or even specialize in these cases, many outside experts are available and private schools have a stake in placement decisions. These we label legal-regulatory districts. Here we expect to find that district defensive strategies play an important role and distort the process.

Second, we have districts where legal conflict has not taken place. These districts tend to be in rural areas or in distant suburbs. Even if parents are organized, they do not have ready access to legal talent and the due process remedies of the law have simply not been used. These districts we label professional to distinguish them from legal-regulatory ones. Here implementation results more from internal cooperative decisions than from pressure from parents.

Why there might be such differences in the level of conflict across districts has to do, in part, with the perceived quality of service and in part with perceived alternatives. Parents will not initiate conflicts regarding placement when they are satisfied. Some districts with adequate resources manage to satisfy most parents. Parents will not initiate conflicts if they believe that nothing will come out of it. This will happen more often if they are not organized, have little legal information, and have no knowledge or even access to alternative private facilities.

But these differences have consequences for implementation. In legal regulatory districts, some of the patterns we have already described take place: the system of R & P is activated mostly as sanctions. These districts are involved in many fair hearings, appeals and legal suits in the courts. Some parents attend the IEP accompanied by their own experts and even by counsel. They do not come to the schools to seek help; they come in an adversary role to establish their rights and those of their children.

Other parents are less able or unwilling to play the role intended for them. Considerable district time and effort goes into seeking them out; getting them to agree to sign what documents are called for.

In these districts, every effort is made to expediate the IEP. To the extent possible, the meeting is a signature gathering exercise. The IEP document remains incomplete or imprecise to protect internal discretion. There is careful adherence to paperwork. These districts take great care to establish a set of forms for referral, evaluation, processing, etc., and spend resources to train teachers to know the criteria needed to select, refer, process, and evaluate handicapped children so that the forms will be properly filled out.

Cautious behavior prevails regarding external cooperation. School experts are careful not to suggest that needed help is available in private schools since any such suggestions may activate the system of R & P — *i.e.*, parents can and do ask the school to pay for such services. Therefore there is a strong tendency to diagnose to fit school capabilities. Obviously, school experts, like all experts, do not obfuscate evident deficiencies, but in gray areas of doubt, school experts tend to fit the child's problem to known school capability.

Meanwhile, some parents are exposed to other sources of advice. Outside experts tend to focus on the child's problem and on a more general or universal view of remedial capability. These parents tend to distrust school diagnosis and are further motivated to seek placement in private institutions, thus accentuating external threat on the district.

In these districts, teachers and school experts are hampered in their ability to cooperate among themselves. Each party is careful to avoid blame for possible negative outcomes and therefore seeks to control the situation. Faced with potential conflict between conventional teachers and special educators and other experts, principals and main office administrators tend to avoid approaches that have to rely heavily on their close cooperation. Since mainstreaming requires close cooperation between classroom teachers, experts and aides, we can therefore assume that in these districts the tendency will be away from mainstreaming while paying lip service attention to its goals.

Since sampling of teacher or expert behavior cannot be carried out on a daily basis, it is doubtful that the protections intended in the law can be implemented. In other words, the appeal procedures will not be used to deal with actual treatment. Instead the appeal procedures will tend to be used by disassociating parents seeking to obtain reimbursement for services or placement in the private sector.

Meanwhile, the protective strategies engendered by these threats mean that considerable and significant portions of teacher and expert time are spent in procedural activities, *i.e.*, filling forms, writing required reports, sending notifications, attending IEPs and fair hearing meetings. This means a reduction in overall district capability to meet the needs of handicapped children.

In professional districts, the system of R & P intended in the law is not activated, therefore the threat of legal intervention is not present. Compliance with the law means accommodation based on district capability.

To be sure there will be compliance with some of the paperwork, procedures will be established to ensure that the IEP meetings take place and, by and large, district capability, teacher inclination and the availability of expert talent will determine how the law is implemented. One might expect that when expert talent is scarce and resources few, the districts will still tend to group children with disabilities and limit mainstreaming to a few token instances (such as having disabled children eat with normal children in the same cafeteria). When expert talent is readily available and the district has considerable resources, we can expect more experimentation with new delivery systems. Children with certain disabilities are placed in classrooms, itinerant experts move from classroom to classroom, specially trained aides help those children needing on-site help, remedial help is provided out of school, in home, etc. That kind of district implementation takes place simply because the resources and commitment are present and risk-taking is not inhibited by the fear of legal interventions and costly payments for private services.

The contrast between legal-regulatory and professional districts is most evident in the running of IEP meetings. Christine Hassell reports preliminary findings based on the observation of eighteen IEP meetings in districts classified as professional.[4] In both kinds of districts, the average length of time of the IEP meeting was about identical averaging 41.2 minutes in legal-regulatory and 43.7 minutes in professional districts. But in legal-regulatory districts 55 per cent of that time is spent purely on matters having to do with elaborating the necessary forms, whereas only 11 per cent of the time is spent on forms in professional districts. She also reports that IEPs in professional districts are twice as much oriented to the child's problem than in legal-regulatory districts — as measured by topics covered, content and involvement of teachers and parents. Many more individuals participate in the IEP in legal-regulatory districts: 7.05 versus 3.8 in professional districts — suggesting both the fact that more talent is perceived to be needed in legal-regulatory districts and that more talent is available — particularly on the parents' side of the table.

These are very preliminary findings and research is still going on. But they already suggest that all is not well with the implementation of PL 94-142. It is suggestive or even disturbing that the IEP meetings which were supposed to be a central decision point in the implementation of the law are run in such different manners and differ so markedly in content. To be sure, the IEP is only one episode in the implementation of the law but the fact defensive strategies play such an important role in legal regulatory IEPs implies that they probably play an important role in other aspects of service delivery.

Implications for the Three Objectives

Given two different types of implementation patterns how do these influence achievement of the different objectives of the act? Obviously, certain tasks are easier to achieve than others and, also, districts will be more motivated to achieve those tasks where compliance can be more easily monitored.

As we saw, the first goal of the statute is to provide services to those children not receiving them at present. Districts are expected to identify this target population. Compliance can be monitored and the task of identifying previously excluded children is relatively straightforward if sufficient resources are allocated. Most districts can therefore be expected to identify and reach this client population and early evidence confirms this. But some differences should be expected between legal-regulatory and professional districts. In the former, sooner or later, there will be a realization that there is a high probability that handicapped children not in the public schools include a higher percentage of cases requiring special treatment, and that the districts can incur high costs when they have to reimburse parents for private education or services. Therefore, while identification may take place, reaching and dealing with these parents will be undertaken cautiously. Every effort will be made to reduce the threat of legal entanglement. In these districts, the tendency will be to end systematic searches or not to use the data unless obligated to by a monitoring agency or an organized group of parents. Selective use of search information will take place as schools seek to enrol those children for whom they have a district capability: there will be a tendency to reach those parents that can be served and to avoid those for whom no service is available.

In professional districts, systematic searches are not perceived to be a potential danger but districts are also cautious not to acquire charges they cannot handle. We can therefore expect that the normal tendency is to seek out children that can be served and to avoid, disregard or kindly discourage, those whose problems are clearly beyond district capabilities.

Empirical evidence of such patterns is suggested in a current evaluation of the implementation of PL 94-142. It indicates that most of the districts surveyed in the evaluation do not find many new cases as a result of searches. Most referrals to special education are done by teachers in conventional classrooms out of the population already enrolled in the school.[5]

These considerations and preliminary evidence suggest that the goal of identifying children previously excluded is easily implemented when enforcement is present. But acting on the information is another matter.

The second goal is to provide safeguards on the arbitrary labeling of children. Here we need to distinguish between effects of PL 94-142 and other statutes. When there is strong political pressure and language to limit minority enrollment in special education, drops of excess enrollments can be expected in both kinds of districts. Quotas on enrollments are output measures and can be easily monitored. When minority political strength is present, the system of R & P is activated. Results are achieved.

But differences will take place between the two kinds of districts when it comes to the use of evaluation instruments and the matching of children's performance with official criteria for referral. Criteria for placement in special education programs differ from state to state, but the degree of professional discretion as to the choice of instrument and how to interpret results will vary between the two kinds of districts. In the legal-regulatory district, much greater attention is given to formalizing procedures and forms. Teachers and other experts are carefully trained in knowing the procedures and in reducing discretion. Routine is encouraged which means that difficult cases that do not fit well with established criteria will tend to be poorly attended to. In contrast, professional districts can be expected to be more flexible, better able to handle difficult cases for which they have the capability of providing services.

But, in general, the implementation of this goal cannot be effectively monitored. To be sure, gross overall statistical controls can be effective in reducing excessive minority enrollments in special education. But whether the right kind of program is provided to the right child is a professional matter and no procedural controls are to alter this fact. Therefore, the conflicts generated by the statute may be considered a net negative effect since these conflicts tend to bring about dysfunctional protective strategies which tend to reduce professional discretion.

Moreover, we need to remember that there is a difference between the IEP and what happens to the child. Parents may be vocal and come to the IEP with all the experts in the world but they cannot sample daily staff behavior. Implementation takes place on a daily basis away from parents and their impact is, even when they are capable of considerable clout, still very limited indeed.

The third goal — the educational goal of mainstreaming or of providing the least restrictive education — is also difficult to monitor. Therefore, implementation is bound to be limited. Some apparent results may be emphasized by districts who have relabeled some children and sent them back to conventional classrooms. Otherwise, real efforts at cooperation between classroom teachers and special educators will only take place when sufficient trust exists and, as we saw, such trust cannot easily flourish in districts under excessive external threat. We would therefore expect more experimentation and more sincere attempts to deal with the spirit of the law in professional districts while we would expect legal regulatory districts to go through the motions (our example of having special education children eat in the same cafeteria) but not the spirit of the law.

Conclusions

PL 94-142 is still a new law. Its implementation is beginning. This chapter suggests a number of pitfalls. Early evidence seems to confirm that some of these problems are real. Obviously, more time and more evaluative research is needed before one may feel confident about the reality content of our more pessimistic assessments.

Some conclusions can nevertheless be sketched out for their policy implication. These have to do with the choice of control points and the choice of system of R & P.

As we saw, PL 94-142 relies on process controls and we have to ask about the wisdom of relying on procedures to achieve what procedures cannot achieve. Our examples are particularly relevant since they show that certain goals of the act are amenable to output controls when these exist: the goal of protecting minority children from excessive incorrect labeling is obviously amenable to routine output controls. But the goal of mainstreaming or of ensuring an adequate education is not amenable to either outputs or process rules. They depend on input controls, namely on the goodwill and intentions of the professionals that provide the service. We therefore must pay far more attention to the needs, rewards, career goals and status of professional staffs. PL 94-142 does not go far enough in that respect. It calls for short-term training but does not suggest why short-term training should be sufficient or might even be implemented. There is evidence it is not.[6] One lesson, therefore, is simple: implementation always requires two components: (a) those who are to act need to learn how to act; and (b) there need exist effective incentives to motivate them to act.

This example also illustrates the potential societal costs of negative sanctions. Negative sanctions generate expensive defensive strategies. Any bureaucracy can defend itself and resist threats. But in so doing it uses resources that are intended for other purposes. It is revealing that in legal regulatory districts a significant portion of teacher or expert time goes into paper pushing. This is wasted motion. It raises the issue of the choice of an appropriate linkage. What kind of monitoring is possible or desirable? When is it desirable to use consumers to ensure compliance? When is it desirable to use outside inspectors and when are third parties, *i.e.*, other professionals, preferable?

Some of the relevant dimensions here include: (i) the extent of distortion the linkage creates; (ii) the consistency, quality and motivation of the outside monitoring; and (iii) the expertise required. The lesson seems to be that parents are not the best choice here. To be sure, they can be important but the distortions caused by their interventions are not desirable. A second lesson therefore is that 'outsiders' can be used effectively when (i) their efforts complement those of insiders; or (ii) their efforts, while in conflict with insiders, are nevertheless predictable and can have the intended impact.

This discussion also suggests that it is useful to emphasize and discuss the concept of excessive control. The pursuit of control objectives generates costs that make them less desirable, but we have no methodology to weigh trade off. At best, we decry the unforeseen consequences of interventions without being able to cost out other alternatives. We can suggest shifts in other directions and insist that process rules be substituted by output controls only to discover that these are also amenable to distortion and manipulation. At some point we have to ask: are controls needed? Will we achieve more if we intervene? Can we justify doing less?

What policy implication can we derive from this? Obviously our main theme has been about the choice of desirable and undesirable controls. Some goals and some tasks can be controlled at output, input and process. But tasks that require considerable professional inputs are *not* amenable to that kind of control. They require far more attention to what motivates professional behavior, to the incentives needed to improve professional role playing, and to the institutions needed to raise the level of professional ethics. In this case this means that one should find out what kind of assistance parents and children need if they are to better play their role. They probably need help to understand about the nature of the handicap. They probably could benefit from some assistance, particularly when economic or other factors impede their ability to deal with the problem.

One might also specify the kind of long-term training teachers and experts might receive to implement mainstreaming. One might specify the nature of support services and provide both short-term and long-term assistance. All this with the recognition that there are many unknowns about 'mainstreaming' and that much learning need take place.

One could also specify the incentives that might ensure that teachers and experts are motivated to implement the statute.

Lastly and importantly, one might specify the kind of peer review that might be used to review compliance and suggest future courses of action.

Such an approach would be more oriented to the role professions can and should play in the implementation of this kind of legislation.

Notes

1 GLASSMAN, R. (1973) 'Persistence and loose coupling,' *Behavioural Science*, 18, pp. 83–98; WEICK, K. (1976) 'Educational organizations as loosely coupled systems,' *Administrative Sciences Quarterly*, 21, pp. 1–19.

2 BERMAN, P. (1978) 'The study of macro and micro implementation,' *Public Policy*, 26, pp. 157–84; ELMORE, R.F. (1978) 'Organizational models of social program implementation,' *Public Policy*, 26, pp. 185–228; SABATIER, P. and MAZMANIAN, D. (1980) 'The conditions of effective implementation: a guide to accomplishing policy objectives,' *Policy Analysis*, 5, pp. 481–504.

3 ALTSCHULD, J.W. and DOWNHOWER, S.G. (1980) 'Issues in evaluating the implementation of Public Law 94–142,' *Educational Evaluation and Policy Analysis*, 2, 4, pp. 31–8; ABESON, A. and ZETTEL, J. (1977) 'The end of the quiet revolution: The Education for All Handicapped Children Act of 1975,' *Exceptional Children*, 44, pp. 114 and 128; BALLARD, J. and ZETTEL, J. (1977) 'Public Law 94–142 and Section 504: What they say about rights and protections,' *Exceptional Children*, 44, pp. 117–85; BALLARD, J. and ZETTEL, J. (1981) 'Fiscal arrangements of Public Law 94–142,' *Exceptional Children*, 44, pp. 457–62; JONES, R.L. *et al* (1978) 'Evaluating mainstream programs: Models, caveats, considerations and guidelines,' *Exceptional Children*, 44, pp. 588–601; SCHLECTY, P.C. and TURNBULL, A.P. (1978) 'The conditions of effective implementation: A guide to accomplishing policy objectives,' *Policy Analysis*, 5, pp. 481–504.

4 HASSELL, C. (1980) Private communication. Ms. Hassell's dissertation in the School of Education, University of California at Berkeley was titled 'Study of the consequences of excessive legal intervention in the local implementation of PL 94–142.' It was completed in March 1981.

5 STANFORD RESEARCH INSTITUTE (1980) Private communication. At the time this chapter was written SRI International was conducting an evaluation of local implementation of PL 94–142 for the Bureau of Education for the handicapped in the US Office of Education.

6 BIRD, P.J. and GANSNEDER, B. (1979) 'Preparation of physical education teachers as required under Public Law 94–142,' *Exceptional Children*, 45, pp. 279–84.

5 The Future

Education and Federalism: Doctrinal, Functional, and Strategic Views

Richard F. Elmore
Graduate School of Public Affairs
University of Washington

> Since the people, being numerous, cannot directly manage their affairs, but must commit them to agents, they have resolved to prevent abuse by trusting each agent as little as possible. . . . There is no reliance on ethical forces to help the government work. . . . The aim of the Constitution seems to be not so much to attain great common ends by securing a good government, as to avert the evils which flow, not merely from bad government, but from any government strong enough to threaten the pre-existing communities of the individual citizens.
>
> Lord Bryce, *The American Commonwealth*

> By and large, the decision of the American people has not been to separate functions by government but to maintain dual institutions which share responsibility for implementation of specific functions.
>
> Daniel Elazar, 'Federal-State Collaboration in the Nineteenth-Century United States'

A large-scale reaction is underway toward federal involvement in education. The question has been posed quite bluntly, both by advocates of the 'new federalism' and by more sympathetic observers of federal education policy over the past decade: is there a federal role in education? On the one hand, critics argue that the federal government has by a steady accumulation of policies usurped a traditional state function and that function should now be returned to the states. On the other hand, supporters of past federal educational interventions acknowledge that the federal government has, in some respects, overreached itself and has demonstrated by its ineptitude that it cannot play as large a role as they once thought. Both sides express skepticism or uncertainty about the federal role, questioning the assumptions that have shaped federal policy over the last fifteen to twenty years.

Underlying this skepticism and uncertainty are a number of basic questions about the nature of the federal system, about the role that education plays in that system, and about how that role should be expressed in policy. The purpose of this paper is to clarify, in some degree, the terms of the debate on these questions by examining alternative meanings of the term 'federalism.' Federalism, I will argue, can mean at least three different things. It can mean a set of principles describing how levels of government *ought* to relate to each other, it can mean a set of functional relationships describing how levels of government actually *do* relate to each other, or it can mean the strategy that one level of government uses to *influence* another. I will call these, respectively, doctrinal, functional, and strategic views of federalism.

Political disputes among levels of government are often argued using all three meanings, without distinguishing among them. Politicians frequently assert that one level of government — states, for example — *ought* to exercise supremacy in a governmental function — education, for example — but day-to-day operating relationships among levels of government suggest a high degree of interdependency. Which definition of federalism should hold: the doctrinal assertion that states are supreme or the functional assertion that states and the federal government are interdependent? Scholars and political figures often argue that the functions of government should be rationalized according to certain well-defined principles (a doctrinal assertion), when in fact the failure to rationalize functions allows one level of government to exercise influence over another through the use of shared functions (a strategic assertion). Which definition should hold: the doctrinal assertion that different levels of government should exercise different functions or the strategic assertion that intergovernmental influence requires shared functions? Different views of federalism, in other words, imply different results; mixing definitions without acknowledging this possibility confuses the debate.

Another source of confusion stems from the failure to distinguish *national* issues and trends from *federal* policy and practice. Policy at all levels of government is subject to national influences — shifts in political ideology, professional and political networks that extend across jurisdictional boundaries, large-scale demographic and economic changes, for example. Sometimes these influences translate directly into national policy, sometimes they don't. Occasionally, they affect state and local policy first and later percolate up to the national level. Sometimes federal policy effectively preempts state and local authority; sometimes it leaves state and local authority in place and adds an incremental federal requirement to it. Just because an issue has national consequences, or a national political constituency, doesn't mean that it must be the subject for federal policy. Likewise, just because an issue has traditionally been the prerogative of state and local government doesn't mean that it can never be the subject of federal policy. In other words, the 'national' questions and 'federal' policy are always distinct, and their relationship is usually ambiguous.

Education presents a particularly difficult array of questions on the meaning of federalism and on the relationship between national issues and federal policy. Education has been the subject of national policy since before the drafting of the Constitution, yet we still persist in raising the question of whether there is a legitimate federal role in the field. A steady growth in functional interdependency among levels of government in education has done little to soften the doctrinal assertion that education is primarily, or purely, a state prerogative. National movements — from the one in the nineteenth century that spread the common school to the one in the twentieth century that fostered racial equality — have done a substantial amount to make education more uniform nationwide, but little to reduce distrust of federal policy. In other words, while policy and practice reflect a strong national interest in education, they also manifest a deep ambivalence toward a federal role. This is the essential contradiction of federal education policy.

Is it possible to make sense of the federal role in education, given this contradiction? Can one say with any assurance what the federal role is or is not? It *is* possible, I will argue, at least to define what federalism means for education in doctrinal, functional, and strategic terms; doing so adds clarity to the debate, even if it doesn't prescribe what federal policy ought to say in every instance.

Briefly, my argument is, first, that there is no doctrinal support for the notion that education is exclusively a state function, or that the federal government has overreached its authority by becoming involved in education; second, that functional interdependence is the central fact of federal-state-local relations in education, even though it raises serious doctrinal questions; and, third, that the past errors of federal education policy have been errors of strategy, not errors of doctrine.

While the federal government may have overextended itself in certain key areas, it has not violated any constitutional principles by becoming involved in education. It follows that the remedies required for past errors of federal policy are strategic remedies, not a fundamental redefinition of the federal role in education. Partisans of the 'new federalism' assert at the doctrinal level that education is uniquely a state function, without accounting either for the important functional interdependencies that have grown up among levels of government or for the national interest in education. Likewise, partisans of a strong federal role in education have tended, without much analytic support, to equate the national interest with the necessity for federal intervention, leaving no way to ration scarce federal resources toward important federal objectives. Neither side of the current debate has disentangled the doctrinal, functional, and strategic questions that precede a definition of the federal role.

Federalism: the Doctrinal View

From a doctrinal standpoint, federalism is the set of principles describing how levels of government *ought* to relate to one another. In the current debate over federal education policy, the central question is whether, within the framework of the Constitution, the federal government has violated principles of federalism by becoming involved in education. If it has, what is the remedy? If it has not, how do the principles of federalism define the federal role in education?

One answer is proposed by advocates of the 'new federalism.' The federal government has, they argue, undermined the essential principles of federalism by intervening in a wide variety of policy areas where it has no authority. The solution is 'reshuffling the division of responsibilities between the federal and state governments and . . . changing the political ground rules between the two levels of government'.[1] The motivation for this reshuffling comes from (i) 'a desire to restore the constitutional balance between the federal government and state and local governments,' (ii) 'a need to reduce the growing number of federal categorical grants,' (iii) 'a belief that state and local governments are more responsive to the needs of both benefit recipients and taxpayers,' and (iv) 'a recognition that dividing responsibility for a program between the federal government and other levels of government results in neither being responsible'.[2] These notions of 'restoring' balance, 'reducing' complexity, 'returning' functions to more responsive levels of government, and 'unifying' responsibility all lead to the conclusion that federalism requires a clear division of labor among levels of government.

Under the 'new federalism,' an issue becomes a subject for federal policy only when it cannot be efficiently performed by lower levels of government.[3] Education is an especially suspect federal activity because of its tradition of state and local control and because the federal government's fiscal contribution is relatively small.

The vehicle for reshuffling responsibilities among levels of government in the short run is block grants coupled with reductions in federal expenditures. Block grants are designed to simplify federal programs and to locate political responsibility for allocation decisions at lower levels. Expenditure reductions are designed not only to trim the federal budget but also to reduce state and local dependence on federal revenues. These measures are, however, 'only an intermediate step' in a more ambitious strategy that entails 'turning back to local and state governments . . . the tax sources (that) have been preempted at the federal level'.[4] Turning back revenue sources presumably also means turning back decisions about how, and at what level, the domestic functions of government will be performed.

The federal system that emerges from this doctrine is one in which levels of government specialize by function, rather like the 'layer cake' model of federalism that is sometimes used to characterize earlier periods of the American federal system.[5] The federal government specializes in truly general and national functions — defense and the regulation of interstate trade, for example — while states and localities specialize in functions requiring adaptation to regional and local circumstances. The division of labor among levels of government must be clean, the argument goes, or higher levels of government begin usurping the authority of lower levels. Sharing authority across levels of government creates a nightmare of 'administrative failures, red tape, poor performance, inadequate results, excessive costs and waste, and lack of control and responsiveness.'[6]

The rationale for a strict division of labor among levels of government, then, is both political and economic. Charging each level of government with a clear list of responsibilities means that each is limited by the authority expressly granted to it, and that decisions about the domestic functions of government are lodged with those units 'closest' to the people. This division of responsibilities also results in an approximation to the laws of comparative advantage, lodging functions at the level of government where they are 'most efficiently' performed. 'Closest' and 'most efficiently' are values to which we will return in a moment.

Finally, the 'new federalism' comes equipped with a theory of the formation of the Union which asserts that, 'The federal government did not create the states,' but 'the states created the federal government'.[7] This theory is historically incorrect, as we shall see in a moment, but it is significant nonetheless because it suggests that the federal government's authority derives from the states, and hence that the federal government is obliged to defer to states in matters of domestic policy.

The clearest rebuttal to this view of federalism was expressed by the drafters of the Constitution. In fact, the current debate over the authority of the federal government relative to the states was anticipated, and resolved in important ways, by the drafting and ratification of the Constitution. The federalists — advocates of a strong central government — took the position in constitutional debates that 'the supreme power' to make and dismantle governments 'resides with the people;' they 'can delegate it in such proportions, to such bodies, on such terms, and such limitations as they think proper'.[8] The anti-federalists — opponents of a strong central government — granted that 'a more efficient federal government was needed,' but refused to concede that it should be constituted by the people, because they felt it should be 'in principle . . . subordinate to the states'.[9]

The federalists prevailed. Anti-federalist Patrick Henry conceded as much when he argued in the ratification debate that the 'question turns on that poor little thing — the expression, we the *people*, instead of the *states* of America'.[10] Lying behind the federalist position was a stark fact of political life learned the hard way under the Articles of Confederation: a government without its own electoral base, and consequently without the authority to reach citizens directly with its actions, is a government at the mercy of rival political units. If the federal government was a government of states, rather than of people, then its authority could be undermined by any assertion of state power, no matter what the consequence for the nation as a whole. 'The great and radical vice' of the Articles of Confederation, according to federalist Alexander Hamilton, was 'the principle of legislation for the States in their corporate or collective capacities'.[11] The federal government is not, in other words, a creature of the states. Instead, 'The federal and state governments are in fact but different agents and trustees of the people, constituted with different powers, and designed for different purposes,' as James Madison argued.[12]

This basic principle — that the federal government derives its authority directly from the people, rather than from the states — contains the essential resolution of what the federal government is authorized to do. As Samuel Beer has put it, the federalists sought by establishing this principle in the Constitution 'to produce . . . a scheme by which (the) nation would act not only as the constituent power, but also as the continuous controlling and directing influence in the political life of the new polity.'[13]

The nationalism of the federalists was, however, tempered by a deep distrust of any concentration of political power. They held a radically skeptical view of human nature, which led them to the conclusion that control over the instruments of power should be 'divided and balanced' so that 'power could be made to check power . . . for the common good.'[14] One source of worry to the federalists was 'faction,' or combinations of individuals pursuing their self interest.[15] The new Constitution was deliberately designed to counteract the negative effects of faction by playing the interests of one level of government off against those of another. The national government, 'thanks to the greater differentiation that goes with larger scale,' would reflect the 'social pluralism' of the nation as a whole and 'counteract tendencies toward factional abuse of power in subordinate governments.' States, on the other hand, would reflect 'territorial pluralism' and 'constitute a safeguard against encroachments by the general government'.[16] Or, as Hamilton argued, 'Power being always the rival of power, the general government will . . . stand ready to check the usurpations of the state governments, and these will have the same disposition towards the general government.' The critical actors in this scheme would be the people, who, 'by throwing themselves into either scale,' would respond to the usurpations of one government by using 'the other as the instrument of redress'.[17]

The federal system works the way it does because it was designed to be a *representational system*, a system for aggregating political demands in a way that prevents concentrations of political power.[18] Neither federal nor state government has a claim to being 'closer' to the people, since both take their authority directly from the people.

Furthermore, if the federal system is designed to work as a representational system, then it should not be evaluated primarily by how efficiently it works as a production system. In policy-making and administration, representative federalism means 'coordinate authority'.[19] Coordinate means that while 'the central government's functions cannot be assumed by (state) governments, or the (state) governments' by the central, . . . the extent of these powers is strictly limited by the simultaneous existence of comparable, though never identical powers in the other unit'.[20] If functions of government are neatly divided by levels, with no overlap or complementarity, then no level of government has a legitimate claim to check the other's exercise of power. On the other hand, if powers and functions are distributed so as to give each level 'comparable, though never identical, powers,' then one level is constantly vigilant about the other's exercise of power. Automony, under representative federalism, means not that one level of government exercises sole ownership of those functions of government in which it holds a comparative advantage, but rather that one level of government may refuse to grant the other exclusive ownership of a function, even though it may concede a comparative advantage in day-to-day administration. Of all the functions of government, only those dealing with foreign affairs and defense can be said to be nearly the monopoly of one level of government, probably because they are instrumental to the survival of government itself.[21] In all other functions, a level of government is 'autonomous' up to the point where its exercise of authority encroaches on another's domain; at that point, some device must be negotiated for the exercise of 'coordinate' authority.

The overlap and inefficiency of contemporary American federalism did not come about, then, by inadvertence or by lack of attention to the 'true' principles of federalism. These attributes were *designed into* the system. To the degree that it works effectively, federalism invites jurisdictional conflict. It does so by dividing the same electoral base in two different ways, which encourages people to use one level of government to redress the shortcommings of another. Those attributes of intergovernmental relations that trouble advocates of the 'new federalism' are precisely the ones that are most consistent with the basic principles of the Constitution.

For education, the significance of representative federalism is three-fold. First, even if the federal government concedes a comparative advantage to states and localities in the finance and administration of education, nothing in the Constitution or the principles of federalism precludes federal involvement in the field. Indeed, a clear understanding of representative federalism would suggest that as education becomes a 'national' enterprise, it will inevitably develop national constituencies that will apply pressure for federal policy. Whether, and in what way, the federal government should respond to these constituencies is a *strategic* question of how it can best use its limited resources, not a question of constitutional doctrine. Second, the fact that federal intervention provokes serious jurisdictional conflicts is not, by itself, sufficient reason for removing the federal government from education. In fact, the existence of these disputes is, to a degree, confirmation that the system is working as it was designed. In strategic terms, the federal government might benefit from a more prudent choice of jurisdictional disputes, but the absence of such disputes is not a sign that federal policy is working. Third, the argument that federal involvement in education produces unnecessary administrative burdens and diffusion of responsibility may be an important practical matter to be considered in the design of federal policy, but it is not the most important doctrinal issue. No sphere of governmental responsibility is exempt, *a priori*, from federal involvement because that involvement results in administrative difficulties. The paramount question is whether the federal system works effectively as a representative mechanism; questions of administrative feasibility and economic efficiency are important, but secondary. The federal system was designed to generate and contain conflict; in that respect, it has worked remarkably well.

Notice, however, that representative federalism is perversely indifferent to prevailing ideological definition of what constitutes 'good' policy. Good policy is whatever electoral constituencies demand, not policy that is 'just' or 'efficient' by some external standard. Electoral constituencies demand different things at different times. Hence, representative federalism does not answer the question of what the federal or state government *should* do. It only answers the question of how power should be divided. *Federalism is a means of distributing and controlling the use of political power, not a set of ends that describe good policy.* As William Riker has cogently argued, the idea that federalism somehow uniquely guarantees freedom or governmental responsiveness is an 'ideological fallacy' which can be proven 'demonstrably false'.[22] Federal systems demonstrate no clear superiority over unitary systems either in guaranteeing individual rights or in providing access to governmental decisions.[23] Federalism, recall, provided the rationale both for the denial of civil rights to blacks in the South and for intervention by the federal government to enforce those rights.[24] Nothing inherent in federalism prevents its use for diametrically opposing goals. To say that federalism requires the federal government to pursue one set of political goals or another — as advocates of all ideological persuasions are prone to do — is to misconstrue profoundly the meaning of federalism. *Electoral preferences* determine the goals of public policy; the federal system only defines the arena in which those ends will be argued out. Federalism is 'nothing more in itself than an institutional device, which (like all such devices) may be used as means indifferent to ends, or as a means which promotes the wrong ends.'[25]

In education, as in other policy areas, the federal structure has done precisely what it was designed to do. First and foremost, it has divided and dispersed power. Secondly, it has made the exercise of federal authority, and consequently the assertion of a federal interest in education, compatible with a high degree of social, political, and economic diversity at the state and local level.

Land grants, the major vehicle for support of education in the eighteenth and nineteenth centuries, were accompanied by strong assertions of the national interest in education. Daniel Webster said of the Northwest Ordinance of 1787 that he doubted 'whether any . . . single law . . . has produced effects of more distinct and lasting character,' and that 'it set forth and declared it to be a high and binding duty of government to support schools and the means of education'.[26] The combined land grants of the Ordinances of 1785 and 1787, the various statehood acts, and the Morrill Act of 1862 probably constitute the largest constant-dollar infusion of federal support for education in the history of the country. In addition to land grants, the national government engaged in a number of policies, like reimbursing states for expenses entailed in raising militias and assuming state debts, that had the effect of freeing state funds for educational purposes.[27] Because these mechanisms were indirect, latter-day analysts have tended to minimize their significance as expressions of a federal role in education. In fact, they contain at least two elements that have characterized the federal role in education continuously for over two hundred years: the first is *promotion* of education as a precondition of citizenship; the second is *collaboration* with states and localities.

Throughout these formative years, the federal government assiduously avoided establishing itself as the dominant presence in education. In 1870, Senator George Hoar of Massachusetts introduced a bill to 'establish a national system of education, ... operated by the states in accordance with federal standards.' The bill was a response to concern that 'only one-fourth of the persons who are growing up to assume the function of citizens will be able to read and write.'[28] It provoked violent opposition in Congress. As long as federal support remained collaborative and indirect, it was regarded as benign. When it threatened to become adversarial and direct, it was regarded as threatening. To many, 'maintenance of local prerogatives loomed far larger than educational improvement; to [others], independence from federal control was essential to that improvement.'[29]

With the Smith-Hughes Act of 1917, the federal government entered the field of education in a manner quite different from the indirect financing of earlier periods. A 'potent and assiduous lobby' of educators, labor leaders, and business representatives combined to assert, for the first time, that the national interest required promotion of particular curricula — agriculture, industrial arts, and home economics — and that the federal government should provide financial support for those curricula.[30] The old elements of promotion and collaboration were still present; the new element was *targeting* federal support on certain categories of *curricula*.

The dominant mode of federal support did not change fundamentally through the 1950s. The federal government continued to use indirect financing in the form of federal compensation for the financial effect of federal installations, 'impact aid.' Targeted support for curricula reappeared in 1958, with the passage of the National Defense Education Act of 1958 (NDEA), designed to stimulate instruction in math, science, and foreign languages. Senate Majority Leader Lyndon Johnson said of NDEA that it 'asserted, more forcefully than at any time in nearly a century, a national interest in the quality of education that states, communities, and private institutions provide.'[31]

The passage of the Elementary and Secondary Education Act of 1965 (ESEA) brought the final new element of federal education policy, *targeting* of federal support on certain populations of *students*. With the construction of the ESEA Title I formula, it became legitimate to identify the federal interest with classes of children defined by certain attributes — low income, educational disadvantage, handicaps, language differences, etc. The programs were always hedged by explicit prohibitions against direct federal supervision of curriculum, administration, personnel, or instructional materials.[32] But the fact remains that, from the mid-1960s, the federal role expanded to include an interest in children of certain types. The logical extension of this interest was the passage in 1975 of the Education for All Handicapped Children Act of 1975 (PL 94-142), which required states and localities to implement procedural guarantees for handicapped children and to provide funding for services to those children from state and local sources.

This gradual accretion of elements from the eighteenth century to the present means, in effect, that no issue of education finance or organization is immune from federal influence. At the same time, the federal government assiduously reinforces state and local control, always stopping far short of assuming responsibility for the provision of public education.

Far from being an aberration of federalism, this ambiguity is entirely consistent with the model of representative federalism underlying the Constitution. There is no avoiding a national interest in education; citizenship and education are inextricable. The federal government, however, is ill-equipped to finance and organize education; nothing incites political hostility from states and localities like the appearance of federal tampering with the schools. The American solution has been to assert and reassert a national interest in education, using indirect, collaborative financing mechanisms and targeting of resources on curricula and on student populations, while at the same time deferring to states and localities on basic questions of finance and organization. In the language of representative federalism, two different aggregations of the same electoral constituency are expressing two different preferences on educational policy. The state or local constituency expresses its preference for decentralized control; the national constituency expresses its preference for attention to certain subjects and populations. Because these preferences are aggregated in different ways, they result in different policies based on different conceptions of national, state, and local interests in education. Citizens are behaving exactly as Hamilton predicted they would in *Federalist* #28: they are throwing their electoral weight first in one direction, then in another.

The fundamental doctrinal flaw in the 'new federalism,' then, is its easy equation of federalism with a very particular ideological view of political responsibility and economic efficiency. In fact, federalism is ideologically agnostic; it does not contain principles for deciding on the ends to which policy is to be directed, or for allocating functions to levels of government. Federalism 'sets itself the enormously difficult task of inserting one political society within another, in such a way that both retain their political character.'[33] It does so by dividing the same electoral constituency in two different ways, making both levels of government accountable to the 'people,' giving neither a claim to primary legitimacy, and allowing the precise determination of governmental functions to vary by the preference of the two constituencies. That such a system results in ambiguity and disagreement over the proper scope of policy at different levels should hardly be surprising. It was designed for precisely that purpose. It was designed on 'the belief that power is evil, that protection against it is only to be found in a notion of balance, of division, of reduction of power to smaller corporate units or to individuals.' Federalism, in other words, is a means of 'making order compatible with power's destruction; . . . a means of reconciling as little government as possible with as much (governmental) autonomy as possible.'[34]

Federalism: the Functional View

From a functional standpoint, federalism is what decision-makers at all levels of government *do*, not what they say ought to be done. Functional relations among levels of government arise out of the self-interested behavior of politicians and administrators, according to the functional view. The question is whether this self-interested behavior serves larger purposes or whether it simply results in 'growth without purpose.'[35]

Some commentators view the growth of functional relations among levels of government with increasing alarm. Before the 1930s, they argue, the functions of federal and state government were relatively distinct, and local governments were regarded as creatures of the states. The period after the 1930s, the argument continues, has seen the steady erosion of the distinctive roles of federal and state government and increasing federal intervention directly in the affairs of local government. These changes have been accompanied by a movement from federal policy based on 'relatively coherent nótions of the government's role in addressing social and economic issues' to 'modern federal goals of "sharing" and "cooperation"' which have resulted in 'extraordinary interdependence and extreme fragmentation,' leading to 'the looming fear . . . of unrestricted intergovernmentalism, (and) of governmental pragmatism out of control.'[36]

There is some support for this view in aggregate data on intergovernmental expenditures. Between 1929 and the present, federal domestic expenditures increased from 1.4 per cent of Gross National Product (GNP) to about 13 per cent; in unadjusted dollars, they have more than doubled since 1974 alone. State government expenditures for all functions increased at a slower rate over the same period, from 1.6 per cent of GNP to 5.3 per cent. Local government expenditures increased from 5.9 per cent of GNP to 7.7 per cent.[37] Between 1950 and 1980, federal grants-in-aid increased as a proportion of state and local expenditures from about 10 per cent to just over 26 per cent.[38] With this growth in federal expenditures came an increase in the number of categories of funding. By the late 1970s, there were at least 490 distinguishable domestic categorical programs, accounting for approximately 80 per cent of federal grants-in-aid to state and local government.[39]

In education, the growth of federal expenditures and categorical grants-in-aid was slower, but followed the same pattern. In 1929, federal revenues accounted for 4 per cent of total revenues spent on education, while state revenues accounted for 17 per cent, and local revenues accounted for about 83 per cent. By 1949, those shares had shifted to about 3 per cent federal, 40 per cent state, and 57 per cent local. Between 1963 and 1967, the federal share doubled, from 4.4 per cent to 8.8 per cent, with the effects of ESEA, and it peaked in 1978 at 9.8 per cent. By the mid-1970s, the state and local shares had become about equal, at around 45 per cent. These relatively modest increases in the federal share were accompanied by relatively large increases in unadjusted dollar expenditures, from $7.3 million in 1929, to $486 million in 1957, to $900 million in 1964, to $2.8 billion in 1967, to $8.6 billion in 1978.[40]

During the period of maximum growth in federal expenditures for education, most new programs were categorical, in the sense that they targeted funds on specific kinds of curricula or children defined by certain attributes. By 1975, federal expenditures for elementary, secondary, and vocational education were being distributed through at least 78 separate categories. Education resisted consolidation attempts that affected other areas of federal policy in the mid-1970s, and by 1980 the number of categorical programs had declined only to 70. At the same time, social services, with a larger federal share, had 47 categorical programs, employment 23, transportation 36, and pollution control 23; only health care, with 78, had more than education.[41]

In political terms, the enormous growth of federal grants-in-aid meant movement from a federal system in which 'shifts of power or function *between* levels of government' were the central issue to one characterized by the 'emergence of new arenas of influence *among* levels of government.'[42] The key constituents of the old regime were levels of government; those of the new regime were vertical networks of federal, state, and local professionals whose careers depended on federal grants and regulations. These vertical networks were connected to 'issue networks' at the federal level, again composed of professionals, whose stock-in-trade was the mobilization of expert knowledge to influence policy.[43] The 'common discipline' of 'similarly trained professionals' across levels of government, sharing strong economic and political incentives to maintain their vertical identification with federal policy, enabled them 'to stand off the claims of rival disciplines and coordinating authorities' in state and local government.[44] The results of this shift were twofold: first, policymaking and implementation tended increasingly to be dominated by professionals who were experts in a narrow sub-specialty of intergovernmental relations, usually identified with a categorical federal program. Second, the distinctive missions of different levels of government were eroded by mutually beneficial functional relations among professionals across levels of government.

The political and economic incentives in this system of vertical networks have had a profound effect on federal policy, substantially weakening federal controls over expenditures and regulations. The beneficiaries of the federal grant-in-aid system are initially the units of government receiving the grants, and ultimately the individuals who receive the services or goods financed by the grants. The cost-bearers are taxpayers at large. Administrators and recipients, while they may disagree on many things, usually agree on the necessity for maintaining or increasing the grants that benefit them directly. In this sense, their interests are 'concentrated'. Taxpayers, on the other hand, don't experience increased grant expenditures as identifiable tax increments.

In this sense, their interests are 'diffuse.' Once the precedent is established for categorical programs, administrators and clients have a stronger incentive to add programs and increase expenditures on existing ones than taxpayers have to resist incremental additions. Hence, the intergovernmental grant system tends to produce an ever-increasing volume of programs and expenditures, with scant regard for budgetary constraints or cumulative effects on state and local administration. Similarly, the system tends, other things being equal, to produce an increasing volume of intergovernmental regulations, designed to assure that grants are properly administered, that they are targeted on the recipients for whom they are intended, and that lower levels of government follow the same procedures in decisions affecting clients.[45]

The effect of these self-reinforcing incentives on federal policy is what underlies current concern about 'unrestricted intergovernmentalism' and 'governmental pragmatism out of control.' Critics fear that functional relations among professionals across levels of government will displace distinctions in authority between levels, creating a system at the mercy of special interest groups and immune to electoral control at any level of government. In fact, this fear is overstated. Functional relations among levels of government carry their own limiting mechanisms and serve purposes beyond those of the self-interest of professionals.

Government through grants-in-aid is inevitably 'government by remote control' or 'third party government.'[46] In undertaking grant-in-aid programs, the federal government chooses, explicitly or inadvertently, to rely on other levels of government, or non-governmental organizations, to administer its policies. This devolution creates strong counter-incentives to those contained in the vertical networks spawned by categorical grants. Elected officials at all levels of government — presidents, congressment, governors, state legislators, mayors, city council members, and school board members — see the erosion of their authority by vertical networks and assert a countervailing interest. Both the executive and legislative branches at the federal level exercise much closer scrutiny now over the proliferation of new categorical programs than they did a decade ago. State executives and legislators are now involved, on a large scale, in reviewing the impact of federal grants on state budgets. More importantly, the 'intergovernmental lobby' — the National Governors Conference, the National Conference of Mayors, the National Conference of State Legislators, the National School Boards Association, etc. — exercises an increasing influence on federal policy. The political strength of these 'horizontal' or 'topocratic' interests, which is largely due to their critical role in making the intergovernmental grant system work, explains the emergence in the mid-1970s of grant consolidation and revenue sharing proposals.

Seen in this light, political support for grant consolidation and revenue sharing are an equilibrating force, explained by the response of elected officials at all levels of government to the erosion of authority implicit in categorical grants. In 1981, the Reagan administration chose to negotiate only with the intergovernmental lobby, or not to negotiate at all, in an effort to break the influence of vertical networks on federal policy. The combination of expenditure controls and appeals to the political interests of the intergovernmental lobby that characterized the 'new federalism' caught education interest groups off guard. Having resisted earlier attempts at consolidation, educators suddenly found themselves the recipients of a new block grant program — Chapter 2 of the Education Consolidation and Improvement Act (ECIA) — which consolidated twenty-eight funded and forty-two authorized categorical programs into a single program.

In other words, the self-interested behavior implicit in functional federalism works two ways, both to create vertical ties among professionals at different levels of government and to reinforce the authority of elected officials at the state and local level. The term 'function' has two meanings in this context: first, it refers to the intergovernmental ties necessary to make federal policy work at state and local levels; second, it refers to the authority of lower levels of government arising from their electoral base. In the first instance, we are interested in how well states and localities perform the 'function' of seeing that national purposes are carried out in practice. In the second, we are interested in how well they perform the 'function' of representing their electoral constituencies. Self-interest plays a role in both, so it is not especially useful to criticize past federal policy because it appeals to the self-interest of one group or another. The question is whether federal policy is sufficiently flexible to respond to both kinds of functions, and whether the self-interested behavior of professionals and elected officials is consistent with representative federalism.

But what of the argument that education is a 'state function,' protected against federal intrusion, if not explicitly by the Constitution, at least by the tradition of federal deference to state and local control? A close reading of history suggests that, contrary to conventional wisdom, education is neither a state or local function, nor a federal one, but a 'national' one. The period from 1840 to 1900 was the most important one for the growth of public education in the United States. During this period, public school enrollments more than tripled, total expenditures on public education increased from $7.6 million to $229 million in constant dollars, and the public share of expenditures on education grew from 47 per cent to 79 per cent.[47] This was also the period during which the local organization of schooling passed from voluntarism and philanthropy through an intermediate phase of neighborhood decentralization to its current locally-centralized bureaucratic form.[48] Out of this period came an educational system that was remarkably homogeneous, in curriculum content, grade structure, staff credentialling, financing, and governance. 'The result of this activity was not thirty different state systems, nor prodigious variations in local districts, but instead great uniformity.'[49] In other words, a kind of national agreement began to emerge on the form and content of public schooling.

Yet this was a period of remarkably little formal policy-making, at least by present-day standards, and even less direct intervention from the federal and state levels in local decisions on curriculum content, finance, and organization. In 1890, the median size of state education agencies was two people.[50] The U.S. Office of Education was a statistical agency, largely staffed by cast-offs from state agencies. How did such broad national agreement emerge without governmental intervention?

The answer appears to lie in 'an institution-building social movement led by men and women who shared a similar ideology and interests and who helped to build a common-school system by persuading and mobilizing their fellow citizens, mostly at the local level.'[51] It was a national movement that worked quite independently of federal and state policy. In its formative stages, the movement was calculatedly anti-government and anti-bureaucratic. 'The polity . . . was not to be consumated in a strong and bureaucratic state; rather it was to be located in individuals and in the exchange relations of a free society.'[52] Hence, the absence of reliance on central control. The cadre of professional reformers behind this movement, including Horace Mann and Henry Barnard, accepted this highly decentralized system and built their strategy around it. Imitating religious evangelists, they formed networks of local influentials who organized others in their communities. They initiated teachers' institutes, they developed national professional associations, and published journals.[53] They occasionally entertained notions of centralizing governmental authority at the national level, but always returned to the pragmatic strategy of working through national networks of reformers.

The single exception to the general pattern of national growth in public education during this period was the South. Southern states lagged well behind the rest of the country on all measure of educational adequacy: illiteracy among whites was on the order of four times what it was in the North; a majority of all pupils were enrolled in private schools in the South decades after enrollment had shifted primarily to public schools in the North; per pupil expenditures in the South were on the order of one-half to one-third those in the North well into the twentieth century; the proportion of school-age children actually enrolled in school in the South lagged well behind the North; and, finally, literacy and school attendance rates among blacks in the South lagged well behind the North.[54]

This regional disparity prompted George Hoar's unsuccessful proposal in 1870 to 'compel by national authority the establishment of a thorough and efficient system of public instruction throughout the whole country.'[55] It also led eventually to the formation of another cadre of professional reformers, the civil rights activists of the 1960s, whose agenda was startlingly similar to that of the earlier reformers, though their tactics were different in some respects. Without reviewing the history of the school desegregation movement, it is sufficient to observe that its *effect* on the South was almost identical to the effect that public school reformers had on the rest of the country a century earlier. It brought the public education system of southern states more closely into alignment with that of the rest of the country.

In the early twentieth century, as states assumed more and more responsibility for rationalizing finance, organization, and professional certification, it became accepted doctrine to say that education was a 'state function,' and to assert that the federal interest in education, if it existed at all, was clearly subordinate to the primary role of the states.[56] The historical evidence suggests another interpretation: that public education came about as a result of a *national* movement; that it was seen by its instigators as a *national* enterprise; and that the division of responsibilities reflected in current policy followed from, rather than preceded, the growth of education as a national enterprise.

In functional terms, then, as well as doctrinal terms, it appears that the federal system is working as it was designed. The present ambiguous division of labor among levels of government in the field of education is a reflection of the fact that education is a national enterprise to which all levels of government have a claim. The combination of growing functional interdependence among levels of government and of growing reassertion of the representative function at state and local levels can hardly be called 'growth without purpose.' The growth of functional interdependence occurred because it was necessary in order to assure that federal *purposes* were carried out; the response of the intergovernmental lobby occurred because it was necessary in order to assure that the *purposes* of state and local government would be taken into account by the federal government. The fact this equilibrating mechanism works with something less than perfect efficiency is reason for strategic concern, but it is not a sign that the federal system is failing in some fundamental sense.

Quite the contrary, functional interdependence and friction are precisely what one would expect from an effectively functioning federal system. In education, the federal government went about creating interdependencies with states and localities by introducing financial incentives, by creating differentiated program units within state and local educational agencies to implement federal objectives, and by generating rules and procedures requiring extensive consultation among federal, state, and local professionals. There are a number of ways these interdependencies can go awry: the financial incentives can be insufficient either to compensate for the incremental cost of implementing federal objectives or to have any lasting effect on state and local practice. Differentiated units within state and local agencies can create counterproductive divisions among staff, giving 'regular staff the sense that the federal government (does) not trust them to do the job' and relieving them of the responsibility to attend to the needs of students targeted by federal policy.[57] Rules and procedures can displace professional judgment and administrative responsibility, creating incentives to regard compliance as more important than effectiveness. In addition, the more interaction that occurs among levels of government, the more opportunities policy-makers and administrators have to observe the weaknesses of their counterparts at other levels. These negative by-products of federal involvement pose serious problems for educational policy, but they are not, by themselves, symptoms of a failing federal system.

The failure occurs when elected representatives at the local, state, and federal level fail to adjust policy and exert control, as negative effects begin to surface. Adjusting policy may require substantial changes in categorical programs, organizational structures, and the incentives that accompany them. These changes may entail conflict among levels of government but they do not necessarily imply any reduction in the level of interdependence, as we shall see in a moment. A federal system without interdependence is one in which mutual influence is impossible, and hence not a 'system' at all.

Federalism: the Strategic View

From a doctrinal standpoint, nothing in the language of the Constitution or the theory of federalism precludes federal involvement in education. Indeed, the history of federal involvement shows that no domain — finance, organization, pupil assignment, personnel, staff development, or curriculum — is immune from federal influence. From a functional standpoint, the growth of interdependence among levels of government, while it raises difficult political and administrative problems, is hardly evidence that the federal system is failing. Indeed, some level of interdependence is required in order for one level of government to influence another. If there are no inherent doctrinal or functional constraints on the range of subjects or the level of interdependence contained in federal policy, there would seem to be no limits at all to what the federal government can presume to do.

In fact, there are limits, but those limits are political and strategic, rather than doctrinal and functional. They are set by the political support that federal policymakers can muster for their objectives and by the resources they put behind those objectives. Cast in these terms, the federal role in education is both more than advocates of the 'new federalism' suggest and less than advocates of past federal intervention have assumed.

The first and most basic limit on federal influence is the federal government's share of educational revenues. Federal funds have never accounted for more than 10 per cent of the total and are not likely to vary from this level under any foreseeable set of political conditions. At current levels, a one per cent increase in the federal share requires something like a $900 million increase in the federal contribution, or a corresponding decrease in state and local contributions with federal expenditures remaining constant.[58] Fiscal leverage, in other words, is expensive. In a period of fiscal retrenchment, declining school enrollments, and a declining proportion of the voting-age population with school-age children, the important strategic question for educational decisionmakers is education's share relative to other public expenditures, not the relative contribution of different levels of government.

From this fiscal limit on federal influence, all others follow. It means, for example, that the federal role in the delivery of education is marginal. Federal policy affects state and local decisions, if at all, by adding some increment of resources to the basic program for certain target groups, by adding staff with certain specialities to the regular complement of professionals, and by requiring that certain rules and procedures be followed over and above those normally observed in the daily administration of schools. Beyond these specific, marginal adjustments, which characterize all federal programs in some combination, the federal government can rely only on its moral authority to influence states and localities.

Federal policy succeeds — in the sense of producing outcomes consistent with politically-determined objectives — to the degree that the 'regular' program succeeds and to the degree that the marginal adjustments added by federal policy work in tandem with the 'regular' program rather than at cross-purposes with it. Playing a marginal role, in other words, puts the federal government in the position of depending heavily on others for its own success.[59]

Furthermore, the marginal role invites an explicit or implicit benefit-cost calculation on the part of state and local administrators and policymakers. While the federal share of total expenditures in any given setting may be a small fraction of the total, this fraction is not an accurate measure of its utility to state and local actors. A more accurate measure of utility is the added discretion bought by the marginal federal dollar. 'Eighty to eighty-five per cent of most local school budgets are in fixed costs, mostly salaries, while the federal share is mostly in that precious portion that is discretionary and is devoted to special services and program innovation.'[60] In other words, the marginal federal dollar is valuable to state and local actors to the degree that it allows them to undertake, and assume credit for, activities that would not be possible under existing budgets. But in order for the marginal federal dollar to work effectively for *federal* objectives, it must be accompanied by restrictions on its use, to assure that it does indeed purchase some incremental value.[61] These restrictions carry a cost to state and local decisionmakers, in the form of added administration and reduced discretion. So the marginal value of federal dollars to state and local decisionmakers is 'discounted' by the marginal cost of lost discretion. When the number of federal categorical programs increases, and the restrictions accompanying them multiply, with only modest increases in marginal federal support, the net value of federal support to states and localities declines. This was the risky strategic game federal education policymakers were playing in the 1970s. When policymakers in other areas were consolidating, those in education were holding steady against the declining net value of federal dollars.

Increased complexity of federal policy carries other costs to federal influence. The multiplication of restrictions and controls that accompanies the growth of categorical programs institutionalize distrust between levels of government in the interest of promoting better education for certain segments of the population. Federal policy was couched, at least implicitly, in an accusatory rhetoric suggesting that federal intervention was necessary because of state and local neglect — of racial, ethnic, and linguistic minorities, of the educationally disadvantaged, of the handicapped. The growth of federal education policy 'occurred in a system of designed skepticism about government,' a 'system intended to protect citizens from government by protecting governments from each other.'[62] The problem with institutionalized distrust is that it doesn't necessarily result in better results for the intended beneficiaries of federal policy; their interests are served by a careful orchestration of the federal government's marginal contribution with the 'regular' program, not by institutionalized conflict between levels of government.

The growth of categorical programs in federal education policy, at first a rational response to limited federal leverage, begins to turn back upon itself and create negative incentives that undermine federal influence. Or, as Elliot Richardson put it, in the early stages of federal involvement 'narrowly drawn categorical grants . . . actually advance the targeted national interest,' but past a certain point 'the leverage exerted by a given program has almost completely dissipated: state and local administrators, having a bunch of carrots held out to them, are free to select those which feed the activities they would have undertaken without any special inducement.'[63] Federal influence depends on the ability of policymakers to find the margin where federal policy is likely to be most effective, to ration the use of federal resources to those purposes where they are most likely to have an effect, and to avoid engaging in activities that erode the base of services upon which marginal federal resources operate.

If federal policymakers have erred, their errors have been strategic: allowing the number of categorical programs to increase beyond the point where the value of any one is diminished by the weight of the total; allowing rules and restrictions to diminish the net value of additional resources to states and localities; allowing an adversarial relationship to develop between levels of government that led to disconnections between marginal federal resources and the 'regular' school program. The degree to which any of these things has actually happened is still a matter of empirical investigation. But the perception is strong that an increasing federal presence has led to a diminishing federal influence.

If the errors have been strategic, then the remedies must be strategic. They are likely to be found in a narrowing of federal purposes, a calculating and skeptical attitude toward the value of federal resources to the units of government receiving them, and a studious regard for the relationship between federally-initiated activities and the 'regular' program. They are *not* likely to be found in shifts of doctrine or function.

Notes

1 Barfield, C. (1981) *Rethinking Federalism: Block Grants and Federal, State and Local Responsibilities*, Washington, D.C., American Enterprise Institute, p. 61.
2 Office of Management and Budget (OMB) (1982) *Major Themes and Additional Details*, Fiscal Year 1983, Washington, D.C., Executive Office of President, p. 18.
3 Barfield, C. (1981), *op. cit.*, pp. 23–4.
4 Reagan, R. (1981) 'Inaugural address,' *Weekly Compilation of Presidential Documents*, vol 17, Monday 26 January, pp. 61–2.

5 GRODZINS, M. (1967) 'The federal system' in WILDAVSKY, A. (Ed.) *American Federalism in Perspective*, Boston, Little, Brown, p. 257.
6 BARFIELD, C. (1981) *op. cit.*, p. 11.
7 REAGAN, R. (1981), *op. cit.*, p. 2.
8 WOOD, G. (1969) *The Creation of the American Republic*, Chapel Hill, University of North Carolina Press, p. 530.
9 STORING, H. (1981) *What the Anti-Federalists Were For*, Chicago, University of Chicago Press, p. 15.
10 *Ibid*, p. 526.
11 *Federalist Papers* (1788/1961), New York, New American Library, p. 15.
12 *Ibid*, 46.
13 BEER, S. (1978) 'Federalism, nationalism and democracy in America,' *American Political Science Review*, vol. 72, March, p. 12.
14 *Ibid*, pp. 12–13.
15 *Federalist Papers*, op. cit., p. 10.
16 BEER, S. (1978) *op. cit.*, pp. 13–14.
17 *Federalist Papers*, *op. cit.*, p. 28.
18 BEER, S. (1978) *op. cit.*, pp. 9 and 15–19.
19 WHEARE, K.C. (1964) *Federal Government*, New York, Oxford University Press, 4th edn, p. 2; and RIKER, W. (1964) *Federalism: Origin, Operation and Significance*, Boston, Little, Brown, pp. 5–6 and 11.
20 LIVINGSTON, W. (1952) 'A note on the nature of federalism,' *Political Science Quarterly*, vol. 77, p. 81.
21 RIKER, W. (1964) *op. cit.*
22 *Ibid*, pp. 13–14 and 139–45.
23 RIKER, W. (1969) 'Six books in search of a subject, or does federalism exist and does it matter?,' *Comparative Politics*, vol. 2, pp. 139–42.
24 RIKER, W. (1964) *op. cit.*, pp. 142–3; and RIKER, W. (1969) *op. cit.*, p. 146.
25 KING, P. (1973) 'Against federalism' in BENEWICK, R., BERKI, R.N. and PREKH, B. (Eds) *Knowledge and Belief in Politics*, London, George Allen and Unwin, p. 153.
26 TIEDT, S. (1966) *The Role of the Federal Government in Education*, New York, Oxford University Press, p. 16.
27 ELAZAR, D. (1967) 'Federal-state collaboration in the nineteenth century United States' in WILDAVSKY, A. (Ed.) *American Federalism in Perspective*, Boston, Little, Brown, pp. 195 and 204–5.
28 ADVISORY COMMISSION ON INTERGOVERNMENTAL RELATIONS (ACIR) (1981a) *Intergovernmentalizing the Classroom: Federal Involvement in Elementary and Secondary Education*, Washington, D.C., p. 14.
29 *Ibid*, pp. 16–17.
30 KAESTLE, C. and SMITH, M. (1982) 'The federal role in elementary and secondary education, 1940–1980,' *Harvard Educational Review*, pp. 8–9.
31 ADVISORY COMMISSION ON INTERGOVERNMENTAL RELATIONS (ACIR) (1981a) *op. cit.*, p. 25; also pp. 20–4.
32 *Ibid*, p. 33
33 VERNON, R. (1979) 'Introduction' in PROUDHON, P. *The Principle of Federation*, Toronto, University of Toronto Press, p. xxxv.
34 KING, P. (1973) *op. cit.*, pp. 155 and 162.
35 ADVISORY COMMISSION ON INTERGOVERNMENTAL RELATIONS (ACIR) (1981b) *The Condition of Contemporary Federalism: Conflicting Theories and Collapsing Constraints*, Washington, D.C., p. 2.
36 *Ibid*, pp. 1–2.
37 Advisory Commission on Intergovernmental Relations (ACIR) (1981c) *Significant Features of Fiscal Federalism*, Washington, D.C., table 2, p. 2.
38 OFFICE OF MANAGEMENT AND BUDGET (OMB) (1982) *op. cit.*, table H-6, p. 17.
39 HALE, G. and PALLEY, M.L. (1981) *The Politics of Federal Grants*, Washington,

D.C., Congressional Quarterly Press, table 5-2. p. 82 and table 6-2, p. 108.

40 NATIONAL CENTER FOR EDUCATIONAL STATISTICS (NCES) (1981) *Digest of Educational Statistics*, Washington, DC, US Department of Education, table 64, p. 74.

41 HALE, G. and PALLEY, M.L. (1981) *op. cit.*, table 5-2, p. 82.

42 BEER, S. (1978) *op. cit.*, p. 9, emphasis added.

43 HECLO, H. (1980) 'Issues networks and the executive establishment' in KING, A. (Ed.) *The New Political System*, Washington, D.C., American Enterprise Institute.

44 BEER, S. (1978) *op, cit.*, p. 18.

45 BEER, S. (1977) 'Political overlord and federalism,' *Polity*, vol. 10, Fall, pp. 5–17; CHUBB, J. (1981) 'Regulating economic opportunity,' paper presented to the Seminar on Law and Education, Institute for Research on Educational Finance and Governance, School of Education, Stanford University; THOMAS, J. (1980) 'Governmental overload in the United States: a problem of distributive policies?', *Administration and Society*, vol. 11, February, pp. 371–91; WILSON, J.Q. (1980) 'The politics of regulation' in WILSON, J.Q. (Ed.) *The Politics of Regulation*, New York, Basic Books, pp. 357–94.

46 HECLO, H. (1980) *op. cit.*; SALAMON, L. (1981) 'Rethinking public management: Third party government and the changing forms of government action,' *Public Policy*, vol. 29, pp. 255–75.

47 FISHLOW, A. (1966) 'Levels of nineteenth-century investment in education,' *Journal of Economic History*, vol. 26, tables 1 and 2, pp. 420 and 423.

48 KATZ, M. (1971) 'From voluntarism to bureaucracy in American education,' *Sociology of Education*, vol. 44, summer, p. 325ff.

49 TYACK, D. and HANSOT, E. (1982) *Managers of Virtue: Public School Leadership in America 1820–1980*, New York, Basic Books, p. 20.

50 MEYER, J. *et al.* (1979) 'Public education as nation-building: Enrollments and bureaucratization in the American states,' *American Journal of Sociology*, vol. 85, p. 546.

51 TYACK, D. and HANSOT, E. (1982) *op. cit.*, p. 19.

52 MEYER, J. *et al* (1979) *op. cit.*, p. 599.

53 TYACK, D. and HANSOT, E. (1982) *op. cit.*, pp. 47–51.

54 *Ibid*, pp. 83–9; MEYER, J. *et al* (1979) *op. cit.*, pp. 594 and 597.

55 ADVISORY COMMISSION ON INTERGOVERNMENTAL RELATIONS (ACIR) (1981a) *op. cit.*, p. 14.

56 WIRT, F. (1976) 'Education politics and policies' in JACOB, H. and VINES, K. (Eds) *Politics in the American States*, Boston, Little, Brown, 3rd edn, pp. 284–348.

57 KAESTLE, C. and SMITH, M. (1982) *op. cit.*, pp. 26–7.

58 NATIONAL CENTER FOR EDUCATIONAL STATISTICS (NCES) (1982) *op. cit.*, table 64, p. 74.

59 ELMORE, R. and MCLAUGHLIN, M. (1982) 'Strategic choice in federal education policy: The compliance-assistance trade-off,' in LIEBERMAN, A. and MCLAUGHLIN, M. (Eds) *Policymaking in Education*, 81st Yearbook of the National Society for the Study of Education, Chicago, University of Chicago Press; ELMORE, R. (1982) 'Differential treatment of states in federal education policy', *Peabody Journal of Education*.

60 KAESTLE, C. and SMITH, M. (1982) *op. cit.*, p. 32.

61 BARRO, S. (1978) 'Federal education goals and policy instruments: an assessment of the "strings" attached to categorial grants in education' in TIMPANE, M. (Ed.) *The Federal Interest in Financing Schooling*, Cambridge, Ballinger, pp. 229–85; VOGEL, M. (1982) 'Education grant consolidation: its potential fiscal and distributive effects', *Harvard Educational Review*, vol. 52, pp. 169–88.

62 COHEN, D. (1982) 'Policy and organization: The impact of educational policy on school governance,' *Harvard Educational Review*, pp. 19–20.

63 HALE, G. and PALLEY, M.L. (1981) *op. cit.*, p. 19.

The Deregulation Critique of the Federal Role in Education

William H. Clune
University of Wisconsin

This chapter is an analysis of the 'deregulation critique' of the federal role in education.[1] The deregulation thesis may be briefly stated as follows: it is possible to reduce the number and intensity of legal obligations on educational organizations without decreasing the quantity or quality of education in any respect. Legal intervention, with its categorical rules and sanctions, is said to be incompatible with the adaptive, flexible, social interaction of teaching and learning. Education, especially, is not the place for 'going by the book.'[2] The principal purpose of this paper is to 'unpack' the largely political debate over deregulation into distinct analytical parts, or separate 'criticisms.'

An important conclusion of this chapter is that while many deregulatory adjustments may be possible and desirable, the idea of costless wholesale deregulation is almost exclusively associated with criticisms of the *goals* of federal intervention rather than with means. The deregulation critique tends to conceal policy judgments with a rhetoric of legal mechanics. In order to counter this tendency, my primary purpose in this essay is to ascertain the 'range' of benefits that might be expected from deregulatory initiatives of various kinds and disentangle objections to goals from objections to means.

Criticisms of the Goals of Federal Intervention

As a logical matter, objections at the level of goals are especially powerful because they assert that, regardless of how well legal means are designed and administered, there are no net benefits from intervention.

Federal Goals are not Worthwhile

A strong, though often latent, theme in the deregulation critique is that the goals of federal intervention are not worthwhile. The criticism is strongly associated with, and perhaps limited to, civil rights type interventions. Beneath a variety of articulations, the touchstone of the criticism seems to be a perceived tension between 'equality' and 'quality.' Equality may be seen as so preoccupied with *relative* advantage and disadvantage that the absolute values of education are ignored. Civil rights may be viewed as a type of 'jealousy,' seeking to make people more equal without producing any other benefit, and, sometimes, actually damaging the educational process.

The 'equality versus quality' theme in the anti-civil rights position has strong and weak versions. The strong version asserts a sharp distinction between equality and quality, and holds the goal of equality to be worthless. Some criticisms of school desegregation, holding it a 'disaster,' are of this variety.[3] The weak version suggests that the problem is one of maldistribution of resources with too much for the civil rights claimants, too little for the 'mainstream.'

There are two problems with the strong version of the quality versus equality criticism. First, if it were true that there is a sharp distinction between goals of equality and educational goals, the goals of equality may be important. Unequal treatment of racial minorities or females is a wrong that is worth eliminating even if the more equal treatment lacks 'educational' value. Second, a sharp distinction is not really justified. Bilingual and special education present the clearest cases of a breakdown of the quality versus equality distinction. In those situations, the right to equal treatment is synonymous, at least in theory, with the right to an effective education. Both bilingual and special education originated in situations of almost total exclusion of the underserved group from the educational process. Thus, to a large extent, claims for equality by underserved groups really are claims for quality education for those groups.[4]

The weak version of the anti-civil rights criticism claims that too much emphasis has been given to the needs of previously underserved groups at the expense of mainstream groups. The problem is one of resources. Federal programs mandating equal rights have not made sufficient resources available to implement the rights. If state and local taxes do not increase, at a certain point the quality of education for mainstream groups must begin to pay for the better treatment of previously underserved groups.

The weak version of the anti-civil rights criticism deserves serious consideration, but it is important to examine carefully exactly what the objection is. Objections to merely equal treatment cannot be taken seriously, even if we are sympathetic to the fiscal problems of school districts. When special education services are much more expensive than mainstream services, the problem is less easy to resolve. One has the impression that judicial and legislative concern for excluded groups may not have been sufficiently tempered with an understanding of limited resources. The question of the right of the handicapped to an appropriate education, for example, was perhaps not sufficiently balanced against the right of the non-handicapped to an appropriate education. Perhaps the ultimate difficulty is the historical inability of the legal process to claim a greater share of public and private resources. Court decrees requiring more resources for a particular purpose usually do not specify where the resources should come from. The political response to a decree is often reduction of other public services rather than an increase in taxes. On the other hand, bureaucratic and judicial decisions during implementation may be seen primarily as compromises of reformist purposes against competing considerations and interests.

Federal Programs are not Effective

One of the basic elements of the recent conservative movement in American politics is a loss of faith in the efficacy of idealistic social programs initiated in the 1960s and 1970s. In the educational context, it is believed that one cannot legislate learning, one cannot produce change in local education with grants or laws from Washington, and one cannot do anything about class-linked achievement patterns. Skepticism about the potential for government intervention is part of the neo-conservative mindset.[5]

Taken literally, as a broad-scale assertion that nothing has happened, this criticism cannot be taken seriously. In the first place, federal programs have been responsible for an enormous amount of change in educational programs and administration. The main criticism is that long-run educational results cannot be demonstrated. But standards for success are unclear. Consider, for example, the right of parents to veto placement in special education programs under PL 94-142.[6] It is sometimes said that this provision has failed because education systems often succeed in diminishing the effective participation of parents (by professional intimidation, by obtaining prior consent, etc.).[7] However, it is also clear that many parents do participate effectively; and it is at least arguable that the availability of the veto right for parents who become concerned enough to exercise it ought to be the primary standard of success. In that case, the availability of the right would itself be a measure of success.

There is, as with most of the deregulation criticisms, an element of truth here. Both the standards of program effectiveness and our knowledge about what constitutes an effective program need to be reviewed. Marshall Smith has suggested the following 'rules of thumb', about what kinds of federal programs are known to have been effective:[8] (i) *Programs giving educational access.* Some education is better than no education, and more education tends to be better than less.[9] Accordingly, federal programs which increase access to education tend to be successful. Examples are Headstart, which provided preschool education to youngsters who had none, the GI Bill and student loan programs, which made higher education more available, and remedial language instruction, to the extent that it offered some services where none existed before (that is, wholly aside from which brand of remediation is appropriate). (ii) *Programs overcoming major gaps in technology.* Occasionally, educators in one segment of the profession learn how to teach a subject in a drastically superior way compared to previous practice. In that situation, centrally sponsored reform has a good chance of success. Federally sponsored reforms in the areas of physics and mathematics fall under this category.[10]

Although it would be a double standard not applied to state and local programs, it would not be unreasonable to hold federal programs to the requirement that they have a high probability of success. The cost would be all hopes for success where technology is uncertain.

Federal Programs are Unnecessary

A common deregulatory criticism is that federal programs are unnecessary in the sense that state and local governments would meet the need if the federal government did not. Few would assert that change would happen as quickly in the absence of federal intervention; but if the change occurred more slowly without federal intervention, the delay might well be worthwhile, so goes the argument, because it would occur in the absence of coercion, costly federal regulation, and the like. The criticism seems ridiculous when applied to the area of racial equality; but the strong need for a federal presence in the race area may have been mistakenly generalized to other areas.

This criticism is ultimately unconvincing. The fact that many programs begin in the states does not mean that they will spread very far. Most federal programs, whether picked up from the states or not, are not politically popular in a great many states. The most straightforward reason is that federal programs often demand a redistribution of resources toward groups which were previously underserved. The requirement to redistribute resources is a painful one; and the fact that groups have been historically underserved, if it does not indicate outright discrimination, at least suggests that these groups are not likely to be high on the list in the painful process of redistributing resources. Moreover, the speed and scope of change may be extremely important. Even with the maximum amount of federal pressure, the desegregation of southern schools took fifteen to twenty years.[11] How long would it take for education of the handicapped, sexual equality, and bilingual education to spread of their own accord?

The weaker version of the criticism that federal programs are unnecessary is that once the federal government has sponsored changes and they are in place for a number of years and established, it is time for the federal government to withdraw. In other words, many people recommend that the federal government play the role of an innovator, but not sponsor educational programs indefinitely.

This criticism has its greatest appeal in situations where the federal innovation actually does seem to have been adopted by the states on a wide scale. Vocational education is probably a good example. Unfortunately, when programs become widely adopted, they also develop strong constituencies.[12] Therefore, when the federal role is least needed because the program has become popular, the political difficulty of terminating the program may be very great. It is the programs whose objectives are still politically unpopular that receive the most vociferous criticism.

Constant innovation is thus difficult on two fronts. Innovation tends to be unpopular at first because it is unfamiliar or is designed to benefit politically weak groups. Once the innovation becomes established, and therefore is no longer innovation, constituencies have developed and termination of the program, even if sensible policy, is likely to be unpopular.

Federal Goals are not Properly Federal

The idea here, often expressed by President Reagan, is that education is a matter of state and local concern, so that even if federal goals are worthwhile, can be effective, and are supplementary to state and local action, they should not be pursued, because of a proper understanding of federalism. Strictly speaking, this criticism is not of the deregulatory variety, because it does not assert the basic deregulatory thesis that there would be the same or greater education with fewer legal requirements. However, in a colloquial rather than a logical sense, the idea of no federal role is one of the strongest elements of the deregulation critique.

As with most of the deregulatory criticisms, there is some merit to the one that asserts a lack of federal role. Federal intervention in education is relatively recent and sporadic. There is no strong theory of why national intervention is needed, such as there is for national defense or national regulation of interstate commerce.[13] Also, it is clear that, regardless of the existence of national programs, the most important part of the educational process must always be local: the interaction between teachers and students and the maintenance of effective educational organizations. There has been no national crisis, such as the Great Depression, which served to justify national interventions in many areas that were previously considered exclusively the province of state and local governments or not the function of government at all.

Even if they are not very clear, the arguments for a federal role are surprisingly tenacious. Although education is not itself a federal purpose, and the connection between education and other purposes is often unclear, a connection is almost certain to be urged on a regular basis. The role of the federal government in maintaining and improving economic productivity is well accepted, and the role of education in economic productivity is likewise established. For this reason, and because the market for employable skills is essentially national, it will be difficult for the federal government to resist all efforts to improve the stock of human capital (as economists would call it). A second strong function of the federal government related to education is the function of immigration and naturalization. Many of our most severe education-al problems originated with the immigration of unschooled or foreign-speaking peoples (including the forced immigration and subsequent mistreatment of black Americans). Rapid and large-scale immigration tends to place an unbearable strain on state and local capacities. At a certain point in the failure of the educational process, the minimum requirements of citizenship are not met. If hundreds of thousands, or even millions, of inner-city youth cannot exercise the basic functions of citizenship, or hold a job in an increasingly technological economy, the philosophical idea that education is exclusively a matter of state and local concern is likely to seem too thin for sustenance.

Criticisms of the Basic Form of the Intervention

This part of the paper asks whether there is some radically different way to structure the relationship between the federal government and the states so as to make it less regulatory or legalistic and more cooperative. Two main avenues have been suggested for achieving this kind of radical 'delegalization': first, that within the existing framework of federal grants, specific requirements simply be relaxed, in favor of something like block grants coupled with precatory purposes; second, that binding legal requirements be relaxed and replaced, not with mere legal exhortations, as recommended by the block grant approach, but with an intense administrative relationship of 'assistance' or 'adaptation.'

Same Educational Effect with Reduction of Strings Only

The thesis of the consolidation movement is that the federal government can achieve its educational goals just as well and at a lower cost by merely reducing the number of legal requirements or strings attached to existing grants.[14] The idea seems to be that groups benefitted by the federal controls will be able to insist upon allocative patterns and educational services approximating the formerly mandated patterns and services; except that, since the services will be more adjusted to local conditions, they will be more efficient.

As background for considering the consolidation thesis, it is helpful to review the various degrees and kinds of legal requirements that have been imposed by the federal government. Table 1 suggests categories of such requirements from most to least mandatory, that is, from least to most discretion for the states.

Category A in the table is regulation, that is, mandatory requirements without the compensation of federal assistance. Intervention of this kind has been associated with civil rights, either judicially declared and enforced, as in the case of desegregation, or legislatively mandated, as in the case of many civil rights type statutes modeled upon the court decrees.[15] It is interesting that unassisted regulation by the federal government in education has apparently been restricted to civil rights-type situations. The ideal seems to be that, if we can assume the violation of a basic right by the states or localities, it is fair to ask them to remedy the situation without federal assistance. In fact, of course, financial assistance has been provided in some civil rights contexts.[16]

Table 1 Basic regulatory options in the federal-state relationship

(From top down: more to less federal regulation; less to more state and local discretion)

A	Regulation (Mandatory Requirements)	1 Court decrees 2 'Civil Rights-type' statutes.
B	Categorical or Conditional. Grants	1 'Any Grantee' type (e.g., § 504, Title IX, Buckley). 2 Service regulations plus compensation (94-142). 3 Effective strings on Use of Funds (e.g., Title I). 4 Ineffective Strings on Use of Funds (Vocational Education). 5 Block Grants with Precatory Purposes
C	General Aid	

The next least restrictive category is categorical or conditional grants. The most fundamental element of discretion allowed under the conditional grants is the ability of the grantee to turn down the money, thereby escaping the legal requirements. In this respect, the first kind of categorical grant, referred to as 'any grantee' type in Table 1, does not realistically allow this sort of discretion, and therefore is probably closer to regulation.[17] Laws like Title IX,[18] Executive Order 11,246,[19] and the Buckley Amendment,[20] apply to all federal contracts or grants. Therefore, in order to escape the conditions enacted by such laws, educational institutions would have to decline all federal support. While this is a theoretical possibility, and has actually been done by institutions receiving very little federal support, the price is too great for most institutions to consider as a realistic possibility.

The next least intensive or intrusive type of intervention is referred to in the table as service regulations plus compensation. The model is Public Law 94-142, the handicapped education act. The conditions on this type of grant are not limited to the use of federal monies but rather are direct service requirements which apply if the federal monies are accepted at all. Relatively few conditions attach to the use of federal money as such; but the federal grant pays for only a fraction of the required services. The reason that this type of grant is more restrictive than conditions which apply only to the use of money is that the amount of the federal compensation is not necessarily sufficient to defray the cost of compliance.[21] States and localities accept this type of relationship and continue in it either because of local pressure groups, which are able to insist upon, in effect, a type of matching aid by the states, or because, for some other reason, the states would have allocated as much or more resources to the general purpose without the federal aid.[22]

The next least restrictive form of legal intervention is referred to as 'effective strings on the use of funds.' Title I is given as an example. Effective strings are less restrictive than direct service requirements because the only restriction is on the use of federal funds.

The term 'effective' requires explanation. An effective grant in these terms is 'additive,' that is, it produces substantial extra state and local educational services for the federally approved purpose.[23] For example, a dollar of aid for compensatory education under Title I actually produces some substantial amount of state and local spending, say at least sixty cents, for compensatory education. Achieving this stimulative effect is not as easy as it may sound. In the case of Title I, it took years of planning and experimentation to design the exact set of legal conditions which achieved some additive effect. The term effective does not necessarily mean a program which works, however. Additional spending is a necessary but not a sufficient condition of program effectiveness. Indeed, conditions which are specific enough to produce additional spending may interfere with program effectiveness.

Although political debate suggests a sharp distinction between categorical grants and general aid, the next three types of federal intervention may be grouped together in terms of restrictiveness. It is generally conceded that many types of federal aid are accompanied by what may be called ineffective strings. If the ratio of federal funds to state funds is too low and very careful fiscal targeting is absent, aid which is categorical in the sense of having restricted purposes in fact operates as general or unrestricted aid.[24] Vocational education is an example. Because the states spend many times the federal contribution from their own resources on vocational education, the federal contribution does not produce much extra state and local spending. If this conclusion is valid in the case of aid, like vocational education,with strong limitations on the use of federal funds, it is true *a fortiori* with respect to both block grants with precatory purposes and general aid. The Reagan Administration has been moving in the direction of block grants with precatory purposes. Under this type of grant, one or more purposes for the spending are recited in the law, but realistic restrictions on the use of federal money are not provided.[25]

The basic point of view contained in Table 1 and the argument just presented is that, without effective strings, states and localities will use federal money for their own purposes; and these will not correspond to federal purposes to any great extent. For this reason, categorical or conditional grants are the least restrictive form of traditional legal intervention consistent with achieving federal purposes effectively. Above effective strings in Table 1, we find a better deal for the federal government in terms of cost effectiveness, in the sense that, at least superficially, more of the desired state and local conduct is obtained for a lower investment of federal resources. Below effective strings in Table 1, the only purpose achieved by the federal intervention is general aid.

There is thus a clear internal contradiction in the deregulation philosophy as applied to the federal role in education. One part of that philosophy insists that federal intervention occur under limited circumstances and for limited purposes. The other part, objecting to federal requirements, insists upon the consolidation of categorical grants. However, when effective strings are dropped, categorical aid becomes general aid; and the limited purpose of federal intervention is lost. The only escape from this contradiction is the suggestion that the states and localities will spend federal aid for the federally declared purposes without mandatory requirements that they do so. This flies in the face of all available research on the subject.[26] The problem is not, as some in the new administration would have it, that the federal government 'distrusts' state and local governments; or that state and local officials are assumed to be 'dishonorable.' The ineffectiveness of block grants is based simply upon the fact that state and local governments have somewhat different priorities for spending than the federal government. If this is not the case, if the priorities are so similar that local spending will completely track federal purposes, then the aid program fails to meet another requirement of the conservative philosophy of the federal role in education, that the federal government act only when state governments are incapable of doing so.

Assistance versus Compliance Orientation

The second way sometimes suggested to remove virtually all legal requirements from the federal-state relationship is to establish what Elmore calls a relationship of pure 'assistance' or what Berman calls 'adaptive implementation.'[27] Under such a relationship, the agent of change (here, an agency of the federal government) does not impose any rules and regulations. Instead, broad goals (such as the education of disadvantaged children) are articulated by the outside agency; more precise goals and means are worked out jointly through discussion and experimentation; and the role of outside agency is to provide financial, technical, organizational and professional assistance. The prototype of this kind of outside change agent would seem to be the organizational development or management consultant. In the relationship between consultant and client, rules and regulations seem obviously out of place; yet the potential for change, even painful change, is significant.

It is much easier to construct attractive imaginary cameos of the assistance relationship than it is to picture the existence of a program on a large scale, however. If 'assistance' is to be administered by anything other than a tiny, elite, closely controlled group of consultants, solutions to a number of fundamental difficulties need to be suggested.

First, many federal programs, especially of the civil rights variety, require states and localities to do things that they do not want to do, at least initially. The Reagan administration is committed to 'negotiation' rather than 'confrontation' in such matters, but historical experience is contrary to the idea that deeply entrenched behavior can be altered without the meaningful threat of coercion.

Even if the confrontational era of race and sex discrimination is tapering off, there are problems of recalcitrance (or 'divergent preferences') even in relatively non-controversial programs. School districts do not object to expanding services for the poor and handicapped in the same way that they resist racial desegregation, but the issue of budgetary priority is almost invariably painful.

Even when the federal government brings new money, school districts usually have a long list of unmet needs, including tax relief, which they regard as more important than the federal priorities.

Second, it seems doubtful that the pure assistance type of intervention can produce rapid change on a nationwide basis. Objective standards are efficient because they simplify the tasks of compliance and monitoring of compliance. They are inefficient in a different sense because compliance with the objective standards often does not achieve underlying program objectives. It may be quite legitimate for the federal government to seek unartfully rapid, broad-scale change, at the cost of frequent missteps. More refined interventions have a higher probability of success, but they would seem to be limited in the scope and pace of change.[28]

Third, strong political and legal forces work against 'pure assistance.' Advocacy groups representing the underserved are distrustful of purely negotiated arrangements because of their secrecy and accommodation to majoritarian values. Political and fiscal conservatives are suspicious of costly programs with a 'do good' mandate and no performance standards. States and school districts may protest the 'arbitrariness' and 'excessive discretion' which are counterparts of a freewheeling, standardless federal intervention.

The wholesale replacement of federal 'regulatory-type' programs, including categorical grants, with pure assistance programs does not seem plausible. There is much that is attractive about the assistance model. However, since assistance and regulation seem to be good for somewhat different purposes, they should not be regarded as substitutes.

Criticisms of the 'Technique' of Intervention: the Search for Less Legalism

Much of the criticism of regulation concerns what may be called 'technique.' If the validity of goals is presumed (as discussed under Criticisms of the Goals of Federal Intervention), and a fundamental regulatory form accepted, whether through regulation or categorical grants (as discussed under Criticisms of the Basic Form of the Intervention), the search for deregulation becomes a search for less 'legalism.' 'Legalism,' which here could be called 'regulationism,' refers to the unpleasant, rigid, formalistic qualities of legal intervention: universally applicable specific standards, procedures, paperwork, compliance-orientation, and so on. Even among those who acclaim the net benefits of legal intervention, legalisms are assumed to be costly, undesirable by-products. For example, even the most ardent proponents of affirmative action in employment do not recommend filling out reports as a good thing in itself. Given the almost universal distaste for legalisms, much thought naturally is given to having less of them. Couldn't the law be more 'reasonable'?[29]

To focus discussion, it is helpful first to arrange some of the separate dimensions of legalism according to regulatory and deregulatory options. That is done in Table 2.

Table 2 Dimensions of legalism

	Regulatory	Deregulatory
A General Characteristics	Measurable, standardized obligatory	Subjective, communal idiosyncratic, discretionary
B Organizational Activity		
1 *Planning or Policymaking*	Procedures — rulemaking, PPBS, school improvement plans, etc.	Spontaneous interaction, muddling through
2 *Influence or Efficaciousness of Client*	Due process, rights	'Politics'
3 *Reliability in Administration*		
(a) How obligations are defined	Standardization and standards, monitoring, paperwork	Loosely defined goals exceptions
(b) How compliance with obligations is obtained	Enforcement	Exhortation, professionalization, assistance, trust

The General Characteristics of Legalistic and Non-legalistic Interventions

The general characteristics of legalism, and the source of its objectionable status, are the measurable, the standardized, and the obligatory. When legalistic interventions are justifiable it is because measurability, standardization and obligation are functional and useful. The opposites of these characteristics which so often seem attractive are the subjective, communal, idiosyncratic and discretionary.

The general characteristics of legalism/non-legalism are found or realized in separate aspects of organizational activity. That is, for each of several important types of activities in organizations, there is a legalistic mode, a non-legalistic mode, and many alternatives in between. Within each dimension of organization activity (B1, 2, and 3 in the table), in moving from the legalistic to the deregulatory mode, two kinds of changes occur: first, there is less supervision by the external, law-making agency; and, second, to the extent supervision and interaction remain, the style (or mode) is more flexible, spontaneous, innovative, discretionary, and so on.

Consider each organizational dimension in turn. In the area of planning or policymaking (B1), the legalistic mode entails formal procedures, including everything from rational decision-making models like PPBS, to regular meetings of school boards with agendas. The deregulatory mode implies spontaneous interaction, muddling through, etc. The next area (B2), is 'influence or efficaciousness of client.' By this, I mean the avenues which are available to the clients of organizations to be heard and be influential, e.g., parents and schoolchildren attempting to influence educational institutions. The legalistic mode establishes formal mechanisms of influence, such as administrative hearings and litigation rights. The deregulatory alternative relies upon unstructured personal influence — what I have called 'politics.'

The third organizational activity I have called 'reliability in administration.' This refers to the means by which an external, supervisory agent seeks to effectuate the continued implementation of any policy in the day-to-day life of an organization. One aspect of reliability is the definition of obligations (B 3 a) — how is it determined that 'non-compliance' exists? Here, the legalistic mode relies upon standardization and standards (which also imply monitoring and paperwork). The non-legalistic mode is to work with loosely defined goals rather than standards and freely grant exceptions. The other aspect of reliability is obtaining compliance with the obligatory policy. Legalistically, this is done by enforcement — the definition of sanctions for non-compliance of varying degrees of seriousness, the imposition of sanctions, and so on. The non-legalistic mode is to 'professionalize' (including policy-supportive values and habit structures), lend assistance, and rely upon trust.

The Possibilities for Wholesale Delegalization or Deregulation

Equipped with a definition of legalism or 'regulationism' at the level of technique, it is now possible to evaluate the deregulation criticism at that level. Here, an important distinction must be made. There frequently are a host of discrete deregulatory options, all perfectly sensible and productive, along all of the dimensions of Table 1. Almost all that is productive about deregulatory initiatives consists of marginal adjustments in particular dimensions of legalism in specific contexts. Careful analysis might reveal, for example, that much of the paperwork associated with IEPs in special education could be dispensed with. That type of context-specific, marginal adjustment is not what I take to be the message of the deregulation critique.

In its strong form, *the deregulation critique tends to assert that,* (i) *across all dimensions of legalism, and in all regulatory contexts, it is most consistent with underlying policy, and least costly, to move as far in the direction of non-legalism as possible*; and that, (ii) *practically all actual regulatory programs undertaken by the federal government are strongly and unnecessarily legalistic in character.*

This thesis of the wholesale deregulation critique is wrong, since sometimes the deregulatory alternative is better, but not always. The generalization that legalisms are always undesirable probably originates in the true perception that legalisms are always more costly and unpleasant than voluntary (unregulated) action toward the same end. However, in this part of the paper, and often in real life, an agency outside the local organization must play the role of stimulating change, if change is to occur at all. Under those circumstances, the question of what technique of intervention will best promote the underlying policy, at the least cost, is problematical and depends upon a close analysis of the particular context. Whether the least costly intervention is nevertheless unjustifiably costly compared to the benefits involves the evaluation of goals as discussed under the section Criticisms of the Goals of Federal Intervention. Assessment of the net benefits of the intervention is, of course, logically dependent upon how far the costs of intervention may be reduced. To that extent, the general conclusion in this section that there is no policy-effective wholesale method to reduce the costs of legalism affects the overall cost-benefit analysis of legal interventions. Conservatives are right in sensing that regulation always carries a high price tag, and right in concluding that ill-conceived and low-return regulatory interventions are almost never worthwhile.

The rest of this section is organized according to a series of propositions and sub-propositions about the *relationships between legalistic and nonlegalistic techniques*. The discussion is structured in light of the relationships displayed in Table 2, and frequent references will be made to that Table.

1 *All real examples of legal interventions are mixtures of legalistic and non-legalistic techniques.*

The foundation for an understanding of legalism is the appreciation that all government interventions lie on a continuum somewhere between the purely legalistic and purely non-legalistic forms. Furthermore, the relevant policy question as to any particular type of intervention usually concerns changing the mixture of legalistic and non-legalistic elements, thereby 'moving' the 'position' of an intervention to the left or right along the dimension of Table 2.

Consider the right of parents to disapprove or veto the placement of their children in special education. A veto right is a legalistic technique (B 2 in Table 2); yet in practice, the operation and effectiveness of the right is determined by political/organizational patterns. How passive and unwilling to exercise the right are parents? Does the system obtain the prior routinized consent of the parents? How prepared are parents to contradict findings of experts influenced by perceptions about the availability and non-availability of appropriate remedial resources?

At the other extreme, relationships considered to be pure assistance have legalistic elements. An effort to enhance the bilingual capability of a school, for example, may translate into the obligatory attendance by teachers at a series of in-services.

2 *Legalisms are always costly and inefficient compared to voluntary action directed at the same end.*

The formal and external nature of legalism inevitably creates costs and inefficiencies compared to equivalently intended voluntary action. Being required to do *anything* and expecially being required to do something *specific* cannot match the effectiveness of internally motivated, adaptive behavior directed at the same underlying end.

Manifestations of the cost and inefficiency of legalism appear endlessly in the study of government programs. Some costs and inefficiencies are so common that they may be expected to occur. Among such universal problems are the following:

(i) Compliance uses scarce resources, such as personnel time for filling out reports.
(ii) Specific legal requirements against a background of divergent preferences almost always produce goal displacement, that is, organizations figure out how to comply with the literal requirement while to some degree maintaining their own contrary substantive purposes.
(iii) Mandatory requirements create unfavorable organizational morale, including dissimulation, resentment and loss of self-esteem rooted in occupational autonomy.
(iv) Because of their formality, legalisms often interfere with the very policy the law is trying to promote, as when the requirements of fiscal allocation in Title I interfere with integrated educational offerings.
(v) Legalisms tend to conflict with each other, especially when a variety of lawmaking authorities and programs regulate the same institution. An example is the complex resolution used to determine the 'eligibility' of students who qualify for both Title I and special education services.[30]

3 *In spite of the costs and inefficiencies, legalisms often are the only or best means of achieving social policy, because they also provide characteristic benefits.*

Just as legalisms are associated with characteristic costs, they tend to provide characteristic benefits. Functionally, legalisms are beneficial because they operationalize, give specific meaning to, or objectify policy. Specification is helpful in several kinds of situations.

First, there may be many possible specific ways to pursue a particular goal, but the different ways are inconsistent with each other, and one (or a limited set) must be selected in order to accomplish anything.

Desegregation is an example. Once it is decided to have racially integrated schools, in an outcome sense, a numerical definition of 'racially balanced' must be chosen. Various definitions would be reasonable, but one, or a permissible range, is necessary for coherent policy. Another example is the federal compensatory education program. The concept of 'poverty schools' must be operationalized. Many definitions are possible. Indeed, so many considerations are involved that every solution seems somewhat arbitrary. Yet, again, one coherent approach is necessary for good policy.

Specification, then, may be an aspect of orderly planning in a complex organization. An obvious question is why organizations such as schools may not be left to find specification on their own. The most common answer is that a problem of recalcitrance, distrust, unwillingness, or divergent preferences exists. If the 'outside' organization believes that the regulated organization will not develop any or sufficiently effective policies on its own, then a standard solution helps both to obtain compliance and monitor it.

In a sense, identifying the problem solved by legalisms as 'recalcitrance' is slightly misleading. A potential problem arises at the moment it is decided to have any kind of centralized policy. If the federal government is determined to accomplish *anything*, as opposed to letting states and localities do their own thing, problems of interorganizational complexity and coordination are likely to demand a coherent, streamlined and therefore highly specified program. Consider budgetary decisions. Once it is decided that budgetary decisions shall be made centrally, whether by the federal government, a school board, or the chairman of an academic department, a considerable demand for specificity and orderliness (what Max Weber called 'rationalization') is 'automatically' established. The only way for the federal government to avoid all legalisms in budgetary matters is not to collect taxes in the first place. Conservatives are right: centralism breeds legalism. Legalism is a tool of complex coordinated action.

We see here a reaffirmation of a conclusion reached earlier, that the only way for the federal government to obtain complete deregulation is to abandon all special goals in education.

4 *Real-world legal interventions often are at the point of trading off the advantages and disadvantages of more and less legalism. Therefore, close examination of particular policies is required to establish productive changes.*

Since legal interventions are designed to obtain results and counter-legalistic interests are well represented, the degree of legalism which exists is thought by its designers to be the least which is consistent with obtaining results. As a result, real legal interventions often are near the point where a decrease in legalism would sacrifice more compliance than justified by savings in cost while an increase in legalism would unacceptably elevate costs compared to gains in compliance. This cannot be taken as a justification for all legalisms, because some may be just plain stupid (teacher certification and PPBS are my candidates). Nevertheless, the possibility that a system already is near the optimum point should always be considered.

The idea of moderation is often said to be incompatible with the bureaucratic mind. Regulators often are portrayed as driven by an insatiable fetish for rules and conformity. Examination of the actual process of designing various legalisms suggests a different picture. Again and again, we see the incremental adjustment of legalism in response to feedback about program effectiveness. The typical pattern is to begin with too little legalism and gradually raise the stakes.

Title I and desegregation are good examples. Both the rules and sanctions utilized in desegregation were made more strict over a period of ten to fifteen years in response to problems of recalcitrance.[31] Similarly, Title I fiscal allocation standards were tightened up in several incremental stages as weaknesses and loopholes in the previous standards were revealed.[32]

The adjustment and compromise of legalistic requirements also occur informally. Many systems which critics of legalism would characterize as dominated by considerations of compliance and enforcement are seen by those who study them as systems of conciliation and compromise. Affirmative action laws, for example, contain legalistic sounding requirements like goals and timetables; but the reality is otherwise. In systems like affirmative action, the question of compliance/non-compliance is negotiable. Pressure toward compliance and degrees of actual compliance are serial, incremental, gradual, and open-ended. Planning to conform often is as important as actual conformity; and the plausible demonstration of good faith or reasonable effort is probably the best way to prove compliance in the practical sense of satisfying regulatory inspectors. There is, in other words, a social reconstruction of compliance at the field level which invariably compromises the stricter sounding legal requirements.[33]

5 *Improvements of legal techniques usually involve substitution of less unreasonable techniques for more unreasonable ones, rather than discovery of ideal techniques. Therefore, criticisms of the imperfections of legalism which do not examine alternative solutions are usually misleading.*[34]

The most common type of critique of legalism is a recitation of its many costs and disadvantages. These are normally taken as an indictment of the underlying program, because 'how could anything so stupid be right.' Notwithstanding its popular appeal, the logic of such criticisms is completely erroneous. A 'stupid' thing cannot be *right*, but it may nevertheless be the best of all the available alternatives and worthwhile in net terms.

Probably the most important insight to be gleaned from studying legal interventions is that there often is not much room for improvement, not because the intervention is enlightened, but because available alternatives are equally unsatisfactory. A good example is the goal of making reasonable exceptions to a law. Regulation always is 'overinclusive' in the sense that many of the regulated institutions would comply without paperwork and inspections, or would have a good reason for claiming an exception to the general rule.[35] Denunciations of this overbreadth are inconclusive, however. The relevant inquiry is a comparison of the various institutional devices available for making exceptions. That inquiry reveals serious flaws in all possibilities. For example, the most flexible possibility, unlimited administrative discretion, allows for unpredictability, arbitrariness and the frustration of protection for underprivileged groups. A system of 'waivers' (exemptions for exemplary compliance) turns out to be administratively laborious and politically unpopular; and it exempts organizations which tend to be relatively unburdened by discretionary systems.[36] A system of 'certification,' exemption of all but the worst cases, may focus enforcement where improved compliance is impossible (because the worst cases sometimes lack the capacity to improve).

A Deregulation-Sensitive Federal Role for the Eighties

In particular circumstances deregulation is a good idea. It may even be conceded that Great Society educational programs were in need of discipline, and, therefore, that there is a presumption in favor of the effectiveness of deregulation. Nevertheless, deregulation must be selective — it cannot be presumed beneficial in any particular context. Examples of what I believe to be promising deregulatory options in federal educational policy are suggested below. To follow the earlier organization of the chapter, examples are given at the level of goals, form and technique.

Deregulation at the Level of Goals: Reordering Federal Priorities

Deregulatory philosophy applied at the level of the goals suggests that emphasis be given to goals which are worthwhile, effective, necessary (in the sense that the states are unwilling or unable to fill the need), and strongly federal in character. Applying these criteria to existing areas of federal intervention suggests a reordering of priorities something like this:

1 *For Emphasis*
   (a) Compensatory Education
   (b) Youth Employment Programs
   (c) Immigration Problems (including language)
2 *For De-emphasis*
   (a) Vocational Education
   (b) Special Education
   (c) Student Loans for Higher Education

The programs to be emphasized: respond to needs which most states do not place a high priority on, or lack capacity (fiscal and technical) to cope with (for example, language training of immigrant groups); involve basic access to education rather than incremental improvements (see 'Federal Programs are not Effective' page 195); and are strongly federal in character because they are concerned with immigration, functioning of the national economy, and equality of opportunity.

One characteristic of the suggested priorities can hardly escape notice: the de-emphasized programs are more popular. This is because of the 'paradox of innovation' mentioned earlier in the chapter.[37] Needs unmet by the states are not popular. Programs which could be carried on by the states without federal help are popular and therefore difficult to terminate.

Deregulation at the Level of Form: the Continued Vitality of Conditional Grants

Deregulatory philosophy does not suggest major changes in the basic form of federal-state relations. The conditional or categorical grant is an effective compromise of federal and state interests; and a better one has not been suggested. States have the option to withdraw from the relationship; and federal money pays for expenses of the state incurred to comply with federal requirements. The existing practice of limiting direct regulation to bona fide civil rights situations is proper. At the other extreme, every evidence suggests that block grants do not work except as general aid (or revenue sharing). And, again, while general aid satisfies the deregulatory goal of few legal requirements, it violates every deregulatory precept about the selection of distinctive federal goals.

Among the types of categorical grants, there is support for a change of emphasis. It may be time to abandon the 'effective strings' type (see Table 1). Although effective strings are the least restrictive form consistent with achieving narrowly-defined federal objectives, because of their strong emphasis on fiscal accountability, they seem to interfere with educational effectiveness. In a sense, the overall lack of restrictiveness comes at the cost of inefficient and counterproductive details.

Streamlining is best obtained by direct service requirements. Under this arrangement, the government specifies a complete educational program or supplement as the condition of receiving funds. Expenditure of the funds is monitored to prevent abuse but not to ensure educational effectiveness. The requirements may be standardized, as with PL 94-142, or custom fit to the local district or school, as in the grant competition model of bilingual education, or the 'negotiated contract' model of the Youth Act.[38]

Deregulation of Technique: a Multitude of Contexts

Neither more nor less regulation can routinely be presumed beneficial and, therefore, all efforts should be concentrated on identifying marginal improvements in particular contexts. Given that perspective, it is impossible to make any comprehensive recommendations for change. On the other hand, the lack of promise of across-the-board deregulation could easily conceal the very great possibilities of deregulation in particular contexts. To prevent that false impression, I would like to suggest a number of specific possibilities here.

Often what seems to make a legal intervention successful is discovering a workable combination of compliance and cooperation. The prototype is probably school desegregation where an early state of recalcitrance and hostility must give way to a later stage of cooperation between court and school system if educational progress is to occur.[39]

One technique for moving in that direction is the use of 'contract' rather than regulation. Grants for bilingual education are awarded on a competitive basis to school districts which submit the best proposals.[40] The ill-fated Youth Act contained provisions by which the federal government could enter into detailed performance contracts with schools serving disadvantaged children. The advantage is that specific, 'tough' goals for change are obtained through consent rather than regulation. Another technique is sharp isolation or confinement of necessary legalisms in such a way that they do not interfere with the educational process. Still another approach is 'assistance with compliance.' Paul Berman correctly reminds us that many school districts do not know how to comply with mandates requiring technical and organizational change.[41]

Finally, much could be accomplished by close examination of what aspects of particular legalisms are functional versus what aspects could be eliminated. Consider as an illustration the problem of conflicts between the requirements of different programs.

Conflicts between federal programs involve redundant, wasteful political and administrative structures; ambiguities, conflicts and wrongheaded rules about how to combine or not combine funds from different programs, and so on.[42] A substantial portion of the problem seems to be the confusion and misunderstanding generated by the complexity and technicality of the programs themselves and the rules for reconciling the requirements of different programs. Conflicts between programs appear to be a blind spot in the regulatory process. Program designers tend to think about the purpose and mechanics of each program in isolation from other programs which apply to the same institution.[43]

The existence of this blind spot suggests the institutionalization of a regulatory counter-force. Research which examines the interaction of programs at the school, district, and state levels is a good beginning. A true solution may need to go further and create an independent regulatory agency with authority to reconcile conflicts in an educationally sensible rather than a legally precise way. Because they think in terms of program purposes, supporters of individual programs are often somewhat imperialistic. It may seem reasonable to an advocate of compensatory education that 'PL 94-142 money' spent on a particular child should not discharge the Title I obligation (otherwise, 'what do "we" get for "our" money?'). From the perspective of the larger federal government and the school, however, the only important issue is that the combined funds promote the objectives of both programs in a general, programmatic sense. An agency with a nonprogrammatic mission may be needed to impose this sort of flexibility on the process.

Conclusion

The constant theme of this chapter has been the need to be careful and precise about the deregulation critique. Benefits of deregulation exist, but they do not exist wholesale, and they must be obtained through carefully designed solutions.

The most conspicuous problem with the theme is the clumsiness and imprecision of politics. A certain amount of undifferentiated social indignation is required to overcome the inertia and lethargy of the regulatory process. If this spirit is applied full strength to government programs, the result is likely to be wreckage rather than efficiency. The typical pattern tends to be one of new programs erected on the ashes of the old. This, too, is wasteful; and there are hopeful signs that, with a growing appreciation of the problem, deregulatory discipline can be institutionalized within the regulatory process itself.

Notes

1 See, PELTZMAN, S. (1976) 'Toward a more general theory of regulation,' *J.L. & Econ.*, 19 p. 211; STIGLER, G. (1971) 'The theory of economic regulation,' *Bell J. Econ. & Management Sci.*, 2, p. 3; STIGLER, G. (1975) *The Citizen In The State: Essays on Regulation.* See also, BREYER, S. *Administrative Law and Regulatory Policy.*

2 BARDACH, E. and KAGAN, R. (1982) *Going By the Book* Temple.

3 See, GRAGLIA, L. (1979) *Disaster by Decree.*

4 For statistics on special education, see KIRP, D.L., BUSS, W. and KURILOFF, P. (1974), 'Legal reform of special education: Empirical studies and procedural proposals,' *Calif. L. Rev.*, 62, pp. 40, 60 and 63. Exclusionary aspects in the bilingual area may be seen in *Lau v. Nichols*, 414 U.S. 563 (1974), codified by Congress in the Equal Educational Opportunity Act of 1974, 20 USC sec. 1703 (1976).

5 'The quality of education today offers no glowing evidence of the magical powers of the federal government, despite years of massive effort.' BELL, T. (1981) 'Comment, Block Grants: The secretary explains the rationale for consolidating federal education programs,' *Education Times*, 2, 4 May.

6 20 USC sec. 1415 (1976).

7 BLASCHKE, C. (1979) *Case Study of the Impact of Implementation of PL 94-142*, Education Turnkey Systems, Executive Summary; STEARNS, M., GREENE, D., DAVID, J. (1979) *Local Implementation of PL 94-142*, Stanford Research Institute, December. See also, BICKEL, W.E., (1981) *The Placement Process in Special Education With Special Reference to Issues of Minority Representation* (unpublished draft, 19 August).

8 SMITH, M.S., Director, Wisconsin Center for Education Research, in conversation with the author.

9 The importance for income and status of educational attainment (years educated) as opposed to quality of education was one of the basic findings of *Inequality.* JENCKS, C., SMITH, M., ACLAND, H., BANE, M.J., COHEN, D., GINTIS, H., HEYNS, B., MICHELSON, S., (1972) *Inequality: A Reassessment of the Effects of Family and Schooling In America*; see also, TURNBULL, B., SMITH, M. and GINSBURG, A. (1981) 'Issues for a new administration: The federal role in education,' *American Journal of Education*, 396, pp. 407–9, August.

10 The basic legislation was the National Defense Education Act, 20 USC sees. 401, pp. 541–2 (1976), COHEN, (1968) 'An idea that grew, the National Defense Education Act,' *American Education*, 4, pp. 2–3, September; NOVAK, J. (1969) 'A case study of curriculum change — science since PSSC,' *School Science and Math*, 69, p. 374, May; ROTHSCHILD, (1968) 'The NDEA decade,' *American Education*, 4, pp. 4–11, September.

11 See, RODGERS, H., and BULLOCK, C., (1976) *Coercion to Compliance.*

12 See, WILSON, J. 'The rise of the bureaucratic state,' in RABIN, R., (1979) *Perspectives on The Administrative Process* 16, pp. 22–8. One source of program self-penetration is the so-called 'iron triangle,' an alliance between local interest groups, the bureaucracy, and supportive special committees in Congress.
13 The power of Congress to regulate interstate commerce rests ultimately on the inability of states to control actions beyond their borders. See *NLRB v. Jones & Laughlin Steel Corp*. 301 US 1 (1937).
14 Cover letter to David Stockman from Education Secretary T.H. Bell transmitting Department's consolidation proposal; BELL, T. (1981) 'Comment, Block Grants: The secretary explains the rationale for consolidating federal education programs', *Education Times* 2, 4 May; Representative JOHN ASHBROOK, (1981), 'Comment,' *Education Times* 2, 10 August.
15 Civil rights statutes which apply to schools and do not depend upon the pressence of federal financial assistance are rare. The main one is 42 USC sec. 1983 (1976), which creates a private cause of action for violations of the Constitution and other federal laws. See YUDOF, M. (1976) 'Liability for constitutional torts and the risk-averse public school official,' *S. Calif. L. Rev*, 49, 1322. Some statues which are commonly thought to be obligatory in fact apply on their face only to programs receiving federal financial assistance. They thus belong in the 'any grantee' type of conditional grant discussed in the next paragraph. See especially Title VI of the Civil Rights Act of 1964, 42 USC sec. 2000d (1976) and Section 504 of the Rehabilitation Act of 1973, 29 USC sec. 794 (1976).
16 For example, The Emergency School Aid Act, 20 USC sec. 1601 (1976) (aid for desegregation).
17 See, HASTINGS, A. (1981) *More Ways Than One: Federal Strategies to Equalize Access in Education and Health Care Policy* (unpublished paper) prepared for the School Finance Project, U.S. Dept. of Education, September. Just how crosscutting Title IX is a matter of dispute. See *City College v. Bell* 104 Sup. Ct. 1211 (1984). (Sex discrimination barred solely in 'program or activity' receiving federal funds.)
18 20 USC secs. 1681–1686 (Supp. III, 1979).
19 3 CFR 339 (1964–1965 Compilation), 30 *Fed. Reg*. 12319 (1965).
20 Family Education Rights and Privacy Act of 1974, 20 USC sec. 438 (a) (1) (A) (1976). See (1976) 'Comment' *Wis L. Rev*. p. 975.
21 The federal share of the estimated costs of complying with services for the handicapped mandated by PL 94-142, 20 USC sec. 1401 (1976), was about 12 per cent in early 1981. TURNBULL, B., SMITH, M. and GINSBURG, A. (1981) *op. cit.* p. 400.
22 In *New Mexico Assoc. for Retarded Citizens v. New Mexico*, 495 F. Supp. 391 (D. New Mexico, 1980), the court held that sec. 504 of the Rehabilitation Act and its regulations required New Mexico to provide a free, appropriate education to all handicapped children. Under that holding, it would not help a state much to withdraw from 94-142, as New Mexico did, because Sec. 504 applies if there is any federal assistance.
23 See BARRO, S. (1978) 'Federal education goals and policy instruments: An assessment of the strings attached to categorical grants in education,' in TIMPANE, M., (Ed.) *The Federal Interest in Financing Schooling*, p. 229.
24 BARRO, S. (1978) *op. cit.*, pp. 257–60.
25 The most conspicuous recent example is Chapter 2 of the Education Consolidation and Improvement Act of 1981, PL 97-35, Subtitle D, Sec. 551-96; 20 USC 3801 (1981).
26 'Nearly all such studies have found that a large fraction of external aid tends to be substituted for the local district's own revenue.' BARRO, S. (1978) *op. cit.*, p. 237.
27 See generally, BERMAN, P. (1980) 'Thinking about program adaptive implementation: matching strategies to situations,' in INGRAM H. and MANN, D. (Eds) *Why*

Policies Succeed or Fail, Sage Yearbooks in Politics and Public Policy, p. 205; Berman, P. (1978) 'The study of macro- and micro- implementation,' *Pub. Policy* 26 (2), p. 157; Elmore, R. & McLauglin, M. (1981) *Strategic Choice in Federal Education Policy* (unpublished paper).

28 If possible, Berman recommends 'matching, mixing and switching' implementation strategies. Berman, P. (1980) *op. cit.* p. 221.

29 See Kagan, R.A., (1981) *Regulating Business, Regulating Schools: The Problem of Regulatory Unreasonableness* Project Report 81A-14, Institute for Research on finance and Governance, Stanford University in this volume.

30 See Berman, P. (1979) *Case Studies of Overlap Between Title I and P.L. 94–142 Services for Handicapped Children*, SRI International, Menlo Park; Hill, (1979) *Do Federal Programs Interfere with One Another?*, Rand Corporation Paper Series, p. 6-6416, September.

31 See Rodgers, H., and Bullock, C., (1976) *op. cit.*

32 See National Institute of Education, (1977) *Administration of Compensatory Education*; Kirst, M., and Jung, R., (1980) 'The utility of a longitudinal approach in assessing implementation: a thirteen year view of Title I ESEA,' *Education Evaluation Policy Analysis* II No.5, Amer. Educ. Research Assoc., September–October.

33 Reis, A. and Bitterman, A. *The Policing of Organizational Life* (unpublished paper); Hawkins, K. (1982) *Environment and Enforcement: The Social Construction of Pollution*, Oxford University Press.

34 The importance of comparing one imperfect institution with another, instead of, by implication, with some non-existent perfect institution, is stressed in Komesar, (1981) 'In search of a general approach to legal analysis,' *Mich. L. Rev*, 79, p. 1350.

35 The central problem of regulatory unreasonableness, and therefore the prime cost of regulation, is often said to be that requirements suitable for controlling worst case offenders are applied to *all*, including those who would comply voluntarily or exceed minimum requirements. Turnbull, B., Smith, M. and Ginsburg, A. (1981) *op. cit*, p. 405; Kagan, R.A. (1981) *op. cit*; Bardach, E. and Kagan, R. (1982) *op. cit*; Berman, P. (1981) *From Compliance to Learning: Implementing Legally-Induced Reform*, Institute for Finance and Governance, Stanford University, August.

36 Murphy, J. (1981) *Differential Treatment of the States, A Good Idea or Wishful Thinking?* (unpublished paper) 25, August.

37 See text accompanying note 12.

38 See, the Youth Act of 1980, secs. 411–13, H.R. 6711, 96th Cong. 2d Sess., 126 *Cong. Rec.* p. 7846, 26, August, 1980.

39 See Clune, W. *Courts and Teaching* (unpublished paper) (forthcoming as a chapter in a National Institute of Education collection).

40 20 USC sec. 8806 (1976).

41 Berman, P. (1981) *op. cit.*

42 See note 29.

43 See Knapp, M., Stearns, M., Turnbull, B., David, J. and Peterson, S. (1983) *The Cumulative Effects of Federal Education Policies on Schools and Districts*, SRI International, Project #3590, January.

Part Two
Legalization and Education

1 Historical Context

Toward a Social History of Law and Public Education

David Tyack
Stanford University

Introduction

Before the last generation, writing on law and education tended to take two directions. One has been the study of landmark decisions of federal and state supreme courts that presumably 'settled' disputed basic questions. That has been the scholarly high road. The second, less lofty tradition of writing on 'school law' has been the pragmatic textbook telling educators (and the lawyers they hired) how court decisions and statutes have shaped what they must and cannot do.[1] Anthropologists, political scientists, sociologists, and historians have gone beyond the written decisions of judges and the structures and processes of legal institutions to ask how law and society interact. 'The legal system, described solely in terms of formal structure and substance, is like an enchanted courtroom, pertrified, immobile, under some odd, eternal spell,' writes Lawrence Friedman. 'What gives life and reality to the legal system is the outside, social world.' A social history of the law and education guided by such a perspective has yet to be written, though the work of Friedman and Willard Hurst on other aspects of legal history and the contemporary analyses of law and education by scholars like David Kirp and Mark Yudof suggest the possible contours of such a study.[2]

Why might a social history of the law and education be of interest? In the last generation there has been much writing about the litigiousness of American society and legal activism in public education has drawn fire from critics. Yet, it is often forgotten that law has always been an important instrument in shaping public schooling as well as a mirror of its goals, structures and processes. Not all groups have had equal access to legislatures or courts, of course, nor have all conflicts been defined as legal ones. The very ability to define an issue as a legal question is an important index of the relative power of groups or individuals. The nature of the legal profession — its concern with precedent, its opaque language — often makes law a screen to obscure social change and to blur conflicts of values and interests. Particularly in times of social stress and structural transformation, people often employ the law to create a real or imaginary continuity with the past which may camouflage — intentionally or unintentionally — what is really happening. For this reason, a social history of the law should attend to the politics of legalization, to whose interests are being served and whose are not. Uproar over recent litigiousness may signal, in part, concern over new and hitherto powerless actors gaining new influence.[3]

In this exploratory chapter, I suggest what might be some of the issues which a social history of the law might address. I am interested in how the functions and operation of the law — both legislative and court-based — changed over time and what were alternative non-legal ways of expressing consensus and resolving disputes. Statutory law and court law often worked in dialectic, I believe, and hence it is a mistake to treat them in isolation from one another. Landmark cases are surely important, but they need to be placed within the broader context of institutional history and societal values and interests, not treated as if they were the result of an hermetic legal evolution or automatically implemented in practice. A social history of the law in education needs to probe as well the origins and consequences of everyday legislation and litigation.

Briefly, the argument runs in this fashion. Advocates of the common school in the mid-nineteenth century used state legislation as a mode of *enticement*, as a way to persuade their fellow citizens through moral appeals or to attract them through state subsidies to establish public schools and to send their children to them. Such laws in education parallel a broader trend, documented by Willard Hurst, to release and channel energies in economic and institutional development. State constitutional provisions and school laws constructed a framework of governance and finance for common schools. Such legislation expressed what reformers believed to be a pervasive belief system. Through such laws, the crusaders reminded Americans of their duty, the educational correlates of their civic and moral convictions. The power of the state to actually enforce such laws, however, was minimal. Local citizens needed to be convinced that they should act. The main concern of leaders at both the state and local levels was to *attract* support for public schools in what was, in effect, a diverse buyers' market of schooling.

Toward the end of the nineteenth century, a somewhat different emphasis appeared in school legislation, that of *normative dominance*. By then, public education had become so firmly established that its only major competitor was the Catholic parochial school system (by 1880, about 98 per cent of rural students went to public schools). But people worried that the older civic and moral values — assumed by the earlier crusaders to be self-evident to responsible citizens — were threatened and hence the destiny of the republic clouded. Self-consciously, they turned to legislatures to give their own values what Friedman calls a 'monopoly of respectability.' The Women's Christian Temperance Union (WCTU), for example, persuaded all of the states to pass laws requiring instruction in the evils of alcohol. Patriotic groups anxious about social conflict or the assimilation of immigrants pressured for compulsory instruction in American principles, including flag salutes. Nativists demanded laws mandating that elementary teaching be in English only, reversing a more tolerant policy that earlier had commonly left such decisions to local communities. The new legislation reflected a breakdown of the older confidence in the force of voluntarism, a fear of pluralism, and an increasing conviction that the child was to be socialized in a manner dictated by the state and not the parents.

Professional leaders from the Progressive era onwards shared many of these concerns for proper socialization, but they also pressed for state legislation to *codify* schooling according to their own 'scientific' administrative models. They sought to standardize education by redesigning school codes and by increasing the power of states to enforce compliance. Centralization of control in city schools and state systems reflected their desire to turn educational decision-making over to the experts and to widen the purview of administrative law. This era saw increased regulation promoted by the professionals themselves — for example, to consolidate rural schools. In turn, such changes weakened previous means of conflict resolution and lessened the powers of local school boards and parents.

In the years following *Brown v. Board of Education* (1954) much has changed. Dispossessed groups have *challenged* through legislation and the courts what they perceived as an unequal and unjust system of public schools. Basic cleavages and inequities in society have become increasingly apparent, and the law has become a new force for social change in education as in the society as a whole.[4]

These emphases in educational law — enticement, normative dominance, codification, and challenge to the existing order — were not mutually exclusive and successive stages. But relative emphases in school legislation did change in different periods, as did the use of the courts to contest such laws. In the formative stage of the public schools, few Americans took their disputes over public education to the courts. People in local communities had many ways of settling conflicts in their one-room schools, much as church members adjudicated differences in small congregations. The cases that did reach appellate courts overwhelmingly involved disputes over finances and governmental arrangements. Going to court was probably a last resort, except to enforce or contest contracts, where legal procedures were common and well-established. When dominant cultural groups used laws to enforce their values on others, however, an increasing number of citizens went to court to protest the right of the state to intervene in matters previously left to the discretion of parents and ethnocultural groups in local communities. And when professional educators used state school codes to enforce their version of the one best system, the courts became a safety valve for opposition once expressed through other channels.

Throughout American history, the bedrock of cases probably continued to consist of the traditional fiscal, contractual, and governmental issues, but new types of law brought new challenges. And in the last generation, advocates of dispossessed groups, spurred on by major movements for social justice, began to introduce new issues of individual rights and equity that pushed the courts into fresh domains of educational policy. The dialectic between statutory and court law shaped the development of public schooling in profound ways.

Consensus and Conflict in the Common School Crusade

The common school crusaders of the mid-nineteenth century sought to persuade, entice, shame, frighten, and inspire their fellow citizens to support public education. They wanted to attract everyone to public schools — rich and poor, native-born and immigrant, male and female, and people of different religious persuasions. They had few powers of coercion in most states and communities, and relied instead on mobilizing a social movement that drew, in its methods, ideology, and membership, on the example of the expansionist Protestant churches of the period.

To understand the use of law in this campaign, it is useful to recall the cultural values and the social and political setting of the educational revival. A large number of the common school leaders believed, quite literally, that the United States was God's country. They assumed that all right-thinking citizens basically shared their Protestant-republican ideology and needed to be reminded of the duties entailed by that system of belief. Thus, when they argued for public education, they based their case not simply on instrumental political and economic values but on common assumptions about a providential plan. They sought to align the institutions and laws of man with the intent of God.[5]

Common school crusaders operating in communities across the settled states and frontiers used multiple strategies to create the public school system. Like ministers building churches, or reformers arousing citizens through voluntary associations, they relied heavily on appeals to common religious and socio-political ideals. They sought action based on shared convictions. State constitutions and statutes provided one kind of idealized framework for this mobilization at the local level. Many of the early hortatory preambles to constitutional provisions for education expressed the values that comprised, they thought, this agreement on cultural values. Over and over again, they declared that intelligence and virtue were necessary for the stability of republican government and the preservation of the rights and liberties of the people, that political wisdom, morality, and religion were inextricable.[6]

Although moral exhortation was the main form of enticement, constitutions and laws also took advantage of monetary inducements and local rivalries. Laws established a framework for creating, governing, and financing local districts (or ratified them where they existed already). But in an era when states had weak or nonexistent machinery for actually enforcing the laws, much depended on local initiative. Districts could receive apportionments from state or county school funds only if they met the (minimal) state regulations, and the strong force of neighborly competition between townships or settlements to secure those funds impelled many to action. Laws in sparsely settled states or territories were often framed to stimulate such emulation. But school codes described ideals as much as they prescribed penalties and rewards. The state superintendent of education was expected to inspire teachers with the latest pedagogical methods, to rouse the citizens to build better schoolhouses, and to try (as best he could) to create a uniform system.[7]

The school laws provided a blueprint to the local citizens for a uniform system of common schools: free, universal, public in support, and unconstrained by sectarian and politically partisan influence. The public, not the bureaucrat, was the real keeper of the model. The law was not the esoteric domain of the professional but a guide accessible to the people who actually built the system: local citizens. Like law in many other fields — land entitlements, business contracts, incorporation — educational law was designed in large part to release and channel energy, not to curb it.

Conflicts clearly did arise over public schools all across the nation, despite the reformers' desire to base public education upon consensus. Local citizens quarreled about who was to run the schools, how, and to what end; about district boundaries and tax rates; about contracts; about questions of religion and partisan politics; and about a host of other issues. But relatively few of these conflicts ended up in court.

The appendix to this chapter describes a foray into quantitative analysis of issues litigated in courts during the nineteenth century. The authors of that appendix and I are quite aware of the limitations of this preliminary study. We rely on the categories of analysis conceived by the lawyers who compiled the *Centennial Digest* for the West Publishing Company, and these categories may reflect more the professional concerns of lawyers of the time than the present-day interests of social historians. No one knows to what degree reported appellate cases are a representative sample of all court cases. But bearing these cautions in mind, and recognizing that this broad analysis should be supplemented by careful state and local studies of court records, we present some of our findings in Table 1 and Figure 1.

There are some tentative observations and hypotheses one may draw from the data and some lurking puzzles. The first observation based on Table 1 is that the absolute number of litigated issues is small. The entire nineteenth century produced fewer cases than did most of the separate decades of the twentieth century (I shall return to this point later). Second, the court volume of school litigation increased over time (the last column, on the 1890s, covers only the years 1890–1896). Third, almost 90 per cent of the issues dealt with finance and governance (for the categories included, see the appendix). Fourth, the category listed as 'other' increased over time to 15 per cent in the 1890s; this includes what the lawyers listed under such rubrics as 'private claims against districts,' 'teachers (appointment and removal),' and 'pupils and conduct and discipline of schools.'

Figure 1 standardizes the rates of litigation by population and plots those

Table 1 Distribution of litigated issues pertaining to schools, by type of issue and by decade (Number of issues in parentheses)

Type of Issue	Before 1820	1820–1829	1830–1839	1840–1849	1850–1859	1860–1869	1870–1879	1880–1889	1890–1896	Totals
Finance	63.2 (12)	60.9 (14)	43.8 (35)	45.5 (97)	52.0 (166)	45.8 (146)	47.7 (305)	49.5 (409)	45.9 (339)	47.8 (1523)
Governance	31.6 (6)	34.8 (8)	50.0 (40)	48.4 (103)	40.0 (130)	43.3 (138)	41.3 (264)	38.1 (315)	39.2 (289)	40.6 (1293)
Other*	5.3 (1)	4.3 (1)	6.2 (5)	6.1 (13)	8.9 (29)	10.9 (35)	11.0 (70)	12.3 (102)	14.9 (110)	11.5 (367)
Totals	0.6 (19)	0.7 (23)	2.5 (80)	6.7 (213)	10.2 (325)	10.0 (319)	20.1 (639)	26.0 (826)	23.2 (738)	100.0 (3182)

* Other includes the selection and appointment of teachers, their removal and discharge; the admission and attendance of pupils, their classification and pupil discipline and instruction.

Figure 1: *Educational litigiousness by region (see Appendix for state listings within region)*

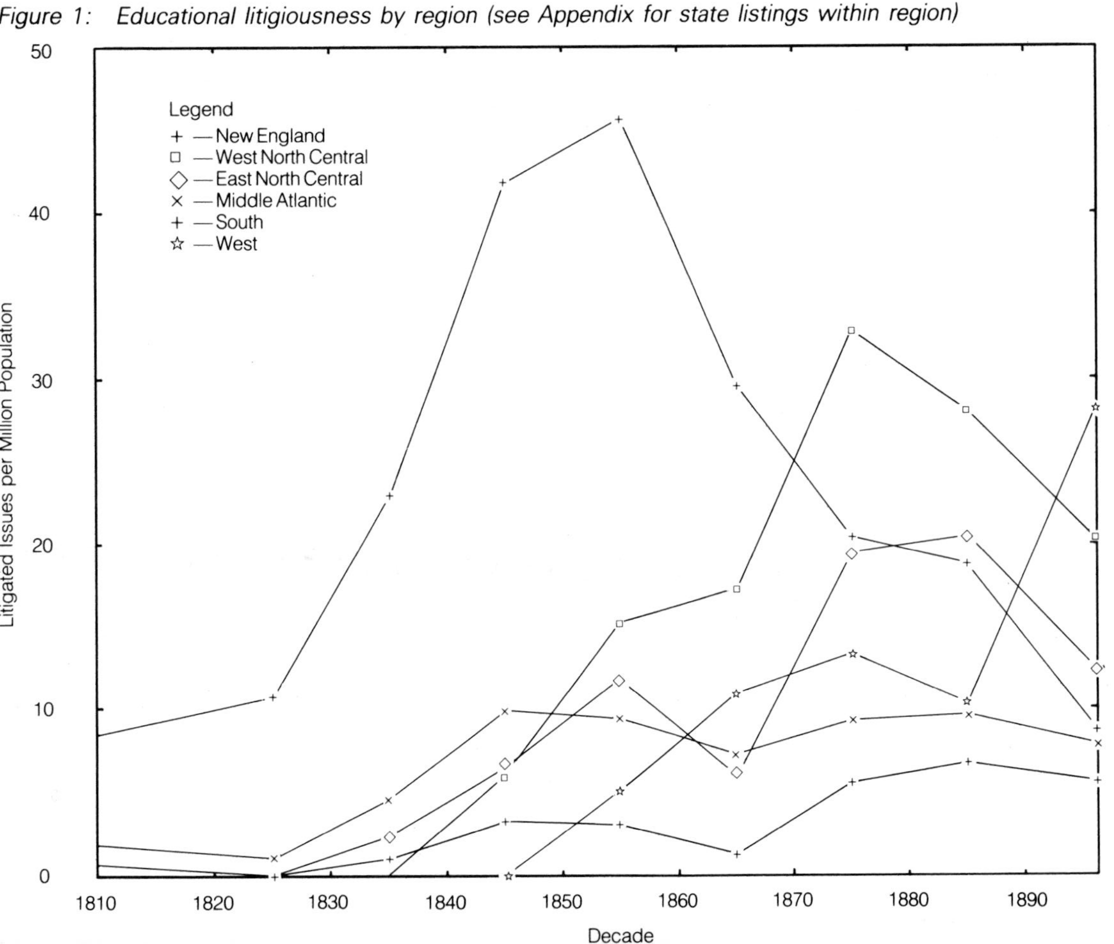

rates over time by census regions. The variations suggest some hypotheses. First, the pattern of a steep rise in rates of litigation followed by drops in New England and the North Central states (paralleled to a degree by the Mountain and Pacific states) suggests a rough correlation between legislation establishing school systems and challenges in the courts, varying over time as the common school moved westward. Second, the relatively high rate of litigation in the early years of the common school crusade may have set legal precedents and clarified certain kinds of issues when later states established their own systems (it was common for western states to copy eastern constitutional provisions and statutes). Third, the very low rates of litigation in the South suggest a quite different political-legal culture as well as retardation in the growth of public education in that region.[8]

The paucity of appellate cases does suggest that it took a strong motive — most often a monetary one — to push Americans into the courthouse over educational disputes. Even the few (seven) school cases that found their way into the US Supreme Court were overwhelmingly fiscal in character during the nineteenth century: with one exception, they primarily involved bonds and taxes.[9]

As Lawrence Friedman points out, average Americans of the nineteenth century generally did not seek redress of grievances in court. Litigation became increasingly costly, decisions were often delayed by logjams in the courts, and legal processes seemed technical and impersonal. The mutual interdependence of people living in small communities probably also discouraged litigation. During the entire nineteenth century, there were only four cases involving compulsory school attendance, for example. A school official in Nevada suggested why: in the rural sections of his state, the compulsory law 'is a dead letter, and will remain so as long as the initiative for the enforcement is in the hands of the trustee. They simply will not swear out warrants for the arrest of their neighbors.'[10]

Americans in local communities did have a particular legal recourse other than the courts, however, if they did not like the general laws their legislatures passed. They could, and did — in large numbers — go to their state legislatures to secure new and special laws adapted to their own local needs. They could ask their own representative to introduce special acts that enabled them to change the rules for electing school directors, alter school boundaries, borrow money, build schoolhouses, and accomplish many other purposes. From 1851 to 1855, the Ohio legislature passed 228 such acts; by 1873, they totaled 982. Legislatures in many other states proved to be similarly responsive to local influentials. Thus, before the movement to establish uniform school codes in the Progressive era, when such special acts were condemned as 'weeds in our legislative garden,' local people who disliked general laws could secure a special dispensation, could settle local disputes by going to the legislature, or could secure legal authorization for new bond levies or taxes.[11]

The most prevalent and important conflicts over public education in the mid-nineteenth century were not battles between state authorities and local officials — for the 'system' of public schools was very loosely articulated — but rather controversies that arose within communities (and between neighboring communities, for local rivalries were common). They argued over which teacher to hire or fire (ability to discipline was often an issue — was the teacher too harsh or soft?); whether to read the Bible, and if so, which version; whether to permit teaching in foreign languages; whether to raise taxes or lower them; what kind of schoolhouse or facilities to provide; what textbooks to use; when to open and close school — important in agricultural communities that needed children's labor; who should get contracts for goods and services; and the list goes on.[12]

People had many other ways of avoiding, settling, or aggravating their quarrels, quite apart from courts or legislative appeals. They could elect new school trustees who agreed with their views. They could take a dispute before a respected member of the community — often a minister, accustomed to controversy in his church. Sometimes a faction might simply solve the matter by force, as when a group of Iowa farmers moved a schoolhouse a mile by oxen one night because they did not like its location. If parents did not like a school policy or a teacher, they could simply withdraw their children. And in the highly mobile society of the nineteenth century, Americans could decide to move on to a new community where the schools were more to their liking.[13]

What is more striking than conflict in the mid-nineteenth-century public school, however, is the relative agreement that prevailed in most communities. People accustomed to competing in religion, in party politics, and in economic life found enough common ground in their values and interests to build together a common school system. In this process, the enticements of law played a part by expressing common aspirations and authorizing a structure of governance and financial reward for compliance. The courts offered a safety valve for some to resolve conflicts. But litigation remained at the periphery of the campaign, not the center.

The Quest for 'Normative Dominance'

In the last quarter of the nineteenth century, when the public school became well-established as the mainstream of elementary education, there was a gradual shift in state legislation from enticement to coercion, from trying to persuade all groups to support the common school to using it as a tool for certain groups to achieve what Friedman calls 'normative dominance,' to give particular values the authority of law. Worried about what they took to be a declining consensus on the earlier Protestant-republican ideology, dismayed by urban ills, concerned about the assimilation of new immigrant groups, and fearful of sectional and class conflicts, organized WASP pressure groups prevailed on states to pass laws that gave them a 'monopoly of respectability' in their competition with other status groups.[14]

'Normative dominance' was, of course, not a new phenomenon. Value-free schooling is an impossibility. Even a highly pluralistic form of education that fosters appreciation for diverse cultures and opinions is itself based on a particular ethical vision and attempts to socialize children to tolerance and appreciation of difference. The founders of public education clearly wished their values to prevail in the classroom. But during the middle of the nineteenth century, many issues that divided the larger society were presumed best solved by local public authorities or by leaving them to voluntary moral suasion. Often school promoters wished to avoid divisive questions in the interest of finding a consensus in which all could share. Mostly Anglo-Saxon Protestant and native born, exemplars of Victorian morality, they assumed that all other responsible people would share their advocacy of Bible reading, civic instruction, teaching about the evils of alcohol and tobacco, and the need to Americanize the foreign-born.[15]

Towards the end of the century and during the Progressive era, however, certain ethnocultural groups decided that they should enforce their values on others in public education through legislation. Americans who believed that the United States was not only God's country but also *their* nation — mostly native-born Anglo-Saxon citizens of pietist Protestant persuasion and respectable station — decided that their preferred future required the force of state sanction and that they could no longer rely on voluntary action or on unselfconscious consensus.

Religion was a major arena of ethnocultural conflict in education. Most of these disputes were fought out in local communities without recourse to the courts or legislatures; indeed, sometimes they led to pitched battles in the streets between Protestants and Catholics. Typically, arguments over religion were not perceived so much as issues of constitutional rights as they were tests of sheer power — who had the majority? Beset by such conflict, school people often preferred a watered-down pan-Protestant moral teaching rather than a decisive legal solution that might alienate important factions, and in most communities teachers did employ prayers and read the Bible.[16]

When contestants in local communities did take religious issues to courts — normally over the use of the Bible — the decisions usually favored majority rule over individual rights of conscience. In a study of twenty-five cases in nineteen states from 1854 to 1924, Otto Hamilton found that three-quarters of the protesters lost (three-fifths of these complainants were Catholic). The chief argument used in favor of religion in the curriculum was that it was essential to the teaching of morality and therefore to the preservation of the state.[17]

Although only Massachusetts had required the reading of the Bible during the nineteenth century, a total of thirty-six states passed legislation during the twentieth century permitting or requiring the reading of the Bible, while some states forbade the teaching of evolution or otherwise specified religious orthodoxy. Once transmitted in an unselfconscious way in homogeneously Protestant communities, religion became in the early twentieth century a matter for legislation by evangelical interest groups. What had once been safely left to voluntary action now seemed so endangered that the state must act.[18]

Impelled by a similar certainty about public evils and the need for educational solutions, other private groups pressed for mandatory instruction in American history and civics. These state laws, reflected a concern for national unity inspired by wars and worry about radicalism and the assimilation of immigrants. A major vehicle for inculcating patriotism was United States history, required in 30 states by 1903. The American Bar Association lobbied so successfully to require teaching about the American constitution that by 1923 twenty-three states prescribed the subject.[19] Legislation on flag salutes and ceremonial uses of the stars and stripes exemplified the doctrinaire character of such socialization in civics. New York enacted the first requirement of a flag salute the day after the Spanish-American War began, and was soon joined by three other states; six states mandated flag salutes as a result of World War I.[20]

Another important kind of state legislation — one that aroused great political controversy between ethnic groups in the latter two decades of the nineteenth century — concerned language policy, especially compulsory instruction in English. During the mid-nineteenth century, such decisions were customarily left to local communities. Fear of unassimilated immigrants and radicalism at the end of the century and during World War I, however, strengthened the power of assimilationists. By 1903, fourteen states required public elementary shcools to teach only in English, a number that swelled to thirty-four by 1923. During World War I, the National Security League also campaigned actively against the teaching of German in both elementary and high schools; partly as a result of their efforts, enrollments in high-school German classes fell from 24.4 per cent of students in 1915 to less than one per cent in 1922.[21]

There were few court cases challenging the new language restrictions and compulsory instruction in patriotism, just as there were few questioning the ceremonial uses of religion in public education. Some cases — including the landmark decisions of *Meyer v. Nebraska* (1923), *Pierce v. Society of the Sisters* (1925), and *West Virginia State Board of Education v. Barnette* (1943) — did test the limits of coercion. What is striking in retrospect in these cases is the large zone of discretion still allowed legislators and public school officials in *Meyer* and *Pierce* and the tardiness of the reversal of earlier state and federal flag salute decisions in *Barnette*. While these opinions may be read as charters of freedom, what is often not stressed is the very wide domain of normative dominance still permitted to those who wished to define truly American instruction. It is this historical perspective rather than later, more liberal, uses of the decisions that I wish to explore here.

The *Meyer* case resulted from a Nebraska law forbidding teaching in any language other than English to children below the ninth grade. It was one of many such statutes passed during the anti-German and 100 percent American climate of the war years. The plaintiff was punished for teaching a ten-year-old boy to read German. The attorneys for the state of Nebraska used arguments for the ban that were common at the time. 'The purpose of the statute is to ensure that the English language shall be the mother tongue and the language of the heart of the children reared in this country,' they told the Supreme Court. 'It is within the police power of the state to compel every resident of Nebraska so to educate his children that the sunshine of American ideals will permeate the life of the future citizens of the Republic.'[22]

The Supreme Court based its decision in *Meyer* primarily on the relatively narrow ground that it interfered with the pursuit of a lawful occupation without any compelling public necessity. The Court recognized 'the desire of the legislature to foster a homogeneous people with American ideals'; what it rejected was the means, which infringed on the rights of the plaintiff. The Court did not question the fundamental right of the state 'to improve the quality of its citizens, physically, mentally and morally,' nor did it seek to limit the legislature's 'power to prescribe a curriculum' or 'the power of the State to compel attendance at some school and to make reasonable regulations for all schools, including a requirement that they shall give instructions in English.' Thus, by implication the Court allowed the state very large discretion short of this specific clause, despite its rhetorical support for individual rights (which encouraged later liberals to regard *Meyer* as a blow for liberty).[23]

The *Pierce* decision of the Supreme Court upheld the right of parents to send their children to private schools. Again the Court based its findings chiefly on the relatively narrow grounds of the property rights of private school educators even though it also referred to 'the liberty of parents and guardians to direct the upbringing and education of children under their control.' In 1922 the voters of Oregon had passed an initiative that required children to attend public schools. The chief organizers of that campaign were the Oregon Scottish Rite Masons and the Ku Klux Klan. Their targets were groups they defined as deviants from their approved version of Americanism: Catholics, immigrants, and elites who escaped the benign influences of the common school. Public school people supported the law in solid phalanx.

The Court ruled that Oregon had no power 'to standardize its children by requiring parents to send children to public schools only.' *Pierce* has thus offered a useful precedent for friends of pluralism and individual rights in education, for it showed the outer limits of considering the child as 'the mere creature of the state.' But it is important to recall that in *Pierce* as in *Meyer* large domains of state police power and 'normative dominance' were left unquestioned: regulation of all schools, public and private; compulsory schooling; and laws decreeing 'that teachers shall be of good moral character and patriotic disposition, that certain studies plainly essential to good citizenship must be taught, and that nothing be taught which is manifestly inimical to the public welfare.'[24]

Indeed the flag salute cases that culminated in *Barnette* indicate how firmly embedded was the assumption that the need for national unity transcended individual rights. Jehovah Witnesses objected to the flag salute on religious grounds, believing the flag to be a 'graven image.' In *Minersville School District v. Gobitis* (1940), the US Supreme Court upheld several state court decisions that regarded refusal to salute the flag as punishable insubordination. *Gobitis* reflected a long tradition of judicial non-intervention in compulsory civic socialization. It affirmed many state court decisions that took the side of school authorities in student rights litigation.[25]

The decision in *West Virginia Board of Education v. Barnette* (1943) — reversing *Gobitis* on the constitutionality of the compulsory flag salute only three years later — marked a sharp departure. The Court declared in *Barnette* that 'if there is any fixed star in our constitutional constellation, it is that no official, high or petty, can prescribe what shall be orthodox in politics, nationalism, religion, or other matters of opinion or force citizens to confess by word or act their faith therein. If there are any circumstances which permit an exception, they do not now occur to us.'[26]

In their eloquent characterization of history, the justices were evidently not thinking of children in public schools, who had, of course, precisely been subject to court-approved prescriptions of orthodoxy in 'politics, nationalism, religion' and other domains like temperance.

When the public schools had been well-established, they were a ready target for politically potent groups that wished to write laws to inculcate their version of truth and virtue on the rising generation. Since it was easier to exercise normative dominance on the captive audience of the young than on adults, WASP citizens found it more feasible to shift the burden of reform to the next generation, to define problems as educational rather than as injustices or evils calling for immediate action. Not until the last generation would excluded groups achieve the voice and power to challenge the results of this earlier legalization of orthodox values, and then their efforts would be labeled litigiousness partly because they came from people who had traditionally lacked power. The values of those who had power seemed self-evidently correct.

Codification of the One Best System in the Twentieth Century

Statutory and administrative law were major means of educational reform employed by professional leaders in public education from the Progressive era onwards. These reformers, whom I shall call the administrative progressives, were a cohesive group of university education professors and deans, leading city and state superintendents, foundation executives, and other administrators who had a new vision of how to create a differentiated, centralized, and 'socially efficient' system of schooling.

More than any other one group, the administrative progressives transformed the character of public education during the twentieth century, often in alliance with business and professional elites. They sought to change the locus and process of decision-making by abolishing the older decentralized mode of school governance and putting in its place a more centralized system in which lay boards deferred to professionals. They wished to legitimize governance by expertise — by the new canons of 'scientific management' — rather than by popular participation. They increased the scope and complexity of city and state school systems until they became large pedagogical conglomerates, patterned in many ways upon the new business corporations. While they sought and won power for the professional, they believed that educators were not just another interest group but experts who understood and served the public good. Their ideal was to replace 'politics' by 'administration.'[27]

Professional leaders wanted to use state legislation not so much to prescribe virtue as to codify and enforce their version of a new standardized and expanded educational system. How to use the political processes of state legislatures to accomplish the purpose of creating a 'non-political' one best system was a bit of a puzzle. One administrative progressive complained that 'No one having the slightest acquaintance with the ignorance, selfishness, greed, partnership, logrolling and hamstringing to be found in the average legislature, can have any great respect for all provisions of law simply because they happened to be passed by the legislature.' Indeed, codification was to clear away the underbrush of obsolete, over-detailed prescriptions that tied the hands of educators, to abolish special legislation that prevented statewide uniformity, and to place the schools beyond the reach of special interest groups, small-minded rural legislators, and machine politicians.[28]

What the progressives wanted was a complex mixture of centralization of certain functions by the state together with professional autonomy for superintendents in the county districts and cities. The state legislature should use 'a perfectly definite yet somewhat complicated scheme for the apportionment of funds . . . to stimulate and reward effort, and to penalize inactivity'; should require higher standards of certification and in-service education for professionals; and should see that compulsory attendance is enforced. The code should reflect the best professional knowledge available and employ strong sanctions in standardizing schools according to expert blueprints.[29]

The administrative progressives used a variety of political-professional strategies in persuading state legislatures to amend or codify school statutes. Foundations and the United States Office of Education sponsored state school surveys which employed experts to compare existing educational laws and practices with their version of an up-to-date system of schools. University education professors and deans served as advisors to state commissions on educational reorganization. National and state educational organizations — expecially those affiliated with the National Education Association (NEA) — lobbied effectively for the professionally-designed legislation.

Of all groups who tried to influence state educational legislation during the twentieth century, public school people (organized in their state educational associations) were the most influential. They had a direct and personal interest in securing better funding, tenure laws, certification requirements restricting entry, better school buildings, expanded structures and content of schooling, greater scope for professional discretion, and consolidation of small schools. They did not always agree on legislation, of course, but by and large they could agree on what constituted appropriate codification of school law.[30]

Partly because they had themselves designed and lobbied for the new legalization of education, educators were effective in implementing the laws in the schools. Compulsory attendance regulations were a case in point. During the nineteenth century school people were ambivalent about laws requiring all children of a certain age to attend school. Such laws were often passed without their strong support and were more symbolic than practical in their effects — a stamping of the foot by virtuous citizens who sent their children to schools and who demanded that other less conscientious parents should do likewise. But there were few effective ways of implementing the laws in most states until the twentieth century. During the Progressive era, however, school leaders joined child labor reformers and labor unions in securing the passage of strong legislation, and the administrative progressives created elaborate 'pupil personnel' departments with truant officers and other means of tracking errant youth and bringing them into schools. Justices of the peace and juvenile courts supplied the sanctions of law when necessary. The new educational experts were effective administrators who knew how to design and implement legislation, particularly when they believed that they — and their schools — stood to benefit from it.[31]

Standardization of rural schools by carrot and stick techniques provided another example. In the twentieth century, it became a common practice for state legislatures, state boards of education, or state superintendents by administrative law to require rural schools to comply with state standards before they could receive state funds. By 1925 thirty four states reported that they had standardized 40,000 local schools. No detail was unimportant. Administrative reformers George Strayer and Nicholaus Englehardt of Columbia created score cards for country schools that rated them on their window shades, the color scheme of floors, globes and dictionaries, sanitary drinking cups, and the types of toilets they had. Like standardization, accreditation of schools enabled the administrative progressives to determine what was normal.[32]

In the nineteenth century, as I have suggested, citizens and parents had many ways to settle disputes over public schooling outside of the courts. As state laws extended their scope and state and local bureaucracies grew more efficient, however, the means of recourse narrowed. Educational officials had more incentives to implement laws and more sanctions to punish dissenters. The decline of popular participation in educational decision-making gave local administrators greater autonomy in making regulations and exercising professional judgment. The courts loomed larger, then, as a means of redress of grievances than in the past. During the nineteenth century, as we have seen, there were only about three thousand cases appealed in state courts. During the next decades the state cases mushroomed.[33]

Although there have been studies of landmark decisions and surveys of court cases in particular domains — curriculum or transportation, for example — there are many questions unanswered about the use of the courts in the period from 1900 to *Brown*. Who brought suit and why? What kinds of cases remained relatively constant in proportion and what changed? What were the uncharacteristic 'out-of-time' cases that were harbingers for later developments in fields like individual rights or desegregation? How did the case load in the courts correlate with new school legislation? How did regional or state variations in political culture and legal systems help to explain different rates of litigation? Some of these issues are taken up in the chapter by Donald Jensen and Thomas Griffin in this volume, and some additional speculations are in order.[34]

Recourse to the courts had many purposes. In the twentieth century school districts increasingly used the judicial process to enforce compulsory attendance. Laws on contracts and tenure gave new rights of due process to teachers. Consolidation statutes created conflicts between levels of government to be settled in the courts. New entitlements such as right of transportation to schools brought parents into courts to claim benefits for their children. There was a good deal of litigation on busing in the 1920s and 1930s — eighty reported cases on pupil transportation between 1926 and 1936 nationwide, for example — in which parents demanded a place on the bus for their sons and daughters (I have found none in those years in which they *opposed* busing). The increased regulation of schooling by the state, the expansion of the scope of the curriculum and elaboration of new structures, and the greater jurisdiction of professionals through increased administrative law also created conflicts with parents that took the form of litigation.[35]

For the most part, the judiciary proved to be highly deferential to the authority of legislatures and school officials when their new powers came into conflict with the desires of parents. Parents usually lost when they challenged compulsory attendance, new curricular or health requirements (such as vaccination), harsh discipline, and seemingly arbitrary regulations controlling pupils or the course of studies. In the nineteenth century the courts typically sought to uphold the dignity of the lone teacher confronting the rural community (though often cautioning the teacher to be tactful and moderate, lest community members take vengeance into their own hands for real or imagined abuses of power). In the first half of the twentieth century, judges largely ratified the centralization of authority in increasingly bureaucratic structures of schooling.[36]

From increased litigation emerged a new specialization in law and in the professional preparation of school administrators: school law. By and large, the authors of the early school law texts took as their premise that the purpose of the study of school law was to prevent litigation or at least ensure that school authorities won their cases.[37]

The principles of organization of the traditional school law texts mirrored the bureaucratic concerns of the administrators and the focus on case precedent of the school lawyers. Using court decisions as the primary and often the sole body of evidence, the textbook writers discussed legal relations of the different levels of government, contracts, finances, tort liability, employment and dismissal of staff, school attendance, pupil transportation, and related matters. Broad issues of constitutional rights seemed anomalous in such a mode of thinking; thus it is not surprising that authors often treated religious controversy as a problem of curriculum or racial segregation as a question of pupil assignment to schools. The courts were seen as interpreters of vague clauses in statutory law or the limits of administrative discretion, clearing away ambiguities so that educators could get about their real business: orderly instruction. The informed administrator supposedly used his knowledge of school law as one tool in the armamentarium of rational decision-making.[38]

To compare such school law texts with recent scholarship is to enter a new world of assumptions about the relation of law to education. The older authors seem to these scholars to be looking through the wrong end of the telescope. The new approach stresses the connections between broad social forces, the schools as complex institutions in flux, and fundamental issues of constitutional rights. The 1974 text *Educational Policy and the Law* by David L. Kirp and Mark G. Yudof, for example, examines how basic social and educational problems became legal issues, drawing on studies by historians and social scientists to plot the demands on the legal system and to demonstrate how law reflected social change. They organize the book according to basic issues of educational policy rather than the older bureaucratic-legal categories, stressing such matters as 'student and teacher liberty,' racial and sexual equality, the relation between school resources and outcomes, and new concepts of equal educational opportunity and classification.[39]

Recent changes in legal scholarship have reflected major transformations in the society since *Brown* and in its public schools. The cleavages of race, religion, sex, class, and ethnicity — once papered over by gentlemen's agreements among the powerful — could no longer be neglected, for newly aroused groups among the governed refused their consent to such agreements. A new era of legal activism began.

Challenges to Business as Usual: Law and Public Education after 1954

Americans have used law in a variety of ways in creating and reshaping their public schools: to exhort local citizens to action, to enforce mainstream cultural values on outsiders, to standardize schools according to 'scientific' specifications, to conduct the ordinary business of education in a commercial-industrial society, to protest, to gain entitlements. The list could go on. The problems of implementation and compliance are not new, nor are complaints over hyperactive use of the law. But today amidst a furor over litigiousness and overregulation it is easy to forget the injustices of the old legal order and to fail to ask why the legal transformation of the last generation took place.

If one went back to the early 1950s, one would find less litigiousness than today, fewer and less complex federal and state regulations, and more acceptance of the authority of educational officials. One would also find legal segregation of the races in the southern half of the nation, legal compulsory religious exercises in a multitude of school districts, legal sex-based discrimination, gross inequities in the funding of schools between districts and within districts, systematic favoring of middle-class and prosperous students, and pervasive lack of due process in the treatment of pupils' rights and in the relations between administrators and teachers.[40]

When low-power protest groups pressed their demands for basic social change, therefore, they tended to appeal not to local oligarchs but rather to outside agencies for redress: to the courts, to state and federal legislatures, and to prosperous liberals in the churches, foundations, and national voluntary groups like the NAACP.[41] One social movement after another mobilized members and broad public support for social change in the 1960s and early 1970s. Blacks, women, Hispanics, the handicapped, native Americans, and many others sought greater equality in education, while public interest lawyers translated their demands into claims to which activist judges could respond. Federal and state legislatures also passed landmark statutes like the Civil Rights Acts, Title I of ESEA, and laws on multicultural education, bilingual instruction, and the handicapped.

The gains were both symbolic and tangible. Ethnic groups sought equality of dignity, a legitimation denied by earlier attempts to define American values in a culturally exclusive manner. In effect, symbolic legislation about multiethnic curricula declared that pluralism of culture was also American. They also won increased funding for their schools, new jobs for minority staff, and new entitlements. Taken together the cases added up to a legal revolution and revealed the impact of protest stemming from the larger society. Increasingly, the Supreme Court has demanded that educational policy respect the constitutional separation of church and state through the Bible and prayer decisions; questioned some assumptions behind compulsory attendance in *Yoder*; demanded greater attention to non-English-speaking students in *Lau*; pressed desegregation in many cases; and upheld student rights to due process and free expression. The number of federal cases increased dramatically:

1946–56:	112
1956–66:	729
1966–76:	1273

State courts, as well, treated basic questions of equity, as in the school finance cases.[42]

In their study of legalization of policy-making in California, Jensen and Griffin show not only the absolute increase in court cases but also important shifts in the issues litigated during the last generation. In the 1962–79 period personnel, tort, and fiscal and governance questions continued to constitute the bedrock of cases, but new issues of individual rights, labor relations, school finance, and school desegregation have arisen, often pressed by public law organizations in class action suits. Increasingly suits have been brought against state officials and educational administrators to enjoin them to alter educational policies. Legal principles have increasingly been evoked as a source of authority in education and other traditional forms of authority, such as professional expertise and local majority rule, have been questioned. One result had been an increased centralization in policy-making, but it is an incomplete and often confusing form of centralization not fully incorporated into standard operating procedures.[43]

As David Kirp has observed, judges have been ambivalent about their powerful new roles in public education. Many have believed themselves lacking in both the expertise and time to supervise the very changes which court decisions required in public schooling. Some observers have seen activist judges as heroes of social justice, while others have condemned an 'imperial judiciary' for exceeding its proper scope. In fact, as Kirp notes, 'many of the questions of equal educational opportunity presented for judicial resolution strain, in one way or another, the competence of the courts.' Court decisions and legislation have worked in tandem in securing changes in educational policies and practices, and many aggrieved groups such as the handicapped, women, and non-English-speaking citizens may have won more pervasive reform through legislatures than through litigation.[44]

For their part, school officials have had mixed reactions toward the new legal activism. Not surprisingly, they have often been bothered by the decline in judicial deference toward school authorities in student rights and due process decisions and by the increase in procedural regulations affecting their everyday work.[45] But educators also have been historically committed to certain visions of equality. In the nineteenth century reformers conceived of equality mostly as free and open access to public schools. The administrative progressives added a new and complicated dimension — equality of opportunity — while believing themselves the best judges of how to achieve that goal. Many of the court decisions and legislative reforms of the last generation can be understood within those two traditional concepts of equality. One could argue that what groups like blacks, or the handicapped, or women really wanted was equality of access and equality of opportunity — in short, to have public education fulfill the promise of the *common* school. Educators could deny that goal only by denying their own best ethical heritage.

The history of law in education in the last generation has thus been one of both continuity and change. New groups have demanded that the old ideals of the common school should include them. Older notions of normative dominance — whether unselfconscious or deliberate — have given way to a new pluralism of values in which equality of dignity has been a goal of excluded groups. Codification of the one best system through law under the guidance of professional experts has been replaced by a plethora of new regulations and overlapping agencies so complex that Rube Goldberg himself could not map the lines of force or master the levers. Legislation and court decisions — always in tension — now have produced the perplexing kind of legalization that is the subject of this book. The strains on the educational system today are formidable, but in large part the present conflicts stem from attempts to remedy injustices for some when justice for all was a dream too long deferred.

Appendix: Using Legal Case Digests in Historical Analysis *by Aaron Benavot, Jill Blackmore, Karen Harbeck, and Susan Looper*

In the preceding text, Table 1 and Figure 1 represent part of an ongoing foray we are conducting into the changing character of litigated issues in education. We thought it would be helpful to describe how we conducted our quantitative analysis because we think that legal case digests can be a useful historical source in studying the relationship of law and society. Although case digests cover only reported cases, they provide a fairly sound basis upon which to raise questions and formulate ideas. We recognize the need to supplement this source with more detailed court records and other materials to gain a fuller sense of how representative were the appellate cases. This would also add to our understanding how legal processes differed by time and place.

In our study we used the *Centennial Digest*, the first nationwide digest of state and federal cases, which spans some fifty volumes and includes over half a million cases decided between 1658 and 1896. Since the first edition was issued, eight subsequent decennial editions based upon the Digest System have been published. For each case indexed, we coded three pieces of information: (i) the year of litigation; (ii) the state in which the case occurred; and (iii) the type of legal issue raised by the litigating parties. What we — and the original compilers — have been interested in is the type of *issues* that have been litigated. As the coding progressed, we found that some *cases* were indexed in more than one category of legal *issues*. In other words, the digest references both cases dealing with a single issue as well as those dealing with multiple issues. Thus, the unit of analysis in Figure 1 and Table 1 is not individual cases but rather litigated issues. Because the latter was our chief concern, duplication of cases was not a major conceptual problem.

We were interested, nonetheless, in estimating the degree to which cases were cited more than once. Accordingly, we made an exploratory study to discover how many cases were cross-referenced more than once *within* each of the eight major categories on the one hand and *across* all categories on the other. Our non-random sample of litigated issues found that *within* categories about one case in seven (15.1 per cent) dealt with more than one issue and was thus cited twice (see Table B). Our estimate of cross-referencing *across* all categories was slightly higher (about 20 to 23 per cent).

With this in mind, we can turn to discuss how Table 1 and Figure 1 were constructed. Upon completing our coding of the *Centennial Digest*, we reclassified the forty-three subcategories into three substantive areas: finance, governance and 'other'. Our grouping of the various subcategories is noted in the last column of Table A. We then looked at the distribution of litigated issues for the three areas we had constructed at different intervals in the nineteenth century. In this way, we demonstrated the tendency of litigated educational issues to be financial or administrative in character throughout the period.

In Figure 1, we changed our focus from the types of litigated issues to whether certain regions in the country tended to have greater rates of litigation

Table A List of major categories and sub-categories found in the Century Digest under the topic, schools and school districts, and their reclassification

		Legal categories and subcategories in Century Digest	*Reclassified Topics*
1		Establishment and Regulation of School Lands and Funds	
	A	Establishment and maintenance	Governance
	B	School lands	Finance
	C	School funds	Finance
	D	Regulation and supervision of schools	Governance
2		Creation and Alteration of School Districts	
	A	Incorporation and organization	Governance
	B	Alternation and creation of new districts	Governance
	C	Adjustment of pre-existing rights and liabilities	Governance
	D	Union or annexation of districts	Governance
	E	Enumeration of children for school purposes	Governance
	F	Dissolution of districts	Governance
3		Government, Officers and District Meetings	
	A	Administration of school affairs	Governance
	B	State boards and officers	Governance
	C	County boards and officers	Governance
	D	Officers of towns	Governance
	E	District meetings in general	Governance
	F	District boards	Governance
	G	Criminal responsibilities and penalties	Governance
4		District Property, Contracts and Liabilities	
	A	Acquisition and use of property	Finance
	B	School buildings	Finance
	C	School furniture, etc.,	Finance
	D	Contracts	Finance
	E	District expenses and statutory liabilities	Finance
	F	Torts	Finance
5		District Debt, Securities and Taxation	
	A	Power to incur indebtedness	Finance
	B	Administration of finance	Finance
	C	Bonds and other securities	Finance
	D	School taxes	Finance
	E	Assessments and special taxes	Finance
	F	Poll taxes	Finance
	G	Disposition of taxes and other revenue	Finance
	H	Rights and remedies of taxpayers	Finance
6		Claims against District and Actions	
	A	Presentation and allowance of claims	Governance
	B	Actions by or against district	Governance
7		Teachers	
	A	Eligibility	Other
	B	Selection and appointment	Other
	C	Contracts of employment	Finance
	D	Removal and discharge	Other
	E	Compensation	Finance
	F	Duties and liabilities	Other
8		Pupils	
	A	Admission and pupil attendence	Other
	B	School terms, pupil classification and instruction	Other
	C	Control of pupils and discipline	Other

Table B *Estimation of the degree of cross-referencing within each of eight major legal categories for all nineteenth-century educational cases*

Major Legal Category	Number of actual issues in category	Number of sampled issues	Percent of sampled issues referring at least once to same case
1 School Lands, School Funds	226	38	2.6
2 Organization of School Districts	495	112	15.9
3 Government and Officers	635	111	21.6
4 District Property and Liabilities	353	79	15.2
5 District Debt and Taxation	768	229	16.6
6 Claims Against District	124	35	14.3
7 Teachers	387	35	0.0
8 Pupils	195	30	6.7
Totals	3183	669 (21.0%)	15.1%

than others and whether certain historical patterns in these rates could be discerned. Our measure, the degree of educational litigiousness, was constructed by taking the total number of litigated issues per decade for a region and dividing by the average population during the decade for that region. Although the average rates of litigation for the whole country generally rose during the nineteenth century (from about two issues per million population to over fifteen issues), the most dramatic rise took place, as might be expected, in the 1840s after the onset of the common school crusade. Most revealing, however, is the variation found in the rates of litigation by region.

Our exploratory investigation clearly raises as many questions as it answers. For example, why the relatively high rates of litigation in the rural Mid-western states as compared to the industrial ones, and why the relative lack of litigation in the populous Middle Atlantic states such as New York and New Jersey? Careful analysis of court records will undoubtedly provide new and more complete material to answer these questions. All in all, we are convinced that the type of research strategy we describe in this appendix highlights the historical value of legal case digests and suggests new ways of studying historical patterns in the relationship of law and society.

Notes

1 A classic school law textbook is EDWARDS, N., (1933) *The Courts and the Public Schools*, Chicago, University of Chicago Press, (reprinted 1933 and 1955).

2 FRIEDMAN, L.M., (1975) *The Legal System: A Social Science Perspective*, New York, Russell Sage Foundation, p. 15; FRIEDMAN, L.M (1973) *A History of American Law*, New York, Simon and Schuster; HURST, J.W., (1977) *Law and Social Order in the United States*, Ithaca, Cornell University Press; KIRP, D.L., and YUDOF, M.G., (1974) *Educational Policy and the Law: Cases and Materials*, Berkeley, McCutchan Publishing Corporation, (new edition forthcoming); SCHEIBER, H.H., (1981) 'American constitutional history and the new legal history: complementary themes in two modes,' *Journal of American History*, 68, pp. 337–50.

3 LIEBERMAN, J.K., (1981) *The Litigious Society*, New York, Basic Books; GLAZER, N. (1975) 'Toward an imperial judiciary?' *The Public Interest*, 41, pp. 104–23; for observations on the creation of continuity I am indebted to Tom James; for analysis of the relation between law and behavior, see LUFLER, H.S. JR. (1970) 'Compliance and the courts,' in BERLINER, D.C. (Ed). *Review of Research in Education*, vol. 8, Washington, D.C., *AERA*, pp. 336–59.

4 Subsequent footnotes document the historical argument: for two recent studies of law and educational policy see: HOOKER, C.P. (Ed.,) (1978) *The Courts and Education*, 77th Yearbook of the National Society for the Study of Education, Chicago, University of Chicago Press; RIST, R.C. and ANSON, R.J. (1977) (Eds.,) *Education, Social Science and the Judicial Process*, New York, Teachers College Press.

5 TYACK, D. and HANSOT, E. (1982) *Managers of Virtue: A History of Leadership in American Public Education: 1820–1930*, New York, Basic Books, Part 1.

6 KOTLIN, L. and AIKMAN, W.F. (1980) *Legal Foundations of Compulsory School Attendance*, Port Washington, N.Y., Kennikat Press, pp. 420–33; FLANDERS, J.K. (1925) *Legislative Control of the Elementary School Curriculum*, New York, Teachers College, pp. 158–9.

7 See, for example, STATE OF CALIFORNIA, (1866) *Revised School Law*, Sacramento, O.M. Clayes; HOLCOMBE, J.W.(Ed)., (1883) *The School Law of Indiana*, Indianapolis, Wm. R. Burford; BLODGETT, J. (1893) *Report of Education in the United States at the Eleventh Census*, Washington, D.C., GPO, introduction; UNITED STATES COMMISSIONER OF EDUCATION, (1889) *Report for 1888–89*, Washington, D.C., GPO, Chapter 18, pp. 79–139.

8 On the pattern of school founding in the North, see TYACK and HANSOT, (1982) *op. cit.*, pp. 28–34 and 44–63; on the South, *Ibid*, pp. 83–93.

9 *Cummings v. Missouri*, 4 Wall 277 (1876) concerning a loyalty oath was the exception (unless one also excludes the case of *Dartmouth College v. Woodward*, 4 Wheat. 518 (1819) which guaranteed the sanctity of contract); private school cases listed in West's *Centennial Digest* showed the same preoccupation with fiscal and governance issues (only three of nineteen cases dealt with pupils).

10 FRIEDMAN, L.M. (1975) 'Notes toward a history of American justice,' in FRIEDMAN L.M. and SCHEIBER, H.N. (Eds)., *American Law and the Constitutional Order: Historical Perspectives*, Cambridge, Harvard University Press, pp. 19–20; Nevada official quoted in BENDER, J.F. (1927) *The Functions of Courts in Enforcing Compulsory School Attendance Laws*, New York, Teachers College, p. 10.

11 ALEXANDER, U.S. (1929) *Special Legislation Affecting Public Schools*, New York, Teachers College, 10, 5–6, 45, 52, 15, 17, 26, 110–12.

12 TYACK, D. (1972) 'The tribe and the common school: Community control in rural education,' *American Quarterly*, 24 pp. 3-19.

13 DICK, E. (1937) *The Sod-House Frontier*, New York, D. Appleton-Century, Chapter 6; John Miller to Oliver Applegate, 21 June, 15 August, 1863, O.C. Applegate Papers, University of Oregon; JOHNSON, C. (1963) *Old-Time Schools and Schoolbooks*, New York, Dover, p. 102.

14 FRIEDMAN, L.M. (1978) *op. cit.* pp. 21-24; LIPPMAN, W. (1928) *American Inquisitors: A Commentary on Dayton and Chicago*, New York, Harper and Row.

15 WIEBE, R. (1969) 'The social functions of public education,' *American Quarterly*, 21 pp. 147–64.

16 McCLOSKEY, R.G. (Ed)., (1967) *The Bible in the Public Schools: Arguments before the Superior Court of Cincinnati in the Case of Minor v. Board of Education of Cincinnati, 1870*, New York, Da Capo Press, p. 213; TYACK, D. (1970) 'Onward christian soldiers: religion in the American common school,' in NASH, P. (Ed)., *History and Education: The Educational Uses of the Past*, New York, Random House, pp. 212--55.

17 HAMILTON, O.T. (1927) *The Courts and the Curriculum*, New York, Teachers College, p. 113.

18 BOLES, D.E. (1963) *The Bible, Religion, and the Public Schools*, New York, Collier Books, p. 53; FLANDERS, J.K. (1925) *op. cit.* p. 155.

19 Shelton, 'Legislative control,' 481; FLANDERS, J.K. (1925) *op. cit.*, p. 40–1; EDELMAN, L.F. (1976) 'Basic American,' *NOLPE School Law Journal*, 6, pp. 92–5.

20 Shelton, 'Legislative control,' 483; FLANDERS, J.K. (1925) *op. cit.* pp. 5–12.

21 HEATH, S.B. (1977) 'Language and politics in the United States,' in TROIKE, M.S. (Ed.) *Georgetown University Round Table on Languages and Linguistics*, Washington, D.C., Georgetown University Press, pp. 267–96; FLANDERS, J.K. (1925) *op. cit.*, pp. 8–9; Shelton, 'Legislative Control,' 480, footnote 30.

22 *Meyer v. Nebraska*, 262 US 390, (1923), 394, 401, 402.

23 *Ibid.*

24 *Pierce v. Society of Sisters*, 268 US 510 (1925).

25 *Minersville School District v. Gobitis* 310 US 586 (1940); KIRP, D.L. and YUDOF, G. (1974) *op. cit.* pp. 134–7; FULBRIGHT, E.R. and BOLMEIER, E.C. (1964) *Courts and the Curriculum*, Cincinnati, W.H. Anderson Company, pp. 70–7.

26 *West Virginia State Board of Education v. Barnette* 319 US 624 (1943).
27 TYACK, D.L. and HANSOT, E. (1982) *op. cit.* Part 2.
28 ALEXANDER, C. (1932) 'Can a school executive afford to ignore the law?' *Nation's Schools*, 9, p. 29.
29 *Ibid.*, vii; for criticisms of Cubberley for being over-specific, see CAULKINS, G,W. (1934) 'A proposed criterion for evaluating state schools laws,' *Nation's Schools*, 14, p. 29.
30 REMMLEIN, M.K. (1955) 'Statutory problems,' *Law and Contemporary Problems*, 20, pp. 125–37.
31 Bender, *Compulsory School Attendance*; TYACK, D. and BERKOWITZ, M. (1977) 'The man nobody liked: Toward a social history of the truant officer, 1840–1940,' *American Quarterly*, 29 pp. 31–54.
32 COLLINS, G.J. (1968) *The Constitution and Legal Basis for State Action in Education*, Boston, Massachusetts Department of Education, pp. 30–2; LATHROP, E. (1925) *The Improvement of Rural Schools by Standardization*, Washington, D.C, GPO, pp. 10–13.
33 HOGAN, J.C. (1974) *The Schools, the Courts, and the Public Interest* Lexington, Lexington Books, 7, chapter 2; CHAMBERS, M.M. (Ed) (1937) *The fifth Yearbook of School Law*, Washington, D.C. American Council on Education.
34 In this volume; see also JENSEN, D.N. and GRIFFIN, T.M. (1981) 'The legalization of state educational policymaking in California,' Institute for Research on Finance and Governance, Stanford University, p. 11.
35 BOLMEIER, E.C. (1955) 'Legal issues in school transportation,' *Law and Contemporary Problems*, 20, pp. 45–59; ANDERSON, E.W. (1927) *The Teacher's Contract and Other Legal Phases of Teacher Status*, New York, Teachers College.
36 LOUGHERY, SISTER M. BERNARD FRANCIS (1952) *Parental Rights in American Educational Law: Their Basis and Implementation*, Washington, D.C., Catholic University of America Press; TRUSLER, H.R. (1927) *Essentials of School Law*, Milwaukee, The Bruce Publishing Company, chapter 13.
37 HODGDON, D.R. (1933) 'School law — a social philosophy,' *Junior-Senior High School Clearing House*, 8 pp. 229–32.
38 VORHEES, H.C. (1961) *The Law of the Public School System of the United States*, Boston, Little, Brown, and Company; TRUSLER, H.W. (1927) *op. cit.* preface; Editorial (1927) 'Education jurisprudence,' *Nation's Schools*, 2, p. 72; DRURY, R.L. (1958) *Law and the School Superintendent* (Cincinnati, W.H. Anderson).
39 KIRP, D.L. and YUDOF, G. (1974) *op. cit.*; for reviews of recent work on the law and education see the essays by ROSSELL, C.H., THURSTON, P. and LUFLER, H. in BERLINER, D.C. (Ed). (1970) *op. cit.* pp. 237–355.
40 GOLDHAMMER, K. (1977) 'Roles of the American school superintendent,' in CUNNINGHAM, L.L., HACK, W.G. and NYSTRAND, R.O. (Eds) *Educational Administration: The Developing Decades*, Berkeley, McCutchan Publishing Company, pp. 148 and 150–1: TYACK, D. and HANSOT, E. (1982) *op. cit.* part 3; on the lack of due process see JAMES, H.T. (1981) 'Educational administration: A forty-year perspective,' Division A, Invited Address, AERA Convention, New York, April.
41 COLEMAN, J.S. (1967) 'The struggle for control of education,' ERIC Report Resume ED 015 158, 7, October, pp. 5–6, 7 and 8.
42 KIRP, D.L. (1982) *Just Schools*, Berkeley, University of California Press; HOGAN, J.C. (1974) *op. cit.* 7, chapters 2–4.
43 GRIFFIN, T.M. and JENSEN, D.N. (1981) *op. cit.* pp. 19–28; MEYER, J.W. (1981) 'Organizational Factors Affecting Legalization in Education,' Institute for Finance and Governance, Stanford University.
44 KIRP, D.L. (1977) 'Law, politics, and equal educational opportunity: The limits of judicial involvement,' 47 *Harvard Ed. Rev.* 117, May.

45 For an excellent review of new literature on governance see BOYD, W.L. (1976) 'The public, the professionals, and educational policy making: who governs?' *Teachers College Record*, 77 pp. 539–77.

Limited Monarchy: The Rise and Fall of Student Rights

Lawrence M. Friedman
Stanford University

Student Rights

This is a survey of reported cases on what, for want of a better term, I will call student rights. These are suits, by or on behalf of public school students, challenging rules or practices of local school boards, principals, or teachers. I will stick to cases about elementary- and high-school pupils and to cases about *substance* — that is, about what the rules say, rather than about *procedures* for handling disciplinary problems. These cases can be, I think, quite revealing. They shed considerable light on the relationship between law and public education.

I will begin with a nineteenth century illustration — one of the rare reported cases of its day. A teacher in Tennessee, James Anderson, was indicted for assault and battery. He had been drilling his class when young Wyatt Layne spoke softly out of turn. Anderson kept the boy after class, and then gave him a whipping: 'He hit him about a dozen licks with a switch, . . . struck him pretty hard, Layne crying all the time.'

Anderson was convicted in the trial court; the Supreme Court of Tennessee affirmed. Young Wyatt's offense had been 'slight and entirely unintentional.' The teacher's cruelty was 'an unauthorized exercise of power.' A teacher had discretion, but he must not abuse it. He can use the rod, but not 'wantonly and without cause.' Punishment must be moderate; the student is 'helpless' and in the teacher's power. When a teacher goes too far, 'courts must afford a proper redress, and prevent the temptation from being presented to parents and relations to take vengeance into their own hands. The government of the school should be patriarchal rather than despotic. If it be a monarchy, it should be a limited one, and not absolute.'[1]

My theme is this limited monarchy: the role of courts in providing, on behalf of students, limits to teacher and school board power. One caution: despite what courts say, we know little about students' rights in practice. Only appellate cases get reported. They may be the tip of an iceberg. No experience or rule of thumb tells us how to estimate numbers of trials from numbers of appeals. We are even more in the dark about the real world of the classroom.

Cases do tell us, of course, about certain events inside the *legal* system. They are an index, for example, of *judicialization*. We can define *judicialization* as the process of converting disputes or conflicts into court cases. Frequently, one can distinguish three stages of a process, and that is true here as well. First is a stage of authority and discretion, of *pre-judicialization*. Decisions made by teachers and school boards go largely unquestioned. Second is the stage of *challenge*, or, in a sense, of judicialization itself. This occurred in the late 1960s, with a bulge of cases that now seems to be subsiding. The third stage is the stage of *absorption*. Institutions digest and accommodate the doctrines the courts have worked out, and develop new grievance procedures. At this point, litigation on the issue dies down.

This is a typical and common pattern, but of course not the only one. The process can become 'stuck' before reaching the third stage. The stages, in other words, are by no means inevitable. Institutions and social groups must acquiesce in some kind of solution. If schools had continued to struggle over hair length, say, or if courts had been unable to agree on lines of doctrine which the schools could absorb, we might still be stuck at stage two.

Here, as always, social forces pull the strings. The great hair-length fuss would have been unthinkable a century ago. And it is an issue that played itself out; the symbolic meaning of hair length dribbled away. Men's hair got longer in the general population, and the issue disappeared. For school desegregation, busing, and the like, no such happy outcome can be expected, at least not in the short run.

Students' Rights: the Nineteenth-Century Prologue

Nineteenth-century cases are few and far between, but are often of uncommon interest. One point has to be made at the outset. 'Student rights' cases in the nineteenth century usually had little to do with the feelings of students. Overwhelmingly the rights of *parents* were at issue. The children were minors, and their parents prosecuted the suits. (Strong-minded high-school students are more a feature of our own generation.)

In one small, rather anomalous group of cases, the issue was whether or not a child had the right to attend some particular school. These are cases on the student's right to be admitted or readmitted. There are also cases about expulsion. Some cases turn on rules of the school board. In *Board of Education v. Bolton* (1899),[2] a rule prohibited children who had just turned six from entering the school at any time except during the first months of the fall and the spring terms. The court held the rule was unreasonable, and struck it down.

A school rarely, if ever, keeps a student out merely because of whim. Usually, some issue of student conduct lurks in the background. In one Massachusetts case, in 1893, the student was excluded from school because he was weak-minded, 'troublesome to other children,' made 'uncouth noises,' pinched others, and could not 'take ordinary, decent physical care of himself.' In another Massachusetts case, a girl was excluded from school because she was 'immoral,' and 'pursued a couse of open and notorious familiarities, and actual illicit intercourse, and that for hire and reward.' In still another Massachusetts case, the court allowed the exclusion of a student guilty of 'whispering, laughing, acts of playfulness and rudeness to other pupils, inattention to study,' and other distracting conduct.[3]

The school board did not win all its cases. Courts sometimes threw out 'unreasonable' rules. In a Wisconsin case, a school required each pupil to bring in a stick of wood after recess. A father complained that his son, who had diphtheria, could not carry the wood. The rule was held unreasonable.[4] Courts were reluctant, however, to let parents sue school boards for damages. In one case, in Indiana (1887), a 10-year-old girl was late for school in the middle of January. The temperature was 18 degrees below zero. When she reached school, she found herself locked out. She had to walk back home, and suffered frostbite. Her parents lost the case against the school.[5]

A small group of cases dealt with corporal punishment. Courts did not question the right of schoolteachers to take a switch to their pupils. The question was, how far could they go? Punishment should not be 'excessive.' In a New Hampshire case, *Heritage v. Dodge* (1886),[6] the teacher whipped a student who coughed and made coughlike noises to attract attention. The student claimed he had whooping cough. The teacher was held not liable. He may have made a mistake; but so long as he acted in good faith and without malice, the law did not require him to be 'infallible.' In an Indiana case, decided in 1888, the pupil, Edward Patrick, 16, was obviously a troublemaker. He 'made some antic demonstrations which created a general laugh,' and later walked off with the teacher's overcoat. The teacher, Tyner Vanvactor, was only 18 himself. He consulted the township trustees, and they told him to give Patrick his choice: whipping or expulsion. Patrick chose the whipping. There was some dispute about how hard he was beaten. (He was whipped with 'a green switch . . . about three feet long, and forked near the middle.') Vanvactor was convicted of assault and battery, and fined one cent. He appealed, on principle no doubt; the appeal court reversed. Still, an Indiana teacher was convicted in 1853 for overpunishing a pupil. He whipped, punched, and kicked the student in the head for misspelling the word *commerce* and refusing to try again. A Texas teacher beat a 17-year-old student sixty-six times for bringing brandied cherries to school and dividing them among the other pupils. This teacher was also convicted.[7]

The right of *parents* to punish their children physically was clear. The teacher — and the school board — had a similar right (up to a point). They stood 'in loco parentis.' The question was how far teachers, during the school day, filled the parents' shoes. The parents had a *general* right to chastise; the teacher's was 'restricted to the limits of his jurisdiction and responsibility as a teacher.' Other kinds of teacher power were in a kind of gray zone. Could a school, for example, forbid parties after school? Probably not — because this invaded the *parents'* domain.[8]

Still, discipline was at the core of the school system. A Maine judge put it this way: 'Free political institutions are possible only where the great body of the people are moral, intelligent, and habituated to self-control, and to obedience to lawful authority.... To become good citizens, children must be taught self-restraint, obedience, and other civic virtues.'[9] The nineteenth century notion of schools was frankly 'didactic'; schools aimed to teach 'a traditional value system,' and they 'genuinely believed that their world view was one that could be shared by all right-thinking people.'[10] Nothing is said, in the literature or the cases, about freedom of speech, or expression, or the dangers of conformity, which liberal judges of the twentieth century have made so much of. Conformity, or obedience, was a virtue, and democracy depended, not on the wilder excesses of 'individualism,' but on a kind of balanced self-control.[11]

A few cases questioned the limits of parental authority. How much must schools concede to the right of parents to decide what is best for their children? Compulsory education is itself, of course, a displacement of parental authority. In an Iowa case, in 1871, the school district allowed only so many absences a month, except for sickness and other good reasons. But one family kept the son home to prepare shrubbery for winter, do marketing, and take care of two cows. The daughter was kept home to keep the parents company. The school board's right to expel these students was sustained.[12]

At the end of the nineteenth century, schools began to require vaccinations before pupils could be admitted. A few parents — Christian Scientists, for example — opposed vaccination on religious grounds. In one case, the parents felt that vaccination produced 'a loathsome constitutional disease, which poisoned the blood.' The court generally sided with the schools in these cases.[13]

Religion cropped up in a few other cases, too. In *Donahoe v. Richards*,[14] a 15-year-old girl, Bridget Donahoe, who was Catholic, was expelled from school for refusing to read the King James version of the Bible. The Maine Supreme Court upheld the Board of Education and its power to decide which books would be used in the schools. Generally speaking, nineteenth century courts went along with school prayers and Bible readings. In one Massachusetts case, decided in 1866, a young girl was suspended for refusing to bow her head during Bible readings and prayers. This was on her father's instructions. But the State Supreme Court affirmed; the school's practice was an 'appropriate method' of reminding 'both teachers and scholars that one of the chief objects of education ... is to impress upon the minds of children and youth ... principles of piety and justice.'[15]

Nineteeth century courts were less finicky than courts today about sectarian encroachments in school. Parents' rights were distinctly subordinate to the power of local majorities to mold the character of local schools. In *Miller v. Board of Education* (1887),[16] parents challenged a school board for renting rooms in the basement of a Catholic church and holding classes there. Catholic children were required to attend mass before regular school hours. The Illinois court saw no violation of rights; neither did the Pennsylvania court in a case where a school district hired nuns to teach public school. The sisters wore habits, crucifixes, and rosaries while teaching.[17] Yet, 150 Catholic children were expelled from schools in Brattleboro, Vermont, for missing school on 4 June 1874 to attend services for the feast of Corpus Christi.[18]

Even in the nineteenth century, there were a few ornery, claims-conscious parents, though probably less than today. Guy Taylor's father refused to sign his report card.[19] Another father in Wisconsin refused to have his 12-year-old son study geography.[20] An Illinois father did not want his 16-year-old girl to study bookkeeping; an Indiana father vetoed music study for his boy.[21] A tempest in a Georgia teapot (1900) turned on whether a 13-year-old girl could be forced to take part in a debate. (The topic was 'Should Trial by Jury Be Abolished?') Her father thought the subject too difficult. The teacher refused to excuse her. Called on in class, the girl read a paper which ridiculed the teacher. The teacher refused to call on her again until she wrote a paper on the proper subject. The Georgia Supreme Court ultimately held that the punishment was proper.[22]

Pupils' Rights in the Twentieth Century[23]

These cases were rarities. Student rights became a more common issue in the twentieth century. Table 1 shows the number of published cases in which a student (or his parent as next friend) challenged the *content* of a school board rule or regulation, up to 1978. (As explained earlier, I have excluded cases in which the rule challenged was not a school board rule, regulation, or policy — for example, those in which the school board merely enforced a state law. I have also excluded cases about processes and procedures — whether a student can be expelled, for example, without a hearing. In the broadest sense, these are part of the phenomenon we are investigating. But they present other complexities as well.)

As the table shows, the rise in the number of such cases was moderate until the 1960s. In the 1950s, indeed, there were fewer such cases than in earlier decades, though the numbers between 1900 and 1960 are so small that fluctuations probably have no meaning. Cases covered by this study ballooned after 1960. Not a single case before the Second World War presented an issue of student rights to a *federal* court. Yet, of the 164 cases decided between 1969 and 1978, 118 were federal — 75 per cent of the total. No less than eighty-seven of these were dress code cases. More dress code cases were decided in the few years before and after 1970 than *all* student rights cases between 1899 and 1958. State court cases also increased; in the last decade of the survey, they were more than double those of the previous decade.

The early twentieth century cases carried on prior themes. The vaccina-

Table 1 Rates of litigation

Years	No. of cases (A)	No. of pupils (B) *	A/B	Won by pupil	Federal court	Most commonly challenged rule
1899–1908	11	15,503,110 (1900)	0.7	3 (27%)	0 (0%)	Vaccination (6)
1909–1918	14	17,813,852 (1910)	0.8	2 (14%)	0 (0%)	Vaccination (7)
1919–1928	15	21,578,316 (1920)	0.7	5 (33%)	0 (0%)	Vaccination (5)
1929–1938	13	25,678,015 (1930)	0.5	1 (8%)	0 (0%)	Flag salute (3)
1939–1948	10	25,433,542 (1940)	0.4	2 (20%)	0 (0%)	Anti-fraternity (5)
1949–1958	5	25,111,427 (1950)	0.2	0 (0%)	1 (20%)	Anti-fraternity (2)
1959–1968	29	36,086,771 (1960)	0.8	3 (10%)	8 (28%)	Married students (6)
1969–1978	164	45,909,088 (1970)	3.6	78 (48%)	118 (75%)	Dress code (87)

SOURCE: *The World Almanac and Book of Facts, 1980*, p. 184.

tion issue, for example, was still significant.[24] In the 1940s and 1950s, the biggest issue was school rules restricting fraternities, sororities, and other student clubs. School board officials claimed that the clubs were bad for morale, and they objected to blackball procedures.[25] Many states enacted anti-fraternity statutes.[26]

In the 1960s, rights of married students became an issue. Some schools limited the right of such students to take part in school activities outside of class. Underlying these cases is a view of public schools as guardians of conventional morality — or at least as places where traditional purity is maintained, even at some risk of unreality. In the 1940s and 1950s, teachers often smoked in secret, just like their students, and many school districts regularly expelled married students, pregnant students, and teenage fathers. Some districts even suspended pregnant married teachers when they started to 'show.'[27]

It is easy to write these policies off as simple bigotry or hypocrisy. They in fact imply a rather complex theory of what school is or ought to be. Cases on censorship of student publications also touch on the theme of schools as guardians of conventional morality. In *Shanley v. Northeast Independent School District, Bexar County, Texas* (1972),[28] five high-school seniors were expelled for printing and giving out a newspaper called *Awakening*, even though they prepared it off the grounds of the school, and there was nothing obscene or scurrilous about the newspaper (it did, however, print a story which favored legalizing marijuana). The school district had a policy that allowed expulsion of pupils who tried to avoid 'established procedure' for approval of 'activities such as the production ... and ... distribution of ... printed documents of any kind.' A federal court upheld the constitutional rights of the students.

It is useful to specify a little more carefully exactly what sort of 'conventional morality' schools have been guarding. In this regard, the cases about married students are crucial. The school boards gave various excuses for restricting these students. There was a deep fear of contamination. In Fremont, Ohio, by a Board of Education rule, any boy who 'contributed to the pregnancy of any girl out of wedlock' could take part in no school activity except classes, for the rest of the year. A *married* student was similarly restricted, until graduation; and the Junior-Senior prom was specifically off limits. One married student, who wanted to play baseball, challenged the rule in federal court and won.[29]

But why have such rules? The policy was stated in *Indiana High School Athletic Association v. Raike* (1975).[30] What was at stake was 'integrity' and a 'wholesome atmosphere.' Married students were 'bad examples' to the other athletes. They might discuss 'marital intimacies' and similar 'corrupting "locker room talk."' The court fortunately struck down the rule as unconstitutional.

The 'locker room talk' of married students could hardly be worse than that of unmarried students; but what the school boards really feared was legitimating teenage sex. The ideal was chastity, strict morality, obedience, respect for authority. The atmosphere of school should be almost monastic — at least officially. (A pregnant teacher, for example, like a married student, advertises sexuality too blatantly for these purposes.) This view of the schoolhouse no doubt reflected the wishes of most parents. Morality and respect were ebbing, they felt. The schoolhouse must not ratify these unfortunate social developments.

Social pressures on schools and school authorities were nothing new. What was different now was the attitude of a handful of mavericks — and judges. School was no longer a kind of surrogate home. At home, children are socialized; children are trained. Parents do the job. Hence, the right to correct the children. The schoolhouse, to a degree, was an extension of the home.

Of course, an extension of the home can easily become a *substitute* for the home, especially when the home falls down on its job. Hence, compulsory education and the development of institutions for juveniles who had no parents or had bad parents. There are faint echoes in a few students' rights cases of this stage in the evolution of school law. I cite here a tiny, one-paragraph case out of Georgia (1918). The school had a rule that no pupil could attend any 'show, moving picture show, or social function' except on Friday and Saturday night. Some students broke the rule by going to the movies — *with* parental consent. They were about to be expelled. The courts refused to intervene.[31]

The modern cases are dramatically different. The simple statement in *Tinker v. Des Moines Independent Community School District*[32] that students do not 'shed their constitutional rights . . . at the schoolhouse gate' is not as self-evident as appears at first glance; it is actually a startling shift in doctrine and attitude. By implication, and necessarily, it reduced the authority of teachers and school boards, over students as individuals. The power of schools no longer derived from parental power. After all, a parent can force his kids to take off black armbands, despite 'freedom of speech.'

In the old cases — about vaccination, for example — 'student rights' were really peripheral. No doubt the students shared their parents' view, but they were very young, and the real conflict was between two zones of discretion: schoolhouse and home. Only in the twentieth century do the cases confront real student rights; that is, rights of young people as individuals — backed, no doubt, by their parents, but nonetheless primarily asserting *their own* interests. Only the twentieth century looks on the schoolhouse, not as an extension of the family, but as one social institution among many; and, like other institutions (hospitals, prisons, business corporations), subject to general rules of law. School is no longer a parental or loco-parental zone. The very idea of student rights, in a sense, prejudges the issue.

To put it another way: the earlier cases did not focus on 'rights' but on *duties* — that is, on authority and its limits. The reader will immediately object, and quite rightly, that a duty is only the flipside of a right. Every right implies a duty, and every duty implies something about rights. Very true, in the world of legal philosophy; but not necessarily true of law as a working reality. It was an important *social* shift to move from thinking of pupils as people whose main job was learning how to obey, to thinking of them as people owning personalities and a bundle of 'rights.'

Not that the courts were of one mind in twentieth century cases. Students won some, but by no means all, of their cases.[33] Until quite recently, in fact, pupils were consistent losers. In no decade did students win more than a third of their cases. In one decade, with only five reported cases, the students struck out completely: they were zero for five. Contrariwise, in the decade of the great dress code brouhaha, they won 48 per cent, or almost half, of their cases.

Judge Not by Looks: the Dress and Hair Case[34]

Nothing is more startling in the history of student rights litigation than the explosion of dress and hair cases. These were decided almost entirely after 1966. The peak was in the early 1970s. They have since dwindled down to nothing.

Apparently, not a single reported case concerned this issue until 1921. The pioneer was a certain young Miss Valentine. She was one of six in her graduating class in Iowa, all young women. The school provided caps and gowns. Three girls refused to wear the gowns because of an 'offensive odor.' The school held back their diplomas. Miss Valentine fought and won.[35] Two years later, in 1923, we hear of a rule in Clay County, Arkansas, against 'transparent hosiery, low necked dresses, or any style of clothing tending toward immodesty in dress,' 'face paint or cosmetics' were also prohibited. Eighteen-year-old Pearl Pugsley came to school with talcum powder on her face, and was expelled. She challenged the rule. The court held against her, with a testy comment about the 'complaints of disaffected students.'[36]

These were isolated cases. The outburst of hair cases came between 1969 and 1973. They were mainly federal cases (by a three-to-one margin); they also raised *constitutional* issues, which were almost totally lacking in earlier cases. They owe something, perhaps, to doctrines that the Supreme Court developed: the second flag-salute case (*Barnette*, 1942),[37] for example, in which the Supreme Court, for the first time, used the 14th Amendment against the action of a school board. *Barnette* was, of course, a religion case. Jehovah's Witnesses refused, on religous grounds, to salute the flag. The case was rather nineteenth century in style (though not in outcome): the rights were parental, and the conflict was between zones of authority. And a full generation went by before the hair cases erupted.

Barnette, however, did point toward a new style of school case: it was federal and constitutional, invoking broad principle. The nineteenth century cases were mostly local and dyadic. Almost none were strategic or had the smell of a class-action or test case. The cases of the 1960s — the hair cases, for example — are cases about individual rights, personal life-style, freedom *from* authority. But they address themselves to courts on the basis of fundamental principle. They use social means, and a socialized remedy, to advance an exaggerated form of individual right.[38]

The first federal hair case was *Ferrell v. Dallas Independent School District* (1966).[39] The school board here had ruled out 'Beatle-style' haircuts. A group of boys, members of a 'combo,' broke the rule. (Young Phillip Ferrell, for example, wore his hair 'down to the ear lobe on the side and to the collar in the back.') The judge had no sympathy: he smelled 'confusion and anarchy' in the classroom; the school officials, on the other hand, had 'acted reasonably under the circumstances.'

In another Fifth Circuit case (1969),[40] the judge was annoyed by the very presence of the case on his docket. It was a 'lilliput of a lawsuit,' which had 'upset everybody in the school system,' even threatening ticklish plans to desegregate schools in his Georgia county. And this 'new school crisis,' he said sarcastically, was over the 'monumental question of the constitutional right of a student to wear a mustache.' Why should a judge, 'overloaded' with work, have to decide when the 'fuzz or down above the lips of a teenager becomes a mustache?' The rule against mustaches and beards was 'reasonable.' Hairy students may be 'distracting.' Teachers have the right to an 'atmosphere conducive to teaching and learning,' without 'unkempt faces' staring at them. If plaintiffs decided to 'place their right to . . . hair . . . on their faces above getting an education,' so be it.

This dash of cold water did not stop the flow of cases. Under the pressure of litigation — not to mention the forces which led to the pressure in the first place — judges began to weaken, they then did an about-face, at least in some circuits. Even in the Fifth Circuit, the hair issue was persistent and troublesome. A 15-judge panel was convened to decide, on a unified rule for the circuit so that what was valid in Hillsborough County, Florida, should also prevail in 'the Pampa, Texas, Independent School District.' Long hair lost in *Karr v. Schmidt* (1972), but just barely (eight to seven).[41]

The district court had found as a 'fact' that 'the haircut rule causes far more disruption of the classroom . . . than the hair it seeks to prohibit.' But this did not stop eight judges from holding otherwise. They were alarmed at the 'burden' on federal courts. The lawsuit in *Karr* took four full days of testimony at the trial level. It came up on appeal with a printed appendix more than 300 pages long. To put an end to all this, the court announced a 'per se rule': hair regulations 'are constitutionally valid,' and cases should be immediately dismissed 'for failure to state a claim.'[42]

This was a classic reaction to a problem of volume and legitimacy. The court laid down a flat rule to end disputes on the trial court level. I have elsewhere argued that this is a standard response to sudden intrusions of unwelcome, troublesome cases.[43] The rule adopted in *Karr* is what we can call a *rule of rejection*. That is, it is a rule which flatly orders courts to hear *none* of a certain brand of case, or to throw out all cases that claim a certain cause of action. A rule of rejection, of course, solves the problem of volume — if it is followed. Notice that it does not solve the *social* problem; it throws it out of court, in this case back into the lap of the school boards. A rule rejection, of this type, thus tends to decentralize decisions.

The hair problem, of course, was not confined to the Fifth Circuit. In the Seventh Circuit, for example, *Breen v. Kahl* (1969),[44] was a clear victory for the student, Thomas Breen. The code of Williams Bay High School (Wisconsin) provided that:

> Hair should be washed, combed and worn so it does not hang below the collar line in the back, over the ears on the side and must be above the eyebrows. Boys should be clean shaven; long sideburns are out.

Breen was tossed out of school for violating the code. The school board defended its action with the usual argument about 'distraction,' and also argued that students whose 'appearance conforms to community standards' tended to do better at school. But the court felt that the school board had the burden of showing why it was interfering with 'personal freedom,' and concluded that the board had not met this burden.

Later cases in this circuit came to mixed results. The judges did tend to agree that the issue was serious. The right to wear long hair was no joke, but a 'vital' matter to some students, who were 'willing to sacrifice' for their claim.[45] For one judge, the issue was 'simple disobedience parading as an assertion of constitutional rights.'[46] Another, however, looked past 'the length of a schoolboy's hair' to the vital core: whether the state had power to restrict a young person's freedom 'to mold his own life style through his personal appearance.'[47] There were mixed results in other circuits, too. The Sixth, Ninth and Tenth Circuits joined the Fifth Circuit in adopting a rule of rejection.[48] The First, Fourth, Seventh, and Eighth Circuits were pro-student. The Third Circuit flip-flopped. The Supreme Court might have put an end to the confusion, but it never did. It denied certiorari in no less than ten different hair cases.[49]

Nobody can read a judge's mind, but if we take text at face value, *Tinker v. Des Moines Independent Community School District*[50] deeply influenced many of the hair cases. *Tinker* was decided in 1969; almost every challenge to a school board since then has cited it. *Tinker*, of course, was not a dress code case. In *Tinker* students wore armbands, during school hours, as symbols of opposition to the war in Vietnam. Three students, including John Tinker, age 15, and his 13-year-old sister Mary, were suspended from school for refusing to take these off. The Supreme Court, looking through the lens of constitutional principle, saw the schoolhouse as a very limited monarchy indeed. Students and teachers do not shed freedom of speech at the schoolhouse gate. Schools are not 'enclaves of totalitarianism.' The state may (of course) regulate school activity, to prevent disorder; but there was no evidence that the armbands caused disturbance. The regulation was unconstitutional.

Thus the majority: Justice Black, however, delivered a furious dissent. He spoke of a 'new revolutionary era of permissiveness ... fostered by the judiciary.' The decision, he felt, encouraged pupils to 'defy and flaunt the orders of school officials to keep their minds on their own school work.'[51] *Tinker* was indeed about authority, if it was about anything at all. But if *Tinker* limited, in some ways, the authority of schools, it also by the same token increased the power of courts. Who would decide which board rules were 'reasonable' and which ones restricted rights unreasonably? The courts, of course. The tests set out in *Tinker* cannot apply themselves automatically at the local level. If challenged, there must be some third party with authority to resolve the issues. This means (in this society) the courts, above all.

Of course, there is nothing new about this rule of reason. As we have seen, it goes back deep into the nineteenth century. It is the idea of the 'limited monarchy.' In the nineteenth century, however, the limits of discretion were rarely tested, so that the rule of reason was essentially toothless. Mapping the boundaries did not present much of a problem, either for the courts or society at large. Only truly egregious violations of local norms were likely to evoke any challenge. When small minority groups protested on the basis of principle, the courts were generally unsympathetic.

On one level, the issue in the hair cases was a similar one: how far did the discretion of teachers and school boards go? From one standpoint, the best rule was a rule of rejection. But this did not fit the mood of potential litigants. No matter that 99 per cent of all students and parents, or more, were willing to abide by the rules. It does not take more than a tiny minority, people with nerve and will, to stir up the waters, to create 'disruption' (as school people see it), or to create a 'litigation explosion' (as the judges see it).

Some courts did try to choke off litigation, as was mentioned. But still the cases came. There were eighty-seven of them between 1969 and 1978; and they split about evenly down the middle. Curiously, neither students nor lawyers nor courts were ever clear exactly *what* in the constitution gave students the right to long hair. According to this or that plaintiff, dress codes violated the 1st, 8th, 9th, 10th, or various pieces of the 14th Amendment. Some courts muttered vaguely about 'personal freedom' or the 'penumbras' of various rights. In one case, a judge rhapsodized over the 'commodious concept of liberty, embracing freedoms great and small,' which apparently lurks inside the 14th Amendment.

Judges and teachers on the other side were almost equally vague and sometimes downright silly. One judge in Pennsylvania defended a rule against beards and mustaches because it prevented 'psychological detriment'. High-school boys who were still beardless might suffer because they were 'unable to compete in the "face race."' (In the actual case, young Darius Lovelace won the right to get back into school, since *his* mustache was 'practically imperceptible' and was 'merely a natural growth, not a cultivated adornment.')[52] In a Florida case, the school board argued that grooming codes were valuable training in 'norms and values'; they helped teach 'that there are consequences if one deviated from the norm.' The board also brought in evidence that long-hairs had lower test scores than short-hairs, more disciplinary problems, and tended to be 'socially maladjusted and to cluster in cliques.'[53] In *Parker v. Fry*, there was the usual testimony about distraction and disruption, but Evans, a history teacher, moved the discussion to a higher plane: in his view, 'Jesus had worn short hair and was clean shaven. . . . In effect, . . . this was a rule that God established.'[54] (This was balanced, perhaps, by a district judge who noted that 'portraits of six great jurists' were on the walls, starting with Moses, and that 'some had mustaches and beards.')[55] In still another case, the principal was afraid that students 'would polarize into camps of "long hairs" and "short hairs."' Besides, if 'boys were allowed to wear long hair so as to look like girls,' there might be 'confusion over appropriate dressing room and restroom facilities.'[56]

After a few furious years of litigation, the hair cases died down, and no more was heard of them. The 'explosion' passed as rapidly and suddenly as it had come. Yet, the issue was (legally speaking) never definitively resolved. Why, then, did the lawsuits stop?

One guess is that student activism faded in general. Nobody wears black armbands in the schools today. There are fewer issues and fewer issue-mongers. The end of the war in Vietnam may have cast its mysterious spell of calm here, too. Some might add that the battle was simply won. Long hair no longer seems to bother anybody. Even school superintendents sometimes wear long hair. Far worse was in store for schools than Beatle-style haircuts. The schools have generally agreed, tacitly or otherwise, to tolerate all sorts of hairstyles. In the Reagan age, there might yet be a backlash, but so far all is quiet.

Yet, *judicialization* has not ended. Far from it. Even some of the cases that rejected hair rights grudgingly conceded the general principle. The message was fairly clear: *this* issue may not be appropriate, but others are. The door is open — has *got* to be open — for students to assert their constitutional rights. In May 1981, the *San Francisco Chronicle* reported on a lawsuit over a high-school grade in an Advanced Algebra class. The student, Janice Anderson, 17, got a B+, but felt she deserved an A.[57] The teacher refused to budge. Appeals were taken within the school system of San Leandro. The superintendent ordered the grade raised. This outraged the teacher, who filed a grievance with the San Leandro Teachers Association. The Association sued the superintendent, on the grounds that he had infringed academic freedom. This time Janice lost. The case displays, in unusually graphic form, how the entire school system, from top to bottom, has been judicialized. There is more here than student rights. Note, too, that while all parties took the case quite seriously, the case still seemed odd enough to catch the *Chronicle*'s eye.

Recognizing 'student rights' does not mean that courts will 'run local school boards,' or even that courts will be flooded with cases. These cases are and will be rare. There may be 'bulges' in the caseload from time to time — some particularly acute social problem, or a particularly controverted one. These 'bulges' (of hair cases, or prisoners' rights cases, or whatever) need not be permanent, and rarely are. Another lesson is that the 'fall' or decline (of hair cases) masked a real change. The cases made their impact, no doubt, on local school boards. They saw that courts were not laughing at 17-year-olds with funny hair. Judicial review of the 'limited monarchy' was at least a *possibility*. Schools adjusted their rules — and perhaps their behavior as well.

Thus, the limited monarchy is more limited than ever. The cause, however, does not lie in court doctrine, but rather in social relations. Public attitudes toward schools are the fundamental fact. These are both deep and volatile. In any event, they are quite beyond the power of courts either to generate or subdue. These attitudes, of course, are also often in conflict. Judges in the hair cases plainly were of two minds: some stressed the function of schools in teaching 'obedience'; others stressed 'individuality' or 'personal life-style,' an idea which was (to say the least) foreign to the mind of the nineteenth century. But the notion of 'individuality' or 'life-style' is central to the very jurisdiction of courts in these cases. Otherwise, suing authorities is not only a nuisance, it is bad modeling and bad training for the young.

It is dangerous, of course, to use reported cases to draw inferences about schools in general, or even about what society thinks of its schools. But the temptation is hard to resist. We start out, in the nineteenth century, with a picture of schools molding young minds, imbuing patriotism, morality, and obedience. Pupils were, in a real sense, 'passive vessels into which education is poured.'

The quote is from an article about *Tinker*. The author observes (quite accurately) that *Tinker* rejects this approach.[58] Is it too farfetched to say that the tables are now turned? Now the *school* is the 'passive vessel.' It is supposed to avoid whatever smacks of 'indoctrination.' A case in point is *Smith v. St. Tammany Parish School Board* (1971).[59] A high-school principal hung the Confederate battle flag in his office. Black students objected. The court agreed with them. The flag was a symbol of segregation, of 'white racism in general.' A 'Black Panther or a Black Power flag,' would be equally out of place. The constitution forbids all such flags in a 'unitary school system where both white and black students attend school together.'

Yet, of course, *students* can fly flags, wear black armbands, whistle or not whistle Dixie, distribute pro-pot or anti-pot literature, and sport whatever hair, hats, berets, buttons, and badges they wish. The constitution protects their freedom of expression, in and out of school. The same constitution frowns on symbols and manifestoes *by* the school — whose job is 'education,' a neutral, professional job. This is, at any rate, the message of modern law.

The courts stand ready to enforce this view of schools. And judicialization here is part of a broader phenomenon: legalization. By this I am referring, basically, to the stiffening of informal norms into networks of rules and regulations, and of informal procedures into procedures that look more or less like those of courts. The two phenomena, of course, interact. A judicialized system warns organizations that they had better legalize their own house or the courts will force them to do it.

The passage from informal to formal norms, and from informal procedures to 'due process,' goes on throughout society. At the most abstract level, it is an inevitable outcome of the complexity of society and the growth of institutions.

Sears Roebuck cannot hire and fire like a mom and pop grocery store. It has a 'personnel department,' which is inevitably more formal. Legalization also reflects the tremendous expansion of government between, say, 1870 and today. Government (federal, state, and local) has its finger in many pies; organs that *control* government (courts, for example) grow too. Moreover, the scope of modern government blurs the line between what is 'legal' and what is not. Leviathan is so large that it seems to swallow the whole ocean, and little fish, like Janice Anderson, begin to think thoughts that were once unthinkable. Like it or not, it is probably an irreversible process.

Notes

1 *Anderson v. State*, 40 Tenn. (Head 3) 348 (1859).
2 85 Ill, App. 82 (1899).
3 See *Watson v. City of Cambridge*, 157 Mass. 561, 32 NE 864 (1893); *Sherman v. Inhabitants of Charlestown*, 62 Mass. (8 Cush.) 160 (1851); *Hodgkins v. Inhabitants of Rockport* 105 Mass. 475 (1870); *Board of Education v. Helston*, 32 Ill. App. 300 (1890).
4 *State ex rel. Bowe v. Board of Education*, 63 Wis. 234, 23 NW 102 (1885).
5 *Fertick v. Michener*, 111 Ind. 472, 111 NE 605 (1887).
6 64 N.H. 297, 9 Atl. 722 (1886).
7 *Vanvactor v. State*, 113 Ind. 276, 15 NE. 341 (1888); *Gardner v. State*, 4 Ind. 632 (1853); *Whitley v. State*, 33 Tex. Cr. R. 172, 25 SW 1072 (1894).
8 See *Dritt v. Snodgrass*, 66 Mo. 286, 298 (1877); but compare *Mangum v. Keith*, 147 Ga. 603, 95 SE 1 (1918).
9 *Patterson v. Nutter*, 78 Me. 509, 7 Atl. 273 (1886). The judge in *Cooper v. McJunkin*, 4 Ind. 290 (1853), warned of this 'evil practice' with its 'inherent proneness to abuse. The very act of whipping engenders passion and generally leads to excess.'
10 TYACK, D. and HANSOT, E. (1981) 'Conflict and consensus in American public education,' *Daedalus*, 110, 3, pp. 1 and 5–6.
11 The point should not be carried too far. School authority was a shade ambiguous. Nineteenth-century teachers were chronically underpaid, often poorly educated, treated dismally by school authorities, and not much older than their pupils. They symbolized authority — but sometimes weakly.
12 *Burdick v. Babcock*, 31 Iowa 562 (1871).
13 *Blue v. Beach*, 155 Ind. 121, 56 NE 89 (1900). See also *Labaugh v. Board of Education*, 177 Ill. 562, 52 NE 850 (1899); *Potts v. Breen*, 167 Ill. 67, 47, NE 81 (1897); *State ex rel. Cox v. Board of Education*, 21 Utah 401, 60 p. 1013 (1900).
14 38 Me. 379 (1854).
15 *Spiller v. Inhabitants of Woburn*, 94 Mass. (12 Allen) 127 (1866). *Pfeiffer v. Board of Education*, 118 Mich. 560, 77 N.W. 250 (1898); *State ex rel. Weiss v. District Board of School, District No. 8*, 76 Wis. 177, 44 NW 967 (1890).
16 121 Ill. 297, 10 NE 669 (1887).
17 *Hysong v. School District*, 164 Pa. 629, 30 Atl. 482 (1894).
18 *Ferriter v. Tyler*, 48 Vt. 444 (1876).
19 *Bourne v. State ex rel. Taylor*, 35 Neb. 1, 52 NW 710 (1892).
20 *Murrow v. Wood*, 35 Wis. 59 (1874).
21 *Trustee of Schools v. People*, 87 Ill. 303 (1877); *State ex rel. Andrew v. Webber*, 108 Ind. 31, 8 NE 708 (1886).

22 *Samuel Benedict School v. Bradford*, 111 Ga. 801, 36 SE 920 (1900).
23 See GOLDSTEIN, S.R. (1969) 'The scope, and sources of school board authority to regulate student conduct and status: a nonconstitutional analysis,' *University of Pennsylvania Law Reivew*, 117, pp. 373–430.
24 Eighteen out of the forty cases in the first three decades were vaccination cases. To some extent the cases disappeared because State law removed the issue from local school boards. For example, *Mass. Ann. Laws*, chapter 76, sec. 15; see *Commonwealth v. Green*, 268 Mass. 585, 168 NE 101 (1929); *Jacobson v. Massachusetts*, 197 US 11 (1905).
25 See *Coggins v. Board of Education of City of Durham*, 223 No. Car. 763, 28 SE 2d 527 (1944).
26 See also *Wilson v. Abilene Independent School District*, 190 SW 2d 406 (Texas, 1945); *Wright v. Board of Education*, 295 Mo. 466, 246 SW 43 (1922). *Iowa Code Ann.* sec. 287.1: 'No pupil may join ... any fraternity or society ... except such societies or associations as are sanctioned by the ... schools.'
27 *Cleveland Board of Education v. LaFleur*, 414 US 632 (1974).
28 344 F. Supp. 298 (ND Ohio, 1972).
29 *Davis v. Meek*, 462 Fed. 2d 960 (CA 5, 1972).
30 329 NE 2d. 66 (Ind. App., 1975); see also *Romans v. Crenshaw*, 354 F. Supp. 868 (SD Tex., 1972); *Nutt v. Board of Education of Goodland*, 128 Kan. 507 278 Pac. 1062 (1929); *Board of Education of Harrodsburg v. Bentley*, 383 SW 2d 677 (Ky., 1964). *States ex rel. Thompson v. Marion County Board of Education*, 302 SW 2d 57 (Tenn., 1957); *Board of Dir. of the School Dist. of Waterloo v. Green*, 259 Iowa 1260, 147 NW #2d 854 (1967). On the early cases, see in general, FLOWERS, A. and BOLMEIER, E.C. (1964) *Law and Pupil Control.*
31 *Mangum v. Keith*, 147 Ga. 603 95 SE 1 (1918).
32 393 US 503 (1969).
33 For example, contrast *Gambino v. Fairfax County School Board*, 429 F. Supp. 731 (ED Va., 1977), aff'd. 564 Fed. 2d 157 (CA 4, 1977), in which students successfully fought a ban on an article ('Sexually Active Students Fail to Use Contraceptives') in the school newspaper, with *Trachtman v. Anker*, 426 F. Supp. 198 (SD NY, 1976), aff'd in part and rev'd in part, 562 Fed. 2d 512 (CA 2, 1977) (a questionnaire was passed out by the students, asking about attitudes about sex; the school called a halt, and was upheld). See also, *Fricke v. Lynch* 491 F. Supp. 381 (DRJ, 1950); *New York Times*, 13 May 1979 and 24 May 1979 on a related issue (gay rights and the senior prom).
34 Dozens of law review articles treat the subject — and at least one book: PUNKE, H.H. (1973) *Social Implications of Lawsuits over Student Hairstyles.*
35 *Valentine v. Independent School District of Casey*, 183 NW 434 (Iowa, 1921). See also *Stromberg v. French*, 60 ND 750 236 NW 477 (1931).
36 158 Ark. 247, 250 SW 538 (1923); *Stromberg v. French*, 60 ND 750, 236 NW 477 (1931).
37 *West Virginia State Board of Education v. Barnette*, 319 US 624 (1942), overruling *Minersville School District v. Gobitis*, 310 US 586 (1940).
38 It is interesting, therefore, to compare the facts of the flag-salute cases with, for example, *Frain v. Baron*, 307 F. Supp. 27 (ED NY, 1969). Here students refused to recite the Pledge of Allegiance, because they thought the words 'with liberty and justice for all' were 'not true in America today.' One student was 'an atheist, who also objected to the words "under God."' The students also 'refused to stand during the Pledge, because that would constitute participation in what they considered a lie. They also refused to leave the room.' The students won a preliminary injunction preventing the school from forcing them to leave the room or from treating them any differently from those who recited the Pledge.
39 261 F. Supp. 545 (1966).

40 *Stephenson v. Wheeler County Board of Education*, 306 F. Supp. 97, (DCSD Ga, 1969); aff'd 426 F. 2d 1154, cert. den. 400 US 957 (1970).
41 460 F. 2d 609 (1972).
42 There were three separate dissents. Judge Wisdom (and four other colleagues) suggested that the school board had violated the equal protection clause, the due process clause, and the First Amendment. Judge Godbold (and three others, some of whom also joined with Judge Wisdom) thought that circuit courts should leave the whole matter to the district courts. Judge Roney dissented on the 'narrow ground' that a hair rule is unconstitutionally oppressive because it 'follows' students 'out of the school house door.' That is, once hair is cut, it is cut (unlike clothes, which are an on-and-off proposition). Hence, the rule tells students what they can do outside of school as well as inside.
43 FRIEDMAN, L.M. (1967), 'Legal rules and the process of social change,' *Stanford Law Review*, 19, pp. 786–840.
44 419 F. 2d 1034 (1969).
45 *Arnold v. Carpenter*, 459 Fed. 2d 939 (1972).
46 Judge Stephenson, dissenting in *Torvik v. Decorah Community Schools*, 453 Fed. 2d 777 (1972).
47 Judge Lay, concurring in *Bishop v. Colaw*, 450 Fed. 2d 1069 (1971). Schoolchildren 'must be given every feasible opportunity to grow in independence to develop their own individualities and to initiate and thrive on creative thought.'
48 See, for example, *King v. Saddleback Jr. College District*, 445 Fed. 2d, 932 (1971); *Freeman v. Flake*, 448 Fed. 2d 258 (1971).
49 On the results in the various circuits, see TROUP, F. (1975) 'Long hair and the law: A look at constitutional and Title VII challenges to public and private regulation of male grooming,' *University of Kansas Law Review*, 24 pp. 142–72 at 156, note 110. On the denials of certiorari, see p. 155, note 106. Justice Douglas felt strongly that the Court should have heard these cases; see 404 US 1042 (1972) (dissent in denial of certiorari in *Olff v. East Side Union High School District*, 445 Fed. 2d 932, CA 9, 1971).
50 393 US 503 (1969).
51 310 F. Supp. (DCWD Pa. 1970).
52 *Dawson v. Hillsborough County, Fla. School Board*, 322 F. Supp. 286, 301 (1971); aff'd, 445 Fed. 2d 308 (1971).
53 *Parker v. Fry*, 323 F. Supp. 728 (DCED Ark, 1971).
54 D.J. Singleton, in *Calbillo v. San Jacinto Junior College*, 305 F. Supp. 857, 861 (SD Tex., 1969).
55 *Bishop v. Colaw*, 450 F. 2d 1069 (8th Cir., 1971).
56 *San Francisco Chronicle*, 28 May 1981, p. 2, col. 2. The result, she said, 'destroyed' her 'faith in the legal system.'
57 GOLDSTEIN, S.R. (1970) 'Reflections on developing trends in the law of student rights,' *University of Pennsylvania Law Review*, 118, pp. 612–20.
58 316 F. Supp. 1174 (ED La., 1970), aff'd, 448 F. 2d 414 (5th Cir., 1971).

2 Theoretical Frame

Organizational Factors Affecting Legalization in Education

John W. Meyer
Stanford University

'Legalization'

Educational systems are deeply institutionalized in society. There are generally shared definitions within them of their main outlines: for instance, the pagentry of progress from kindergarten through the post-doctorate is clearly understood, and so are the broad outlines of the curriculum. These shared definitions unite education as much as any special organizational mechanisms or rules: parents, the wider community, teachers, administrators, legislatures, and interest groups of all kinds, know the main outlines. In one sense, education is more a ritual system than a technical organizational one: more of what a third-grade teacher is to do is communicated by the common culture than by any combination of administrators (or socializers in teacher education programs). Occasionally some confrontation arises, sometimes from the legal system — an anomalous right or a pupil, or programmatic rule, or special requirement — some external social presupposition that all is not well, and that special virtues must be enforced. A drama of opposition is created between education and society. This is colloquially what we mean when we talk about 'legalization' — a court case or order intruding into the system, a special administrative requirement imposed on it by the state, or special legislative action. These anomalies are what we really mean by 'legalization.' But a formal definition is not so easy, because even though the actors in the system are not routinely conscious of it, the whole institutionalized structure itself is embedded in legal rules. The third-grade teacher teaching arithmetic is not conscious of these rules, because arithmetic is part of a deeply-institutionalized national routine — but the rules are there in the law and regulations. We need a definition of legalization that separates the anomalies from the routine: otherwise, legalization refers to the whole system.

Thus, throughout the world, modern educational systems are legally based. Laws and state regulations define, compel, and classify pupils; specify days, hours, and years of attendance; and define much of the impact of education in later life by occupational credentialling rules. They credential teachers, and specify their relevant properties. They lay out the required curricula, and sometimes even define the proper materials. They define and periodize the conjunction of pupils, teachers, and curricula; they also specify in detail the physical space in which this conjunction is to occur; the size of classrooms, the size and height of their windows, the number and character of toilets and water fountains, and detailed features of school design and construction. And the entire assembly of elements — pupils, teachers, curricula, and space — is approved by the state. The school is or is not accredited, and thereby its resources are mainly determined, as well as the social positions of its students and graduates.

Beyond the school itself, laws and state regulations establish a larger organizational structure: defining, requiring, and legitimating the elements of this system. There are principals, districts, superintendents (in some systems, inspectors), and a variety of state functionaries in ministries or offices or departments of education.

All these materials make up an educational organization and an educational order. And all of it, essentially, is legal in foundation. It makes little sense to speak of legalization as a variable by this criterion — though one can find a little variation around the world in legalization in this sense.

One could argue that all of these standard legal ingredients of the system are so deeply institutionalized in the educational order itself that their legal bases are taken for granted by the actors involved. Legalization, then, might be restricted to legally induced changes in the system: since much educational change has some base in legal authority, this directs our attention to educational change in general. It is not useful to treat as legalization every enactment of a properly constituted hillbilly school board, every routine complaint by an authorized citizen-parent, every curricular change installed by a legally mandated subminister of education, or every funding modification in the routine order enacted by a legislative body. Most legal changes are not 'legalization' — they are the routine modification, through the established chain of command, of the established order. These legal changes are part of the organizational order itself — they are part of its standard linkages with the environment. They are, in short, too orderly.

We mean by legalization the disorderly introduction of legal authority into the educational order: instances of the exercise of authority which violate the routinized order and chain of command, which introduce new rules without their integration into the established set. We mean decisions of the courts or of administrative agencies, or of legislative bodies creating a specific program or compelling a specific line of action outside the routinized command structure. But we also mean any court or legislative actions legitimizing a new interest with specific rights within the system.

Thus, suppose a concern about the inadequate educational treatment of the handicapped arises in society, and demands are made through the legal system. If these are responded to by the national legislature in its routine management of the educational system, it is not by our definition legalization. If the national ministry of education adapts the national educational system's rules in a routine and integrated way, it is also not legalization. But if the national legislature creates new rights for classes of handicapped citizens which they can impose on education through the courts, or funds a new special program in no way linked to other aspects of the educational system, or imposes direct controls on schools bypassing intervening administrative layers, our criteria for legalization are met. They are also met if such programs are created administratively by national officials. And it is legalization by our account if the courts on their own discover and adapt to the new claims for the handicapped, and impose new demands on the educational system. The key to our definition is lack of integration of the new rules with the main rules constituting the system, or the lack of integration of the new channels of control with the old ones. Thus, we contrast legalization by our definition — disorderly legalization — with the routine legal controls managing and changing every educational system in the world. Our definition may seem arbitrary, but no other is of much use in discussing so quintessentially public an education in the modern world: other definitions make legalization coterminous with centralization, or with rates of administrative action, or with rates of change.

Legalization, thus, is likely to be a transitory phenomenon, like a social movement: the routinization and integration of its claims in the established structure are likely to eliminate it as a main process on any specific issue. We focus, then, on the rise and fall of waves of court actions and special-purpose legislation outside the regular chain of educational command: on the legal introduction of disorder into the educational order.

The Problem

We consider the conditions under which demands against the educational system arise in society — confrontations between social rights and interests, on the one hand, and the putatively recalcitrant educators on the other; and the conditions under which these demands become legal rules penetrating the system from outside rather than through its routine administrative structure. We call the demands arising outside the system *disorders* — depictions of needs and rights in society unmet by the educational system — and the special results of interest here *legalization*.

The special nature of the educational order in modern societies affects both the process of development of external disorders and the extent to which they are resolved by legalization — that is, by the transfer of the external disorder into one internal to the educational system. We turn to an examination of the educational order.

Nature of the Educational Order

One can imagine an institutional order so closed and complete that almost no sources of disorder are left — almost no sources or grounds of legalization. In practice, this is quite unrealistic, and the educational order shares with all others some potential sources of disorder:

1 Orders are connected to society through some principles of collective authority and purpose. Interests may arise or change in society altering or reweighting the goals of the educational system (e.g., a concern with radically improving the services provided the poor or the handicapped). If authority within the order is weak enough or if the rearrangement of interests is substantial enough, a disorderly penetration of the system may result.

2 The internal structure of any order is also subject to a variety of social constraints (e.g., the required forms of treatment of workers). Interest readjustments in society may lead to the alteration or delegitimation of elements of the educational processing system itself (e.g., certain groups are not properly funded or employed in the system).

But beyond these ordinary possibilities for the creation of disorders, the educational system contains extra potential, arising from the special nature of educational order. Education is a rationalized and clearly defined organizational system, like many others. But this organizational system is imposed on an extraordinarily chaotic domain: the human inputs are highly and unpredictably variable, technologies of instruction are non-existent or variable in nature and consequence, outputs are unpredictable and uncertain in measurement, and an organizational system of controls over all this would be impossible or impossibly expensive. The real world of the educational domain is, as the current phrase in organizational theory has it, 'loosely coupled' in the extreme[1]. In this situation, the rationalized educational order has a highly ritualized character, disconnected at every point of technical substance from the variability of the domain over which it exercises control.[2] In fact, the creation of a coherent and rational educational order requires such disconnection. Thus, order in the classification of pupils is achieved by ignoring their substantive properties and attending to ritual ones: they are admitted to Algebra II because they 'have had' Algebra I, not because they know it; they enter college because they 'have graduated' from high school, not by virtue of substantive properties or competencies. They enter school by virtue of age, not competence. Order in the definition of teachers is achieved by reference to 'professionalism' and credentials, not substantive capacities or skills. Order in the definition of the curriculum is achieved by abstract specification and by avoidance of inspection that is renowned and quite extreme.[3] And arching over this technical domain is an organizational system that attends carefully to ritual matters (attendance, credentials, formal program categories and labels) and sheds information on matters of substance[4]. Administrators disinform themselves on matters of classroom processes and outcomes[5] — if outcome data are forced on them by exogenous processes, they ignore them.[6] In sharp contrast to organizational orders resting in technical action and consequence and in which information is a resource, education is a highly institutionalized order with ritual characteristics — information on the technical world is a cost.[7] Imagine a religious organization trying to deal with the actual evaluations by God of the souls of its members and elites.

All this is fairly well understood in the field, though in a rationalist world it is delegitimated and treated as wrong or archaic or almost scatological. We are in chronic postures of rationalizing educational reform: professors of education ordinarily pursue these reforms for primary and secondary education, while sustaining the ritual structures in their own universities. There are, thus, substantial literatures blaming each of the parties to the educational order (parents are unconcerned and inattentive; teachers are ignorant and reactionary and self-protective; administrators are lazy and self-serving; and politicians bow down too much to irrational pressures). From a more serious point of view, this is unrealistic: many parties have a stake in educational order, and it is quite clear that any educational order must most of the time keep its head in the sand, given a substantive domain so filled with variability and unpredictability. The extension of modern rationality so far into social life requires a great deal of sustained ignorance.

But this means that the educational order is surrounded by much potential (legalizable) disorder:

3 Pupils and their properties are in fact infinitely variable. Any new virtue or handicap may be 'discovered' and licensed and made basis for legitimate claims on the order. Recently, a number of new educational handicaps have been discovered with the support of some researchers, and made grounds for claims.[8]

4 The substantive effects of education are enormously uncontrolled and variable. Order is obtained by the social definition that all products of Algebra I are in important ways alike, as with all high school graduates. They are not. Any 'discovery' of this creates a disorder, and with some interpretation, an injustice and a claim.

5 The actual processes of classroom life are uncontrolled and variable. This may be discovered, treated as a violation of putative technical rules, and made basis of a claim.

6 The higher levels of management and funding of the system are based on ritual categories, and relatively uncontrolled in substance. Variabilities and claims may arise. (For example, in a school with more troublesome students, any individual student with given properties receives fewer resources than would be the case in another school with the same overall per-pupil resources.)

Overall, it should be apparent that educational orders are more likely loci of perceived disorder than other orders.

But in important ways, all educational systems around the world have these common properties. We need to go on to consider conditions under which perceived disorders produce legalization. Much more routine responses are more common: in every educational system, routine administrative structures are constantly adapting education to new groups, new curricular themes, new problems, and so on. The special feature of American education in the recent period is probably not the rate of expansion of social claims or disorders — many educational systems, for instance in developing countries, are under much more extreme pressures — but the extent to which these are turned into legalized responses.

Structural Conditions of Legalization in Education

Waves of socially perceived disorders in the system lead to controls. But most of these occur through the routine operations of the structure itself. Our problem is to understand the conditions under which this does not happen (a necessary aspect of legalization, by definition), and the further conditions under which legalization is a possible outcome.

Assume the available disorders. Consider two variables that may affect their outcomes:

1 Educational orders vary in degree of organizational centralization. Many national systems are highly centralized. A ministry of education defines pupils, teachers, curricula, and so on, and coordinates these in a rationalized myth of education. Every aspect of the educational system has as its referent the rules of the ministry.

The American system is highly decentralized. The national state has practically no jurisdiction over the content of education. There are no national state curricula. There are no national state definitions of teachers, and very few accrediting principles for schools. There are the weakest national state definitions of pupils and their general educational categories (specifying, for instance, the definition of the fourth grade, or of high school graduation). The national state department of education is a collection of disorganized special programs — a situation clearly resulting from the absence of legitimated national state authority over education itself.

States do have substantial controls, though they vary greatly in this, from centralized Hawaii to many states with very weak central rules.[9] By and large, states do build up an integrated myth of education, specifying general categories of pupils and their attendance rules, certifying teachers in various categories, requiring some elements of standard curricula, establishing funding rules and their district bases, defining school and classroom space, accrediting schools, and so on. These integrated control systems are substantially weaker than those built into many national states, but they are nonetheless very real, and have been built up over a long history (for instance, state laws making education compulsory were passed between eighty and 110 years ago; state credentialling of teachers has a history almost as long).

School districts have much autonomy of their own, defined in state law. Within state rules, they have many legitimated powers over pupils, teachers, and curricula. And they are, of course, subjected to legitimated political influences from their own constituencies.

Schools themselves often have considerable autonomy over their own programs. And the tradition of local influence over school policy is substantial (aided by a structure in which many administrators have no tenure rights).

Overall, the American system is one in which most educational authority of an organizational kind is reserved for the state or local levels. This has extremely important consequences for legalization rates, as we will subsequently argue.

2 Issues and disorders also vary in their loci. Some are local, as when a given group of parents is dissatisfied with the educational progress of their children. Others are national in scope, as when American economic failures are attributed to a lax national educational system, or a national problem in the treatment of the handicapped or of minorities is discerned, or the 'Sputnik crisis' is attributed to failures of American engineering training, or the 'Watergate crisis' is seen to result from the ethical failures of American legal education.

The locus of a disorder is socially determined. We discuss in the section on the Social Generation of Waves of Perceived Educational Disorders how wider social forces have shifted many disorders to the national level, and in the section on the Intersection of Waves of Disorder and Centralization how this has affected legalization. At present, however, our interest lies in the consequences of the interaction between system centralization and disorder loci for the creation of legalization. Our two variables create four distinct situations.

Centralized Disorders in Centralized Systems

In these systems, national disorders do not tend to generate legalization. The centralized system provides routine channels for the management of new interests and claims, and for the management of the discovery of new forms of variation to which adaptation is required. The legislature may act, the ministry creates new rules of curriculum or program or new types of pupils, and the legitimately subordinated levels of the structure comply with more or less precision. New claims are integrated in the ongoing myth of education: the loose ends that might make possible court cases are tidied up in the standard bureaucratic ways. The same processes that specify the rights, say, of the poor also specify the educational procedures that meet these rights. Such systems, carrying central responsibility for and authority over education, typically do not endow groups in society with the kind of standing to make possible such court actions. Similarly, central legislative bodies carry the responsibility to integrate the whole educational system — to create the rules under which the responsible ministry functions. They infrequently perpetrate legalization — the anomalous introduction of rules violating extant ones or of procedures violating the regular chain of command — for doing so would constitute a form of violation of their own authority.

Localized Disorders in Centralized Systems

Complaints are, of course, endemic to educational systems. But in centralized systems, local complaints are relatively unlikely to take legalization forms (though these complaints make up much of what little legalization there is in such systems). Elaborated bureaucratic systems contain elaborated procedures to manage or suppress complaints within the routinized order. And they occur in states that are likely to keep access to extra-educational machinery for local complaints at a low level: the same state which assumes general educational responsibility preempts under this responsibility the possibilities for autonomous educational action through the state legal system.

Nevertheless, there is undoubtedly considerable variation among states here: it seems likely that states with both elaborated centralized control systems and substantial development of the rights of relatively autonomous citizenship make possible legal action by local sub-groups more than states in which citizenship is itself mainly seen as a creature of the state itself. This situation could relatively easily be studied empirically.[10]

A further issue here is the degree of implementation of the national system in a nominally centralized order. Many developing countries have high levels of educational centralization,[11] without much effective implementation. This might make possible a variety of legal actions on the part of local groups. It would be relatively easy to investigate what happens when national legislative and constitutional guarantees for educational access are accompanied by an educational system that does not contain many schools — a common situation in developing countries. But such countries often have structures restricting the access of local groups to either courts or legislative and administrative authority.

Localized Disorders in Decentralized Systems

Here we anticipate limited legalization. Such systems are designed to manage local disorders in their routine structure: the classic American school board election, or local movement to fire a school principal or superintendent, take this form.

On the other hand, the same American processes that maintained a decentralized educational system also legitimized much individual and group action in the courts. So while other forms of legalization (i.e., legislative and administrative penetration of the system) may have been limited, fairly high levels of litigation may have been common. Even today, substantial proportions of the education cases in the courts are traditional kinds of local litigation:[12] business conflicts between local companies and the schools; conflicts over school construction and location or over loci of school closings; conflicts between individual children and families and the local schools; and so on. In one sense, the frequency of such suits in American courts suggests we are really discussing a different structure: such claims are local in one sense, but take advantage of nationally conferred rights. Genuinely decentralized disorder — those claims of local groups not built around the elaborated citizenship rights of the American system — might generate little legalization of any kind. The relatively extensive procedural rights of American citizens has, as is well known, led to court-generated legalization in many areas of American life, and has done so over long periods of time.

Centralized Disorders in Decentralized Systems

This case, clearly, generates the maximal amount of legalization. Equally clearly, it describes the current American scene, as well as some aspects of the historical situation: we believe it accounts for the high historical levels of legalization in American education (especially through court action) and the very high levels of legalization in the recent period (through court, administrative and legislative action). In this situation, legalizable disorders arise in a number of ways.

First, central legislative bodies legalize. The American Congress, vested with no *general* educational responsibility or authority, responds to many disorder-discovering interest groups by the creation of special rights or programs in no way integrated into the regular educational system and frequently bypassing many levels of this system. There are special and unintegrated rules about a number of minorities, the poor, the pregnant, special vocational training, female students, a few special curricula of national interest, many types of handicapped or special students, and so on and on. With a general mandate to insure equality, and none to assume responsibility for the educational order, the Congress almost at random emits equalization programs for ever more groups. This process is enhanced by interest groups, which quickly adapt to the language of equality and the possibilities for national action.

Further, the Congress discovers national disorders in relation to national purposes, not simply in reaction to interest groups: a need for foreign language specialists, or doctors, or more engineers, or mathematics instruction in high schools. Each of these is enacted as a special program, bypassing the institutionalized order. All this is legalization in itself, by our definition. And most national action has this character, since there is little by way of a routinized structure of national educational management.

Second, central administrative agencies, in state and federal governments, legalize. They create categorical programs with special rules and controls for special problems or groups of students. These rules and controls bypass the main lines of educational organization, reaching down in the system to impact certain specific points. They are unintegrated with the rest of the educational system. Thus, Title I funds and requirements define rules governing certain special resources and groups of students without relating these to the rest of the work of the school and district: they do not redefine the main structure of education and funding to fit in the new elements in an integrated way.

Third, the continued expansion in national action and in nationally certified rights, provides many possibilities for local actors to legalize their claims through court action. Both central legislatures and central courts define these new rights, but make no coherent provision for how these rights are to be fit in with the rest of the educational system.

The recent legislation for the handicapped (PL 94-142) provides an excellent example. It creates legalization on its own — special legal rules bypassing levels of the regular educational system — but far beyond the structure of funding it creates, scatters legal rights throughout the citizenry. Many new types of handicapped pupils (some undiscovered as of a decade or two ago) are endowed with educational rights that probably cannot be met even in principle. A fertile field for private legal action in the courts is created.

Argument

Our main overall argument is quite clear. The centralization of perceived educational disorders, combined with a decentralized educational order, increases legalization, both from the center and from peripheral groups (which employ centrally-conferred rights).

This argument explains what may turn out to be a puzzling fact about American educational history. There have been many periods during which the educational agenda (disorder) underwent centralization: why does the present period seem so distinctive in the amount of created legalization? An answer would be that previous waves of disorder involved shifts in control from the local to the state level — and the American states, with legitimate educational authority, could respond by elaborating the routine management system. For many decades, American states responded to issues through the steady and integrated expansion of their institutionalized myths of education — altering the curriculum, expanding requirements for teacher credentialling, raising building standards, raising requirements for attendance, changing rules of pupil classification, and so on. There were occasional special programs and requirements, but most of the rules were built into relatively integrated codes and funded through general educational funds. The myth of education came down to the district and the school in an orderly way, as a package.

But the shift to a national educational agenda cannot take the same form, in the absence of the possibility of legitimated central integration and authority. A national aganda simply adds to a disorganized list of programs, each posing special requirements for the system: legalization from the center, making possible much legal action in the periphery. We now have scores of federal programs, and many state programs, defining special rules, protections, and resources, little integrated with the main required structure of education. Schools must be schools within the standard myths; but they must also contain the additional elements, some of which are inconsistent with the standard requirements. They are to treat the poor and minority children equally, but also using the special resources unequally; they are to mainstream the handicapped in the schooling process, but also to treat them with special resources. And over and above the federal programs, we have an expanded set of citizen rights enforceable through the courts: a competent psychologist could almost certainly find in any of our children one or another special disability which required the school system — in the name of equality — to make special provision. And many of these have at least some chance of court enforcement.

Notes on Additional Variables

Some other aspects of American education and society make legalization especially likely, and suggest that rates of legalization should generally (over long periods of time, not only in the present) be higher in this country.

1 The American polity endows citizens and associated groups with more rights and capacities for legal action than most. As is well known, this is combined with a generally decentralized state system.

The character of American constitutionalism, with its separate court system descending from the center to each village, passing along a quite extensive set of substantive and procedural rights to each citizen and group of citizens, is a permanent invitation to legalization. The extraordinary American inclination to employ the services of lawyers and the courts is not an irrational litigiousness: it reflects the structure of the American polity.

Further, there has in the recent period been a general extension of rights through the courts. Attacks on many institutions as unjust, using these rights and the mechanisms of courts, have been common. This general wave of expansion of rights — and the broadening of their application to racial, sexual, and social inequalities — has made for a considerable increase in legalization, entirely aside from any feature of the educational system or its problems.

2 The American cultural theory of education is unusually broad. This is true in several senses. First, educational scope is less restricted by vested

academic interests than in most countries and includes many more elements and issues (for example, driver training, etc.).[13] Second, in an individualist political culture, more emphasis is placed on the importance of institutions of socialization, and these institutions are employed for more legitimate purposes. Third, more differentiated aspects of persons come under the scrutiny of the educational system in this context (i.e., properties of personality, not simply of intellect). All these factors increase the possibilities for legalization.

3 Intrinsic educational authority (an ingredient in any educational order) is less developed in America than elsewhere, as part of a general political pattern. The autonomous authority of teachers and higher-level educational authorities is less rooted in traditional status definitions and corporate powers, and is more rooted in technical myths. The technical character of educational myths, in a highly ritualized system, provides many grounds for legalization (both from the center and from peripheries). If the teacher's authority is justified by a highly institutionalized social contract, little room for legal action is created. If this authority is justified by technical considerations, technical objections can be raised — and American educational culture is, at any point, filled with hundreds of candidate technologies compared to whose claims every feature of the present educational system is illegitimate. Squadrons of educational and developmental psychologists will testify in legislative committee hearings, or sometimes in court, to the injustices contained in the present in contrast to the new techniques.

A system that justifies authority by technical considerations leaves highly ritualized orders, which shelter themselves from technical variabilities, open to many social and legal objections. It creates the continuing sense of 'status-deprivation' of American educators.[14] Note that the early studies of occupational prestige[15] were done at teachers' colleges by researchers concerned with the 'declining status of teachers' in American society — the concern goes on over a long period of time.[16] The problem arises, not because the social *rank* of teachers is low in America, but because this rank is not accompanied by the broader status rights and authority necessary to the protected functioning of a ritualized order.

The Social Generation of Waves of Perceived Educational Disorders

We have traced legalization to the intersection of a decentralized educational order with the creation of centralized conceptions of educational disorders. In this section, we discuss the factors affecting the latter variable. Two questions, in reality, are at issue. First, what factors create a national awareness of urgent problems in education that require collective resolution? And second, what factors tend to lead these formulations in the direction of legalization? We have already answered the second question in part — arguing that organizational decentralization eliminates the possibility of routinized solutions. But a number of features of American society and education amplify this tendency to adopt legalizational solutions.

First, it must be understood that, whatever the organizational structure of the educational order, modern educational systems are not simply the creatures of emergent local interests and networks of interest: they have substantial general ideological components. Education is advocated, not only for the children of the interested groups, but for all children in the community and society. This is strikingly true of American educational history, even in the absence of much organizational centralization. In the northern and western states, practically universal education was built up by a sweeping set of social movements long in advance of state rules (including even compulsory education rules; American society had a legal notion of truancy long before education was compulsory). It did not arise earlier in the urban centers, where local economic demands might have been highest, but expanded as part of a general cultural pattern.[17] Education was, from the first, a generally collective concern. This is strikingly the case in developing countries now,[18] but also characterized American educational development. The point here is that a collective, and to some extent national, educational agenda was present from the start, with at least some potential for the legalization of disorder perceptions.

Second, the educational agenda has been centralized further over time. Many factors are involved here: (i) the creation of national customs of occupational certification and a nationwide system of higher education created pressures for educational standardization at lower levels; (ii) the general expansion of state control in other societies provided models for the nationalization of educational issues; (iii) the general expansion of national state power in the world and in America has tended to produce the redefinition of many issues as national ones. For example, the development of explicit national concerns with the management of the economy in the twentieth century, combined with the conception that education is a vital *productive* investment after World War II, has legitimated much national concern about education: a host of 'manpower planning' and occupational training issues both take on educational meaning and become national concerns; (iv) the general process of state expansion both aids in the redefinition of more and more rights and citizenship dimensions (e.g., for minorities) as national concerns, and is in some respects a response to the nationalization of such issues. The expansion of citizenship rights and their location in the national state fuels potential educational disorders; (v) perhaps over and above the expansion in state power, recent decades have generated a wave of concerns — education entirely aside — about citizen rights and equality. Stemming from the historic problems of racial equality, a variety of pressures to expand equality, and the role of the constitutional system in protecting equality, have gone on. Over and above specific educational problems, these claims have fed into the educational system. This is part of the general logic of modern systems, in which social problems are traced back to the socialization of individuals, and urgent repair requirements in the socialization system are seen as necessary. A variety of problems of general inequality — racial, sexual, income, and the like — are seen as resulting from unequal socialization, and an extension of constitutional rules of equality results.

Third, the historic American process of creating a national educational agenda without a centralized national organizational order has built up and institutionalized sources of continuing *formulation* of disorders in ways that promote legalization. American society is not unique in the overall amount of perceived educational disorder — the total number of claims made against the educational system by society at any specific time; developing societies, for instance, have much larger gaps between educational ideals and educational reality. American society is distinctive in that perceived educational disorders tend to lead to legalization rather than routine administrative implementation. And one reason for this is that a whole structure of interest groups tends to arise and become legitimated apart from the standard educational apparatus. These interest groups *mobilize* their constituencies more than their authority within the bureaucracy, they organize their appeals to the national consciousness, and they formulate their demands in terms of special rights and needs, not smoothly integrated alterations in the (barely extant) central administrative myth of education. Our point here is in some contrast with the picture of interest groups sometimes taken by traditional political scientists — that their mobilization and forms of mobilization are natural to the social relations and ideas of their constituents. Our argument is sociological: the claims of interest groups often arise out of rights conferred from the center (often, the courts); their mobilization is determined by the possibilities for action opened up in the center; and their organization reflects the structure of possibilities for action, not some natural reflection of their internal constituent interests. Thus, (i) in America, many interest groups come to be organized as national legalization-creators. They are not oriented toward becoming coopted by the central administrative apparatus, because there has not been one. So they pursue special claims and rights built around court-conferred and constitution-conferred rights, around new national purposes, around special interests, around equality, and so on: they do not organize claims to modify the integrated national educational control system; (ii) national educational authorities rise up outside the organizational order. In other countries, the educational elites come to be built into the national policy-making and administrative system: the connections in America are loose. These elites, in America, rest on various technical or 'scientific' justifications: at one time professionals of all sorts, they are increasingly university professors. They are formally unintegrated in the command and control system, and thus formally irresponsible. Their calling is to create and discover disorders. But they make up a kind of national school board with no line authority or line responsibility and so they organize their disorders so as to promote legalization. Recent members of this school board have included, for instance, James Conant, James Coleman, Coons and Sugarman, and Jencks. There are a great many candidate members:

the educational journals and NIE reports are filled with their campaign statements suggesting disorders and often legal solutions. The national educational agenda has, at any one time, room for only a few disorders; the great majority of proposed disorders never really enter this agenda. Some are excluded by the presence of others; others are excluded by political priorities or interest group processes. Prediction here is extremely difficult: no one can predict which new disorders will enter the agenda in the 1990s, and past predictions have by and large been failures. There is a little stability in this system in that one can ascertain rough life cycles for disorders. They rise, build up support, peak, and decay, leaving a greater or smaller institutional precipitate in the established order. Our main point here is that the disorders created tend especially to lead to legalization. It may also be that the lack of formal responsibility of American disorder-creators tends to increase the *amount* of disorder they perceive, relative to real educational problems, since they are less capable of cooptation than similar elites in other systems.

Fourth, a variety of financial problems in American society, education, and structure of taxation, have led to greatly increased demands for federal educational funding. And state funding, relative to local funding, has increased. The shift upward in fundings, with no corresponding shifts in authority and responsibility, creates an invitation for legalization. As part of this process, for instance, the National Institute for Education, with no line responsibility in the system, has throughout its short history been engaged in a search for disorders and legalizational solutions. Most of its funds go into the maintenance of disorders.

The Intersection of Waves of Disorder and Centralization

Our point here is simple. Waves of disorder may produce little legalization if legitimate centralization, or the modification of central controls, are possible. As the agenda of educational disorders is centralized without much possibility for centralization organizationally, legalization results. Programs and rights are created without organizational integration or management. Both directly and indirectly, legalization results.

This is an important aspect of the present condition of American education.[19] If one examines the structure of an American school district of substantial size, one finds programs and fundings reflecting thirty or forty different state and federal programs and agencies. These programs are not integrated in any coherent way in the federal government, which has neither general educational authority nor general responsibility. Nor are they integrated at the state governmental level — the states have fragmented structures reflecting federal programs and funds. This is legalization in itself, by our definition: district officials cannot conform to a general federal myth of education, which doesn't exist. They can only be in *compliance* or *not in compliance* with specific regulations which were never intended to make general educational sense for the whole system. Much work is created for accountants. And for lawyers. There is no real process that might make federal programs and requirements consistent with each other: one has to elaborate special treatment for various handicapped groups; but at the same time 'mainstream' them.

And there is no attempted integration with the policies and purposes of states and districts themselves — the levels at which general education policies and myths are to be formulated. To comply with federal rules, one has to have a resources teacher whose services are restricted to certain groups of students: an ostentatious inequality and violation of district policy is thus created.

Some of this process occurs through legislative action, aided by interest groups focused on legalization, rather than general educational modification. Some of it is amplified by administrative action in the state. But much of it occurs through the courts, which discover and extend private rights, making legal solutions available to a variety of interest groups. Even more than the legislature and central administration, the courts are formally irresponsible for the main conduct of education, and thus exceptionally likely to promote legalizational penetrations of the system — rules poorly linked to the ongoing educational system as a whole.

Consequences of Legalization

A result of the great expansion in unintegrated rules and pressures pouring into the educational system from central authorities is an enormous administrative expansion in state and district offices, and a considerable administrative expansion in the school itself. A school or district needs functionaries to deal with each of the special rules and findings and programs that now control it: to write proposals, to collect the specially required data, to write reports, to keep separate accounts. It also needs expanded legal services to fend off a variety of groups taking advantage of court-extended rights. It is clear that administrative work in American schools and districts has greatly increased in response to this burden: one estimate has it that each new dollar of federal funds creates nine times the increase in administrative personnel that each new dollar of local money creates.[20] Similar expansions have taken place at the state level: the typical state department of education has large numbers of people whose main role is to respond to and monitor the federal funds, programs, and court-conferred rights that make up the legalized system. In some states, these functionaries make up a majority of the personnel.

Still, administrative expense is a relatively minor part of the American educational budget. And even though educational administration is made cumbersome and inefficient and even more decoupled (both horizontally and vertically[21]) than in the past, it is not clear that we should regard it as a major educational problem. The American polity has historically tended toward inefficient public administration as a result of the general policy of maintaining a plethora of social controls and citizen rights; a Prussian bureaucracy is not the American dream. So it is in education: a system which maintains an unwieldy list of educational disorders, and which turns many of them into legalizational solutions may nevertheless be more responsive to societal claims than a tidily integrated centralized administrative structure. The disorganized character of the American educational bureaucracy, and its chronic crisis of legitimation, may be an effective and desirable state, giving much room for the expression of diverse public interests.

Consider simply the symbolic value of all this legalization. Consider it especially in a highly institutionalized and ritualized domain like education, which mainly operates by highly symbolic processes (for example, authority built into unimplemented curricula, policies, and so on). Legalizational solutions are often not effectively implemented *organizationally* — especially in such a decoupled system as education, and especially when the legalization itself increases organizational inefficiency and decoupling. But they are ways of defining to the educational establishment as a highly institutionalized ritual organization important new rights and public desiderata. Even if the legalized solutions to racial inequality are ineffectively implemented, they mark new public standards, which are now widely shared by administrators, teachers, and parents. Even if the handicapped legislation is legalizational beyond belief, and ineffectively implemented, it communicates to the institutionalized educational community a new emphasis — even unimplemented organizationally, it may affect the judgments of teachers and administrators. Note that one hallmark of American education innovation is that adopted innovations are poorly implemented: but note that another hallmark of the same system is that rates of change in response to national trends are very high — these changes occur more through the institutional features of the system than the organizational ones, so any given change is about as likely to occur where it has not been formally adopted as where it has been adopted. But change does occur, and the structures of legalization — court action, symbolic actions of the central legislature and central administrators — may be a main mechanism, operating through altered symbolic agreements. The failure of legalizational pressures for desegregation is often noted; less often noted is that a major new national norm is firmly in place, subscribed to by many of the most vocal opponents of organizational implementation.

Prospects for Delegalization

The peculiar structure of the American educational system, and the prospect for a continuing national educational agenda, make it likely that rates of legalization will continue to remain fairly high. Nevertheless, even within this system, some processes of routinization and the absorption of disorders and legal pressures are at work. Anomalous pressures from the center, and expanded rights in the periphery, come to be incorporated in the regular organizational structure, though at considerable cost. Consider some of the ways in which the pressures from the recent waves of educational disorder are being absorbed:

1 State control systems are expanding, and federal demands are increasingly passed down through the regular state structure. Increasingly federal requirements and funds are handled in this manner, rather than through direct legalized controls over districts and even schools. Given state authority and continuing educational responsibility, this provides some integration and routinization.
2 Similarly, district administrative structures have expanded, and increasingly come to build in federal requirements. At present, these structures are still highly fragmented, but some possibilities for routinization and integration exist.
3 At the federal level, in response to much lower-level complaint, there are a number of attempts at simplification and integration. States and districts complain bitterly about the 'reporting burden', and the federal officials try to create more integrated and simplified controls and reporting requirements (among other ways, through the creation of FEDAC). The Chief State School Officers organization has gained much power in the federal educational establishment, and is a strong pressure group on behalf of routinization.
4 Part of the problem is that recent expansions of local rights and federal rules have been organized around the discovery of variabilities in the real world of education. They demand inspection and control of outputs (for example, test scores), try to control particular processes of instruction and control, and in general try to force the educational order to relate to the real technical educational domain; this is highly destabilizing. But now these efforts are being given up in favor of routinization. Federal and state requirements for program evaluation using output data are weakening and becoming ritualized. Requirements for detailed evaluation of instructional processes are being weakened.

Increasingly, the causal chains managed by the federal myth of education are ending, not in real educational *outcomes*, but in easily ritualizable *structures*. They do not require that the treated pupil learn something, or even be treated in a specific educational process; they require that the pupil be located in the proper category, subjected to teachers with proper certificates, and so on. The causal chains of the new myths, thus, end where educational order has always ended up, in stabilized ritual categories.

This is a fairly stable solution. Of course, because of the absence of much integration among various programs (resulting from the lack of general federal theory of education), much administrative cumbersomeness is created. Schools must have a much wider variety of categories of pupils than they used to, a much more elaborate accounting system, a more elaborate reporting system, and many more categories of 'specialist' teachers. But it does promote delegalization: a given parent has less legal action available if the school can demonstrate that the incompetence of its treatment of a child nevertheless took place under the proper categorical labels.

The administrative complexity will remain. With older processes of centralization to the state level, given state authority, pressures for change could be responded to by routine redefinition of the standard teacher. If we wanted more emphasis on moral training, we got teachers with seven more semester hours preparation in moral instruction. The fragmented federal system ends up creating many more special categories of teachers and specialists.

This solution — delegalization by folding elaborated ritual categories into the traditional structure — is unattractive in many ways. But it may be the only stable solution. A genuine, integrated federal myth of education is not in the offing.

Notes

1 Weick, K. (1976) 'Educational organizations as loosely coupled systems,' *Administrative Science Quarterly*, March; March, J. and Olsen, J. (1976) *Ambiguity and Choice in Organizations*, Bergen, Universitetsforlaget.

2 Meyer, J. and Rowan, B. (1977) 'Institutionalized organizations: formal structure as myth and ceremony,' *American Journal of Sociology*, September, 83, 2, p. 340; Meyer, J. and Rowan, B. (1978) 'The structure of educational organizations' in Meyer, M. *et al. Environments and Organizations*, San Francisco, Jossey Bass.

3 For example, Dornbusch, S. and Scott, W.R. (1975) *Evaluation and the Exercise of Authority*, San Francisco, Jossey Bass.

4 Meyer, J. and Rowan, B. (1977) *op. cit*.; Berman, P. and McLaughlin, M. (1975–78) *Federal Programs Supporting Educational Change*, 1–8, Santa Monica, The Rand Corporation; David, J. (1978) *Local Uses of Title I Evaluations*, Menlo Park, SRI International.

5 Meyer, M. *et al* (1978) *op. cit*.

6 David, J. (1978) *op. cit*; Davis, M. and Stackhouse, E.A. (1977) 'The importance of formal appearances' in Davis, M. *et al. The Structure of Educational Systems: Explorations in the Theory of Loosely-Coupled Organizations*, Stanford University, June.

7 Meyer, M., Scott, W.R. and Deal, T. (1979) 'Institutional and technical sources of organizational structure: explaining the structure of educational organizations,' Conference on Human Service Organizations, Center for Advanced Study in the Behavioural Sciences, Stanford, March.

8 Hobbs, N. (1975) *Issues in the Classification of Children*, San Francisco, Jossey Bass.

9 Wirt, F.M. (1977) 'School policy, culture and state decentralization' in Scribner, J.D. (Ed.) *The Politics of Education*, Chicago, University of Chicago Press.

10 See Boli-Bennett, J. (1980) 'Human rights or state expansion?', (unpublished paper) Department of Sociology, Stanford University.

11 Ramirez, F. and Rubinson, R. (1979) 'Creating members: the political incorporation and expansion of public education' in Meyer, J.W. and Hannan, M. (Eds) *National Development and the World System*, Chicago, University of Chicago Press.

12 See the cases discussed in Kirp, D.L. *et al* (Eds) (1980) *Educational Policy, Governance and the Law*, San Francisco, Jossey Bass.
13 Van de Graaff J. (1978) *Academic Power: Patterns of Authority in National Systems of Higher Education*, New York, Praeger.
14 Meyer, J.W. and Roth, J. (1970) 'A reinterpretation of American status politics', *Pacific Sociological Review*, Spring, 13, 2.
15 For example, Counts, G.S. (1925) 'The social status of occupations', *The School Review*, January, pp. 16–27.
16 Hofstadter, R. (1964) *Anti-Intellectualism in American Life*, New York, Random House; Lipset, S.M. (1960) 'American intellectuals: Their politics and status' in Lipset, S.M. *Political Man*, New York, Doubleday.
17 Meyer, J.W. *et al* (1979) *op. cit.*; Tyack, D. (1974) *The One Best System: A History of American Urban Education*, Cambridge, Harvard University Press.
18 Boli-Bennett, J. (1980) *op. cit.*; Meyer, M. *et al* (1978) *op. cit.*
19 Meyer, J.W. (1979) 'The impact of centralization of educational funding and control on state and local organizational governance,' Institute for Research on Educational Finance and Governance, Stanford University, August.
20 Freeman, J.H., Hannan, M. and Hannaway, J. (1978) *The Dynamics of the School District Administrative Intensity*, Cambridge, Mass., ABT.
21 Meyer, J.W. (1979) *op. cit.*

3 Perspective

Conflicts of Interest in Educational Reform Litigation

Deborah L. Rhode
Stanford University

Over the last quarter of a century, courts have become an increasingly significant force in shaping educational institutions. Opposition to this judicial involvement has never been lacking, but it has changed markedly in tone and direction during the last decade. The shrill and avowedly racist outcries that greeted the first desegregation decrees have largely given way to more muted and reflective skepticism about the institutional competence and accountability of courts in superintending educational policy.[1] This essay addresses one of the primary targets of recent critics, the procedures through which education issues reach the courts.

Most 'educational reform' cases — lawsuits seeking structural change in school programs, policies or racial composition — proceed as class actions. In such cases, there is no single aggrieved plaintiff with clearly identifiable views, but rather an aggregation of individuals, often with unstable, inchoate or divergent preferences. As in other institutional reform adjudication involving prisons, mental hospitals and employment programs, those alleging unconstitutional conduct will rarely be of one view as to what should be done about it. And there is comparable dissension among courts, commentators, and counsel over how to identify and resolve such conflicts.

The following discussion evaluates existing procedural mechanisms for coping with intra-class conflicts in educational reform litigation. Although the focus is on suits challenging racial segregation and institutional programs for the disabled, the problems arising in these cases are representative of those presented in other educational and civil rights contexts.

In exploring these problems, this chapter takes one central proposition for granted. On the whole, educational reform class actions have made, and continue to make, an enormous contribution to the realization of fundamental constitutional values — a contribution that no other governmental construct has proved able to duplicate. That contention has been defended at length elsewhere, and the arguments need not be recounted here.[2] Thus, the following discussion should not be taken to suggest that education class actions are misused or misconceived, or that there are preferable alternatives.[3] Rather, the intent is to identify deficiencies in class adjudication that might be amenable to improvement.

To that end, the essay draws on reported decisions, case histories, and interviews with individuals involved in educational reform litigation. Analysis first focuses on the range of conflicts that have surfaced within plaintiff constituencies and the inadequacy of existing procedures in ensuring that the full range of class sentiment is exposed. Discussion then focuses on the bounded potential of structural reforms in improving judicial responsiveness to class conflict.

Intra-Class Conflicts and Disclosure Obligations

A Typology of Conflicts

For those seeking educational reforms, class actions afford a number of obvious procedural advantages over single-plaintiff suits. By definition, class litigation focuses on institutional practices rather than individual grievances. It also averts problems of mootness if the named litigant graduates or has his personal objectives satisfied during the pendancy of litigation. Yet by the same token, class status can also generate substantial problems in accommodating divergent client interests. Those who prefer the certainty of the status quo to the risks of judicial rearrangement will oppose litigation from the outset. More common, however, are schisms that develop during remedial deliberations. Often when a suit is filed, neither the parties nor their attorneys have focused on issues of relief. The impetus for litigation will be a general sense that rights have been infringed or needs ignored, rather than a shared conviction about appropriate remedies. However, once it becomes clear that some relief will be forthcoming, sharp divisions in preferences frequently emerge.

School desegregation cases provide the most well-documented instances of conflict. Derek Bell, Curtis Berger, and Stephen Yeazell have described in some detail the balkanization within minority communities in Boston, Atlanta, Detroit, New York and Los Angeles over fundamental questions of educational policy.[4] Dispute has centered on the relative importance of integration, financial resources, minority control, and ethnic identification in enriching school environments. Constituencies that support integration in principle have disagreed over its value in particular settings where extended bus rides, racial tension, or white flight seem likely concomitants of judicial redistricting.[5] Comparable cleavages arise in other education contexts. Parents challenging the adequacy of existing bilingual or special remedial programs have disagreed over whether mainstreaming or upgrading separate classes represents the better solution. In suits against the Pennhurst, Pennsylvania, and Willowbrook, New York, schools for the retarded and the California School for the

Blind, plaintiff families divided over whether to press for improvements in the institutions or creation of community-care alternatives.[6]

Moreover, as with any form of collective litigation, parties often differ in their assessment of settlement offers. Given the uncertainty of outcome and indeterminancy of relief available in many civil rights actions, risk-averse plaintiff will often be willing to make substantial concessions. Other class members will prefer to fight, if not to the death, at least until the Supreme Court denies certiorari. And, as the following discussion suggests, doctrinal responses to such conflict have not been altogether instructive.

The Requirement of Adequate Representation

Most civil rights actions seeking injunctive relief proceed under Rule 23 of the Federal Rules of Civil Procedure, which requires, *inter alia*, that 'representative parties will fairly and adequately protect the interests of the class.' This requirement is of critical importance since all members will be bound by the judgment; they cannot opt out of the action. Yet, despite the centrality of the representation concept to class action theory and practice, judicial pronouncements on the subject have been notably unilluminating.

The Advisory Committee that drafted Rule 23 provided no amplification of the terms 'adequately protect' or 'interests,'[7] and judges applying the standard have done little to fill the lacunae. Among the primary questions left unaddressed is whether interest ever means more than preference and, if so, when, and what. Must the named representative and counsel serve primarily as 'instructed delegates,'[8] pursuing objectives to which a majority of class members have subscribed? If so, how are those objectives to be identified, particularly if the class comprises a diffuse and changing constituency of past, present and future members? Alternatively, is the representative role more that of a 'Burkean trustee,' who makes an independent assessment of class concerns?[9] Under that advocacy model, what resource is available to individuals who do not share their trustee's vision? These issues, addressed at some length below, are easily elided under prevailing doctrine. In general, the courts have insisted only that attorneys be competent and that the claims of the named representatives be 'similar', 'common', or 'not antagonistic' to those of the membership generally.[10] Even where there is demonstrable polarization among the membership, courts frequently grant class status.

On balance, that ís a necessary result. To deny class certification whenever a substantial number of members may have diverging remedial preferences would often preempt use of a valuable procedural device without improving adjudicative processes. Most lawsuits now proceeding as class actions could be brought as personal claims. For example, if, in an individual desegregation suit, the named plaintiff established unconstitutional conduct warranting institutional relief, a court must so declare; the breadth of remedy will depend on the scope of violation, not the number of names in the caption of the complaint.[11]

In such cases, those who disagree with named plaintiffs' remedial proposals may have even less opportunity for notice and participation if the case proceeds as an individual rather than collective action. Thus, denial of class certification hardly secures, and may even impede, full protection of all interests affected by judicial decree. From a due process perspective, the preferable strategy for most conflicts is to grant class status and create sufficient institutional safeguards to ensure disclosure of dissenting views.

Disclosure Mandates and Process Values

On one level, the rationale for requiring disclosure of class preferences seems so obvious as to require no further elaboration. In a legal culture that places such an extraordinary premium on client autonomy and procedural values, class members' right to have their concerns counted appears almost axiomatic. Yet on closer scrutiny, a number of sticky questions arise.

Whatever our rhetorical posturings, our adjudicative structures by no means contemplate a hearing for all interests implicated by a given decree. In much litigation brought by single individuals, *Bakke v. California Board of Regents*[12] being an obvious example, the plaintiff will not adequately represent the views of all individuals affected by the judgment. To be sure, those individuals, unlike class members, will not be bound directly by the court's decree and can challenge application of a prior decision to their own circumstances. But given the force of *stare decisis*, the practical consequences for unrepresented constituencies are often the same, whether or not they are part of a certified class.

Moreover, insofar as courts perceive their decisions to be dictated by applicable legal principles and underlying policies, the remedial preferences of present or future litigants may be of relatively little significance. Had *Bakke* been brought as a class action, it is unlikely that plaintiffs' evaluations of various affirmative action plans would have significantly affected the Court's judgment. Thus, two fundamental threshold enquiries are why disclosure of conflicting preferences matters and whether it matters more in class actions than private adjudication.

Apprising the court of class preferences can enhance both the rationality and legitimacy of decision-making. Full disclosure reduces the chance that courts will overlook, undervalue, or otherwise misconstrue relevant considerations.[13] Parties who believe that their perspectives have been fairly presented may also display more confidence in the judicial process and greater willingness to abide by its result.[14] Moreover, sensitivity to such values is of particular importance in educational reform cases, given the nature of the underlying dispute. Such litigation tends to involve complex indeterminate remedies, fundamental personal values, non-apparent preferences, and politically vulnerable forms of intervention, all of which counsel special concern.

As noted previously, the civil rights violations in most education reform cases do not point to any single remedial solution. Typically, the final decree will reflect at least some choices as to which prevailing doctrine is largely indifferent. Of course, on many of those issues, plaintiff preferences will not be controlling; concerns of comity, federalism, and the needs of future class members may mandate a different course. But even if their views are not dispositive, plaintiffs have a strong stake in seeing their preferences put forward on matters of considerable personal significance.

Frequently these preferences will not be self-revealing. The nature of relief available in much educational reform litigation creates opportunities for dispute less easily identified than in other class actions or individual suits. Where the claim is for monetary damages alone, the interests of various plaintiff sub-groups are readily apparent. An adequate working assumption is that for any such faction, more compensation is better than less. When remedial choices involve complex forms of injunctive relief, with many opportunities for trade-offs among sub-groups within a plaintiff class, prediction becomes far more difficult.

Inaccurate assessment of class concerns can be troubling in several respects. Most obviously, it may increase the expense and delay of proceedings, if disaffected parties belatedly appeal the adequacy of their representation and the court's decree. A more fundamental problem is that misperceptions about party preferences could unnecessarily compromise the legitimacy of advocacy structures in general, as well as the success of judicial intervention in particular educational reform cases.

In both concept and implementation, all systems of representation demand some measure of consent. As political theorists since Burke have argued, no governance structure dependent on representative relationships can have a 'long or sure existence' without some grounding in constituent support.[15] Largely for that reason constitutional law is, in John Hart Ely's phrase, 'overwhelmingly concerned ... with ensuring broad participation in the processes and distributions of government.'[16] The need for a consensual foundation is especially pronounced when non-elected or self-appointed advocates arrogate seemingly legislative or administrative decision-making roles. To restructure a school district effectively, or assure adequate programs for retarded children, often required considerable cooperation from the affected constituencies. Yet the further the judge strays into social planning provinces, the greater his difficulty in commanding the moral force of adjudication.

Doubts concerning the courts' institutional competence to manage educational reform disputes have surfaced with increasing frequency over the last decade. That skepticism now threatens to take tangible form in legislative restraints on the courts' jurisdiction and remedial authority in civil rights cases.[17] Judges' inability to assess and accommodate class preferences cannot help but erode political support among constituencies who should be most favorably disposed toward judicial intervention. In cases where the court's legitimacy, and indeed jurisdiction, are so much at risk, disclosing plaintiff sentiment is of particular importance. What is disturbing about current class action structures is that, all too frequently, none of the participants has sufficient incentive or information to ensure such disclosure.

The Participants' Roles in Disclosing Conflict: Rules and Realities

The Named Plaintiffs

In theory, as federal courts frequently have emphasized, the preeminent duty of the class representative is to ensure that the absent members' interests are adequately protected.[18] As a practical matter, however, once a class attains certification, named plaintiffs generally are not highly motivated or well-situated to monitor the congruence between counsel's conduct and class preferences. Although nominal parties' stake in educational reform in litigation varies considerably, such individuals rarely have any incentive to rise above parochialism when speaking for their constituents. Why should named representatives make special efforts to expose conflict that could result in delay, expense, or impairment of their own litigation objectives? At best, the named plaintiffs may attempt to see that counsel is pursuing their own interest; the objectives of fellow litigants could well remain uncertain and unarticulated.

Moreover, many nominal representatives are paper organizations or individuals who lack the expertise, organization, and resources to play a meaningful role in formulating directives. Educational reform cases in general and school desegregation actions in particular provide ample illustrations of plaintiffs who had virtually no communication with their attorney or each other.[19] Particularly where the class membership is diffuse, the issue complicated, or the proceedings protracted, the function of nominal plaintiffs may be no more than what the label implies. Since, as one federal court candidly acknowledged, 'it is counsel . . . not the named parties, who direct and manage these actions,'[20] his role in exposing conflicts is of central importance.

Class Counsel

A familiar refrain among courts and commentators is that attorneys assume special responsibilities in class litigation. Principal among those duties is the obligation to 'discuss the range of interests held by class members (and) . . . to report conflicts of interest . . . to the judge so that he can consider whether disaggregation of the class is necessary for adequate representation.'[21]

Although unobjectionable in concept, that role definition has frequently proved unworkable in practice. To be sure, many attorneys make extraordinary efforts to appreciate and accommodate the broadest possible spectrum of class sentiment. But particularly where the range and intensity of divergent preferences within the class would be unlikely to surface without counsel's assistance, he will often have strong prudential and ideological reasons not to provide it. One need not be a raving realist to suppose that such motivations play a more dominant role in shaping attorneys' conduct than Rule 23's injunctions and accompanying judicial gloss.

A lawyer active in educational reform litigation is subject to a variety of financial, tactical, and professional pressures that constrain his response to class conflicts. To be sure, none of these constraints are unique to this form of practice. Nonetheless, it is appropriate to identify, in generic form, the range of prudential concerns that can inform counsel's management of intra-class disputes.

The most patent of these concerns arise from the financial underpinnings of educational reform litigation. Under various federal civil rights statutes, a trial court may grant counsel fees to prevailing parties. Among the factors affecting the attorney's net award is the amount of the class's recovery, the costs of obtaining it, and the number of attorneys entitled to a share. Given the expense and the marginal budget on which many litigators operate, few can remain impervious to all worldly concerns. And flushing out dissension among class members can be costly in several respects.

In many instances, opposing parties will seek to capitalize on class dissension by filing motions for decertification. If successful, counsel could lose a substantial investment in time and resources that he cannot, as a practical matter, recoup from former class members. At a minimum, such motions may result in expense, delay and loss of bargaining leverage, while deflecting attention from trial preparation. They might also trigger involvement of additional lawyers, who share the limelight, the control over litigation decisions and, under some circumstances, the funds available for attorneys' fees.

So too, exposing conflict can impede settlement arrangements that are attractive to class counsel on a number of grounds. Wherever class members are not underwriting the costs of litigation, they might well prefer a larger investment of legal time than their attorney is inclined or able to provide. If the prospects for prevailing on appeal appear dubious many plaintiffs will nonetheless see little to lose and everything to gain from persistence. Their views may not find an enthusiastic spokesman in class counsel, who has concerns for his reputation as well as competing claims on his time and his organization's resources to consider.

The obverse situation can emerge in test-case litigation. Once a lawyer has prepared a lawsuit that could have significant legal impact, he may not share some plaintiffs' enthusiasm for settlements promising generous terms for the litigants but little recognition and no precedential value for similarly-situated victims. Like other professionals, class action attorneys cannot make decisions wholly independent of concerns about their careers and reputation among peers, potential clients, and funding sources. Involvement in well-publicized educational reform litigation may provide desirable trial experience, generate attractive new cases, legitimate organizational objectives in the eyes of private donors, and enhance attorneys' personal standing in the legal community.[22] Where such rewards are likely, counsel might tend to discount preferences for a low-visibility settlement, particularly if it falls short of achieving substantive objectives to which he is strongly committed.

Although there is little systematic research on point, many commentators have noted the potential for ideological divergence between class and counsel's litigation goals. Summoning case histories from Boston, Atlanta, and Detroit, Derek Bell submits the NAACP attorneys' 'single-minded commitment' to maximum integration has led them to ignore a shift in priorities among many black parents from racial balance to quality education.[23] Similar indictments have been or could be made against attorneys in other educational reform contexts. For example, in 1974, parents and guardians brought suit on behalf of all present and future residents of the Pennhurst, Pennsylvania facility for the retarded. Class counsel, who advocated community care, made no effort to air the views of parents and guardians preferring institutional improvements.[24] After the district court ordered removal of Pennhurst residents to community facilities, a systematic survey of their parents and guardians revealed that only 19 per cent of respondents favored deinstitutionalization.[25]

It does not follow, however, that attorneys in these and comparable cases necessarily failed to represent their clients' interests. Much depends on how one defines 'the client.' As the subsequent discussion will suggest, parents often are not sufficiently informed or disinterested to act as spokesmen for all children who will be affected by a judicial decree. But neither is an attorney with strong prudential or ideological preferences well positioned to decide which class members deserve a hearing and which do not. And one critical problem with existing class action procedures is that they provide no assurance that other institutional participants will raise conflicts that counsel would prefer to ignore.

Courts, Opposing Parties, and Dissenting Litigants

Both the federal rules and the due process clause vest ultimate responsibility for ensuring adequate representation in the trial judge.[26] To discharge that obligation, he has a broad range of procedural options, discussed more fully below. As a threshold matter, however, what bears emphasis is the court's frequent lack of information — or incentive to demand it — concerning the need to invoke such procedural devices.

An adversarial system of justice presupposes that the parties will act as the primary sources of factual data. Yet insofar as a judge relies on these participants for evidence of class schisms, he will often remain uninformed. It is frequently implausible to expect counsel or the named parties to expose interests at odds with their own, and other class members might know little about litigation objectives, let alone the extent to which their particular concerns have been addressed. For example, plaintiffs in the Pennhurst litigation, most of whom favored institutionalization, had no apparent apprecia-tion of their counsel's insistence on community care alternatives until after the court entered a decree. Even if knowledgeable, dissenters will frequently face the precise common action problem that class procedures seek to address; no single individual perceives a sufficient stake in the outcome to warrant the expense of organizing a constituency and obtaining separate representation.[27]

So too, in some instances, opposing parties will lack the facts or motive to challenge the adequacy of class representation. To prevent misleading or coercive communication, prevailing doctrine severely limits adversaries' contact with class members, thereby restricting their ability to document disaffectation.[28] And not all opponents will wish to jeopardize relations with class counsel by challenging their representation. Of course, as noted previously, many defendants will perceive decertification motions as useful tactics in a war of attrition. But in some cases, opposing parties will see little long-range benefit from exploiting conflicts if the probable consequence is simply a slight delay, fewer plaintiffs, or more attorneys. Depending on their relationships with current class counsel and their probable liability for attorneys' fees, defendants may prefer dealing with one rather than multiple adversaries. Moreover, some defendant school officials operating on inadequate budgets may be sympathetic to the named representatives' objectives.[29] If a broad remedial order will give them bargaining leverage with funding sources, such officials might be unwilling to take action that could jeopardize a mutually desired result.

Given these incentive and information barriers, courts that do not undertake independent investigation are often poorly situated to assess the adequacy of class representation. Yet constraints of time and role militate against an activist judicial posture. For many trial courts, the pressures to clear dockets are considerable and the cost of ferreting out conflict substantial. To question the fairness of a settlement proposed by class counsel may require more factual investigation and personal innuendo than trial courts are disposed to supply. In addition, if finding one set of named plaintiffs and their counsel inadequate does not terminate proceedings, it will likely prolong them. From a trial court's perspective, more is seldom merrier. Multiple representation multiplies problems both administratively and substantively. More parties means more papers, more scheduling difficulties, and more potential for objection to any given ruling or settlement proposal.

This is not to imply that most trial courts are more concerned with clearing calendars than protecting a class, or that they deliberately overlook potential conflicts. The problem is generally one of institutional rather than individual insensitivity. Certification is the only stage at which the court must confront the adequacy of representation, and that is the time at which conflicts are least visible. Adversarial norms and habits may enhance the likelihood that nonparticipants' concerns will fall through the cracks. If neither the litigants nor governing rules demand ongoing factual scrutiny, trial judges understandably are ill-disposed to provide it. Moreover, even where conflicts are apparent, participants may doubt the utility of addressing them through available procedural devices. It is to that kind of cost-benefit calculation that the next section is addressed.

Procedural Mechanisms for Coping with Conflicts: The Practical Limits of Theoretical Alternatives

Confronted with the kinds of conflicts discussed above, courts and counsel have responded with two, not mutually exclusive, strategies. A majoritarian approach is to create opportunities for class members to express their preferences directly, through notice, polls, or public hearings. A pluralist alternative is to have separate factions speak through separate representatives.

Although useful in many instances, neither of these strategies provides anything approaching a full solution to class schisms. A generic weakness stems from the information and incentive structures discussed above. If, as is often the case, participants lack the facts or motive to disclose conflicts and the court is insufficiently informed or inclined to pursue the question *sua sponte*, then the theoretical availability of such alternatives is irrelevant. Moreover, each device has certain practical limitations that further impair its value in addressing conflicts.

The Pluralist Response: Separate Representation

Once significant class cleavages become apparent, the conventional judicial response is to recognize separate constituencies by creating sub-classes or admitting intervenors or *amicus curiae*. The potential benefits attending independent advocacy are readily apparent. Broad participation may assist courts in formulating remedies that best accommodate all interests affected by judicial decree. Since many civil rights litigators operate under severe resource constraints, the inclusion of additional advocates with independent funding may significantly improve factual deliberations. And insofar as dissenters believe their views have been advocated forcefully, they may be more supportive of both the process and result of judicial deliberations. Yet problems of bias, timing, manageability, and expense all render the pluralist model less attractive in practice than in theory.

Since a given constituency's views are still mediated through self-appointed representatives and their counsel, the potential for skewed advocacy remains. Certainly the pluralist response cannot fully redress problems arising from attorneys' prudential or ideological concerns. If, for example, separate counsel has commitments to a particular remedial strategy, he may consciously or unconsciously shade the choices or explanations put to clients. Given the absence of any adequate mechanisms for assuring accountability between counsel and his constituents, multiplying the number of lawyers may at times simply exacerbate problems of bias.

So too, involvement of separate attorneys can be counter-productive if it provides a composite portrait of membership concerns even less representative than that emerging from class counsel's presentation. Like other pressure groups, litigants may tend to overstate the extent and intensity of their support, and the judge will frequently have no sense of how substantial a constituency each separate counsel represents. Given that would-be intervenors or amici need not voice interests other than their own, their involvement may distort the trial court's perception of aggregate class preferences and skew settlement negotiations accordingly. This is not, of course, to suggest that separate representation is inadvisable wherever distortion might occur. Excluding some concerned participants solely because others have not stepped forward may enhance neither the quality nor perceived legitimacy of decision making. The point, rather, is that where the court is interested in understanding and accommodating the broadest possible range of class preferences, separate representation is not of itself an adequate response.

Related difficulties with the pluralist strategy involve issues of timing. To avoid unnecessary expense and complication, courts certifying diverse classes may resist subdivision at the outset but reserve it as an option if schisms develop. Yet the extent of conflict frequently will not be apparent until the parties propose a settlement or the court enters a remedial order. At that point, dissenters may seek to reopen issues already — but in their view inadequately — litigated.[30] For courts to deny such intervention as untimely ill-serves constituencies that did not appreciate the need for full participation until the precise terms of the remedy became apparent. Yet, to set aside the results of protracted deliberation can be costly to all concerned. Precisely when conflicts are most concrete, the pressures on the parties and courts to overlook them are most intense.

Even where proposals for separate counsel present no difficulties of timing, they may raise questions of manageability. In complex cases with diffuse classes, how many overlapping interests warrant independent advocacy? On that issue, prevailing doctrine is notably closed-mouthed. Federal intervention rules, in granting courts discretion to admit any applicant whose claim involves issues of fact or law 'in common' with the principal litigation, subsume a broad universe of claimants.[31] Neither courts nor commentators have supplied much in the way of useful limiting principles. In desegregation cases, judges have focused on whether the prospective intervenor or subclass representative will make a substantial contribution or merely seek to raise claims that already have been competently advanced by existing parties.[32] What constitutes 'competence' or a 'substantial' contribution will often be subject to considerable dispute.

That question becomes particularly sticky when the applicants are plaintiffs whose contentions have been pressed by defendants. Faced with such situations in school cases, courts have divided. In some instances, they have denied intervenor or sub-class status to disaffected minority groups on the sole ground that school boards already had raised the same objections.[33] Such reasoning is inadequate in two respects. It overlooks the possibility that many arguments, such as those supporting neighborhood schools or shorter bus routes, may be launched with greater force and credibility by concerned plaintiff parents than recalcitrant defendant school boards. Even were that not the case, such decisions appear strangely insensitive to participatory values and the perceived fairness of judicial processes. Given the premises of our adversarial system, excluding a would-be participant on the theory that opponents have adequately protected his interests seems almost disingenuous.

Conversely, decisions mandating full participation for disaffected parties have all too often overlooked problems of manageability. The Los Angeles school desegregation suit is a case in point. Invoking a state statute similar to the federal rules, a California appellate court permitted intervention by an organization advocating neighborhood schools, notwithstanding the trial judge's determination that the group sought to present no new arguments and that additional parties would unduly complicate proceedings. As Steven Yeazell's extensive analysis of that opinion demonstrates, the appellate court's rationale for participation admits of no logical stopping point; virtually anyone interested in intervening should be allowed to do so.[34] Indeed, that seems to have been the lower court's understanding of the decision. Following his reversal on appeal, the trial judge admitted a dissenting school board member and two citizen groups, one of which candidly disavowed having any position regarding any integration plan, but alleged that its members would develop views by the time they got to court. The result was a trial involving as many as twenty-four to twenty-eight attorneys, with the judge occupying a role he described as 'somewhat akin to a trainer in the middle ring of a circus.'[35]

The difficulties of conducting reasoned deliberations under such circumstances are self-evident. As one attorney in a civil rights case involving far fewer intervenors put it, 'every time someone sneezed, the gesundheits took ten pages of transcript.'[36] Although trial courts are empowered to limit intervenors' role, the path of least resistance will often be to allow whatever evidence and argument these parties wish to offer. Moreover, where intervenors enjoy only a limited role, they may feel correspondingly limited obligations to propose constructive solutions for the problems they identify. Thus, adding participants will at times elongate without significantly improving adjudicative processes.

That observation points up one final weakness in the pluralist response to class conflicts: its expense. Full participation in educational reform litigation can be extraordinarily costly. It took the ACLU years to locate volunteer counsel willing and able to bring the Los Angeles school case, a commitment that ended up spanning a decade.[37] In less celebrated cases, it frequently will prove impossible to attract qualified counsel on a pro bono basis, and at current funding levels, public interest organizations have extremely limited litigation resources. Moreover, the uncertainties surrounding statutory authorization of fees for intervenors[38] have undoubtedly affected both the courts' exercise of discretion in inviting separate representatives, and attorneys' responsiveness to requests for assistance.

That is not to imply that such sensitivity is misplaced or regrettable. Presumably even the most fervent defenders of the pluralist approach would concede that at some point the law of diminishing marginal returns renders further participation wasteful as well as unwieldly. In a vast array of adjudicative and administrative contexts we are unwilling to underwrite the costs of flushing out all perspectives. The difficulty, however, is that current class action structures do little to ensure the allocation of separate representatives along utilitarian lines. As in other decision making contexts, the pluralist response biases decision-making in favor of those with the organizational acumen and financial resources to make themselves heard.[39] Obvious as this deficiency appears, it receives virtually no attention among defendants of the pluralist faith in class adjudication. Yet to accept their solution as appropriate in theory implies a strong indictment of class representation in practice. If significant separate interests warrant separate voices, it is hard to justify a structure that supplies them only to those willing and able to pay.

Of course, on one level, that objection simply expresses a problem with civil adjudication generally: a hearing is available, but only at a price. But the critique has special force in educational reform litigation, where most class members are involuntary parties to actions of considerable personal significance and indeterminate doctrinal outcome. Adequate decision-making under those circumstances requires information about the full spectrum of plaintiff concerns. Such data will not be forthcoming in a system heavily dependent on class members' own resources and organizational initiative. While those deficiences in the pluralist strategy are by no means unique to class action adjudication, their presence counsels some attention to majoritarian alternatives.

The Majoritarian Response: Direct Participation

Under the federal rules governing injunctive suits, courts must afford class members notice and an opportunity to be heard before approving a pretrial settlement and may mandate such notification at other times as a matter of discretion. As a means of conveying information to the court and a sense of participation to class members, majoritarion strategies seemingly offer several advantages over pluralist devices. The first concerns expense. Relatively speaking, talk is cheap, at least when it occurs among class members rather than through separate counsel. Even with large classes, notice costs can be minimized through carefully targeted publicity in public announcements. More important, soliciting class preferences directly, rather than through the mediating influence of attorneys or named representatives, may reduce opportunities for distortion and enhance individuals' confidence in the decision-making process. In practice, however, majoritarian devices are vulnerable to three serious objections. Absent extraordinary expenditures, the views elicited from notice and hearings will frequently be unrepresentative, uninformed, and unresponsive to a range of concerns particularly significant in institutional reform litigation.

To provide meaningful evidence of class preferences, responses to written notice or attendance at open meetings must reflect a fair cross-section of the class as a whole. The scant empirical data available raise significant doubts about how frequently this condition is met. Response rates to written notices are notoriously low, and attorneys who have held public meetings in educational reform cases generally report poor attendance.[40]

Although class members' failure to register dissent has often been taken to denote satisfaction, such inferences are troubling on several grounds. Rarely will most class members have sufficient understanding of the meaning of notice, the positions of counsel, and the remedial alternatives available to make informed decisions about whether or how to respond.

A threshold problem stems from the frequent unintelligibility of formal notices. Particularly in civil rights cases, where many class members' educational background is limited, comprehension may be strikingly low. Even lawsuits involving fewer disadvantaged plaintiffs have confronted severe communication barriers. An illustration outside the educational reform context suggests the extent of the problem. The case involved an antitrust claim against several major drug companies, seeking damages for purchasers of antibiotics. Class members received notices stating that unless they indicated a desire to opt out of the litigation, they would be bound by its result. Of the responses received, 'many if not most' evidenced some degree of misunderstanding, for example:

> Dear Sir:
>
> I received your pamphlet on drugs, which I think will be of great value to me in the future.
>
> Due to circumstances beyond my control I will not be able to attend this class at the time prescribed on your letter due to the fact that my working hours are from 7:00 until 4:30.

> Dear Sir:
>
> Our son is in the Navy, stationed in the Caribbean some place. Please let us know exactly what kind of drugs he is accused of taking.
>
> From a mother who will help if properly informed.[41]

Moreover, written notices and open meetings regarding settlement proposals often fails to convey sufficient facts to permit informed decision-making. Once prospects for a happy ending are in view, neither the parties who draft a notice nor the judge who approves it have much interest in highlighting features that might prolong the narrative. The Tucson desegregation illustrates how participants can intentionally or inadvertently mask controversial provisions. Rather than specifying that three schools would be closed under a proposed settlement plan, a feature opposed by a 'significant number' of parents, the notice stated only that those schools would be operated in accordance with unspecified options of previously submitted plans.[42] So too, public meetings are of limited use in eliciting informed preferences. The complexity of the bargaining process and the range of remedial alternatives are often impossible to convey to large groups. Excessive posturing by vocal participants may divert audience attention from difficult trade-offs that negotiators cannot so readily avoid. Public votes or petition signatures might more accurately reflect peer pressure than reflective judgment. And of course, simple plebiscites cannot adjust for differentials in voter comprehension, acuity, or intensity of concerns. As political theorists have submitted, the more technical the issue, the less the point in counting noses.[43]

In some instances, class members are uninformed in a still more fundamental sense. Individuals who lack experience with controversial remedial options may tend to fear the worst and vote accordingly. Although empirical evidence is limited, several studies suggest that black families subject to metropolitan busing programs are far more supportive of the concept than the black population generally.[44] So too, a survey of families involved in the *Pennhurst* litigation found that after their relatives had gone into community facilities individuals who had strongly opposed such placements were 'very happy' with the result.[45] That study also disclosed that much of the opposition to deinstitutionalization was attributable to concerns that community-based alternatives were not on solid financial ground, and therefore could not guarantee necessary support services and trained personnel. If only experience will effectively allay such fears, there is reason to discount family members' *ex ante* preferences.

Moreover, these same illustrations point up a final problem with relying on majoritarian methods in educational reform litigation. Often, eligible voters comprise only part of the class affected by judicial decree, and are insufficiently responsive to benefits that will redound primarily to others. For example, actions against facilities for the retarded typically proceed 'in behalf of' all current and future institutionalized residents 'speaking through' their parents or legal guardians.[46] Yet, in point of fact, the latter may be speaking for other personal and family interests as well. Parents' primary fear may be that closure of a centralized state facility, without an adequate community alternative, would force them to assume care of their disabled children, a task for which they lack adequate resources and fortitude.[47] The risks of that even may overshadow evidence suggesting that most of those now committed to institutions would lead fuller lives in less restrictive settings. Even absent such direct conflicts, eligible voters cannot always adequately represent a class that includes their successors. Minority parents, whose children will bear the immediate consequences of disruptive school closures or white hostility, are poorly situated to speak for future generations. The inequity of busing only blacks is immediately apparent; the principal benefits, in preempting white flight and maintaining an adequate tax base, are by comparison remote and conjectural. So too, a defendant school board's offer to increase dramatically the funds available for ghetto schools may seem attractive to existing class members. Yet from the perspective of future generations, the 'gold-plated school house' without any stable fiscal foundations has far less appeal. In some circumstances, the more volatile the issues and the greater the demand for class participation, the less comfortable we may be in abiding by majority vote.

Recognition of these factors doubtless accounts for many judges' reluctance to demand systematic evidence of class sentiment, or to view it as controlling. Thus, settlement hearings are often pro forma gestures; only where class opposition is overwhelming are trial or appellate courts likely to reject a proposed agreement. Even then, they generally are at pains to emphasize that vigorous vocal dissent by 'large numbers' of class members does not necessarily render a settlement unfair.[48] Although these opinions fail to explain why majority votes should not control in instances of conflict, their reasoning may well rest on the central unarticulated premise. In many institutional reform contexts, we do not believe that those class members able and willing to express their views provide an informed or representative cross-section of all who will be affected by a judicial decree. And if, in the final analysis, courts often are unprepared to defer to majoritarian sentiment, there are obvious reasons not to solicit it. Persuading either the class or the public of the legitimacy of a particular outcome is far more difficult once eligible voters have registered their opposition. From this perspective, the virtues of relying on class counsel as a mediating presence become apparent. Such reliance maintains a convenient legitimating myth of client control and participation, without an inconvenient substantive reality. That we have more frequently employed pluralist than majoritarian responses to class conflicts is at least partly, albeit not openly, explained on these grounds. In many instances, we wish to provide some limited channel for class members to express a preference without exposing the limits of our confidence in their judgments.

So also, we might at times hope to avoid underscoring the very constitutional indeterminacy that makes such preferences relevant. Even assuming a judge could present intelligible choices to a fair cross-section of the affected constituencies, the institutional costs of doing so would be considerable. To put courts in the business of reading election returns or survey results on a regular basis triggers questions about whether our counter-majoritarian branch ought to be grappling with these issues in the first instance. Insofar as we believe that courts are appropriately or inescapably enmeshed in educational reform, prudence counsels some restraint in open resort to plebiscites. Although majoritarian sentiment would generally cast more light on remedial alternatives than the constitutional text or congressional pronouncements, it is risky for trial judges to talk of entitlements and follow polls. Thus, as David Kirp has documented, resorting to 'legalist' analysis rather than empirical data is a common survival strategy by courts enmeshed in volatile school desegregation cases.[49] To preserve the credibility of judicial office, we make some compromises in the techniques available for particular decisions.

Alternatives and Apologia

Politics, by Reinhold Niebuhr's definition, is a realm where ethical and technical issues meet. In that sense, the problem of class action conflicts is eminently political and, to a considerable extent, intractable. For we have no wholly satisfactory answers to either the mechanical or moral questions that such conflicts pose. In practice, our procedural devices suffer from all the weaknesses of pluralist or majoritarian strategies generally. And in principle, our legal doctrines mask fundamental uncertainties about the meaning of representation, the proper scope for paternalism, and the distribution of legal resources. Yet to acknowledge the limits of our technical expertise and ethical certitude is not, of course, to abandon all hope of improvement. From a prescriptive standpoint, the preceding discussion suggests a number of useful adjustments in class action procedures.

As that discussion has emphasized, current class action structures make see-no-evil hear-no-evil postures far too attractive. Whatever their nominal responsibilities, courts, counsel, named parties, and class opponents may feel that the real obligation to monitor conflicts lies elsewhere. Courts assign it to attorneys, attorneys to each other or to dissenting class members, and so on. As a result, diverging preferences may never fully surface, or emerge only belatedly, when it is most costly to cope with them.

These structural problems suggest two sorts of reforms. One set of strategies should seek to increase judicial awareness of class schisms at an earlier, more meaningful stage of litigation. A second type of prescription would be directed toward improving courts' responses to such conflict. The central objective of both reform strategies should be to enhance the quality and perceived legitimacy of educational reform litigation, without unduly encumbering class procedures. The last qualification bears emphasis, since many cases now brought as class actions could, and presumably would, proceed as individual suits if the burdens on courts and counsel became too great. Given that those now excluded from decision making would generally have even fewer opportunities to be heard in private litigation, concerns about chilling class certification assume special significance.

One potentially promising means of ensuring greater judicial sensitivity to conflicts would be to require that trial courts make a factual record concerning notice and representation. Under current procedures, judges address those issues in too perfunctory a fashion at too early a stage in litigation. A more useful enquiry could occur if trial courts, before entering any remedial or consent decree, were obligated to make specific findings of fact as to the representativeness of positions advanced by existing parties and the adequacy of notice to the class. More specifically, the judge should have to determine that a fair cross-section of class views has been presented and that no significant constituency has been excluded.

To support its determination, the court should require class counsel to submit statements detailing consultations with class members and any evidence of dissension within the class. In addition, the trial judge's findings should explore any divergence between class sentiment, as expressed in response to notice, and the views espoused by named parties and their counsel. Where indicia of substantial conflict or widespread ignorance among class members were present, or where the financial or ideological interests of attorneys raised special concerns, the judge would be obligated to specify what steps were taken to canvass class sentiment.

An assessment of trial courts' and counsel's current ability to monitor class preferences suggests a second avenue for reform. Prevailing doctrine had failed to identify convincing standards for intervention, or for appointment and compensation of independent attorneys. Although neither problem lends itself to tidy resolution, some partial correctives are available.

Many of the difficulties with prevailing intervention analysis stem from insensitivity to the special procedural concerns at issue in educational reform litigation. Decisions denying intervention as untimely have often seemed unresponsive both to the information structures that made earlier participation unlikely, and to the remedial dynamics that make even belated involvement desirable. Decisions denying intervenor status on the theory that defendants have adequately presented dissident plaintiffs' views are similarly unsatisfying. Since dissenters may provide additional evidence or credibility on relevant issues, and are unlikely to perceive a defendant school board as an effective advocate for their concerns, their participation should be tolerated, absent a more convincing basis for exclusion than mere redundancy.

What could, however, provide such a basis are manageability concerns of the dimension present in the Los Angeles desegregation case. Within an adjucative framework, we cannot indefinitely increase access without diminishing capacity. When the cacophony of separate counsel precludes effective decision-making, or belated intervention requires extensive reopening of issues, participatory values may have to yield. Although there is obviously no magic tipping point, uniform for all cases, the costs of additional participants at some stage becomes prohibitive.

Thus, intervention analysis in institutional reform adjudication should reflect a more broad-gauged enquiry into the potential contribution of intervenors and a more particularized assessment of its expense. Insofar as these intervenors make substantial contributions to the resolution of contested issues or the formulation of a workable decree, they should be entitled to compensation.

Absent circumstances warranting separate counsel, trial judges could make greater use of expert witnesses, special masters, and magistrates for surrogate representation functions. Especially where the objectives are primarily majoritarian — to obtain information about aggregate plaintiff preferences or to give class members some direct participatory role — neutral court-appointed advisors could play a more prominent role. Non-partisan experts could, for example, minimize many of the inadequacies in notice and survey procedures described above. So too, where 'exceptional condition(s)' warrant appointment of special masters,[50] they can prove useful in soliciting class preference through surveys, open meetings, and confidential interviews. Given the resources, expertise, and explicit responsibility for these tasks, masters can play a useful role in 'unclog(ging) the channels of participation.'[51]

The ultimate effect of such procedural reforms is difficult to predict. There remains the possibility that greater reliance on separate counsel or court-appointed experts will simply increase the numbers of non-accountable platonic guardians involved in educational reform litigation. And requiring fact finders to make more detailed records in support of their conclusions has had mixed success in various administrative and judicial contexts. According to Joseph Sax, 'emphasis on the redemptive quality of procedural reforms' in administrative decision making is 'about nine parts myth and one part coconut oil.'[52] Yet while systematic data are lacking, most commentators would probably agree with Richard Stewart's less dire assessment. In his view, forcing the decision maker to 'direct attention to factors that may have been disregarded' has in some instances proved of real prophylactic value.[53] Moreover, more explicit requirements for class attorneys could at least narrow their capacity for self-delusion about whose views they were or were not representing.

Pennhurst provides a useful paradigm for speculating on the potential benefits of the proposals set out above. Granting all the dangers of counterfactual analysis, there is reason to suppose that improved procedures could have improved outcomes in that case. If, for example, the trial judge had been required to make a record concerning notice and representation, parental concerns might well have surfaced at a much earlier stage of litigation.

One obvious option would have been to suggest or appoint separate counsel for disaffected parents, a strategy that might have proved beneficial in several respects. Most obviously, it would have preempted an acrimonious and costly post-decree appeal challenging the adequacy of class representation. Separate counsel for the parents also might have minimized the opposition to Pennhurst's closure that followed the court's decree. By explaining the evidence supporting deinstitutionalization, preparing families for the possibility of closure, and providing reassurance that any placement plan would reflect their concerns, an attorney representing parents could have served a useful conciliatory function. As it was, many family members felt that their reservations about community care had never been present. After the district judge's closure order, these individuals joined forces with Pennhurst staff, who had a stake in opposing deinstitutionalization regardless of the adequacy of community-based alternatives. Earlier parental involvement might have averted an alliance that has now cemented resistance to the trial court's decree, as well as legitimated opposition from other quarters.

Continuous appeals, staff recalcitrance, and legislative parsimony all have plagued implementation efforts. During the two years that the trial court's decree was in full force, fewer residents were placed in less restrictive settings than in seven of the eight preceding years: only 184 of some 1156 residents were transferred to community facilities.[54] Since the Supreme Court's stay now limits relocations from Pennhurst to voluntary transfers, parental opposition can severely impede further deinstitutionalization efforts.[55] That result is particularly disturbing given all the evidence that both patients and their families benefit from community placements.

To be sure, none of the proposals outlined here can guarantee better results in cases like *Pennhurst*. But that conclusion, if disheartening, is not necessarily damning. Our other political structures suffer from comparable pluralist or majoritarian weaknesses. Though neither courts, counsel, nor parties will always be inclined or able to protect class interests, we have no reason to expect legislators or bureaucrats to do better. Indeed, the strongest defense of any of our governmental constructs is equally available to class actions. While we cannot depend on disinterested and informed judgment by any single groups of institutional participants, we can create sufficient procedural checks and balances to prevent at least the worst abuses.

Moreover, to acknowledge that the formal mandates governing class advocacy promise far more than they deliver does not necessarily indict the pretense. No current or hypothesized procedures can guarantee that class interests will always be 'adequately represented' or that counsel will single-mindedly pursue his 'client's' objectives. But the risk of abandoning either fiction may be too great.

No matter how faulty the enforcement mechanism, such mandates serve important precatory and legitimating functions. Amorphous injunctions concerning client autonomy and adequate representation allow us to affirm each individual's right to be heard without in fact paying the entire price. To give fixed content to those terms might force us toward greater pluralism, in which case we would face certain difficult questions about the distribution of legal resources and the marginal contributions of counsel. Alternatively, we would totter towards majoritarianism, only to confront the awkward fact that paternalism is often offensive in principle but desirable in practice. Like other 'white lies of the law' those governing class action conflicts spare us such discomfitting choices by papering over 'certain weak spots in our intellectual structure.'[56] Given the extraordinary achievements of educational reform litigation, that is a useful, if sometimes unbecoming, role.

Notes

1 See Graglia, L. (1976) *Disaster by Decree*; Horowitz, D. (1977) *The Courts and Social Policy*; Hazard, G. (1970) 'Social justice through civil justice,' *U. Chi. L. Rev*, 36, p. 699; Mishkin, P. (1978) 'Federal courts as state reformers,' *Wash & Lee L. Rev*, 35, pp. 949 and 959–61.

2 For relatively positive assessments of courts' intervention in institutional reform litigation, see Cavanagh, R. and Sarat, A. (1980) 'Thinking about courts: Toward and beyond a jurisprudence of judicial competence,' *Law & Soc'y Rev*, 14, p. 371; Eisenberg, T. & Yeazell, S. (1980) 'The ordinary and extraordinary in institutional reform litigation,' *Harv. L. Rev*, 93, p. 465; Fisso. (1979) 'Forward: The forms of

justice,' *Harv. L. Rev*, 93, p. 1. For more critical evaluations, see sources cited in note 1.

3 Many of the problems presented by educational reform litigation would arise with equal force if the issues were addressed in administrative or legislative, rather than judicial contexts. See CHAYES, A. (1976) 'The role of the judge in public law litigation,' *Harv.. L. Rev*, 89, p. 1311; TRUBECK, D. (1979) 'Public advocacy: Administrative government and the representation of diffused interests,' in CAPPELLETTI, M. and GARTH, B. *Access to Justice* pp. 447 and 464–8.

4 BELL, D. (1976) 'Serving two masters: Integration interests and client interests in school desegregation litigation,' *Yale L. J*. 85, p. 470; BERGER, C. (1978) 'Away from the court house and into the field: The odyssey of a special master,' *Colum. L. Rev*, 98, p. 707; YEAZELL, S. (1977) 'Intervention and the idea of litigation: A comment on the Los Angeles school case,' *UCLA L. Rev*, 25, p. 244.

5 See ORFIELD, G. (1978) *Must We Bus* (discussing Tucson, Arizona, desegregation suit). Interview with Clyde Murphy, NAACP Legal Defense Fund, in New York City (25 June 1981) (discussing Austin, Texas, desegregation suit); *Calhoun v. Cook*, 487 F. 2d 620 (5th Cir. 1973), 522 F. 2d 717 (5th Cir. 1975). *Norwalk CORE v. Norwalk Board of Educ.*, 298 F. Supp. 203, 298 F. Supp. 208 (D. Conn. 1968), 298 F. Supp. 210 (1969), *aff'd* 423 F. 2d 121 (2d Cir. 1970); *Hart v. Community School Board*, 383 F. Supp. 699, Supp. 383 F. Supp. 769 (EDNY 1974), *aff'd* 512 F. 2d 37 (2d Cir. 1976).

6 *Halderman v. Pennhurst State School & Hospital*, 612 F. 2d 84 (3rd Cir. 1979), discussed in BURT, R. (1981) *Pennhurst — A Parable* (unpublished manuscript); *New York State Ass'n for Retarded Children, Inc. v. Rockefeller*, 357 F. Supp. 752 (EDNY 1973), Interview with Armando M. Menocal III, Public Advocate, Inc., in Stanford, California (10 February 1982) (discussing *Students of the California School for the Blind v. Riles*, No. 5-80-473 (ED Cal., 15 Aug., 1980)).

7 See Advisory Committee Note, 39 F.R.D. 100 (1966).

8 See CHOPER, J. (1974) 'The Supreme Court and the political branches: Democratic theory and practice,' *U. Pa. L. Rev*, 122, pp. 808 and 810. See generally, PENNOCK, J. (1968) 'Political representation: An overview,' in PENNOCK, J. and CHAPMAN, J. (Eds) *Representation* 3, pp. 6–16.

9 See generally, BURKE, E. (1970) *Reflections on the Revolution in France* and (1770) *Thoughts on the Cause of Present Discontents.* For an excellent account of the application of Burkean theories to class representation, see YEAZELL, S. (1980) 'From group litigation to class action — part II: interest, class, and representation,' *UCLA L. Rev*, 27, pp. 1–67.

10 *Long v. Thornton Township High School District 205*, 82 F.R.D. 186 (N. D. Ill. 1979). See generally DEGNAN, R. (1972) 'Forward: Adequate representation in class actions,' *Calif. L. Rev*, 60, p. 705.

11 *Swann v. Charlotte-Mecklenburg Board of Education*, 402 U.S. 1 (1971): see *Potts v. Flax*, 313 F. 2d 284 (5th Cir. 1963).

12 438 US 265 (1978).

13 SUMMERS, C. (1974) 'Evaluation and improving legal processes — a plea for process values,' *Cornell L. Rev*, 60, pp. 1 and 21–5; TRIBE (1975) 'Structural due process,' *Harv. CRCLL Rev*, 12, p. 267.

14 KADISH, S. (1957) 'Methodology and criteria in due process adjudication: A survey and criticism, *Yale L.J.*, 66, pp. 319 and 346–63; MICHAELMAN, F. (1973) 'The Supreme Court and litigation access fees: The right to protect one's rights' (pt. 1) *Duke L.J.* pp. 1153 and 1172–3. But see SIMON, W. (1975) 'The ideology of advocacy: Procedural justice and professional ethics' *Wisc. L. Rev.* 30 (challenging the premise that participation in legal proceedings enhances their perceived legitimacy).

15 BURKE, E. (1969) 'Representative as Trustee,' in PITKIN, H. (Ed.) *Representation*, p. 170.

16 Ely, J., (1980) *Democracy and Distrust*, p. 87.
17 For a description of various statutory proposal, see Wicker, T. (1981) 'Court stripping,' *New York Times*, 24 April, at 31, col. 1. See also (1982) *Crawford v. Board of Educ.*, 50 *US L. W.* 5016 (U.S. 30 June) (upholding California constitutional amendment limiting state court authority to order mandatory pupil assignment or transportation).
18 See (1981) 'Developments in the law — conflicts of interest,' 94 *Harv. L. Rev*, 94, pp. 1244, 1449–50, 1453 and cases cited therein.
19 The trial judge in the Los Angeles school desegregation case believes that plaintiff parents had no real contact with their attorneys and were 'totally uninformed' about the litigation. Interview with former Judge Paul Egly, in San Francisco (4 June 1981). See Lubenaw, G. (1972) 'The petition lawyers,' *Saturday Review*, 39, 26 August.
20 *Greenfield v. Villager Industries, Inc.*, 483 F. 2d 824, 832 n. 9 (3d Cir. 1973).
21 (1970) 'Developments in the law — class actions,' *Harv. L. Rev*, 89, pp. 1270 and 1595 and sources cited therein.
22 Weisbrod, B., Handler, J. and Komesar, N. (Eds) (1978) *Public Interest Law* 88; Handler, J. (1976) 'Public interest law: Problems and prospects,' in Schwartz, M. (Ed.) *Law and the American Future*, 99, pp. 106–8; Rabin, (1976) 'Lawyers for social change: Perspectives on public interest law,' *Stan. L. Rev*, 28, pp. 207 and 233.
23 Bell, D. (1976) *op. cit.*, p. 516.
24 Brief of *Amicus Curiae*, in *Halderman v. Pennhurst State School & Hospital*, 612 F. 2d 104 (3rd Cir. 1979).
25 Keating, D., Conroy, J. and Walker, S. (1980) 'Longitudinal study of the court-ordered deinstitutionalization of Pennhurst,' 16, 30 October, Temple University Institute for Survey Research.
26 *Fed. Rules Civ. Proc.*, Rule 23; *Kremens v. Burley*, 431 U.S. 019, 135 (1977).
27 Weisbrod, B. (1978) 'Conceptual perspective on the public interest,' in Weisbrod, B., Handler, J. and Komisar, N. (Eds), *Public Interest Law: An Economic and Institutional Analysis*, 4, p. 29. For general discussion of the common action problem, see, for example, Olson, M. (1965) *The Logic of Collective Action*.
28 See *Am. Fin. Sys., Inc. v. Pickrel*, 18 Fed. Rules Serv. 2d, 292, 295 (D. Md. 1974); Federal Judicial Center (1978) *Manual for Complex Litigation*, pt. 1 See. 1.41. DR 7-104 of the ABA's *Code of Professional Responsibility* prohibits attorneys' communication with opposing parties represented by counsel absent counsel's consent.
29 See, for example, Borow, Minneapolis, in Kirp, D. *et al* (1979) *Judicial Management of School Desegregation Cases*; interview with Jan Costello, Juvenile Justice Legal Advocacy Project, Youth Law Center, in San Francisco (17 January 1981).
30 *Bustop v. Superior Court*, 69 Cal. App. 3d 66, 137 Cal. Rptr. 793 (2d Dist. 1977); *Jones v. Caddo Parish School Board*, 499 F. 2d 914, 915 (5th Cir. 1974); *Calhoun. v. Cook*, 487 F. 2d 680, 682–83 (Sup. ar 1973). For example in *Pennhurst*, disaffected parents did not seek to intervene until 4 years after the suit began and a year after trial, Burt, R. (1981) *op. cit.*
31 *Fed. R. Civ. P.* 24 (b).
32 See, for example, *Mendoza v. United States*, 623 F. 2d 1338 (9th Cir. 1980); *Hinds v. Rapides Parish School Board*, 479 F. 2d 762 (5th Cir. 1963); *Accord, Calhoun v. Cook* 487 F. 2d 680 (5th Cir. 1973).
33 *Cisneros v. Corpus Christi Indep. School Dist.* 560 F. 2d 190 (5th Cir. 1977); *Bradley v. Millikin*, 620 F. 2d 1141 (6th Cir. 1980).
34 Yeazell, S. (1977) *op. cit.*, p. 260, n. 69 (analyzing *Bustop v. Superior Court*, 69 Cal. App. 3rd 66, 137 Cal. Rptr. 793 (2d Dist. 1977)).
35 (1977) 'Busing hearings to resume: Judge still skeptical but will hear board's case,' *Los Angeles Times*, 15 April, Sec. 1, at 1, col. 5; interview with former Judge Paul Egly, in San Francisco (4 June 1981).
36 Chambers, D. and Wald, M. (1981), *Smith v. Offer: A Case Study*, p. 47

37 ORFIELD, G. (1978) *op. cit.*, pp. 376–7.
38 The Civil Rights Attorneys Fees Act of 1976, 42 USC 1988 (1976), grants courts discretion to award fees to 'prevailing parties' other than the United States. In many educational reform suits involving intervenors, success is a matter of degree. See RHODE, D. (1982) 'Class conflicts in class actions,' *Stan. L. Rev*, 34, pp. 1183 and 1229, and cases cited therein.
39 See generally LOWI, T. (1969) *The End of Liberalism* New York, Norton; CONNOLLY, W. (Ed.) (1969) *The Bias of Pluralism* New York, Norton; KARIEL, H. (1961) *The Decline of American Pluralism* Stanford, Stanford University Press.
40 See SIMON, (1972) *Class Actions — Useful Tools or Engines of Destruction* 55 F.R.D. pp. 375 and 379. In the Pittsburgh school desegregation case, twenty-five to thirty individuals out of a class of 2000 students and 4000 parents typically attended open meetings. Interview with James Liebman, NAACP Legal Defense Fund, in New York City (25 June 1981).
41 HERNE and KING (1972), 'I am sorry, but I cannot attend your class action,' *Virginia Law Weekly*, Friday, 4 February.
42 *Mendoza v. United States*, 623 F. 2d 1338, 1349–50 (9th Cir. 1980).
43 PITKIN, H. (1969) *op. cit.*, p. 20; DAHL, R., (1970) *After the Revolution* pp. 67–88; WOLFF, R., (1968) *The Poverty of Liberalism*, p. 35.
44 For example, in one Gallup Poll asking black respondents which policy they favoured, 18 per cent supported 'integration even with long-distance busing,' and 14 per cent preferred 'minimum integration with short-distance busing,' while 25 per cent endorsed voluntary open enrollment with busing, and 33 per cent favored neighborhood schools. Potomac Associates poll conducted by Gallup, reported in *Watts and Free, State of the Nation* 1974, pp. 109–10. By contrast, surveys of black families in several Florida school districts indicated that only 25 per cent of respondents opposed their districts' busing plan, *ID.* at 414.
45 KEATING, D., CONROY, J. and WALKER, S. (1980) *op. cit.*, p. 44.
46 See, for example, *Halderman v. Pennhurst State Hospital*, 446 F. Supp. 1295 (E.D. Pa. 1977).
47 See KEATING, D., CONROY, J. and WALKER, S. (1980) *op. cit.*, 25 pp.3–6 (citing surveys); SKELTON, M. (1972) 'Areas of parental concern about retarded children,' *Mental Retardation*, 10, 1, pp. 38–41.
48 *Bryan v. Pittsburgh Plate Glass Co.*, 494 F. 2d 799, 863 (3d Cir.), *cert. denied*, 419 U.S. 900 (1974); *Pettway v. American Cast Iron Pipe Co.*, 576 F. 2d 1157, 1216 (5th Cir. 1978).
49 KIRP, D. (1981) 'The bounded politics of school desegregation litigation,' *Harv. Ed. Rev*, 51, pp. 395 and 407–8.
50 Fed. R. Civ. p. 53.
51 KIRP, D.L. & BABCOCK, G. (1981) 'Judge and company: court-appointed masters, school desegregation and institutional reform,' *Ala. L. Rev*, 33, pp. 313 and 392. See BRAKEI, S. (1979) 'Special masters in institutional reform litigation,' *Am. B. Found. Research J.* pp. 513 and 549.
52 SAX, J. (1973) 'The (unhappy) truth about NRPA,' *Okla, L. Rev*, 26, p. 239.
53 STEWART, R. (1975) 'The reformation of American administrative law,' 88 *Harv. L. Rev*, 88, pp. 1669, 1702, 1680 and nns. 524–526 (citing commentary). For an attempt to determine the impact of procedural formality on outcome, see NONET, P. (1969) *Administrative Justice.*
54 HUMAN SERVICES RESEARCH INSTITUTE (1980) *Longitudinal Study of the Court-Ordered Deinstitutionalization of Pennhurst: Historical Overview* 56, 7 April; *Halderman v. Pennhurst State School & Hosp.*, No. 74-1345, at 5 (E.D. Pa., 11 Sept., 1981) (mem.).
55 *Pennhurst State School & Hospital v. Halderman*, 449 U.S. 930 (1981).
56 FULLER, L. (1967) *Legal Fictions*, pp. 51–2 (quoting R. von Ihering).

4 Case Studies

Just Schools

Doris Fine
University of California, Berkeley

'. . . The Board must be required to formulate a new plan and . . . to fashion steps which promise . . . a system without a "white" school and a "Negro" school, but just schools.'

(*Green v. School Board of New Kent County*, 391 US 430, 1968)

This is a study of the school board, several courts, and a special commission of inquiry as they attempted to come to terms with the problems of the San Francisco School District over the past several years. Following them has been like accompanying helpless rescue teams through a disaster area. Since the 1960s, San Francisco schools have, like most metropolitan school systems, been in a permanent state of crisis. Theirs is a familiar story: court-ordered integration; declining enrollments and the flight of the middle class; dropping standards of student performance, and the continuing gap between white and minority student achievement; an epidemic of vandalism and violence; the demoralization and growing militancy of teachers; all the above in a context of budget crises, program cutbacks, and constant administrative dislocations.

The study began in 1975, at a time of growing public concern about the apparent incapacity of the schools to discharge their responsibility for teaching 'basic skills'. The San Francisco Unified School District (SFUSD) had recently been shaken by evidence of a dramatic decline in the levels of achievement of its pupils. A law suit, claiming educational malpractice, had been filed against it on behalf of an illiterate high school graduate. With the support of the state Superintendent of Public Instruction, and under pressure by parents and civic leaders, the district established a special commission of inquiry, the San Francisco Public Schools Commission (SFPSC), to study and recommend means of restoring the competence of the schools. The school board itself was confronted with the need to reaffirm academic standards.

In sum, there was a pervasive sense that, after a decade of agitation over issues of 'justice,' the public schools needed to be recalled to their more central institutional responsibilities. Like other special purpose institutions, schools are expected in principle to be guided by, and responsible for, the specific mission for which they are constituted. Granted all the ambiguities of that mission — the goals of education are multi-faceted, sometimes contradictory, and often elusive — there is no doubt that basic instruction is among the tasks to which public schools must give a high priority. But American public schools have never been 'just schools.' Throughout their history, they have been objects of a wide range of public demands and expectations that extend far beyond instruction and are sometimes only most tenuously related to educational ends. However legitimate such expectations may be, they entail serious costs, including administrative burdens and constraints. When their urgency is too distracting, those who govern tend to lose sight of the basic mission of the schools.

This study describes three different policy agencies — the school board, the SFPSC, and the courts — that tried to cope with the tension between social accountability and institutional purpose during a period when the schools' competence had become a central object of public concern.

The School Board: Opportunism and Drift

Until 1972, the San Francisco Board of Education was appointed by the Mayor from among distinguished civic leaders representative of the city's progressive and cosmopolitan outlook, and beholden to no particular constituencies. That year, following protests against district plans for racial integration, the voters endorsed a charter amendment calling for election of board members. The change was expected to make the board more responsive to public concerns. But basic patterns of board decision-making had been set before the charter amendment, and they persisted. The appointed board had lost legitimacy, but its problems did not arise from its insulation, but rather from its excessive exposure to political pressures, and its critical lack of leadership.

Meddling in Administration

During the 1960s, a major shift had occurred in the relationship between the school board and the school administration: the board has lost confidence in the staff's competence, and gradually had assumed ever greater initiative and responsibility in the conduct of school affairs. This evolution began in 1962 when the Superintendent determined that there was no educationally sound plan for racial integration of the schools. To many board members, the superintendent's position did not offer an adequate response to this highly sensitive issue, and an *od hoc* committee was formed to formulate the board's own approach to the demands of civil rights groups. Public hearings were held and the board retained outside consultants to study and recommend plans for eliminating racial imbalance.

The school integration issue set the precedent for an extension of school

Board concerns to ever more numerous areas of policy, marking the end of an era when separation of politics from administration had been a central tenet of school management. Although the board formally held the authority to make all decisions regarding the budget, buildings and grounds, personnel, textbooks, and the like, for the most part those matters had been delegated to the administration. The arrangement broke down in the late 1960s when pressing political demands began forcing their way on the board's agenda. Although veteran school administrators resisted the trend, their attitude contributed only further to strain relations between the staff and the board. In 1971, when the time came to draw plans for implementing court ordered desegregation, confidence in the administration was so low that the board chose to avoid relying upon the staff. A citizens' committee developed the plan with almost no administrative support.

The administration is the executive arm of the board; but in addition, the superintendent and other top administrators are also the board's chief advisors. Unlike other legislative bodies, the school board does not have its own independent staff. The board's dependence upon administrative advice became a frequent source of embarrassment and frustration, and the board began circumventing the staff by hiring outside management consultants and appointing citizen advisory committees to monitor every sort of school or district-wide program. Ever smaller details of budget and program design became matters for intense school board and public debate. Nothing remained out of the board's purview. As one member remarked, 'for want of a nail, the kingdom might be lost.'

The board offered no structural support for leadership. The presidency was treated as a norminal office, which rotated among the members, and carried no special authority. Divisions within the board further complicated responsible decision-making.

A typical board meeting (18 May 1972) covered the following topics. The board reviewed a management consultant report regarding reorganization of the office of budget and planning, and decided to extend the study and to authorize implementation of a new 'management system.' A board member requested a staff report on bilingual programs in the intermediate (grades 4 to 6) schools. Enquiries regarding recent disruptions in the high schools were referred to special committee. A citizens' committee report on a new counseling program utilizing parent volunteers was heard. The board voted to place a special 10¢ tax increase for school reconstruction on the ballot. In response to a Superintendent request for an allocation of $30,000 for bus monitors, the board insisted that a study be done to justify the need for the expense. Parent councils asked for more bilingual education classes and more involvement in decisions concerning particular schools, and a board member suggested that minutes of parent council meetings be distributed to the board. A draft Student Bill of Rights was presented by a city-wide youth committee, and referred to the administration for comments. A board member questioned the practice of using federal grant moneys to pay for consultants and teacher travel, only to learn from the administration that these expenditures were required by federal program regulations. The administration recommended a moratorium on teacher hiring. A preliminary budget was presented. A parent-teacher group requested space for an alternative school and was tentatively granted a location. The legal advisor reported that a lawsuit demanding desegregation of the secondary schools had been filed by the NAACP, and the board referred to an *ad hoc* committee the question whether to retain special counsel for the district's defense. And so on.

Although board membership is not expected to be a full-time job, agendas of that sort made it a heavy burden. Biweekly evening meetings that lasted often into the early hours of the morning, executive sessions, committee assignments, and oversight activities, not to mention the homework needed to absorb volumes of reports, took their toll. Board members used to serve terms of twelve to fifteen years, providing sustained and experienced guidance to the schools. Since the mid-1960s, however, turnover has been rapid: average tenure in office has been three years; many board members resign before their terms expire, largely on account of the excessive burdens of the office.

Superintendents have consistently criticized the board's intrusion in administrative matters. One complained that the board's meddling in administration' was responsible for the district's budget crises and the loss of public confidence in the schools. Others have charged that board accommodations to various special interests undermine budgetary restraints, forcing last-minute staff transfers and program adjustments, and frustrating efforts to streamline school organization.

An Agenda of Special Interest Issues

An explosion of social activism broke down the separation of board and administration responsibilities. The policies that emerged from the board reflect that pattern. Acting in reaction to pressure, the board kept endorsing all kinds of special interest programs. Although many of them were supported by state and federal funds, only a few were mandated by law; most benefited only from permissive legislation or were purely local initiatives. Within the limits of available resources, the board was inclined to approve any 'innovative' program for which there was sufficiently persistent and vocal support.

In such a context, it is difficult to maintain any sense of priorities. The very word 'priority' loses meaning. The seeming urgency of special interest issues distracts attention, diverts energies, and dilutes the sense of purpose. In the midst of 'innovations,' critical issues become unattended. Among those most vulnerable to neglect were issues without active constituencies, and issues visible only from a long-range perspective. Even with regard to less sensitive programs, no efforts were made to assess the countless 'experiments' and 'innovations' of the time. When cutbacks later became necessary to avoid budget deficits, the Board set some 'priorities', but these did not, and could not, rest on judgments regarding the programs' educational merits. And, although much evidence indicated that pupil performance in core subjects was reaching alarmingly low levels, the board did not begin to act on the matter until 1975, when the problem had become a major public embarrassment. No special interest spoke for the basic curriculum.

On some matters, the board did exert sustained and conscientious efforts, but even there one is struck by its short-sightedness. In order to meet the requirements of state earthquake safety laws, the board undertook a massive reconstruction project affecting half the district's schools at a cost of more than $50 million. But its plans overlooked the implications of declining enrollment trends. Thus, unsafe buildings were brought up to standards, only to be closed down for lack of pupils, while other structures fell into disrepair owing to growing vandalism and declining maintenance budgets.

In sum, the San Francisco school board provides a vivid example of opportunism. It was open to its constituencies, disposed to undertake new social responsibilities, tolerant of change and even chaos; but it was not governed by any sense of direction. Distracted by its many vocal and conflicting publics, and careless of what it had inherited, the school board failed to offer leadership in re-establishing the centrality of basic educational values.

The Schools in Court

The issues of that period were fought only partly before the school district's own governing forum. Several, including the most important one, namely school integration, developed also through lawsuits in state and federal courts. How the district fared under the relatively distant, dispassionate and sober scrutiny of the courts, is the concern of this section.

The analysis concentrates on three cases that addressed the problem of remedying failures on the part of the schools to discharge their basic educational responsibilities. The *Johnson* case, filed in the Federal District Court in 1970, spoke to the educational needs of black elementary school children. The *Lau* case, also filed in the Federal District Court in 1970, concerned the plight of non-English-speaking children of Chinese origin, and raised questions regarding the education of similar students of other national origins. The *Doe* case, filed in 1972 in the San Francisco Superior Court on behalf of a white, English-speaking recent high school graduate, examined an alleged and apparently more general failure of the schools to teach basic skills.[1]

Reframing Issues for Legal Action

Although all three cases involved challenges to the schools' educational competence, they differ with respect to the legal frameworks and doctrines that they invoke. When a claim is pressed in the form of a lawsuit, issues must be framed in the terms of some available and authoritative legal doctrine. There follows, of necessity, a reshaping of the underlying policy problem so as to take into account the current legal doctrine. The latter fixes the legal pegs on which a claim can be hung. In the *Johnson* case, that peg happened to be the constitutional doctrine of equal protection, as elaborated by the Federal courts in the wake of *Brown v. Board of Education* and later school desegregation decisions.[2]

The *Lau* plaintiffs also first rested their case on equal protection grounds. But there had not been, with respect to foreign origin or foreign language, any line of precedents even remotely comparable to the chain of decisions on racial segregation. After a brief hearing, the case was dismissed by the district court, and the dismissal was later affirmed by the Court of Appeals.[3] Four years after its inception, the case was remanded to district court when the Supreme Court found a potential, and far narrower ground for a claim under Title VI of the 1964 Civil Rights Act, which provides that 'no person in the United States shall, on the ground of race, color or national origin, be excluded from participation in, be denied the benefits of, or be subjected to discrimination under any program or activity receiving Federal financial assistance.'[4] This decision had the effect of making the case quite contingent upon what bilingual education policy the HEW Office of Civil Rights, responsible for enforcing Title VI, would support.

The third case, *Doe*, took a radically different tack. Here, no 'civil rights' issues were involved. This complaint also struck at an educational failure of the schools, but one that could hardly be characterized as discriminatory. The equal protection clause cannot protect one from equal neglect. *Doe* took shape within the legal framework of a private lawsuit in torts, in which the plaintiff undertook to show educational malpractice on the part of the schools.

These three cases highlight a basic dilemma of the effort to reform school policy through legal action. *Either* the court's attention is brought sharply to bear on the educational policy issues at stake; but this is an area in which courts have gravely doubted their own competence, and the outcome is likely to be a judgment of deference to administrative authority. *Or* the issue is legally couched in a way that detaches it from educational problems, and while the court may then act more confidently, the outcome will likely be a judgment that ignores its educational ramifications, and whose bluntness in that regard may spell disaster. In both *Lau* and *Doe* educational policy issues became central, and in both the courts opted for restraint and non-intervention. In *Johnson*, on the contrary, no educational question was ever raised and the court, confident in its constitutional expertise, ordered a remedy that tore apart the fabric of the school district.

In *Lau*, the court was asked to order that the schools provide Chinese-speaking students with 'special, full-time instruction in English, taught by bilingual teachers'.[5] In its defense, the school district insisted that it was quite aware of the language handicaps of its ethnic minority pupils, Chinese, Spanish, and others; but that its limited resources compelled it to set priorities among many competing and equally legitimate needs. The district also emphasized the controversy among educators with regard to the advantages and disadvantages of different approaches to teaching English to foreign language speaking children.[6] One approach, called English as a Second Language (ESL), seemed to be more beneficial to students with some command of English; it stressed speedier learning through intensive supplementary classes. In another approach, the one advocated by the plaintiffs, and called Bilingual Bicultural Education (BBE), pupils were taught all subjects by a bilingual teacher for the entire school day.

In dismissing the complaint, the district court pointed out that the educational needs, not the constitutional rights of the plaintiffs, were at stake, and that this was a matter for the schools, not the courts to decide.[7] The Court of Appeals agreed that the case was 'one calling for significant amounts of executive and legislative expertise, and non-judicial value judgments.'[8] Finally, the consent decree which ended the proceedings on remand fully preserved the school district's discretion to develop remedial English instruction as it saw fit.[9]

The court's restraint in matters of educational policy is also illustrated in the *Doe* case. In sustaining the district's demurrer, the San Francisco Superior Court found there was no statutory basis for the plantiff's claim that schools have a duty of care to deliver actual mastery of basic skills.[10] The Court of Appeals, in affirming this decision, was impressed by the absence of consensus among professional educators as to applicable standards of educational responsibility.[11]

In the *Johnson* case, educational concerns never moved to the foreground. The 1965 Coleman Report had fostered the belief that racially mixed elementary schools were necessary conditions for the improvement of black pupils' education, but that proposition had not been the focus of litigation. Before the courts, it was not more than a remote and unexamined assumption. Constitutional, not educational issues were the key preoccupation. In *Johnson*, the elimination of racially 'imbalanced' schools, not the quality of school services to black pupils, was the plaintiff's objective. When, early in the trial, one of the plaintiffs' attorneys questioned whether racial 'balance' would redress the educational handicaps of black pupils, and urged stressing the inferior quality of ghetto schools rather than school population patterns *per se*, he was advised to withdraw from the case, and did so.[12]

Confident in its authority, the Federal District Court found that the school district had engaged in *de jure* segregation, and went on to order a reorganization of the elementary schools, such that 'the ratio of black children to white children will be ... substantially the same in each school.'[13] Six weeks were allowed for the parties to prepare alternative plans of reorganization. A motion by the school district, protesting the impossibly short amount of time allotted to a planning process involving ninety-six schools and 48,000 pupils, was summarily denied by the court. Both the plaintiffs' and the school district's plans were hastily constructed, utilizing a formula set by California statutory guidelines according to which the racial composition of any school's population should not differ from that of the overall school-age population by more than 15 per cent margins of error,[14] and neither addressed any consideration of educational policy.

Pyrrhic Outcomes

In retrospect, the three legal battles are mostly to be remembered for their pyrrhic outcomes: to the plaintiffs, *Lau* and *Doe* ended in apparent defeat, *Johnson* in apparent victory. However, having 'lost' in court, bilingual education and the teaching of basic skills proceeded to become targets of considerable district action and public concern. The *Johnson* decree, a 'victory' for racial integration, never gained more than formal and shallow administrative compliance, and was eventually abandoned. In each case, administrative commitments and public support, not judicial verdicts, made the difference that mattered.

Concern for the issues raised in the *Lau* case increased following dismissal of the suit. Significant program changes were made by the school district. Thus, by the time the Supreme Court remanded the case to trial for reconsideration under Title VI, the Office of Civil Rights informed the school district that no particular program change was required and that, if it received assurance from the district that affirmative program efforts would continue, no sanctions would be imposed. The matter was left for the district to settle in negotiations with the plantiffs. The district adopted a general statement of objectives for remedial English programs. Competing needs and limited resources prevented going further. The plaintiffs yielded, on the condition that the district file annual reports on the progress of its efforts. This agreement formed the basis of a consent decree with concluded the matter.[15]

The *Doe* case followed a similar pattern. Although ostensibly a private law suit involving only the individual plaintiff, the complaint raised far-reaching issues of public concern. Following its dismissal, there was a wave of agitation for educational reform.

The State of California's annual testing program makes it possible to compare levels of achievements in each local school system with other school districts and with state-wide averages. In 1975, those tests indicated that the average San Francisco twelfth graders' reading performance ranked in eighteenth percentile of the state-wide distribution, below other districts with similar socio-economic background characteristics. This meant that only 17 per cent of California twelfth graders scored lower than the average SF high-school graduate. Public alarm over this situation shook the district. A new Minimum Graduation Requirements Committee, consisting of parents and staff, promptly recommended that minimum requirements for promotion be set for all grade levels, and the recommendation won strong administrative support.[16] The school district adopted minimal standards for high school graduation, and implemented a grade structure reorganization designed to provide better articulation of programs for teaching basic skills. San Francisco, a new superintendent promised, was committed to 'end social promotion and meaningless diplomas.'[17]

In contrast to the heightened activity that followed the *Lau* and *Doe* 'defeats', the aftermath of the *Johnson* 'victory' was marked by growing frustration and disaffection, culminating in the eventual abandonment of the integration plan. Following the court order, the school district underwent a period of disruption at all levels. In a wave of public protest, a new school board was elected, after passage of a charter amendment that did away with the earlier system of mayoral appointment. The superintendent was fired. Most unsettling was the massive reorganization that the court's plan required. Ninety-six elementary schools were dismantled to create two new sets of primary and intermediate schools. Patterns of parent involvement in school affairs were disrupted; special programs of all kinds were ended, as their staff was dispersed; administrative continuity was ruptured, and demoralization spread. A year after the court order, there was an abrupt 14 per cent decline in the population of elementary schools. That fact alone would have prevented the plan from achieving its demographic objectives.

Five years after the court-ordered plan went into effect, as the number of racially unbalanced schools grew, the administration announced that it was time to develop a new and more realistic pupil assignment plan. The point of the new plan was to redefine the criterion of a racially balanced school. Instead of striving for a 15 per cent approximation of the composition of the school-age population, the district settled for a system wherein each school would comprise no fewer than 4 ethnic groups, none of which would exceed 45 per cent of the school's population. This plan was adopted by the school district in 1978. Without approving it, the federal district court proceeded to dismiss the original suit. Thus the legal battle ended, with few regrets.

Problems of 'Public Law' Litigation

Among its reasons for eventually dismissing the *Johnson* suit, the district court invoked the plaintiffs' failure to prosecute their case against the school district. As the court noted in its final memorandum, the plaintiffs had virtually lost interest in the matter.[18] So had all their opponents, the defense as well as all potential intervenors. This outcome is surprising when considered in the light of the extensive opportunities for representation that federal procedure allows various affected parties in 'public law' litigation. Why did all the parties abandon the legal forum where they could in principle have succeeded in presenting themselves?

In contrast to traditional adjudication, a 'public law' model as proposed by legal theorist Abram Chayes, promises several advantages:

(1) The judge can bring to bear his familiarity with the political context, while remaining insulated from political pressure and special interests.
(2) Remedies can be tailored to fit the requirements of a specific situation; the court is not hindered by bureaucratic or legalistic constraints.
(3) The process requires and encourages a relatively high degree of participation by representatives of those potentially affected by the decision; insofar as the party structure is representative of the interests at stake, a considerable range of information will be forthcoming, effectively focused, and reviewed by independent experts.[19]

Although it appears to fit within the broad category of 'public law' litigation, the *Johnson* case meets none of those expectations. The policy issues it raised were drastically narrowed to fall within the range of earlier desegregation decisions; the court made no effort to respond to the specifics of San Francisco's residential segregation patterns, and did not take into account the multi-racial and multi-ethnic composition of the pupil population. The court's familiarity with the local political process and with the historical background of the dispute did not affect the scope of judicial inquiry. The court remained narrowly focused on rules governing the racial composition of school populations, with no concern for the constitutional values at stake, and in isolation from all other issues and interests, however salient. Throughout the proceedings, the court exhibited a distinct preference for a simplified adversary presentation of the issues: it limited effective participation to two parties, the plaintiffs and the school administration, assumed to be in sharp conflict over clearly specifiable questions of fact and law. Although this policy reduced the risk of escalating and politicizing the issues before the court, it did so at the price of radically curtailing the representation of affected interests. This curtailment was especially severe because of the character of the parties themselves.

The 'public law' model inadequately addresses this and other important issues raised by the three cases:

1 *For whom do plaintiffs speak?*

The plaintiffs in the *Johnson* case were six black elementary school children, purposely chosen and represented by the local branch of NAACP. Although the case did not proceed as a class action, the remedy that was sought presumed that the plaintiffs were not acting only as individuals, but also as representatives of a larger 'public' whose general interests in the matter were such as to require sweeping institutional reforms. At no time did the Court examine the grounds for this assumption. Early in the proceedings, an opportunity occurred to test it, when one of the NAACP counsel, in conflict with his two colleagues, sought certification of the suit as a class action. The Court precluded any test by ruling the issue out of order. In support of his motion, the dissident attorney had argued that substantial portions of the black community opposed school desegregation and demanded other remedies for the educational needs of black school children. His defeat meant that those interests would never be represented to the court.[20]

The *Johnson* case illustrates a more general point, also evident in *Lau:* the growth of 'public' actions of various kinds has rendered the courts highly vulnerable to activist organizations whose competence and responsibility as the purported representatives of larger interests is always variable and often dubious. Courts have only a limited capacity to check the credentials of such groups, or to ascertain the reality of the interests they claim to represent. The *Lau* plaintiffs also were organized by a small group, called Chinese for Affirmative Action. This group advocated 'comprehensive *bilingual, bicultural* instruction . . . by *bilingual* teachers.'[21] Although the program promised large employment opportunities for a relatively rare breed of teachers and teacher aides, its educational worth was highly uncertain.

The *Doe* case poses the obverse of the same problem. Whereas the plaintiffs' claims to speak for larger classes of children in *Johnson* and *Lau* appear doubtful, it is rather striking that the large (though likely embarrassed) class of potential plaintiffs to which Peter Doe belongs was not in any way made a party to his complaint. The attorneys for Doe were members of the Youth Law Center, a federally funded 'public interest' law firm, hardly unmindful of the goals of institutional reform. One can only speculate as to whether a class action, or at any rate one combining multiple plaintiffs, would have obtained a better hearing.[22] Perhaps some showing of a widespread pattern of educational neglect would have made the case more persuasive. Be that as it may, the plaintiff opted for a standard private law suit on behalf of an isolated aggrieved individual. Here one who could truly have spoken for many, ended up speaking only for himself.

2 *What role do third parties play?*

Third parties, such as intervenors and *amici curiae*, are a familiar resource for correcting failures of representation in the adversary process. The 'public law' model of litigation is expected to encourage their ample use, if only because the policy issues before the court have ramifications that extend far beyond the immediate plaintiffs and defendants.

In the *Johnson* case, however, the court chose to restrict the participation of third parties. Only one small group, representing twelve racially-mixed elementary school children who were just then suing in Superior Court to enjoin the school district from implementing the voluntary desegregation of several neighbourhood schools, was permitted to intervene.

After the trial, when the court was considering what remedy to order, another group representing Chinatown interests claimed standing to intervene, on the ground that their children were innocent bystanders who would be adversely affected by any city-wide desegregation plan. Their petition was denied and the Supreme Court further denied their request for a stay of the desegregation decree.[23] Only three years later did they obtain satisfaction when the Court of Appeals reversed the district court judgment and ordered that they be allowed to intervene on remand.[24]

A host of *amici curiae* were allowed to enter the *Lau* case before the Appeals Court and the Supreme Court. They included the Solicitor General, whose concern was the government's enforcement responsibilities under Title VI; the Center for Law and Education; and assorted other committees and organizations interested in 'affirmative action' for linguistic minorities. All spoke more or less in support of the plaintiffs, but none contributed to enlarging the scope of the courts' enquiry.

3 *For whom does the defendant speak?*

In denying the Chinese group standing to intervene, the *Johnson* court reasoned that their interests were adequately protected by the immediate parties to the case. The court had in mind not the plaintiffs, of course, but the defendant. Just as it neglected to examine what actual constituency was represented by the plaintiffs, the court also took for granted that the school district was competent to speak for the main interests opposed to the plaintiffs' demands. It did so despite the presence of the intervenors, which by itself was evidence of some division between the school community and the district. That the school district in fact did *not* represent interests at odds with the plaintiffs' demands is apparent from the actions it took in its defense.

For several years the district had promoted the improvement of educational opportunities for black children by developing remedial or 'compensatory' educational programs and by facilitating voluntary integration projects. There was much potential evidence to support a defense that the district did not condone discriminatory, much less segregationist, policies, and that it was in fact faithfully discharging all its constitutional obligations to the plaintiffs. But no attempt was made to build up such a defense. No rebuttal evidence was submitted against facts presented by the plaintiffs to document an alleged pattern of increasing segregation of blacks in the school district.[25] In addition, a school board member and a high administration official agreed to testify that the school district had deliberately, and by acts of evasion and delay, contributed to racial segregation.[26] Later only by an agonizing 4-3 vote did the board decide to appeal the trial court's adverse judgment; and when the Court of Appeals ruled in its favor, the district opted not to press the advantage it had won.

Thus, the trappings of adversary court proceedings hid an absence of genuine dispute. Of course the desegregation issue was controversial. But the true conflicts lay elsewhere, not between the seemingly adverse parties, but rather between both of them, on the one hand, and a large number of other groups, including substantial segments of the black community, other minorities, and a host of alarmed, but hardly racist, white parents. The district was not competent to speak for the multiple interests at stake.

The school administration's competence to represent school interests is thus always problematic. It is bound to vary from case to case, depending upon the issue, what constituencies are involved, and what the administration's own commitments may be. In the *Lau* case, the district built a forceful and effective defense on behalf of the numerous categories of educationally handicapped children, from whom resources would be diverted by the policies that the plaintiffs advocated. And in *Doe*, the school administration spoke from a compelling interest in avoiding a liability that, in the long run, would have severely restricted its discretion to allocate resources according to its own sense of priorities.

Conclusion

In explicating these issues inadequately addressed by the Chayes' model what is at issue is the quality of judicial inquiry. There is a close and generally well understood connection between the quality of representation and the quality of enquiry that the court conducts. The point was dramatically illustrated in the *Johnson* case where failures of representation combined with the court's own predilections on matters of both procedural and substantive law drastically to curtail the court's factual and legal enquiries. There was virtually no trial prior to the determination of relevant facts. A crucial legal issue — whether evidence of deliberate discrimination is necessary to establish a case of unlawful segregation — was neglected. The Court of Appeals for the 9th Circuit later reprimanded the district court on this issue, and reversed the judgment.

In the *Lau* and *Doe* decisions, where prudent inaction was the outcome, it did not matter quite as much whether the decision followed thorough or shallow enquiry. Both suits were quickly aborted, a few plaintiffs were rebuffed, but no irreversible institutional change ensued.

From the above, it does not follow that third parties are any panacea. They too suffer from defects of representativeness, and the range of concerns for which they happen to speak, in any particular case, is never more than a partial, and potentially distorting, selection.

Ordinarily, legal action does not become an attractive way of seeking redress until other channels — persuasion, negotiation, inducement, and all the political arts — appear to have failed. That condition also states an important limit on what legal action can do: it is generally ineffective at achieving ends that cannot be reached without a genuinely collaborative effort. If any lesson can be drawn from this analysis of San Francisco schools in court, it is a reminder that the prospects for reforming any institution are profoundly dependent upon that institution's own capacities and commitments. In complex organizations, nothing gets done by simple command; change requires administrative action that is sustained and reaches in depth to all whose concerted efforts must be enlisted. There is no reason to expect that the limits of command should not also affect the orders of a court.

The Schools under Commission Inquiry

In 1974, in the wake of a teachers' strike, groups of parents and civic leaders, alarmed by a new report indicating that San Francisco pupils were falling lower and lower below state and national standards of achievement,[27] began mounting efforts to obtain assistance for the schools from the state Superintendent of Public Instruction. Interviewed in Washington, DC, state Superintendent Wilson Riles had casually remarked to a reporter that San Francisco schools were 'so bad they are embarrassing,' and that 'the system urgently needs total reform and overhaul.'[28] Seizing upon these remarks, parents pleaded with Riles to take some corrective action.

By law, the Office of State Superintendent has virtually no authority over the affairs of local school districts. But after some informal consultations, Superintendent Riles resolved to propose the creation of a commission of inquiry 'to take a comprehensive look at the entire system, . . . assess the needs and effect reforms.'[29] In January 1975, twenty-four members were appointed to the San Francisco Public Schools Commission (SFPSC). The 'Riles Commission,' as it was later called, had a broadly representative prestigious membership, including officers of major corporations, the San Francisco Labor Council, the Rosenberg Foundation, the United Way, a judge, a former Undersecretary of the Department of Health, Education and Welfare, a former member of the federal Equal Employment Opportunities Commission, and the like. Its chairman was William Matson Roth, a distinguished business leader and former Democratic party gubernatorial candidate.

The commission was to report within two years. It received no public monies, but was able to raise sufficient private funds to hire a staff and retain independent consultants.[30] No restriction was placed on the scope of its enquiries. Unlike a court, it was neither confined to the special concerns of a particular class of grievants, nor hampered by the terms of any legal doctrine, nor exposed to the limitations of adversary fact-finding. Its mandate was broad and open-ended, informed only by the diffuse community concerns that had precipitated its creation.

After eighteen months of work, the commission published a 'Summary Report,' reviewing all its activities and its major recommendations.[31] Among the most striking features of this report were the topics on which it was silent. No attention was given to declining standards of student performance, which had been a central preoccupation of the founders of the commission. Ignored also was the epidemic of vandalism and student violence. The administrative disruptions and the demoralization of the staff, which had plagued the system after years of constant reorganization, were similarly neglected. The exodus of students, and the resulting decline of revenues, were noted but not studied.

On some other topics that the commission did address, the report concluded with statements of the following sort.

School Management

The school board should revise its policies to make clear that in fact the principal is the chief executive officer for each school . . . It should be district policy to give principals the authority to make all critical decisions at the school site and to hold them accountable for effective performance through a system of regular evaluation.[32]

Parent Participation

The school board should adopt a policy that there be a School Site Advisory Council for each school.'[33]

Student Participation

There should be a student forum at each high school each year, attended by the school board and the superintendent, as well as a city-wide forum organized by a Student Advisory Council.[34]

Relations with City Government

The district should make increased use of joint task forces and staff committees to improve cooperation and communication with city departments.[35] Our findings can best be used to stimulate further discussions among those responsible for improving these relationships.[36]

Balancing the Budget

The school board must anticipate the fiscal future of the district in order to make reasoned choices about reducing expenditures.[37]

Beside those and other equally vague and innocuous recommendations, the Commission did produce a few more detailed and substantial studies, of a narrowly technical sort, concerning accounting and budgetary procedures, procurement, and the implementation of collective bargaining legislation. Those technical reports, which were its most substantial accomplishment, did not differ in character from other reports the school district had earlier obtained from accountants and management consultants. In some cases, for example, purchasing and the cash flow between school and city treasuries, the commission's conclusions built directly upon the suggestions of previous studies.

If we consider the sense of crisis which led to the creation of the SFPSC, the breadth of the commission's mandate, and the apparent authority of its prominent membership, the poverty of the commission's accomplishments is disappointing and also rather surprising. Why did this promising and resourceful body fail to address the serious issues at stake?

Management and Politics

Part of the answer to that question lies in early and quite conscious decisions that shaped the character and outlook of the SFPSC. It quickly became commission doctrine that political interferences with administrative problem-solving were the chief cause of the district's problems; that strengthening the autonomy and competence of school management was the chief contribution the SFPSC could make; and that, if the schools' administrative procedures were put in order, all other problems would eventually take care of themselves. The fact that the most substantial of the commission's final recommendations were its management consultant reports, is largely traceable to that initial choice of mission.

A by-product of this choice was that the parent groups and civic organizations who had initially pressed for the creation of the SFPSC were shunted. Not only were they not represented in the commission's membership, the commission conceived its authority as flowing from the credentials of its members and from its administrative expertise, rather than from political sources. Indeed the commission feared its authority would be weakened if it appeared to become 'entangled' with any of the numerous special interest groups that make up school politics. Avoiding politics, the commission concentrated on issues of administration and management. At his first appearance at a public meeting of the school board, the chairman condemned the board's 'meddling in administration' as the chief obstacle to school reform: 'A business or government agency that managed its affairs in this cumbersome and redundant manner would soon grind to a halt.'[38]

Thus a pattern became established whereby the school board was identified as the chief impediment to commission efforts, and the school administration as the chief source of support for those efforts. In effect, the administration became the SFPSC's first and favored client. One of the duties assigned by the commission to its executive director was to serve as a staff resources for the new Superintendent who took office shortly after the commission enquiry began. There developed a close collaboration between commission and school district staff on all kinds of managerial concerns, such as procurement, data-processing, staff decision-making, and the like. The SFPSC made successive efforts to hold the board to the 'basic principles of sound management.' As the chairman put it in a letter to the school board, '. . . From the very first, we have made the point that unless some *basic principles of sound management* were accepted by the board, nothing we did would be of value. . . . As the months go on, however, and we see our work continually frustrated by unwillingness on the part of a majority of the board to accept any limitation whatsoever on the right to meddle in the administrative processes of the district, our concern with our ability to assist you deepens.'[39]

Retreat from Controversy

A critical aspect (and source) of the commission's preoccupation with management problems was an acute concern for avoiding involvement in controversy. The posture of neutrality that the SFPSC assumed is best understood as solving a problem of legitimacy. Designed to bring to the district the benefit of an independent and authoritative review, the commission was pressed to remain 'above politics' and untainted by any appearance of partisanship. Thus, any involvement in controversial debates exposed it to some risk of losing its credibility as a neutral third party. By confining itself to managerial concerns — generally matters of administrative procedure without substantive import — the SFPSC was able at once to affirm its objectivity and to invoke the authority of a special expertise. Furthermore, those were issues over which its own ranks were unlikely to divide, and it would be able to 'speak with one voice.'

Of course even matters of management procedure can cause controversy, and when they did, the commission retreated. For example, problems of collective bargaining were studied, but to avoid any risk of alienating the unions, the SFPSC confined itself to recommending that the district hire a full-time employee relations officer. The district felt seriously hampered by the City Civil Service Commission, which claimed control over hiring and other personnel decisions concerning the school support staff; but that also was too controversial to permit any substantive recommendation.

Administrative decentralization, especially the delegation to school principals of greater authority on budget and personnel, was very high on the commission's initial agenda. But disagreements emerged within the SFPSC, because some members wanted to avoid undermining central control over sensitive matters of policy, especially relations with unions and minority groups. In the end, 'speaking with one voice,' the commission was able only to say that principals be designated as 'chief executive officers,' that each school establish an advisory council, and that decentralization remain a 'fundamental objective which will require time and detailed study to implement.'[40]

It was almost a foregone conclusion that a body so inclined to run away from controversy would ignore the thorny problems of student achievement, faculty performance, and racial integration. When the Superintendent submitted to the commission an 'educational redesign' plan, which did away with the court-ordered desegregation guidelines, the SFPSC simply decided not to comment.

'Just Another Report'

To some extent, the commission's focus upon management concerns was set by its initial mandate, which made it responsible for seeing to the implementation of its recommendations. The SFPSC took this duty very seriously; it wanted to assure that it would not be 'just another report,'[41] fated to be shelved and forgotten. Unlike other advisory commissions, the SFPSC would get things done. A corollary of this responsibility for implementation was a heightened preoccupation with the feasibility of policy recommendations. In defining its mission, the commission gave priority to those tasks from which tangible outcomes could be expected. In that perspective, the problems that recommended themselves most to the commission's attention were those which (a) were amenable to relatively quick study; and (b) appeared remediable by actions that the School administration would be ready to take. By such criteria, difficult and/or divisive issues were bound to be low on the SFPSC's agenda.

Shortly after the SFPSC was created, a serious disagreement occurred between the chairman and the vice-chairman as to what the commission should do regarding the matter of collective bargaining. The vice-chairman was concerned that collective bargaining had critical implications for school governance and finances. In his view, there was a need for the commission to examine what mechanisms of negotiation were compatible with the proper distribution of administrative and political authority in the district, and to explore how collective bargaining would affect the direction of, and the allocation of funds to, educational programs. To the chairman, however, such a study seemed to promise only a waste of SFPSC resources: it would take a long time, reach matters beyond the power of the commission, and raise all kinds of questions to which no firm answer could be given. The commission would be more helpful, he thought, if it confined itself to preparing a competent review of what was required to the district under new state legislation on collective bargaining, and then persuading the school board to hire the help of a full-time specialist in labor relations. The chairman prevailed, and all that the commission produced was a superficial legal analysis of statutory requirements.[42] To that, no one would object. Indeed, the school board quickly agreed to hire an employee relations officer.

On the surface, the chairman's approach seemed innocent enough. The commission had to be selective in determining the problems to which it would devote its energies. Even under the best circumstances its success in tackling those problems would have required it to skirt some issues, to accept compromises, and to avoid needlessly alienating powerful interests.

The problem of the SFPSC was not so much that it sought to be effective, but rather that it did so without any conception of educational ends. Detached from substantive concerns, the focus on effectiveness made short-run feasibility the criterion by which the commission chose its tasks. Anything doable within its short lifetime had a claim on commission resources. Nothing that met that test appeared too trivial; whatever failed to meet the test was dismissed as unworthy.

By this measure, petty matters of management were especially suitable. A quick cost-benefits analysis indicated that the district would do better if it assumed direct control of purchasing, transporting, and storing its supplies; the school board agreed, and the SFPSC immediately set about implementing the proposed changes. On more thorny matters, the commission proposed what was, in effect, administrative patchwork. For instance, the central administration had been hampered by the district's practice of granting tenure to school principals. Although a 1971 amendment to the city charter had formally abolished the practice and required that principals be appointed under four-year contracts, the district had managed to evade compliance. A commission consultant reported on the subject with a suggestion that the commission take the district to court to compel enforcement of the charter. This almost brought about a confrontation with the threatened administrators. But the commission found a solution: the problem, it concluded, was not tenure, but inadequate training. Its remedy was to revise job descriptions and institute in-service training.

Perhaps the most striking manifestation of the SFPSC's preoccupation with results was the scant attention it paid to fact-finding. To the commission, enquiries that promised no tangible administrative outcome were not worth undertaking; furthermore, its schedule had to allow time for implementation, leaving little opportunity for in-depth study.

Much could have been accomplished by an authoritative factual report on the state of San Francisco public schools. Even when they do not issue in specific policy conclusions, findings can help diagnose problems, bring more factual objectivity to public debate, recall officials to neglected responsibilities, and in other ways give new direction to policy-making. The SFPSC, however, did not see such tasks as part of its mission. Impatient with politics, and fearful of controversy, it preferred to turn away from all troublesome facts. More important perhaps, the small place of findings in its final reports indicates that the commission tended generally to discount the authority of facts. Wanting immediate results, it saw no point in producing a document that would 'only' help set the premises of further and more sober thinking.

Summary: 'Just' Schools or 'Just Schools'

The SFPSC's enquiry ended in early 1977. The days of activism and social reform have since passed, and the school board's agenda is now set by the exigencies of the district's financial crisis: laying off and firing teachers, cutting salaries, terminating programs and closing schools. It is unclear that any lasting institutional achievement has resulted from the turmoil of the 1960s and early 1970s. The damages, on the other hand, are all too apparent. Some, especially the loss of confidence on the part of parents who hold reasonably strong educational aspirations for their children, will not be soon repaired.

This assessment of the three policy agencies has shown that the resolution of tensions between social accountability and institutional purpose favors more powerful social pressures at the price of educational values. Regardless of their different approaches and resources, none of the agencies was able to focus on or develop capacities to sustain the more precarious values of education. The school board suffered all the disadvantages of opportunism: it was open to its constituencies and disposed to undertake new responsibilities for policy-making, but its efforts were ungoverned by any sense of direction, and were easily distracted by numerous vocal and conflicting publics.

The analysis of the three court cases reveals an important limitation of legal action: courts cannot simply order change; sustained efforts must be enlisted to achieve substantive ends, such as racial justice and equality of opportunity. School capacities and commitments, not court orders, are the decisive factors in this endeavor. In framing issues for legal action, adjustments to the court's competence entail serious distortions of the educational issues at stake.

Finally, the special commission, composed of elite civic leaders, despite its generous mandate and independent resources, failed to attend to the serious issues facing the schools, concentrating instead on shortrun and narrowly technical problems. The commission's impatience with politics, fear of controversy and scant attention to findings resulted from a self-imposed restriction of responsibility, and from a false assumption regarding the power of management, namely, that if only the administration of the schools could be strengthened and made to operate smoothly, all other problems would resolve themselves.

However they thus differed in their responses, the review institutions exhibited equal impotence. They served to restage, and sometimes to amplify, the controversies that beset the schools; they changed neither the terms in which issues were argued, nor the criteria by which conflicting claims were weighed. In this respect, the commission's avoidance of controversy had the same effect as the school board's opportunistic involvement; and when the courts acted, it was largely to finalize settlements reached without them. In those controversies, except for the diffuse protest of some parent groups, isolated teachers and disparaged administrators, no forceful or persistent voice spoke for educational values. No instance of review was able to redress that critical imbalance; even the SFPSC, which had been constituted especially for that purpose, left it untouched.

Looking back at the experience of those review institutions, one can see many occasions at which more candor, more questioning, more firmness or more daring could have changed the course of their deliberations. There were some genuine opportunities to give thought to the issues, to moderate some excesses, and to indicate new directions. But the question remains: would such leadership have made a difference in the fate of the SFUSD? Or were the forces propelling the district on its course largely beyond its control and *a fortiori* beyond that of any institution of review? Much had been determined by the sheer fact that public schools had become symbols and targets of a national crisis of conscience on questions of racial and social justice. Their vulnerability resulted in part from their own politically charged conception of their mission. American public education has historically sought its justification in promises of equal opportunity, upward mobility and civic indoctrination. When schools are criticized by such standards, they tend to respond with a bad conscience, thus giving legitimacy to demands that distract them for more mundane but essential tasks.

Without denying that a closer approximation to social justice is among the benefits of public education, if there is a lesson to be drawn from this study, it is that we must not expect that benefit other than as a secondary and highly contingent outcome of schooling. Moreover, to hold such an expectation of schools that fail to meet the educational needs of their pupils, degrades the ideal of 'just' schools. More justice may reside in schools that are 'just schools'.

Notes

1 *Johnson v. SFUSD*, 339 F. Supp. 1315 (1971); vacated and remanded, 500 F. 2nd 349 (1074); Memorandum and Order of Dismissal, 22 June 1978; *Lau v. Nichols*, 414 US 565 (1974); *Peter W. Doe v. SFUSD*, 131 Cal 854 (1976).
2 347 US 483 (1954); 349 US 294 (1955).
3 483 F. 2nd 791 (1971).
4 42 USCA 2000 (d), Section 601.
5 Complaint for Injunction and Declaratory Relief, filed 25 March 1970, U.S. District Court, ND California, p. A-3.
6 Answer to Complaint for Injunction and Declaratory Relief, filed 26 May 1970, US District Court, ND California. See also Affidavit of Edward Goldman (Associate Superintendent of Instruction), filed 26 May 1970, US District Court, ND Calif., and Affidavit of Yvon Johnson (Acting Director of Research and Evaluation), filed 4 May 1970, US District Court, ND California.
7 Civil No. C-70-627, May 26, 1970, US District Court, ND California, p. 35.
8 483 F. 2nd 791 (1973).
9 Civil No. C-70-627, 22 October 1976, US District Court, ND California.
10 Superior Court #653312, 6 September 1974.
11 131 Cal, 854 (1976).
12 Transcript, 12 August 1970, p. 206; also Memorandum and Order of Dismissal, 22 June 1978, Footnote 9.
13 339 F. Supp. 1315, ND California (1971).
14 California Administrative Code, Title 2, Section #14020–21. The statute was subsequently repealed.
15 Civil # C-70-627, 22 October 1976.
16 San Francisco Unified School District, hereafter, SFUSD, (1976) *Report and Recommendation of the Educational Standards Committee*, 25 May.
17 SFUSD, (1978) *A Proposal for Educational Redesign*, January.
18 Memorandum and Order of Dismissal, 22 June 1976, US District Court, ND California.
19 When 'the argument is about whether or how a government policy or program shall

be carried out, as custodian of the law, the court is inevitably to some degree enlisted in the service of the legislative purpose ... Simple prohibitory orders are inadequate to provide relief ... If the litigation discloses that the purpose has been frustrated in the situation before the court, the relief called for is an affirmative program to implement the purpose. And the undeniable presence of competing interests of all sorts, many of them unrepresented by the litigants, requires that the program be shaped so as to take those interests into account.' CHAYES A. (1976) 'The role of the judge in public law litigation,' *Harvard Law Review*, pp. 1304–5.

20 Memorandum and Order of Dismissal, 22 June 1978, Footnote 9.

21 Testimony of L. Ling-Chi Wang before the US House of Representatives, Committee on Education and Labor, Washington, DC, 12 March 1974, p. 12 (emphasis added).

22 On this issue, see Note, (1976) 'Educational malpractice,' *University of Pennsylvania Law Review*, 124, p. 755, January; SUGARMAN, S. (1974) 'Accountability through the courts,' *School Review*, 82, p. 233, February; RATNER, G. (1974) 'Remedying failure to teach basic skills,' *Inequality in education*, 17, p. 15, June.

23 404 US 1214 (1971).

24 500 F. 2nd 349 (1974).

25 See Memorandum in Opposition to Motion for Preliminary Injunction, filed in US District Court, ND, California, 20 July 1970.

26 Deposition of Laurel Glass, filed in US District Court, ND California, 24 July 1970; deposition of Dr. William L. Cobb, filed in US District Court, ND California 22 July 1970.

27 SFUSD, 'Standardized Test Report, 1973–74.'

28 *San Francisco Chronicle*, 23 March 1974.

29 *Ibid*. See also *San Francisco Chronicle*, 1 April 1974; 5 April 1974; and 9 April 1974.

30 The Commission's budget for the first 18 months of operation was $250,000, of which the SFUSD contributed $25,000 in in-kind services. The remaining funds were obtained from several local private foundations, including the San Francisco Foundation. See San Francisco Public Schools Commission (hereafter SFPSC), (1975) *Minutes of the San Francisco Public Schools Commission*, 5 February, p. 7.

31 SFPSC, (1976) *Summary Report*, June.

32 *Ibid*, p. 6 and 8.

33 *Ibid*, p. 7.

34 *Ibid*, p. 10.

35 *Ibid*, p. 13.

36 SFPSC, (1976) *School District: City and County of San Francisco — An Analysis of Relationships*, May, preface, n.p.

37 SFPSC, (1976) *Summary Report*, June, p. 11.

38 SFPSC, (1975) *Statement of William M. Roth, Chairman*, 5 May.

39 Letter of William M. Roth to the San Francisco Board of Education, 10 December 1975.

40 SFPSC, (1976) *Rewrite of the Site Management Paper*, 13 February 1976.

41 SFPSC, (1976) *Summary Report*, June, p. 15. Also, according to an official of the California State Department of Education, 'There won't be a final report that can be stuck on somebody's shelf.' 'State of siege at 135 Van Ness,' *Saturday Review*, 3 May 1975, p. 39.

42 SFPSC, (1976) *Collective Bargaining: The Impact of the Rodda Act*, 12 April.

The Legalization of State Educational Policymaking in California

Donald N. Jensen
Stanford University and

Thomas M. Griffin
Department of Education, State of California

Much has been written about the extent to which the administration of the public schools has been affected by law and the courts. School superintendents often complain that one must be a lawyer to operate school districts. Court decisions seem to affect every aspect of their professional lives. A related complaint is that both state legislatures and state education agencies are exercising ever more control over local educational policy. The result is that there are fewer areas of educational policy now left to local discretion than ever before.

Court decisions in at least one state, California, support these intuitions of school administrators. We examine in this chapter the published decisions of the California appellate courts that have involved educational issues, and consider the number of cases, the issues raised, and the type of plaintiff raising appeals. We will include every case decided between 1858 and 1980 for the California Supreme Court and between 1900 and 1980 for the state courts of appeal.

We also examine those court cases raising educational issues in which the state or one of its agencies was a defendant.[1] This group of cases includes all decisions of the state appellate courts — to that extent it duplicates the first set of cases. It also includes suits filed and later dropped, and those resolved at the trial court level by stipulation or judgment without appeal. The sample embraces both state and federal decisions.

These data confirm that the courts have been deciding more education cases in the past few years, the cases are increasingly likely to involve educational issues traditionally considered more suitable for resolution by the other political branches and the type of plaintiff involved in these cases recently has been changing. Moreover, in recent years the state of California has been a defendant in education cases more frequently than ever before.

This growing legalization contributes to the centralization of educational policymaking in California. Potential plaintiffs look with greater frequency to the state for the redress of rights allegedly violated at the local level. These trends toward higher overall rates of litigation, more litigation involving educational policy issues usually addressed by other branches, and toward more litigation against the state, require a reexamination of how a state defends its legal interests in court.

Court Involvement in State Educational Policy

Number of Cases

During the past century there has been a continuing increase in the number of higher court cases concerning education in California (see Table 1). It took 68 years, from 1858 to 1926, to decide one-quarter of the 811 education cases resolved by the California courts since they began hearing such issues. It required barely the last decade for the appellate courts to decide the same number of cases concerning educational issues.

This growing involvement of the courts is most evident if we examine those cases decided only by the courts of appeal. It took 48 years for those

Table 1 *The number of court of appeals and Supreme Court decisions concerning education in california rose dramatically between 1858 and 1979*[1]

Decade	No. of Supreme Court Cases	No. of Court of Appeal Cases[2]	Total Cases
1858–69	3	—	3
1870–79	3	—	3
1880–89	13	—	13
1890–99	44	—	44
1900–09	36	13	49
1910–19	14	34	48
1920–29	21	57	78
1930–39	36	104	140
1940–49	11	57	68
1950–59	18	64	82
1960–69	24	82	106
1970–79	23	154	177
Total	246	565	811

1 Does not include decisions in which community college districts were a party.
2 Includes only those court of appeals decisions published after January 1, 1964, that were certified by the issuing court for publication (See Rule 976, California Supreme Court). Since that date approximately 15 per cent of court of appeal decisions have been published. All decisions of the California Supreme Court are published.

Table 2 The number of court of appeal and Supreme Court cases concerning education have increased rapidly in recent years

Year	No. of Supreme Court Cases	No. of Court of Appeal Cases	Total Cases
1970	0	14	14
1971	0	13	13
1972	2	12	14
1973	2	14	16
1974	1	13	14
1975	1	8	9
1976	4	17	21
1977	7	27	34
1978	3	14	17
1979	3	22	25
Total	23	154	177

courts to decide the first 100 cases raising educational issues. The most recent 100 cases were handed down in slightly more than five years. The number of state supreme court decisions concerning education also has increased since 1858.

Table 2 shows the number of education cases decided by the courts of appeal and the California Supreme Court during the past decade and that most of these decisions were handed down during the past five years. Thus, the courts in California have played an especially active role in educational policy in the very recent past. That trend may portend increased legalization in the 1980s.[2]

Appellate Court Decisions: Subject Matter

The issues involved in the education decisions of appellate courts in California have changed markedly in the twentieth century. Table 3 shows that 42 per cent of the 811 reported decisions of the higher courts in California in this century have involved personnel issues (dismissal, salary, tenure, and related matters). Personal injury cases were the second most frequent type of case decided by those courts (almost 14 per cent). Cases concerning contracts to which a school district was a party was the third most frequent type of case (almost 7 per cent). Disputes involving the reorganization of school districts, individual rights, property, administration, and several other categories also have been raised. Individual rights cases including school desegregation suits make up slightly more than four per cent of school disputes decided by the appellate courts.

Different kinds of issues are now being raised before the appellate courts. The number of labor relations cases has increased significantly since 1960.

Table 3 *Suits involving rights issues are increasingly frequent in California*

Year	Personnel (Salary, Dismissal etc.)	Tort Liability	Contracts	Organization	Property
1858–69	0	0	0	0	1
1870–79	0	0	0	0	1
1880–89	3	0	2	0	3
1890–99	7	1	2	5	6
1900–09	14	0	6	3	4
1910–19	15	0	11	6	2
1920–29	20	2	8	14	7
1930–39	73	34	6	2	1
1940–49	29	19	0	4	5
1950–59	31	21	8	4	6
1960–69	41	22	8	5	8
1970–79	108	13	5	0	5
Total (By issue)	341	112	56	43	49

Data between 1858 and 1899 include only decisions of California Supreme Court.
Data from 1900 to 1979 include decisions of California Supreme Court and state courts of appeal.

Table 3 (Cont'd.)

Year	Administration	Teacher Credentials	School Elections	Bonds	Tax Computation & Liability	Individual Rights	Labor Relations	Governance Powers
1858–69	0	0	0	0	1	0	0	0
1870–79	0	0	0	0	0	0	0	0
1880–89	0	0	1	0	0	0	0	1
1890–99	0	1	0	2	13	0	0	4
1900–09	0	2	0	4	6	0	0	1
1910–19	2	1	1	2	2	2	0	3
1920–29	4	0	3	4	4	3	0	3
1930–39	4	1	4	2	6	2	0	0
1940–49	3	0	2	2	0	1	0	0
1950–59	2	2	1	1	3	1	0	1
1960–69	3	4	0	1	0	6	3	1
1970–79	4	6	1	0	3	12	11	1
Total (By issue)	22	17	13	18	38	27	14	15

Table 3 (Cont'd)

Year	Textbooks	Education Programs	Finance	Desegregation	Other Miscellaneous	Total (By Decade)
1858–69	0	0	1	0	0	3
1870–79	1	0	0	1	0	3
1880–89	2	0	0	1	0	13
1890–99	0	1	0	1	1	44
1900–09	1	1	4	0	3	49
1910–19	0	0	0	0	1	48
1920–29	1	3	0	1	1	78
1930–39	2	2	1	0	0	140
1940–49	1	0	0	0	2	68
1950–59	1	0	0	0	0	82
1960–69	0	0	2	1	1	106
1970–79	0	0	3	4	1	177
Total (By issue)	9	7	11	9	10	811

Cases concerning teachers seeking reinstatement of revoked teaching credentials have more than doubled in frequency since that time. More significantly, suits involving school desegregation, school finance disputes and individual rights have shown the largest increase of any category since 1960.

Most dramaticaly of all, five-eighths of all individual rights cases (including school desegregation cases) decided by the higher court in the state of California have been decided since 1960. When one remembers that many cases in other categories can also be cast in 'rights rhetoric',[3] it is evident that cases involving rights questions are now a significant portion of the business of appellate courts in California.

Suits involving personnel injuries and suits for damages moreover usually go no further than the courts of appeal. Those two categories of suits comprise 65 per cent of the courts of appeal decisions, but just one-third of the decisions of the state supreme court. This is not surprising since these types of cases usually involve a few plaintiffs and have little strategic impact. They also pose claims that do not involve the courts in complicated fact-finding tasks or new doctrinal adventures.

It is much more likely that cases concerning educational rights will be appealed to the Supreme Court. These more complicated suits involve detailed analysis of factual occurrences, concern plaintiff 'classes' and draw the courts into areas of educational policy traditionally not considered suitable for judicial resolution. Each of the seven cases concerning educational program issues that were appealed from the trial courts in California was taken to the California Supreme Court. By contrast, just one of the fifteen suits involving labor relations was appealed to the Supreme Court.

The Legalization of Education: Who Is the Plaintiff?

The type of plaintiff bringing certain education suits is changing along with the issues raised. 557 of 811 decisions (68.7 per cent) in cases decided by the appellate courts were brought by private parties. Other frequent plaintiffs have been school districts (16.6 per cent), and employee unions (5.1 per cent). Private organizations were plaintiffs in 14 of the 811 cases decided by the appellate courts. These organizations included the American Civil Liberties Union, a legal aid organization, a private antibusing group, and an association of property owners. Eleven of these cases were brought since 1960, and thus they are an ever more frequent source of business for the appellate courts in California (See Table 4). These organizational litigants are more likely to focus their efforts on educational controversies involving policy or rights issues than are private litigants. Organizational plaintiffs tend to use class action suits as vehicles for the adjudication of these policy issues more frequently than private litigants, school districts, or the other kinds of plaintiffs.[4]

Many of these private organizations are publicly funded legal centers or advocacy groups that are 'repeater' plaintiffs: they have been in court many

Table 4 Private organizations and school districts are increasingly active in educational litigation in California

Years	Private	Private Company	School District	County	City	State	Private Organization	Unions	Total
1858–69	0	0	2	1	0	0	0	0	3
1870–79	2	0	1	0	0	0	0	0	3
1880–89	9	0	4	0	0	0	0	0	13
1890–99	28	3	9	0	3	1	0	0	44
1900–09	31	3	12	1	1	1	0	0	49
1910–19	34	6	9	0	1	1	0	0	48
1920–29	57	4	14	0	0	3	0	0	78
1930–39	114	0	17	2	2	1	0	0	140
1940–49	57	3	5	2	0	0	1	0	68
1950–59	55	2	16	1	2	4	2	0	82
1960–69	72	2	28	0	0	1	5	8	106
1970–79	101	1	28	2	2	3	6	34	177
Totals	557	28	135	9	11	15	17	42	811

Data between 1858 and 1899 include only decisions of the California Supreme Court. Data from 1900 to 1979 include decisions of the California Supreme Court and State Courts of Appeal.

times in various educational disputes; they care about general policy issues (not just the particular dispute), and they have acquired considerable legal expertise. These repeaters carefully select plaintiffs to represent; they identify issues in order to maximize their chances of success. These plaintiffs also enjoy low start-up costs when beginning a suit and enjoy organizational economies of scale. Other advantages possessed by repeaters include the ability to adopt legal strategies to maximize gain over a long series of cases, and the ability to play the litigation 'game' for changes in the rules of litigation rather than only for a favorable outcome. The lawyers working for repeat players are themselves repeaters who profit from long experience in litigation. Thus, the strategic advantages are augmented by advantages in the distribution of legal services.[5]

Cases Filed Against the State

Another measure of the growth of legalization in state educational policy-making is the filing of suits against the state. When successful, in such cases, the plaintiff is able to alter state education policy. Here, too, the data show the growing role of the law and the courts: state educational administrators in California — the State Board of Education, and the State Department of Education — increasingly are being sued. Such suits often involve demands that the state compel local school districts to obey their legal obligations.

The State as Defendant: Number of Suits

Table 5 shows the distribution by subject of the 247 cases filed since 1968 against the California Department of Education, the California Board of Education, and the California Superintendent of Public Instruction. There has been a rapid recent increase in the number of cases filed against the state of California.

Only 85 of the 247 cases filed against the state were filed during the first half of this twelve-year period. An equal number were filed in the two years between 1978 and 1980. This growth in suits against the state is even more dramatic when we examine litigation rates over the twelve-year period studied. In 1969, California was sued only four times — an average of once every three months. In 1980, by contrast, the state was sued 36 times — an average of one suit every 1.44 weeks. This is an increase of more than 1200 per cent in only slightly more than a single decade. In 1981 alone the California Board of Education was named defendant in 108 active lawsuits.

This growth assumes even greater significance if we exclude those cases involving the revocation of teaching credentials by the state of California.[6] If these 37 credentials cases are excluded from consideration, the increase in the number of lawsuits against the state of California is even more apparent. There were 210 other education suits filed against the state between 1968 and 1980. Only one-quarter of these cases were filed between 1968 and 1973; the remaining cases were brought during the last seven years of that period.[7]

The State as Defendant

The increased numbers of lawsuits filed against the state of California often involve the rights issues raised before the appellate courts. While the subject matter of litigation against the state reflects the wide variety of educational concerns that attend the operation of a modern state education system, since 1978 there has been a rapid growth in the number of lawsuits pertaining to special education, other school program matters, school finance, and other constitutional issues. Over two-thirds of all lawsuits against the state of California concerning special education have been filed since 1978, and more than half of the other cases involving educational programs also have been filed since that year. More than 80 per cent of all school finance cases have been filed since 1979, and almost half of the other cases raising constitutional questions have been filed since that year. The state of California has been caught up in the same general increase in litigation over rights questions.

The State as Defendant: Plaintiffs Bringing Lawsuits

The type of plaintiff bringing suit against the state of California has changed in the past decade. Table 6 shows the 247 cases filed against the state of California

Table 5 Suits against the state of California have grown in frequency during the past decade

	Credential	Education Program	School Approvals	Tort Liability	Surplus Property	School Finance	Admin.	Food Service	Const. Pupil Civil Rights	Text-Books	Deseg.	Organi-zations	Contracts	Total
1968	2	0		2										4
1969	1	0			2		1		2					6
1970	6	3		2	1		3	1	2		1			19
1971	9	1			1				2		1			14
1972	12	4	3			1		1	2				1	24
1973	3	8				1	1		3	1	1			18
1974	1	3	4	1				1	2	1				13
1975		3	2	4	2		1	1	0				1	14
1976		8	3	1	3				3		1	1		20
1977		2	2				1	2	0	1		4		16
1978		11	2	1	2		1	1	0	1	1		1	21
1979		7	3			3	1	3	4	3	3	2		29
1980	1	19	2	4	2	4	1		2	1				36
Unk.	2		3			2	2		1	1	1		1	13
Total	37	69	24	19	13	11	12	10	23	9	9	7	4	247

Table 6 *There has been an increase in legal aid centers and private organizations bringing suits against the state since 1958*

	Private	Legal Aid	State	Private Company	Private Organization	School District	Union	Federal	County	Unknown[1]	Total
68	2			1						1	4
69	2									4	6
70	9	3			1					6	19
71	10				1					3	14
72	16	2	1	1		1				3	24
73	1	8			1	1	3			4	18
74	4	1	3		1					4	13
75	4	2	3	2	2					1	14
76	3	6	5	1	2	2				1	20
77	5		1	3	2	2				3	16
78	8	3	3	3	1			2		1	21
79	5	4	7	2	5	5				1	29
80	14	3	2	4	4	5			1	2	36
Unknown	2	1	4	1	1	1				3	13
Total	85	33	29	18	22	17	3	2	1	37	247

[1] The nature of the plaintiff cannot be determined in these cases due to the unavailability of case files for analysis.

by type of plaintiff bringing the lawsuit. The largest single group of plaintiffs, approximately one-third, are private litigants represented by private attorneys. The next largest group of cases, 13.4 per cent, were brought by publicly funded legal organizations.

The state of California itself was a plaintiff in 29 (11.7 per cent) of all cases. These suits were brought for several purposes: to revoke state approval of a private post-secondary vocational school (12 cases), to recover the cost of erroneously purchased surplus property (8 cases). Others include those involving the violation of contract by textbook publishers, the violation by school districts of Title I or food services program requirements, the enforcement by the state of the program requirements for special education, and unpaid wages due an employee by a school district.

Private organizations were plaintiffs in 22 of the cases (8.9 per cent) brought against the state of California. These private organizations included the NAACP (3 cases), an association for retarded persons (2 cases), the American Civil Liberties Union, and an assortment of other private advocacy groups (1 case each). Lawsuits filed against the state of California by public organizational plaintiffs such as these have constituted over 22 per cent of all education suits against the state since 1968.

This growth of involvement by private organizational plaintiffs and legal aid societies is important because of the tactical advantages mentioned earlier that are possessed by repeat plaintiffs. In addition, repeaters have the resources to pursue their long-term interests, they benefit from their experience, the ability to structure the next transaction and to build a legal record. Repeat players have expertise in litigation and ready access to legal specialists.

Although the state of California and organizational plaintiffs such as the NAACP are both repeat players in educational litigation, organizational plaintiffs have a considerable advantage over the state in one very important way: unlike the state, they pursue only certain kinds of issues — generally those educational issues that have been brought only recently before the courts. In desegregation cases and school finance litigation, for example, cases, issues, and plaintiffs are carefully selected by organizational repeat players. The state can only react. Organizational repeaters have gained considerable experience in states in litigating certain issues. A single state often has little such experience.

Entangling the state as a defendant in educational litigation is also tactically prudent for organizational plaintiffs. Change often can be achieved best if the state, acting as supervisor over individual school districts, is ordered by a court to enforce certain legal or constitutional minima. Suing individual school districts requires more time and money than an organizational plaintiff may possess and raises the possibility that different courts will decide the same fundamental educational questions differently. Making the state enforce the law against local districts promises a plaintiff the greatest potential for effecting widespread reform.

The state of California has recently been drawn into a disproportionate number of lawsuits that raise issues concerning educational rights or program issues. Between 1970 and 1979, nine of 154 court decisions of the California Courts of Appeal have concerned individual rights questions, and even if we include all those cases classified as miscellaneous, the total is barely doubled. In that same decade only one-fifth of the Supreme Court cases involved such issues. Yet from 1970 to 1979, nearly half of the 237 disputes involving the state as a defendant raised educational program issues, special education issues, and other rights questions.

If these trends continue, there should be an even larger percentage of cases filed against the state, more cases filed that seek to change general educational policies rather than an individual grievance, and more appeals to the California Supreme Court. These tendencies toward greater legalization of educational policy have important implications for educational policymaking.

The Legalization of California Education: Policy Implications

The increasing rate of educational litigation and the more frequent involvement of the state as a defendant encourage the centralization of educational policymaking. Although 'local control of education has been a hallmark of American education,'[8] that pattern has shifted notably in the past two decades. Judicial decisions have encouraged and hastened this centralization. Courts hand down opinions that bind local school administrators to statewide legal and constitutional standards. The tendency to seek redress at the state level for the local violation of educational rights is another contribution to this centralization.

Increased centralization of educational policy occurs even without court impetus. In his analysis of the patterns of state control of educational policy, a study in which California ranked as a state with 'moderate state control,' Frederick M. Wirt found that the areas of teacher certification, vocational education, attendance, accreditation and financial records were typically the areas with the highest levels of state control around the country.[9] Policies of less extreme, but still high, state control included teacher employment, calendar matters, record keeping, revenue controls and special education. These areas of traditionally high state control reflected those issues that, as we have seen, were always the focus of court attention in education: teacher employment, revenue issues, accreditation and the like. The recent involvement of the courts in educational litigation has occurred in areas that are *not* traditional loci of state control. Individual rights and desegregation, especially, have not been subject to litigation until the past two decades.[10]

Because the California appellate courts contribute to the formulation of statewide legal principles, this new stress by the courts on issues that have not historically been matters of high state control has resulted in increased centralization of educational policy. Policymakers now must take into account the new legal and constitutional standards, established by the courts and applicable throughout the state. That many of these decisions result in the articulation of educational rights and entitlements in education, and are thus much less susceptible to political bargaining and compromise, means that the job of educational policymakers in California is affected. The courts add to the political agenda. They also influence the decisions policymakers reach about such issues.

Court involvement may cause significant problems for policymakers. Courts often articulate legal principles too abstract to be useful to legislators anxious to formulate educational policies. In the famous California school finance case, *Serrano v. Priest*, the California Supreme Court declared a new legal standard, 'fiscal neutrality,' which meant that support of the state public schools could not be a function of wealth, other than the wealth of the entire state. Yet this standard gave little guidance to legislators as to how this principle could be put into effect — whether taxpayers or school children were to be the beneficiaries of the reform, and whether the California legislature should be concerned with making the tax effort of school districts more equal or with eliminating major expenditure differences between school districts.

This trend toward increased court-induced educational policy centralization at the state level has had serious implications for the defense by the state of its legal interests in court. The growth in the number of cases challenging the education programs of local school districts needs to be accompanied by a greater coordination between the state and local school districts in shaping a coherent legal strategy. The state's formulation of its legal position in a controversy — what ought to happen — should be consistent with the school district's view of what is possible. A partnership between state and local authorities is also vital in handling litigation.

The growing number of education cases involving general policy issues and rights issues also require a more sophisticated legal defense. A legal defense not only must take into consideration questions of legal duty and responsibility. Educational philosophies, purposes and programs must also be appraised in light of their local implications. If a teacher is fired and the teacher appeals the dismissal to the courts, the task of the attorney for the district is relatively simple: defend the dismissal. When an attack is made on educational practices — for example on the reliance on standardized intelligence tests to identify schoolchildren for placement in programs for the retarded — the state's task is more complex. To win a lawsuit is not enough; a position consistent with the state's general educational policies also must be articulated.

This need to link legal tactics to general educational goals can be difficult. The educational decision-maker involved in these suits is usually a board of education not an individual policymaker. The state board of education is frequently called upon to decide a strategy of legal defense and to make decisions on questions raised in the lawsuits. Even a single individual has difficulty reconciling the various political, fiscal, educational, and other considerations that a lawsuit entails into a coherent legal position; that problem is compounded when the defendant is the ten member California Board of Education. Stances in lawsuits are determined by a six-member majority of the board, and members may vote the same way on a specific question for different reasons. Problems attributable to the instability of the board's position are compounded by the need of the state to coordinate its position with that of local school boards, who also must reconcile competing fiscal, political, and educational concerns. Both the state board of education and local boards are composed of lay-persons who are neither legal experts nor often experienced educational policymakers. School board members rely exclusively on their common sense; that is often not enough to adequately evaluate many legal problems.

School board members also lack the time to involve themselves in the details of educational lawsuits. Board members pay little attention to lawsuits that affect educational policy until crises arise, problems develop, or the state counsel informs the board that an issue must be considered. Yet the legal process will continue, whether or not the state board of education acts. Legal deadlines still must be observed and legal positions taken. When board members are unable to articulate legal positions, as often happens, there is an inevitable result: the lawyers representing the state decide on a legal position for the state quite independent of the positions of the state board.

It also takes too much time for the board to establish legal positions on matters before the courts. Proposed legal positions usually are discussed and decided in executive sessions which are closed to the public. Thus, there is none of the public comment that helps a lay board make policy positions. The state board of education, as a defendant in a case in which a plaintiff raises specific issues, also has to be specific in its response to the legal allegations made. It is hard enough to obtain the consensus of state board members on a general education question;[11] it is more difficult yet when the board must reach a consensus on the meaning of certain laws or regulations under legal attack. As educational policymaking is centralized at the state level, scrutiny of prior state educational decisions by 'repeater' law firms increases. The state becomes the target of those seeking educational change even when it may have no position on an issue, since it is easier to determine whether a single state board of education has violated the law than it is to determine whether California's 1043 local school boards have violated the law.

Because a large amount of time and effort is required to prepare an adequate legal defense for the state, some consideration must be given to whether some lawsuits ought to be defended at all. In California, the attorney general automatically assumes that when a party sues the state, it must be defended — even when the members of the State Board of Education do not wish to make a legal defense. The former California State Superintendent of Public Instruction, Wilson Riles, expressed from time to time a desire to keep the state's lawyers entirely out of some educational disputes.[12]

The way legal services are provided to state educational policymakers in California is also ineffective. In state government, legal responsibilities typically are divided between a 'house' counsel for the state board of education and the state attorney general. Positions toward legal disputes are formulated by the state board of education with the assistance of the attorneys employed by the state education department — in itself an occasional source of legal conflict. These attorneys assist the state board in analyzing proposed statutes, writing regulations, deciding various legal policy questions, and in formulating legal strategy. However, when cases are filed, the state board of education is represented by a deputy attorney general who has not participated in formulating the policy under legal challenge, and who only occasionally handles education litigation.

This division of legal responsibility causes two difficulties. The deputy attorney general assigned to the case is rarely an expert in educational policy and almost never has a detailed grasp of the nuances of the policy being litigated. Generally, the deputy who handles the case does so along with literally dozens of other pending lawsuits involving non-educational issues. No one keeps track of the progress of the cases, watching trends as they develop or assessing their possible policy impact. Sometimes the need for intensive, expert legal counsel is strong enough to require that outside lawyers be hired to assist in the state's defense.

The state attorney general also cannot defend the state in a way that preserves the traditional lawyer-client relationship. The board of education meets only once a month. Decisions on legal strategy and tactics must be hurriedly made, often without sufficient attention to the details of a legal dispute.

More importantly, the state attorney general is a constitutional officer independent of the state board of education. The lawyers assigned to attend to the legal needs of the state board of education owe their allegiance to the attorney general, not to the state board of education. Thus, the attorney general has taken the position that his responsibility to the people of the state transcends his allegiance to a particular client — even if that client is an important state agency. For this reason, the attorney general's office almost always has refused to act as co-counsel with the lawyers for the state department of education, insisting that only the attorney general's office has the right to manage litigation in which that office participates. This attitude may be appropriate when the issues are primarily legal. It is more difficult to support when the issues at stake have significant educational or political consequences.

Many cases filed against the state are not tried but rather are settled by negotiation and stipulation. For example, the famous case of *Pennsylvania Association of Retarded Children v. Commonwealth of Pennsylvania*[13] was instrumental in establishing that retarded children have a constitutional right to an appropriate education. It was settled by a consent decree entered by the court after all the parties to the suit negotiated the terms of a settlement. These negotiated settlements in educational litigation, while often valuable, place a burdensome responsibility on the state defendants because they often state what the parties think the law ought to be, not what it actually is or can reasonably be made to be.

For several reasons, the problems of formulating educational policy by consent decree are even more significant than formulating educational policy through reliance on lawsuits that are settled through trial, judgment, and appeal. Settlement negotiations are conducted in private, without the public discussion and testimony that accompanies the formulation of educational policy by the state legislature or by the state board of education. Elected representatives and school officials must adhere to laws requiring that meetings be open to the public. Not only are the negotiations on the terms of the consent decree kept secret, but also the debate by the state board on whether to approve the decree's final form usually takes place in closed executive session; it is protected by the attorney-client privilege. Even the state board does not participate in negotiations on the terms of the consent decree, which are conducted by an attorney. The entire state board of education is thus isolated from the bargaining that is supposedly taking place on its behalf. The attorney conducting such negotiations must, in turn, be well versed in the educational policy. This familiarity is difficult to acquire when, as we have seen, the counsel for the state board and the attorney general have different responsibilities and work in different offices. The deputy attorney general working on educational litigation almost never has a true 'feel' for the positions of the state board members.

Use of consent decrees also prevents an assessment by public officials of the cost of alternative proposed settlements. Political and social costs must be weighed, as well as legal requirements set. This balancing can be accomplished only when negotiations are carried out in public, when competing political constituencies are alerted to the details of proposed settlements, and when the attorneys working on behalf of the interests of the state are made aware of all relevant policy implications of a proposed course of action.

Conclusion

These factors — the increasing number of suits in California involving education, the change in the kinds of issues those suits raise, the naming of the state as the defendant and the problem inherent in preparing an adequate legal defense to these lawsuits — are likely to be more frequently and importantly felt. They portend a further reduction of local school autonomy and an increased role for the courts in education. They also require a reexamination of the way a state defends its interests in court.[14]

Notes

1 One would surmise that suits against the state of California raise different issues than do suits against school districts. School districts deal directly with pupils and school employees. The bulk of cases involving districts ought to reflect those concerns: pupil relations (curriculum, discipline) or employment relations (hiring and dismissals).

State agencies generally are concerned with program development in local school districts and, to a lesser extent, in the monitoring and implementation of educational programs. One would naturally expect that the issues raised by lawsuits against the state to be quite different. For example, because state employment relations are handled by departments other than the state department of education, it would seem reasonable to expect that lawsuits against the state education agencies would involve few employment issues. This is what actually occurs.

It is possible that cases brought to the Court of Appeal or to the State Supreme Court may not be representative of the kinds of cases decided at the trial court level. The importance of certain issues to the parties, and the availability of attorneys for the filing and prosecution of appeals may result in some types of cases being appealed in disproportionate numbers.

When lawsuits are appealed, cases involving educational issues gain an importance that transcends the interests of the litigants involved by becoming binding or observed precedent. Thus, although the number of education appeals, the plaintiffs they involve, and the issues they raise may not reflect accurately the issues about which the trial courts are concerned, our focus on the statewide impact of legalization requires that only cases decided by the higher courts be considered.

2 This phenomenon may not continue. In 1980, only one case concerning education was decided by the California Supreme Court. The courts of appeal decided 21 education cases. This total of 22 cases is a slight decrease from the 25 decided by the same courts in 1979. It remains to be seen whether this drop is temporary, or reflects a new stage in the relationship of the courts to educational policymakers.

3 Dworkin, R. (1977) *Taking Rights Seriously*, Cambridge, Harvard University Press.

4 Mayhew, L. (1978) *Law and Equal Opportunity: A Study of the Massachusetts Commission Against Discrimination*, Cambridge, Harvard University Press.

5 Galanter, M. (1974) 'Why the "haves" come out ahead: Speculations on the limits of legal change,' *Law and Society Review*, 9, p. 95.

6 In 1972, the power of revocation of teaching credentials and of credential suspension was transferred from the California Board of Education to the newly created Commission on Teacher Preparation and Licensing. Many of the lawsuits filed against the state of California between 1968 and 1974, therefore, were by teachers whose credentials were revoked by local boards of education. The State Board continued action on those cases in progress as of 1972, but the new commission took action on all cases beginning after that date. Since the liability of the State Board to suit on these issues effectively ended in 1972, it skews the statistics somewhat to include these cases at the beginning of the period but not at the end of that period.

7 The year in which the remaining eleven cases were filed is not known.

8 Kirst, M.W. (1981) 'The state role in educational policy innovation.' *IFG Policy Paper No. 81-C1*, Institute for Research on Educational Finance and Governance, Stanford University, April, p. 20.

9 Wirt, F.M. (1978) 'What state laws say about local control,' *Phi Delta Kappan* 59, April, pp. 517–70.

10 Special education litigation presents an anomalous example: while historically an issue characterized by high state centralization, litigation concerning it is relatively recent. This recent involvement of the courts may be due to recent statutory declarations that access to suitable educational opportunities for the handicapped is a constitutional right.

11 There are extreme examples of the difficulty the board faces in achieving a consensus, In the *Larry, P.* case, a minority of the state board offered testimony at trial which helped undercut the position already approved by the board majority.

12 Interview, Kirst, M.W., Stanford, California, 27 July 1981.

13 *PARC v. Commonwealth of Penna.*, 334 F. Supp. 1257 (1971).

14 See also, Kirst, M.W., (1981), *op. cit.* p. 25.

The Allure of Legalization Reconsidered: The Case of Special Education

David Neal
University of New South Wales and

David L. Kirp
University of California, Berkeley

Introduction

American public policy has recently witnessed the legalization of a host of issues previously left to political or professional solution.[1] The declaration of substantive rights, coupled with reliance on law-like procedures, has become a characteristic way of framing policy. While legalization has been studied in a number of contexts — industry,[2] regulation,[3] education[4] and race relations[5] among them — we lack a precise specification of how legalization comes to dominate an area of policy and its effects in various contexts.[6]

This article contributes to the understanding of these issues by focusing on special education policy. Special education is an ideal case from which to mount a study of legalization. From the first articulated claims to the recognition of the rights of the handicapped to education, the development of the policy at the federal level, and the implementation of that policy in schools, we can trace the evolution of the phenomenon and analyze the appropriateness of this style of policymaking to its policy setting. Before undertaking that analysis, however, a fuller treatment of the process we have characterized as legalization, comparing it to other policymaking styles, is in order.

Legalization

Legalization is only one of several modes of giving substance to a policy objective[7] and one which, at least in the fully-developed form it takes in the Education for All Handicapped Children Act, (commonly referred to as Public Law 94-142), is fairly new to policymaking in the United States. It is nonetheless a style close to the mainstream of American social and political culture.

The characteristic features of legalization include a focus on the individual as the bearer of rights, the use of legal concepts and modes of reasoning, and the provision of legal techniques such as written agreements and court-like procedures to enforce and protect rights. PL 94-142 comes shot through with legal concepts and procedures: the notion of right or entitlement; the quasi-contractual IEP meeting in which the right is elaborated; the provision of due process guarantees and appeal procedures; and, implicitly, the development of principles through the mechanism of precedent.

A preference for legalization is premised on the classically liberal belief that individuals, and not the organization charged with delivering a good or service, can best safeguard their own interests. Paradoxically, the very fact that the individual has not been an effective self-guardian is the rationale for offering him or her the resources of the state, thus empowering the individual to pursue this interest. The individuals to be entitled cannot attain the policy goal unaided, either because of ill-will on the part of the service provider, or absence of consensus between them and the service deliverer on the goal to be achieved.

Legalization also betokens a mistrust of other forms of accountability, particularly accountability based on bureaucratic norms of fairness, using statistical tests across classes of affected people. It defines accountability in individual terms: a person polices his or her own interests. Individual accountability also implies singling out a party responsible for malfeasance in a way that group compliance procedures do not.

The aspirations of underlying legalization include a desire for principled decision-making, minimization of arbitrariness, and a concern for the rights of the individual. In an extreme case, where an organization is frozen into traditional ways of doing things, legalization may be needed to bring about a reorientation of goals and priorities. This may entail changes in the power relations between clients and service providers and, as in the case of special education, may involve rearrangement of status positions *within* the hierarchy of the delivery agency. At the same time, the dangers of this approach should not be minimized. One danger is that professionals in key positions may be alienated. More generally, legalization may degenerate into legalism, as law and procedures become ends in themselves and substantive goals are lost in mechanical adherence to form.[8]

The distinctive features of legalization become clearer if one compares this approach to other characteristic modes of government policymaking. Under a professional model, experts administer and enforce a policy mandate. The beneficiary occupies a passive role, deferring to the professionals' expertise. This model has been widely prevalent: it is exemplified in the federal vocational education program[9] and — outside education — in the Legal Services Program.[10] That mode of service provision leaves little or no room for the recipient to define the nature and extent of the benefit; that is accomplished in the legislation itself or, more likely in the professional model, by the professionals administering the program. Nor does the recipient have any significant role in maintaining accountability in the system; that function is carried out by units of the bureaucracy, through agency review focusing on regularity of systems and procedures. Such agency review relies on policy impacts on classes of people using probabilistic statistical testing rather than case by case review which can be triggered by an individual. Indeed the very notion of a right is foreign to this approach.

Programs providing money payments — welfare, social security and the like — constitute a second variant. These bureaucratic models leave less scope to program administrators than the professional model. Legislation specifies the type of benefit and eligibility criteria and is administered by a government department. The notion of an individual right has more relevance in this model compared to the professional model; the greater emphasis is placed on safeguards built into the legislative apparatus. The right, however, is a very limited one in comparison to the legalization model. Unless the claimant can show that the exercise of administrative discretion was either 'outrageous or stupid',[11] the best that the claimant can hope for is that the court will ask the agency to review the matter. By contrast, the PL 94-142 framework gives force to an agreement between the parties which defines the substance and extent of the service to be delivered. The due process hearing is not limited to a *review* of administrative discretion but may rely on the written agreement, individualized educational plan (IEP), to provide substance for a ruling on the merits of the case. The existence of a written agreement, possibly some sort of record of the negotiations and the opportunity to pass on the substance of the right make this a much more congenial atmosphere for the legal model, allowing much more scope for the claimant than the narrow review of administrative discretion.[12]

Choice among styles of policy implementation — legal, professional and bureaucratic — has important consequences in terms of the services provided, as the history of policy concerning the handicapped reveals. It determines the type of service offered, who receives it and on what terms. It limits the degree of variation and affects the stake the client group has in the service offered. It also fixes the extent of regulatory control and the means of redress available to the client group.[13]

Evolution of a Right

Two million handicapped children aged between seven and seventeen years were not enrolled in school in 1970.[14] Many were excluded by the state laws, like the Pennsylvania statutes attacked in the *PARC* case,[15] which designated them as ineducable or untrainable. Other handicapped children were consigned to institutions offering only custodial care. By the late 1960s, the wretchedness of the treatment meted out to the handicapped at institutions such as Willowbrook and Pennhurst,[16] and the specious nature of the rationale for excluding handicapped children from schools,[17] led reformers to demand a radical change in the way handicapped people generally and handicapped children in particular were treated. The means adopted for effecting this change were distinctively legal. The language of rights and the mechanisms of due process were introduced into an area that had previously relied on the professional discretion of teachers, psychologists and school administrators.[18]

From Proclamations to Courts

The civil rights movement and the War on Poverty provided the key ideas and context for the movement on behalf of handicapped people. Both heavily emphasized legal rights and focused the idealism of a generation of policy makers whose interests brought them in contact with powerless groups. The emphasis on rights and the active participation of those who had previously been treated as dependants in decisions affecting their lives, as well as more direct analogies from the emphasis on due process in the student rights movement,[19] suggested strategies to activists in the area of special education. The position of the retarded could be and was analogized to that of blacks, Native Americans, and the poor. For many of these groups the courts were the only effective point of entry into the political system. The courts gave power to groups which otherwise had none, and for that reason could not attract the attention of legislatures at state or federal level.

The way in which a claim is defined, and the orchestration of the campaign to have it ratified, are crucial in determining whether it will be recognized at all, and, if recognized, the level at which recognition comes. As noted, the transformation of the political perception about the claims of the handicapped from charity to right began in the 1950s. The formation of associations for retarded citizens at national and state levels was a most significant step. The most influential of these was the National Association for Retarded Children.[20] Key figures in this movement carried out research establishing the educability of all children, and publicized their findings through an extended national network. The associations became active not only on the political level, but also as service deliverers. So, for example, the Pennsylvania Association for Retarded Children (PARC) developed and ran programs for handicapped children funded by state agencies.

Two crucial research findings were becoming widely accepted in the education community. The determination that all children could benefit from education[21] undermined the rationale for excluding retarded children from public schooling as ineducable. Research also suggested that testing procedures for the assignment of children to classes for the retarded were racially discriminatory,[22] thus strengthening the analogy between the retarded and racial minorities. The issue of educating handicapped children had undoubted appeal. Once one could argue that such children were educable it became well-nigh impossible to mount a politically palatable argument denying handicapped children's claims to education; while educating handicapped youngsters might be expensive, how could costs be weighed against reclaimed lives?

The handicapped rights movement had gained considerable momentum by the late 1960s. While organizations representing the interests of the handicapped had been formed, they had been able to extract only expressions of good intent from the States. One such group, PARC, decided that court action was the only way to break the impasse. The initial focus of PARC's attention was the Pennhurst State School and Hospital, the subject of considerable press and political attention for inhumane treatment of its patients.[23] PARC had engaged in a long battle with Pennsylvania authorities about the conditions at Pennhurst, but to little avail, and so turned to legal counsel. The influence of legal modes of thought in framing and defining the issues even at this early stage is noteworthy. PARC's attorney, Thomas Gilhool, advised that the most promising strategy for attacking the Pennhurst situation was to insist upon handicapped youngsters' legal right to education.

The case that Gilhool mounted was formidable. He was able to assemble a group of witnesses with overwhelming expertise in the field of special education[24] and to forge a link with the Council for Exceptional Children (CEC), a group which had already demonstrated its effectiveness at state level, and was to become the major federal lobbyist for handicapped children.[25] The plaintiff's monopoly of expertise and weight of evidence swamped the defense. After one day of testimony the Commonwealth withdrew its opposition to the complaint.[26]

The final court order, which was handed down in May 1972,[27] enjoined the defendants from applying statutes excluding mentally retarded children from public education. It required them to provide every retarded child access to a free public program of education and training appropriate to his learning capacities.[28]

The order also included a detailed stipulation as to the procedures that had to be followed in classifying mentally retarded children. It specified a full range of due process procedures, including written notice of changes in educational status; the opportunity for a due process hearing, at which the parents may be represented by counsel, call and cross-examine witnesses, examine records relating to the child; and a verbatim record of the proceedings.

The consent agreement in *PARC* was the culmination of the first stage of the legalization of special education. Political pronouncements about the rights of the retarded had been translated into legal arguments and formally recognized in a court of law as protected by the United States Constitution. The federal district court judgment in *Mills*,[29] issued the following August, reiterated the rights established in *PARC* and extended them to all handicapped children. There was more to come. *PARC* and *Mills* precipitated a rash of litigation across the country, both inspired and orchestrated by lobby groups on behalf of the handicapped, in order to pressure state governments into action. Some thirty-six cases were filed in twenty-one jurisdictions.[30]

The commitment of a policy area to the hands of courts and lawyers has significant policy ramifications. Rights take on a life of their own in the hands of attorneys, who bring a particular conceptual framework to the problems with which they deal. Analogizing the claims of the retarded to the legally cognizable right to education preempts other potential ways of conceiving the issues. To cast a claim in terms of a Fourteenth Amendment right also implies creating a set of procedures to protect that right; in the consent agreement drawn up between the lawyers for the parties in *PARC*, relied upon in subsequent cases, a detailed set of due process procedures figures prominently. Similar provisions were incorporated in the model statute drafted by the Council for Exceptional Children (CEC). Using the threat of litigation as leverage, organizations such as CEC lobbied successfully for new state legislation. By 1974, twenty-five states required due process procedures.[31]

From Test Case to Federal Legislation

Publicity about the treatment of the handicapped led to the introduction of bills adding handicap to Title VI of the Civil Rights Act;[32] discrimination against the handicapped in education was specifically mentioned as one reason for the proposed amendment.[33] The emergence of these issues prompted formation of the Senate Sub-Committee on the Handicapped early in 1972. These developments spurred lobby groups for the handicapped to respond; groups which had traditionally focused their efforts at state and local level were drawn into the Washington orbit.

Issues involving the handicapped were thus tentatively placed on the federal agenda. The court cases, however, proved to be the decisive factor. The financial pressure generated by these cases forced the states to turn to Washington for assistance and convinced policymakers in Washington of the need for federal initiatives.

The court opinion also led lobby groups for the handicapped to focus on Washington. The CEC, which had played an influential role in orchestrating the litigation and using it to force states to enact special education legislation, had doubts about the constitutional firmness of the court decisions, none of which had been tested on appeal. Moreover, a federal statute would establish an authoritative national standard. While maintaining pressure by continuing to bring suits, the primary focus of the lobby groups for the handicapped changed from seeking substantive change at state level to forcing states to accept — even to promote — federal legislation. The strategy dictated that states be obliged to accept conditions to be imposed in new federal legislation in order to obtain the funds necessary to comply with court orders.

The courts were thus a crucial factor in the combination of events which put special education on the federal agenda. The influence of the courts, however, went beyond this, shaping the substance of policy at federal level.

The Individual Education Program (IEP)

The approach of the courts to the issue of special education had been to determine that handicapped children have a right to education. Since courts are used to dealing with individuals as bearers of rights, casting the issue in this way made it legally cognizable, for rights could then be protected by due process procedures. This emphasis on individual needs suited both the professional concerns of the CEC as well as the processual biases of the legalized model. That congruence in turn predisposed policymakers to deal with further policy questions in a legalized mode. Individualism was critical to the next step in the process of legalization.

The courts had declared the right of handicapped children to a free and appropriate public education, with a presumption that a student be placed in the least restrictive school environment (the environment as similar to the regular classroom as possible). Beyond that, though, the substance of the right was unspecified. Once the idea of an individual right to an appropriate education was accepted, it became nearly impossible to define the substance of the right to education in general terms, for the needs of individuals varied so greatly from person to person. Moreover, even if a categorical definition could have been produced it would have been politically difficult to do so. Since education was still regarded essentially as a local responsibility, even in this interventionist era, federal substantive mandates would have seemed excessive.

The device settled on to elaborate the right to education, as it appeared in the first Senate bill, was the IEP 'a written educational plan for a child developed and agreed upon jointly by the local educational agency, the parents or guardians of the child and the child when appropriate . . .'[34] The program was to contain a statement of the child's level of educational performance, long-range educational goals, intermediate objectives, the specific services to be provided, the date of commencement and the duration of the services, and objective criteria and evaluation procedures to determine whether the goals were being achieved.[35]

The character of the IEP process is legal, not administrative, in character. Rather than empowering an administrator to exercise discretion in delivering pre-ordained services to a recipient, the act recognizes that the handicapped child has a right. This right entitles the child or the parents to negotiate as parties with school officials and involves them in the task of defining the nature and extent of the services to be delivered. The character of the IEP is legal and quasi-contractual, a logical extension of the fact that handicapped children had been accorded rights.[36]

The IEP is also an ingenious device in terms of political acceptability. It avoids attempting to mandate specific services; it recognizes the rights of recipients, empowers them, and involves them in the process; it avoids trenching on the professional discretion of teachers and potentially enhances their influence over placement decisions; it provides a means of holding local administrators accountable while paying some deference to the belief that the federal government should not interfere too much with local autonomy in education; and it appeals to local school officials by fixing the upper limit of the liabilities with respect to the child.[37]

Compliance: Legalization Begets More Legalization

If the IEP was to be a meaningful contract, some means of enforcing its provisions, and more generally of assuring compliance with the aims of the law, had to be found. A way for parents to express dissatisfaction with the IEP procedure or the performance of local officials was required, as was an assurance that federal funds were being spent in accordance with the objectives of the legislation.

Early legislative drafts emphasized agency review, a bureaucratic mode of accountability. As the legislation took final form, however, due process guarantees and not administrative monitoring became the primary compliance mechanism.[38] This outcome constitutes a further extension of the legalization process, building on the already established themes of individual entitlement and the quasi-contractual IEP. The due process procedures, a natural concomitant of the legalized model, would not only serve as a means of redress for parents but also as a device for policing the expenditure of federal funds by local officials.

The history of this aspect of the legislation begins in the 1973 Senate bill[39] with the monstrously impractical notion of forwarding all IEPs to the U.S. Commissioner of Education for review. The idea of detailed central oversight was abandoned when it was realized that the requirement entailed sending some eight million IEPs to Washington each year. The Senate's alternative was a state-level independent complaints agency called 'the entity,'[40] which would conduct periodic evaluations of state and local compliance, receive complaints from individuals and provide opportunity for hearings, notify the state or local agency of a violation and take steps to correct it. The House bill, by contrast, had developed a local school district grievance procedure, to receive complaints from the handicapped and carry out investigations. Neither bill entitled an individual to a hearing.[41]

Conflict in the House-Senate Conference Committee over these competing compliance mechanisms became acute when the decision was taken to fund local school districts directly rather than give the states the discretion in distributing the federal money. Could administrative oversight assure accountability from some 16,000 school districts? Some did not want to see 'federal money being poured down the same old rat holes,' as one policymaker put it, referring to misuse of funds under earlier federal education legislation. The advocacy and civil rights groups did not trust local schools administrators and teachers and pushed for due process protections. The Children's Defense Fund (CDF) and the California Rural Legal Assistance Foundation (CRLA), both of which played a key role at this stage as advisors to the congressional conferees, were heavily involved in civil rights and poverty law litigation. Their experience in those fields produced a belief in the efficacy of rights, courts and the court-like procedures, and profound mistrust of bureaucratic accountability.

Quite apart from the inconsistency of agency review with individual entitlement, however, political factors militated against agency review. Any watchdog agency large enough to police 16,000 school districts would have done too much violence to traditions of local governance in education. The due process provisions fitted perfectly into the federal legislative scheme. They carried through the notion of individual entitlement developed in the IEP. They also enabled client and advocacy groups to undertake their own enforcement initiatives. Enlightened self-interest would obviate the need for a large watchdog agency and reassure advocacy groups like CDF, which believed that courts and court-like procedures were the only way to counteract the power of local school boards. The due process provision offered a means of resolving the deadlock between the House and the Senate over compliance mechanisms that was consistent with the legalized model of the legislation. The conferees could embrace a solution that both embodied a logically coherent development of all that had gone before and also solved their more pragmatic political problems. Although the states remained legally obliged to monitor local behavior, the due process procedures assumed primary importance as a means of ensuring compliance and providing a forum for individual grievances.

The Appropriateness of the Legalized Model: The Empirical Evidence

Introduction

The evolutionary nature of legalization in special education policy precluded any detailed consideration of the appropriateness of a legalized model in the education setting, at least in the policy formulation stage. Now that some of the major abuses that led to the court decisions and ultimately the legislation have been corrected, questions are being raised about the appropriateness of legalization in the education setting.[42]

This reappraisal poses serious issues of policy. Does it make sense to impose on education a policy mold which does not place much faith in the professional discretion of the service provider?[43] The implications of this shift are not lost on educators who may understandably resent the implicit loss of confidence. More generally, does legalization fit the needs and demands of schools — or of children? The impositioon of legalization onto ongoing complex organizations, such as schools, also creates particular problems.[44] Studies of the implementation history speak less of the promise of legalization and more of its pathology: compliance with the letter rather than the spirit of the law; preparation of standard form IEPs, resentment that handicapped children have gained a priority that does or may gain them more than their fair share of the education dollar; and defensive strategies, such as the tape recording of IEP meetings, to protect the interests of the school district and teachers.

Yet the story is more complex than this. While implementation studies view the due process procedures as a separate and severable part of the federal legislation, these procedures are an integral part of a legislative scheme which adopts a legalized policy style. The appropriateness of this policy style must be judged with reference to the place of special education in the school system, not by focusing only on the due process hearings ignoring this overall context. To be sure, the benefits to special education flowing from the federal presence — more money, more initiatives, and the like — must be offset by the costs of the due process hearings. Yet the question is whether these gains could have been achieved without the legalized policy style of PL 94-142.

A radical reorientation of priorities in special education was needed in the American context and those who shaped PL 94-142 judged that legalization was the only way to bring it about. That view has much to recommend it. In certain situations shock treatment is called for to convince service deliverers in an ongoing institution that established patterns and values must be changed. Legalization was not the first but the last in a series of approaches taken by educators of the handicapped. Years of campaigning had not convinced the education community of the justice of the claims made on behalf of the handicapped.

Legalization was a plausible approach. While law may not be the only way to reorder priorities or legitimate claims — the availability of a great deal of new money for special education or the operation of a competitive market, for example, might have brought about the same result — law and legal sanctions offered a surer and more direct means of institutionalizing the values promoted by the proponents of change. The embodiment of values in law and the possibility of sanctions offer powerful reference points to those implementing a reform, serving as a rallying point for claims on the system and a powerful mechanism for responding to arguments from competing value positions. The law also provides a frame in which values can be translated into services and new values and services can emerge, for it requires the adjustment of power positions of the various groups with a system. Proponents of the new values gain power in the institution and can introduce still further changes on behalf of their interests.

In short, legalization is neither so cost-free as its proponents suggested nor so defective as subsequent analyses contend. In what follows we explore the effects of legalization by examining the implementation of PL 94-142 and the due process mechanisms in particular.

Implementation: The Due Process Procedures

The studies of the implementation of the due process aspects of PL 94-142 are the best available indicators of the effects of legalization but they need to be evaluated with caution.[45] For one thing, they report a fairly short experience of the legislation and necessarily do not deal with the possibility that implementation improves over time.[46] For another, they are flawed in a variety of ways. The research typically relies on small, non-random samples of individuals involved in the hearings. While valid as a guide to the experience of those who undertake a hearing, these cases focus on the deficiencies of the process. They do not speak to the appropriateness of the due process procedures generally, nor to the level of satisfaction in general of parents of handicapped children with the new law. This research approach shortchanges the systemic effect of the procedural reforms. Moreover, since the studies only report the post-legislation experience, the ill-effects attributed to the due process procedures may simply be old problems transferred from other forms or made more visible by the existence of the hearings.

1 *The IEP Meeting*

The notification and procedures required to draw up the IEP and hold the meeting are generally in place.[47] After some early hearings where schools failed to comply with notice deadlines, and the like, the mechanics of the IEP procedures seem to be operating.

The qualitative picture is not as clear. Two types of IEP meeting have been identified: a legalistic form in which half the time is devoted to narrow procedural requirements, and a child-oriented form, faithful to the spirit of the law.[48] IEP sessions in which the parents are overwhelmed with professional jargon and other strategies used by schools to minimize the portion of their resources devoted to meetings have been reported in two states.[49] There are also hearsay accounts of IEPs prepared in advance where the parent is pressured to sign on the dotted line, but little evidence to indicate how widespread this practice is.

Reactions of the IEP process are mixed. Parents generally seem satisfied, even enthusiastic, about the development of the IEP, but in the districts characterized as legalistic, one third of the parents describe the meetings as formalistic.[50] Teachers generally regard the IEP as useful but reports differ as to whether there is a high degree of actual use of the IEP as an instructional tool,[51] or such use is the exception rather than the rule.[52] Even this more pessimistic accounting acknowledges that the IEP has the force of law and serves as new found leverage both within the school and the district and provides a basis for a due process hearing.[53]

2 *Due Process Hearings*

(i) Number of hearings

The total number of due process hearings held pursuant to the Education for All Handicapped Children Act is not known. Scattered reports suggest wide variations from state to state. In California, 278 hearings were held in 1978–79, the first year of uniform state regulations, and one-third of these were held in two school districts. That number represents just 0.08 per cent of California's special education population.[54] A nationwide study of twenty-two sites found half had experienced hearings; seven had only one hearing.[55] Massachusetts had 350 hearings between 1974 and 1979.[56]

As with litigation generally, it is difficult to say whether those figures represent a large percentage of hearings relative to the number of people who had grievances. Data from other comparable contexts — welfare, for instance — suggest that hearings are highly unusual phenomena in relation to the number of people or even the number of complaints in a given area.[57] Right to education hearings are not atypical in this regard.

The impact of hearings, however, cannot be measured simply in terms of the number of hearings held.[58] The prospect of a hearing and estimations of its likely outcome shape the behavior of participants, both in the formulation of their basic relationships and in the way they handle their disputes. The 'shadow of the law'[59] extends well beyond the formally affected parties.

(ii) Who uses the hearings and for what end?

Middle class parents bring the majority of hearings[60] — the proportion of middle class users was as high as 82 per cent in one study[61] — leading one commentator to observe that '(d)ue process and appeal procedures are used to advantage by the well-to-do and almost not at all by the poor.'[62]

The middle class are usually best able to press their claims. Factors similar to those identified in other contexts seem to be at work in relation to reliance on hearings in the special education context. People in ongoing relationships are unlikely to resort to legal sanctions.[63] Parents who know that their children will have to deal with the local school district personnel for twelve years are understandably reluctant to resort to legal action, with the anxieties that such undertakings generate, in all but the most serious cases. The opportunities for reprisal even after an outcome favorable to the parents, and the difficulties of enforcing such a decision in the face of an intransigent school district,[64] pose too great a risk.

Middle and upper class parents do not face such high odds, for they have an exit strategy.[65] Their complaints typically assert the inability of the local school district to provide 'appropriate' education and claim reimbursement for tuition in private schools. If this proves unsuccessful, these parents can pay for the private schooling themselves. Lower class parents do not have this option; when they are involved in hearings at all, it is most often to resist changes proposed by the school, rather than to initiate change.[66] The ongoing nature of their relationship with the school system means that circumspection is probably in the best interests of these parents. This pattern points up an important limitation on the capacity of due process to bring about change in professionally-run bureaucracies. It also raises questions about the wisdom of placing primary reliance on due process to effect policy change.

(iii) Style of hearings

Adversariness and legalism seem to characterize the conduct of hearings.[67] Rather than adopting an informal negotiating format, the due process hearings tend to provide a forum for culmination of long-term bad relations between the school and the parents involved.[68] Involving lawyers aggravates the situation, rendering proceedings more legalistic.[69] Emphasis on compliance with procedural matters such as notices, signatures, and time deadlines offers an easy substitute for harder substantive questions, such as the meaning to be given to the word 'appropriate' in the phrase 'free, appropriate, public education' in a given case. This legalistic pattern seems particularly evident in the earlier stages of implementation. As schools have learned to comply with the forms of the law opportunities for evasion have diminished, and there is some evidence of reduced formalism, as in reliance on 'pre-hearing hearings' and negotiations among the participants.[70]

Parents generally reported both considerable expense and psychological cost in the hearing process. They often felt themselves blamed either for being bad parents or for being troublemakers.

School districts regarded the hearings as expensive, time-consuming and a threat to their professional judgment and skill. The private school placements which parents often sought are enormously costly and also carry an implied criticism of the public school program. Directors of special education programs often regarded parents seeking these placements as 'ripping off' the school system, depriving other children of the benefits that would otherwise accrue to the public school program.[71] They complained about inconsistency in interpreting the appropriateness criterion from one hearing to the next and difficulties in accounting to the school board for expensive new services endorsed in hearings.[72] Special education administrators see themselves as caught in a cross-fire between parents and hearings officers who charge them with denying entitlements and school boards who blame them for failing to hold the line on expensive new services.

Some school districts which have experienced a number of hearings have developed an array of defensive strategies. There are reports of districts tape-recording IEP meetings, retaining lawyers, tightening up on procedures[73] and interpreting education and related services narrowly; all ways of sticking to the letter of the law.[74] Other districts negotiated extra services with parents who promised not to pursue a hearing, or threatened to demand a hearing in order to coerce parents into accepting an IEP.[75]

While a few participants in due process hearings regarded them as positive experiences, allowing some sort of catharsis and a forum in which an independent party could suggest a solution,[76] most held a negative view. In many instances, hearings have become an additional weapon with which the disputants can bludgeon one another. Parents see themselves as pursuing the best interests of their child while the school district is anxious to preserve limited resources.

The negative effects of the due process hearings should not be exaggerated. Even though they impose a high economic and psychological cost on all involved, their incidence is concentrated on relatively few school districts. Furthermore, these are districts where parents have a long history of dissatisfaction with the school system.[77] The hearings provide an arena in which old conflicts are played out, and sometimes escalated. In view of this the assertion that the introduction of due process procedures has caused relations between schools and parents to deteriorate must be treated with extreme caution.

The Appropriateness of the Legalization Model: the Wider Context

Introduction

The implementation studies discussed in the previous section assess the appropriateness of legalization in special education without either attending to the wider context of the education system or proposing plausible alternative means of rectifying the indisputable abuses of the past. To focus exclusively on the due process procedures in isolation and to identify the undesirable effects associated with them misses the broader institutional changes associated with the legislation, of which the due process procedures form an integral component.

Passage of PL 94-142 has had an enormous effect on special education. More than 230,000 children were identified and provided with education within the first two years after passage of the law and the rate of increase is steady.[78] Although appropriations are now falling below authorizations, there has been an infusion of $950 million in federal funds over the first two years of the program, increasing to over $800 million in 1980 and 1981.[79] While reduced substantially under the Reagan administration, special education has proved to be less of a casualty than other social welfare programs.[80] This represents an enormous increase in special education expenditure which has produced not only cash benefits, but also augmented the prestige and attractiveness of special education as a field of endeavor. The formal procedures mandated by the Education for All Handicapped Children Act are in place and many new programs are being developed in school districts.

Much of this change might have been achieved without reliance on such a legalized policy style. Implicit in the criticisms of due process procedures is the suggestion that the policymakers were wrong in believing that the legalized model was essential to achieve their purposes, and that legalization is inappropriate in the context of education. Even if we remain skeptical about the causal links between the due process hearings and the effect attributed to them by the studies canvassed in the previous section, there is reason enough to raise concerns about the appropriateness of the due process procedures in the school setting.[81] It may be that some issues are not amenable to legalized treatment[82] and that education is one of these, but in our view that will depend on analysis of the particular situation. In the context of special education, it involves studying the effects of legalization going beyond mere consideration of the hearings process to look at the impact of legalization on the wider institutional setting.

Legalization and De-Legalization

Legalization, a relatively new phenomenon in the schools context,[83] is more familiar in public life generally, where trends alternate between reliance on formal, procedural justice on the one hand and informal, substantive justice on the other.[84] The civil rights era and the War on Poverty heavily emphasized rights, lawyers, courts and formal procedures.[85] Those who studied those movements in the late 1960s and early 1970s began to doubt the extent to which substantive goals could be achieved through the legal model, especially where the poor were the intended beneficiaries.[86] The mid 1970s, by contrast, saw a growing interest in delegalization, emphasizing informal methods of dispute resolution, arbitration, mediation, negotiation, ombudsmen and community dispute resolution centers.[87]

Underlying this dynamic is the Janus-faced nature of legalization. In its positive aspect, legalization makes several promises. It is a vehicle by which individual citizens may redress the balance between themselves and the state or other powerful opposing interests. It provides access to individuals unable to summon the political resources needed to obtain a legislative majority in modern politics. It offers principled decision-making in an impartial, procedurally balanced forum. It emphasizes accountability, administrative regularity and the reduction of arbitrariness.[88] In its other face, legalization can turn into legalism, arid formality.[89] Equality before the law is too often dependent on access to resources. It can also lead to the sorts of pathologies — defensiveness, delay, hostility, expense — adverted to in the previous section. Emphasis on accountability and reduction of arbitrariness imply a mistrust of those administering policy; that in turn may inhibit the creative exercise of professional discretion and judgment.

This duality of the legal model plays itself out in the special education area. Previously, handicapped children were excluded from school and from their share of the education dollar; those given some instruction were often badly treated by the education system. After years of unsuccessful political efforts, the courts were called on to restructure power relationships in the education organization that excluded the handicapped, and to legitimate their claims by declaring that they had a right to a free and appropriate public education.

The argument has now moved on beyond the question of admission to the question of the quality of education to which the handicapped are entitled.

Leaving substantive determinations to due process hearings had both the virtues and the vices of legalization. It contemplates principled arguments about the amount and type of services due to a given child. This may be preferable to such alternatives as centralized bureaucratic decision-making with its attendant problems of distance and rigid categorizations or professional judgments which are often paternalistic and give undue weight to the needs of the professionals at the expense of the handicapped student. The legalized model also creates problems.[90] Handicapped children are accorded formal rights not made available to other children in the education system. There is, for instance, a tendency for rights to know no dollar limitations.[91] Yet the reality that school administrators face is that they have limited budgets and must make difficult decisions about the just distribution of those funds among competing sectors of the school system.

Ambiguity surrounding the word 'appropriate' also produces tension between schools and parents.[92] School officials complain about parents looting the public treasury to obtain private school placements and express frustration that they feel unable to put these sorts of arguments to the hearings officers. This limitation may be attributable to the tendency of due process hearings to individualize problems but it is not a necessary interpretation of the legislation. Acting on this perception, school administrators are resorting to indirect means of protecting funds, adopting defensive or delaying tactics, and attempting to translate arguments based on the needs of the school system in general into arguments about a particular child. For their part, parents' expectations may have been raised to unrealistic levels by the law. Their concern is likely to reside exclusively with their child; in their eyes the word 'appropriate' may have come to mean whatever is appropriate regardless of the cost. This would explain parental frustration with school districts, and their perception concerning the lack of candor in the school officials with whom they deal.

While this dispute over the relevance of costs is partly attributable to the fact that entitlements of handicapped children, but not those of non-handicapped children, are clearly spelled out, it is also partly a function of the adjudicative process itself. The hearing mechanism is, in its ideal form, a case-by-case process; it formally assumes that two parties are disputing in a contextual vacuum. That fiction alone is enough to give rise to considerable frustrations. Moreover, different hearing officers will render different decisions on similar cases. There is no consistent interpretation of 'appropriate,' and there does not appear to be much communication among hearing officers about their decisions.[93] While this may change as precedents develop, several factors — the variegated nature of appropriateness, the fact that hearings officers lack either the legal or educational expertise to render consistent judgments, and the variability of schools and handicapping conditions — make consistency unlikely.

Modest changes in the law would improve the situation. For one, the legislation should be amended to make it clear that arguments based on the overall needs of the school system (subject to proof and open to challenge in the hearing) are germane to the question of appropriateness.[94] Use of informal dispute resolution techniques seems to be producing good results, and should be encouraged.[95] Greater information, attention to problems at an early stage of development, and the use of mediation techniques prevent the escalation of conflict in a significant number of cases.[97]

The broadest concerns relate to the effects of legalization of special education on the school as a bureaucratic/professional organization.[97] Schools face serious problems of coordination, confronting acutely complex questions of distributive justice among different elements of their program, of management *vis-à-vis* theirr own professional staff, and of accountability to the community, especially to the parents of currently enrolled students. The meaning of a good education is controversial, and limited in any case by funding realities. Potential lines of conflict run in every direction: between school board and teachers, teachers and principal, teacher and student, and teacher and parents.

The effect of legalization on special education entails a radical reorientation of this complex network. It empowers what was previously an out group: the handicapped must now be included in policy decisions. No one in the school system can maintain that handicapped children should be excluded from school, at least not publicly. The force of the state and the moral authority of the law is available to the handicapped.

Legalization has also improved the status of the special education professional. In an era of shrinking education budgets, special education has received an infusion of new money. It has become an attractive area for new teachers and a way for existing teachers to earn additional salary and avoid retrenchment. Special education teachers are assuming places in school administrations which, hitherto, they had not held, and this too will affect the organizational goals of schools and strengthen the perceived legitimacy of the claims of the handicapped.

The pathologies of legalization must also be owned. There is some evidence that the values promoted by the legislation are provoking resistance from the education community.

Despite increased funding there are too few resources to treat all handicapped children individually.[98] By distinguishing the handicapped children from the regular school network and granting them rights not enjoyed by other school children, the law potentially distorts the allocation of resources. This potential is aggravated by the legal model which treats the parties to a dispute as discrete from the system in which they are located.

Finally, legalization betrays a mistrust of schools. It may inhibit the discretion of professionals[99] whose judgment should be exercised creatively on behalf of the child.[100] In the past that distrust may have been deserved. But legalization can be a blunt instrument, undermining healthy as well as malevolent exercise of discretion. Special education teachers now find themselves as 'defendants' in due process hearings. This represents a marked change from their self-perception, prior to passage of PL 94-142 as lone advocates for the handicapped child. From the viewpoint of the handicapped it would be disastrous to alienate this group, particularly in view of their role as primary service providers and their new status in the school hierarchy. Encouraging mediation and negotiation, rather than due process hearings, should diminish this danger. Moreover, resolution of the appropriateness issue should release special educators from the somewhat false position in which they now find themselves covertly having to argue on behalf of the needs of the school system. Once recognized as legitimate, the system's needs could be advanced openly by representatives of the wider interests, leaving special educators to put the case for the components of the system. Parents would maintain unreal expectations. In this way, parents and teachers could be reunited in the task of providing the best education, within budget constraints, for handicapped children.

Finally, the utility of the due process hearing as a compliance device is dubious. Individualization, lack of coordination and the settlement of strategic cases to avoid hearings suggest systemic problems which may be missed by the individualized nature of the hearings. Hearings alone are ill-suited for the task of precipitating systemic review and reform.[101] Agency-wide review, litigation, and political change remain key parts of appraising and modifying any program.

Only in the context of those wider considerations may the appropriateness of legalization be assessed. Legalization jolted the education system into according handicapped children a fair share of the education pie. As the system comes to accept the presence of handicapped children and recognizes the legitimacy of their claims and, as special education teachers acquire new status in school hierarchies, there are sound reasons to diminish reliance on some aspects of the legalized structure of special education.

Conclusion

Development of special education policy occurred during the heyday of legalization, but the continued prominence of legalization as a policymaking style seems less likely. The force of the civil rights era, which gave so much impetus to the development of the special education policy, is spent. The rhetoric of rights has waned as calls for smaller government, lower taxes and budget cuts produce a climate skeptical of new claims on the public sector and doubtful about many of the old ones. These rights may themselves be trimmed back by budget cuts, legislative repeal, and judicial circumspection.

This is not to suggest, however, that legalization will disappear from public life, for the values it symbolizes are too deeply embedded in the political culture. The lessons to be learned from the special education history speak to individuals' rights to enjoy essential public services and to participate in decisions affecting delivery of those services. These values remain fundamental in American public life. Yet there are also lessons to be learned about the impact of law on complex organizations and the balancing of all interests within those organizations.

Legalization is a powerful tool which needs to be understood and used sensitively. In the long run, there can be no easy solution to the difficult questions of distribution in organizations with conflicting interests competing for limited funds. Outright exclusion such as handicapped children suffered is no answer; neither is the enfranchisement of one group with little effort to relate that group's needs to those of other claimants. Those who would undertake the legalization of a policy area must take careful account of the context into which the policy is introduced, for only in this way can the appropriateness of legalization be weighed against alternative policy courses.

Notes

1 See, for a discussion of these policy frameworks, KIRP, D.L. (1982) 'Professionalization as a policy choice: British special education in comparative perspective,' *World Politics*, 34, p. 137.

2 SELZNICK, P. (1969) *Law Society and Industrial Justice*.

3 KEGAN, R. (1978) *Regulatory Justice*.

4 KIRP, D.L. (1976) 'Proceduralism and bureaucracy: Due process in the school setting', *Stanford Law Review*, 25, p. 841.

5 MAYHEW, L. (1968) *Law and Equal Opportunity*.

6 See ABEL, R. (1979) 'Delegalization: A critical review of its ideology, manifestations and social consequences,' in BLANKENBURG, E., KLAUSA, E. and ROTTLEUTHNER, H. (Eds). *Alternativem zum Recht: Jahrbuch fur Rechtssoziologie und Rechtstheorie*, band 6, Opladen, Westdeutscher Verlag, p. 29.

7 There is a sense in which any time Congress makes a law about anything one can say that the policy area has been 'legalized,' i.e., a law about it has been enacted. That is not the sense we intend to convey here. Rather we attempt to identify and characterize a particular method or style of policymaking and distinguish it from other ways of achieving policy objectives.

8 Selzick described the problem of legalism in this way in SELZNICK, P. (1969) *op. cit.*, p. 13.

9 Distinguish that usage of legalism from that of Judith Skhlar who means something synonymous with the rule of law, SKHAR, J. (1964) *Legalism*, Cambridge, Harvard University Press. We are indebted to Martin Shapiro for this example. For a history of federal vocational education policy see BENSON, C. (1980) 'Centralization and legalization in vocational education: Limits and possibilities,' Institute for Research on Educational Finance and Governance, Stanford University, December.

10 See HANDLER, J., HOLLINGWORTH, E. and ERLANGER, H. (1978) *Lawyers and the Pursuit of Legal Rights*, pp. 29–39.

11 See HANDLER, J. (1966) 'Controlling official behaviour in welfare administration,' in TEN BROEK, J. (Ed.), *The Law of the Poor*, pp. 155, 160–1 and 170–6.

12 *Ibid.*

13 KIRP, D.L. (1982) *op. cit.*, pp. 138–9.

14 CHILDREN'S DEFENSE FUND, (1974) *Children Out of School*. See also, 3 *U.S. Cong. and Admin. News*, 93rd Congress, 2 Sess. 1974, 4138.

15 *Pennsylvania Association for Retarded Children, v. Commonwealth of Pennsylvania 343 F. Supp. 279 (E.D. Pa 1972).*

16 See LIPPMAN, L. and GOLDBERG, I. (1973) *The Right to Education*, Chapter 4.

17 *Ibid.*, p. 29.

18 See SCHEINGOLD, S. (1974) *The Politics of Rights: Lawyers, Public Policy and Political Change*, pp. 8–9.

19 See *Goss v Lopez* 419 U.S. 565, 576 n. 8 (1975). See generally KIRP, D.L., (1976) *op. cit.*

20 LIPPMAN, L. and GOLDBERG, I. (1973) *op. cit.*, p. 20.

21 *Ibid*, p. 29.

22 *Ibid.*, pp. 8–9. See also *Diana v. State of New York* 70 Misc. 2d 660; 335 NYS 3.
23 LIPPMAN, L. and GOLDBERG, I. (1973) *op. cit.*, pp. 8–9.
24 They are listed in LIPPMAN, L. and GOLDBERG, I. (1973), *op. cit.*, pp. 28–9.
25 The CEC is a national professional organization with 90 per cent of its membership composed of special education teachers. Unlike teacher unions it has no responsibility to its membership for wages and conditions. Its purpose is to develop policy in the field of special education.
26 LIPPMAN, L. and GOLDBERG, I. (1973) *op. cit.*, p. 29.
27 343 F. Supp. 279, 302.
28 *Ibid.*
29 *Mills v. Board of Education of the District of Columbia* 348 F. Supp. 866 (D.D.C. 1972).
30 MARTIN, R. (n.d.) *Educating Handicapped Children: The Legal Mandate*, p. 15.
31 ABESON, A., BOLICK, N. and HASS, J., (1976) 'Due process of law: Background and intent in WEINTRAUB, F. *et al.* (Eds), *Public Policy and the Education of Exceptional Children*, p. 30.
32 The House Bill was introduced by Congressman Charles Vanik of Ohio on 9 December 1971 (117 Cong. Rec. 45974–5) and Senator Hubert Humphrey introduced similar bill into the Senate on 20 January 1972 (118 Cong. Rec. 106–07). These later became §504 of the Rehabilitation Act, PL 93–112.
33 MARTIN, R. *op. cit.*, pp. 16–17.
34 Sec. 3(9). The teacher was added by the 1975 bill.
35 *Ibid.*
36 The term quasi-contractual is used advisedly. The National School Boards Association was at pains to ensure that the IEP not be seen as a contract from which specific performance and other court remedies would flow. CEC agreed to this. *House Select Education Subcommittee Hearings*, 10 April 1975, p. 76. The Senate Labor and Education Committee expressed a similar concern *Senate Report (Labor and Public Welfare Committee)* No. 94–168, 2 June 1975, p. 11. One of the first expressions of the idea of a contract was in GALLAGHER, (1972) 'The special education contract for mildly handicapped children,' *Exceptional Children*, 35, p. 527. As one of the policymakers we interviewed summed it up:

> We intended to strengthen the hands of parents.... It was a way of individualizing and contractualizing the relationships and involving parents in the process.... It's a way of enforcing what should be delivered to kids. While it's said not to be a contract, it is a contract for service delivery.

Note in passing the commitment to the involvement and empowerment of the recipient. The interviewee made the attribution to the 1960s and the War on Poverty explicitly later in the interview.
37 One of our respondents informed us that this last item was a good selling point for the IEP to local boards.
38 The first bill proposed in January 1973 contained a number of due process measures which looked almost identical to those contained in the *PARC* consent agreement. That bill did not, however, contain the full range of due process provisions ordered by the court in *PARC*. From our interviews it seems that there was little discussion of the due process procedures until the conference committee stage when there was heated debate under the pressure of the need to secure a compromise between the House and Senate bills. These bills contained agency review type bodies, called 'the entity' in the Senate bill, while the House bill included a set of 'grievance procedures.' These were at odds with one another and with the legalized concepts already implanted in the early drafts. We take this up below.
39 S. 6, §7a.
40 S. 6, §614(8).

41 HR 7217, 617.
42 PITTENGER, J. and KURILOFF, P. (1982) 'Educating the handicapped: Reforming a radical law,' *Public Interest*, 66, Winter, p. 72.
43 See ILLICH, I. (1973) *Tools for Conviviality*; GOFFMAN, E., (1961) 'Asylums' in WASSERSTROM, R. *Lawyers as Professionals: Some Moral Issues, 5 Human Rights* 1 (1975) considers them in relation to the legal profession.
44 MAYHEW, L. (1968) *op. cit.*, pp. 1–30, especially p. 23, and pp. 258–84. On implementation in special education see WEATHERLEY, R. (1979) *Reforming Special Education: Policy Implementation from State Level to Street Level* and on implementation generally, see BARDACH, E. (1977) *The Implementation Game.* See WEATHERLEY, R. (1979); STEARNS, M., GREEN, D. and DAVID, J. (1979) *Local Implementation of PL 94-142*, Discussion Draft, SRI International; KIRST, M. and BERTKEN, K. (1980) 'Due Process in Special Education: Exploration of Who Benefits,' paper presented to the Special Education Collaborative Conference, Institute for Research on Educational Finance and Governance, Stanford University, 8–10 October; HASSELL, C. (1981); BUDOFF M. and ORENSTEIN, A. (1983) *Special Education Appeals Hearings: Their Form, and the Response to Their Participants*; BENVENISTE, G. (1985) 'Implementation and intervention strategies: the case of PL 94–142,' in this volume. Note the studies by WEATHERLEY, R. and BUDOFF, M. and ORENSTEIN, A. are of the equivalent Massachusetts legislation, Chapter 766, the *Comprehensive Special Education Law of 1972.*
45 See KIRP, D.L. and JENSEN, D. (1983) 'What does due process do?' *The Public Interest* 73, Fall, pp. 75–90.
46 *Ibid.*
47 STEARNS, M., GREEN, D. and DAVID, J. (1979) *op. cit.*, p. 51.
48 HASSELL, C. (1981) *A Study of the Consequences of Excessive Legal Intervention on the Local Implementation of PL 94–142*, PhD thesis, University of California, Berkeley and San Francisco State University.
49 *Ibid*, p. 60 and WEATHERLEY, R. (1979) *op. cit.*
50 HASSELL, C. (1981) *op. cit.*, p. 113.
51 *Ibid.* p. 104.
52 STEARNS, M. GREEN, D. and DAVID, J. (1979) *op. cit.*, p. 79–82.
53 *Ibid.*
54 KIRST, M. and BERTKEN, K. (1980) *op. cit.*, pp. 6–7.
55 STEARNS, M. GREEN, D. and DAVID, J. (1979) *op. cit.*, p. 98
56 BUDOFF, M. and ORENSTEIN, A. (1983) *op. cit.*, p. 5–1.
57 Data cited in ROSS, H.L. (1970) *Settled Out of Court*, p. 5. The figures he uses are for 1963 and taken from DAVIS, K. (1965) *Administrative Law: Cases — Text — Problems*, p. 5. See also KIRP, D.L. (1976) *op. cit.*, p. 840, n. 113.
58 ROSS, H.L. (1970) *op. cit.*, MNOOKIN, R. and KORNHAUSER, L. (1979) 'Bargaining in the shadow of the law: the case of divorce' *Yale L.J.*, 88, p. 950; WEATHERLEY, R. (1979) *op. cit.*
59 The phrase is borrowed from MNOOKIN, R. and KORNHAUSER, L. *ibid.*
60 BUDOFF, M. and ORENSTEIN, A. (1983) *op. cit.*, p. 6–11, 6–12; KIRST, M. and BERTKEN, K. (1980) *op. cit.*, p. 21; STEARNS, M. GREEN, D. and DAVID, J. (1979) *op. cit.*, p. 104. On private school placement see BUDOFF, M. *ibid.* at 6–1; KIRST, M. and BERTKEN, K. *ibid*; STEARNS *et al.*, *ibid.* p. 104.
61 KIRST, M. and BERTKEN, K. *ibid.* p. 9.
62 WEATHERLEY, R. (1979) *op. cit.*, p. 10. But see KIRST, M. and BERTKEN, K. *ibid.* p. 23 for hearings that have a higher success rate.
63 GALANTER, M. (1974) 'Why the "haves" come out ahead: Speculations on the limits of legal change,' *Law and Society Review*, 9, p. 95; MACAULAY, S. (1963) 'Non-contractual relations in business: A preliminary study,' *Am. Soc. Rev*, 25, p. 55; HANDLER, J. (1966) *op. cit.*

64 See Budoff, M. and Orenstein, A. (1983) *op. cit.*, chapter 10.
65 Hirchman, A. (1970) *Exit, Voice and Loyalty.*
66 See note 86.
67 Budoff, M. and Orenstein, A. (1983) *op. cit.*, p. 9–1; Stearns, M. Green, D. and David, J. (1979) *op. cit.*, p. 104.
68 Budoff, M. *ibid*, at 9–1, 13–15 and 14–27; Stearns, M. Green, D. and David, J. *ibid*, p. 10.
69 Budoff, M. *ibid.* pp. 9–19.
70 *Ibid.* pp. 13–25; Stearns, M. Green, D. and David, J. (1979) *op. cit.*, p. 104.
71 Budoff, M. and Orenstein, A. (1983) *ibid.*, chapter 13; Stearns, M. Green, D. and David, J. *ibid*, p. 108. Kirst, M. and Bertken, K. (1980) *op. cit.*, p. 34 warn of distortions in the allocation of public funds.
72 Budoff, M. and Orenstein, A. (1983) at 13–24 — 13–25.
73 Kirst, M. and Bertken, K. (1980) *op. cit.*, p. 29.
74 Budoff, M. and Orenstein, A. (1983).
75 *Ibid.*
76 Stearns, M. Green, D. and David, J. (1979) *op. cit.*, p. 103; Budoff, M. and Orenstein, A. (1983) *op. cit.*, p. 13–10.
77 See note 95. Compare Hassell, C. (1981) who seems to attribute the pathologies of the school districts which have a number of hearings to 'excessive legal intervention.'
78 Evidence of E.W. Martin, Deputy Commissioner, Bureau of Education for the Handicapped, Office of Education, Department of Health, Education and Welfare in the *Report of the House Sub-committee on Select Education* 297, 299 (96th Congress, First Session, October 1979).
79 Evidence of J. Weintraub, Assistant Executive Director for Governmental Relations of the Council for Exceptional Children in the *Report of the Subcommittee on Select Education.*
80 The cutbacks for fiscal years 1982 and 1983 amount to 29.6 per cent. Children's Defense Fund. (1982) *A Children's Defense Budget: An Analysis of the President's Budget and Children*, p. 4.
81 See Kirp, D.L. (1976) *op. cit.*, and in schools generally, Pittenger, J. and Kuriloff, P. (1982) *op. cit.*, pp. 89–90.
82 Fuller, L. (1975) 'The forms and limits of adjudication,' *Harv. L. Rev*, 92, p. 353.
83 See Kirp, D.L. (1976), *op. cit.*
84 See Abel, R. (1979) *op. cit.*
85 See for example the three articles by Reich, C. (1963) 'Midnight welfare searches and the Social Security Act,' *Yale L.J.*, 72, p. 1347; (1964); 'The new property,' *Yale L.J*, 73; (1965) 'Individual rights and social welfare: the emerging legal issues,' *Yale L.J*, 74, p. 1245.
86 See Galanter, M. (1974) *op. cit.*, and Handler, J. (1966) *op. cit.*
87 Mnookin, R. and Kornhauser, L., *op. cit.*, Note 59.
88 We owe a number of these points to a talk on legalization given by Philip Selznick to the Berkeley/Stanford Faculty Seminar of Law, Governance and Education, October 1980.
89 See note 9.
90 See generally Fuller, L. (1978) *op. cit.*
91 *Mills v Board of Education of the District of Columbia*, 348 F. Supp. 1257 (1971).
92 Budoff, M. and Orenstein, A. (1983) *op. cit.*, p. 8–48. See, too, Kirst, M. and Bertken, K. (1980) *op. cit.*, on the potential for distorting funds.
93 Budoff, M. *ibid.* chapter 12.
94 *Armstrong v. Kline*, 476 F. Supp. 583 (ED. Pa., 1979) *aff' d sub nom. Scanlon v. Battle*, 629 F. 2d 269 (3d Cir., 1980).
95 Budoff, M. and Orenstein, A. (1983) *op. cit.*, chapter 12 and Stearns, M.

GREEN, D. and DAVID, J. (1979) *op. cit.*, p. 107.
96 BUDOFF, M. *ibid.*
97 See the discussion of law in the context of discrimination.
98 WEATHERLEY, R. (1979) *op. cit.*, pp. 73 and 141–50.
99 See SCHLECHTY, P. and TURNBULL, A. (1978) 'Bureaucracy or professionalism,' *Journal of Teacher Education*, 29, No. 6, p. 34.
100 On the subject of growing government intervention in the classroom see ATKIN, (1980) 'The government in the classroom,' *Daedal Daedalus*, 109: 3, p. 85.
101 See MASHAW, J. (1974) 'The mangement side of due process: some theoretical litigation notes on the assurance of accuracy, fairness and timeliness in the adjudication of social welfare claims,' *Corn, L. Rev*, 59, 772.

5 The Future

The New Federalism Goes to Court

David L. Kirp
University of California, Berkeley and

Donald N. Jensen
Stanford University

I

The heyday of educational policymaking by the courts seems to have run its course. The landmark events — the desegregation cases, the student rights opinions, the right to education suits — occurred a decade or more ago. With the *Rodriguez* decision, upholding prevailing school finance arrangements, the Supreme Court signalled that there were limits to the judges' willingness to reconfigure policy and practice in the schools. Though the intervening period has not been devoid of noteworthy litigation, attention has largely shifted away from the courts and back to the legislature, first at the national, and latterly at the state, level.[1]

One might imagine that judicialization in education was a thing of the past, but this is not necessarily so. Those benchmark decisions set in motion an altered system of decision which has generated a host of rights for historically disadvantaged groups. The judiciary put in place the basic constitutional framework, which has been elaborated and refined in subsequent federal legislation. The process of educational policy formulation is dynamic and interactive, with courts continuing to respond to claimed denials of rights. Should the role of the national government concerning educational policy change, one can anticipate a judicial response. Even a second major wave of legalization in education is not inconceivable.

The Reagan administration's New Federalism offers an opportunity to rethink the judicial stance. In conception, the New Federalism is simple enough.[2] The national government is to play less of a role in setting educational priorities and providing support for education. Washington would largely abandon its responsibility to the have-nots. Much more political discretion would reside with the states and localities, concerning both the kinds of programs that would be provided and the level of resources to be expended.

This abdication of leadership at the national level is epitomized by the proposal to consolidate federal education support at the primary and secondary level into two large block grants, providing funds to the states with almost no strings attached; by the substantial reduction in federal education expenditures; and by the proposal to demote the Department of Education, established under President Carter, to sub-cabinet status.

The Reagan administration has had some success in turning its preferences into policy. Though the largest federal education programs, those focusing on handicapped children and the economically disadvantaged, remain in place, and the Department of Education still stands, thirty small education programs have been consolidated into a block-grant package. Federal financial aid to school districts undergoing desegregation has been eliminated. The number of regulations governing the Title I compensatory education program has been reduced, and the *Lau* bilingual education regulations have been withdrawn. Total federal spending for elementary and secondary education dropped from $5.61 billion in the 1981/82 academic year to $5.3 billion for 1982/83. (Federal spending in 1981/82 already had declined 8 per cent from the previous year.) Adjusted for inflation, federal aid for bilingual and handicapped education dropped more than 50 per cent between 1980 and 1983, while spending for handicapped education declined by 32 per cent during those years.

More changes, consistent with the New Federalism, may be on the way. An Administration Bill to provide tuition tax credits to parents of children in private schools is now pending before Congress and the 1984 budget request calls for basic changes in the way education money is spent, including experimenting with vouchers for distributing money under the Chapter 1 (formerly Title I) program for disadvantaged children.

The anticipated impact of the New Federalism on education governance is clear. Less power in the hands of Washington lawmakers and bureaucrats is supposed to translate into greater decision-making authority on the part of those who, by virtue of propinquity, are presumed to know the needs of their constituents. The likely role of the courts has gone ignored in these discussions. Yet reducing national education aid and repealing legislatively-granted rights to such groups as the limited English speaking and the handicapped will not only have a political impact. Its repercussions will be felt in the courts as well.

II

The wave of legalization of education following the *Brown* decision affords useful historical perspective for this issue.[3] Courts first began to play a central role in shaping educational policy at a time when the very concept of 'right' was not part of the educators' lexicon. Individuals and groups received what school professionals and the sustaining political network regarded as their due. That system was skewed in favor of the interests of the white and well-off, at the expense of racial and ethnic minorities; it emphasized the needs of normal children, not their disabled brethren. Those groups left out of the dominant professional political coalition had long and unsuccessfully struggled in the political arena for minimally adequate support; only out of desperation did they turn to the courts.[4] It bears remembering, in this context, that the Clarendon County segregation suit, one of the four consolidated in the *Brown* decision, would not have arisen had an all-white school board acceded to the black community request for a new bus so that black children could reach the all-black school.[5]

Court decisions altered the balance of authority. They afforded blacks — and, later, limited-English speakers, the handicapped, women, and those living in property-poor school districts — legal rights that they had not previously enjoyed. Those decisions also had a second significant consequence: they gave the have-nots new legitimacy and political clout. The rights-creating court decisions do not incorporate detailed remedies or order new expenditures, but serve instead as charters of principle. Legislatures, state and especially federal, have subsequently filled in the details, securing kinds and levels of assistance undreamed-of in the court cases.[6]

The responsiveness of the political branches through the 1970s shifted the locus of reform efforts away from the courts. Legislative action offered several advantages as compared to litigation. Legislation was broader in scope and backed by substantial resources. The congressional commitment could be safeguarded by a bureaucracy already in place. This resembled the earlier attempts to enlist Congress and the Executive as allies in the effort to dismantle racially separate schools. Yet even as the have-nots had earlier sought judicial support for entitlements, denied by the political system, which they thought rightfully theirs, a return to the courts has always remained a possibility; indeed, that is precisely what occurred in the area of race in the 1970s, when Congress ceased to ally itself with the desegregation campaign. Should the federal government withdraw or water down rights previously placed on the statute books, a second wave of legalization might well be anticipated.

III

This 'new legalization', if it transpires, is likely to take a number of forms. The courts may offer a forum for challenges to proposed federal cutbacks. They may also be called upon to create new legal rights and to 'reconstitutionalize' matters which had been left to the legislative province. Finally, state courts may continue expanding their domain. 'Within the grand design of the "old federalism,"' said federal appellate Judge Jon O. Newman of the U.S. Court of Appeals for the Second Circuit, 'there is room for a little chemistry to be practiced by state court judges construing the fundamental legal document of their state — the state constitution.'[7]

Each of these forms of legalization diminishes the discretion of federal and state-level political actors.

The Constitution does not speak in terms of minimum financial obligations, only of inequalities in how individuals are treated.[8] For that reason, it is hard to construct an argument that a group of beneficiaries has an entitlement to some specified level of federal education aid; hence, fund cutbacks *per se* are not likely to evoke successful legal challenges. Washington could cease to provide any help to educationally disadvantaged students without risking a lawsuit. Yet the way in which cutbacks are carried out may raise legal questions: for instance, when government imposes assertedly arbitrary eligibility requirements or adopts procedures for determining eligibility that are thought constitutionally infirm. At least one effort by the Reagan administration to trim funds, in the school lunch program, has been stalled by legal challenges.[9] In that instance, a coalition of indigent parents and litigant interest groups has contested an administration regulation requiring that a social security number be presented before their children could receive a free or low priced meal. That requirement reflects the desire by the Reagan administration to tighten eligibility for children's food programs; it allegedly has the effect of scaring the needy as well as the undeserving off the rolls.[10]

Should Washington choose to implement the New Federalism not by rewriting the laws but through non-enforcement of existing statutes, legal challenge is also possible. Judges have gone to some pains in detailing the obligations of federal administrators, rejecting the contention that management is a wholly discretionary affair: suits insisting that the Office of Civil Rights move vigorously to dismantle dual higher education systems in the South offer the clearest example.[11] Here too the New Federalism already has wrought change: when deregulation funding was folded into the education block grants, the civil rights compliance survey, the Office of Civil Rights' major tool in determining who practices racial, sex, and other kinds of discrimination, was shelved. In October 1982 'school segregation' was dropped from the list of issues to be examined by the Office of Civil Rights; it was replaced by 'within district comparability — discriminatory delivery of services' — making a distinct shift in federal priorities.[12]

Legal challenges to the way laws are being administered need to be appreciated as delaying actions. Over time, cutbacks can be accomplished in legally permissible ways and legislative authorization can be obtained for a reduced bureaucratic role. But delay is an important policy weapon. It makes the proposed policy harder and more expensive to implement; it gives the opposition time to mobilize. The legal opinions themselves also may undermine policy change. In emphasizing the need for fair procedures or noting the plight of those disadvantaged by the New Federalism, court rulings offer a potential rallying point for the resisters.

The federal judiciary remains in the rights-creating business. And newly-fashioned rights will influence the course of the New Federalism, for what the courts do necessarily influences political contentions. The recent *Plyler v. Doe*[13] decision offers an apt illustration. In *Plyler*, the Supreme Court held that it was unconstitutional for school districts to exclude the children of illegal aliens previously barred from the schools. The effects of this decision are felt most immediately and directly by the district whose practices have been challenged, and by other border districts with similar policies. The discretion of such communities to spend resources as they wish is limited after *Plyler:* these school districts now must take into account the needs of a sizable number of children previously barred from the schools. This obligation alters budgeting in the affected school districts: either less money is spent on other educational needs or taxes are raised. Where the proportion of illegal alien children is high, the effect of *Plyler* is substantial indeed.

Nor is the impact of *Plyler* on the freedom of educational authorities to tax and spend as they wish confined to local districts. Such districts will predictably demand state support for the education of illegal alien children, arguing — and not without force — that the burden of such instruction is more equitably borne by the state. A new claimant group, districts with numerous illegal aliens, will enter the political bargaining arena, its claim premised on a judicial decision.

The story is unlikely to stop there. Texas, California, and Florida, the three states most vulnerable to the influx of illegal aliens, may well turn to Congress for federal educational aid. After all, these states may argue — again, not without force — illegal immigration is an artifact of federal, not state, policy; is it not fair that Washington accept responsibility for the predictable consequences of its policy?[14] Thus, a new judicially-created legal right potentially reshapes the politics of education at each level of government. Meanwhile, litigation begets new litigation. If illegal alien children are entitled to a free education, are they also entitled to participate in the free lunch program? This legal dynamic threatens continuously to alter the political calculus.

Not all rights-based claims will be newly generated. Efforts to turn statutory promises which the administration would like to withdraw into unbreakable constitutional guarantees may also be anticipated, and these efforts too would diminish the political flexibility that the New Federalism promises. The treatment of handicapped children offers an apt illustration.[15] On at least one occasion, the judiciary has demonstrated that it is willing to provide detailed and continuing protection of the constitutional rights of the handicapped when the state seems unable to do so. In *PARC v. Commonwealth of Pennsylvania*[16] a decade ago, a federal district court broadly defined the terms of an 'appropriate' education that was the constitutional due of handicapped children. It left detailed specification of appropriateness to be determined by the Pennsylvania education bureaucracy and in administrative hearings and appeals. When that system proved inattentive to new and plausible claims of right, unduly rigid in its application of the *PARC* norms, the federal courts were not hesitant to intervene again. In a series of subsequent decisions, federal judges have ordered Pennsylvania to offer year-round instruction for one group of handicapped students, second-guessed the quality of education provided to institutionalized retardates, and questioned the adequacy of the legal appeals procedure to vindicate the claims of handicapped youngsters.[17] These court decisions have added detail and particularization to rights roughly sketched out in *PARC*.

Similar demands for judicial vindication are likely to be heard in a host of contexts if the New Federalism achieves what its architects intend. Handicapped children may become the test case, for the administration has tried hardest to deregulate this policy domain. In 1982, it proposed major amendments to the Education for All Handicapped Children Act. Parental involvement in educational decisions would be curtailed; school officials would be allowed to take into account the 'disruptive' impact of placing a handicapped child in a regular educational class; the requirement that children be educated as close to home as possible would be eliminated. Although the administration retreated in the face of substantial and well-orchestrated opposition (six of the proposals were withdrawn for further study), Secretary Bell left open the possibility that similar changes later would be sought. The effect of these changes would be to diminish federal support for the rights of the handicapped.

The Office of Management and Budget has also joined the fray, urging that Section 504 of the Rehabilitation Act, which applies to the education of the handicapped, be rewritten. The amended law would oblige local agencies to secure a particular benefit to the handicapped only if that benefit exceeds the cost of provision; and a determination of how to calculate costs and benefits would be left to the discretion of local authorities. Advocates for the handicapped would then find themselves back where they were a decade ago, at the mercy of school officials who had proven unsympathetic in the past. They might turn to state legislatures for help, but these days the states have fewer resources than needy claimants. Since groups with constitutionally-based mandates will fare best with the states, advocates for the handicapped will inevitably look to the courts. If they succeed in that arena, federal legislative protections contained in the Education for All Handicapped Children Act would be constitutionalized, an outcome which only diminishes political discretion at the lower reaches of government. That, of course, is the opposite result from what the New Federalism intends.

Similar scenarios may be envisioned in other policy arenas. Take bilingual education, for instance. In its first months in office, the Reagan administration reversed detailed guidelines for bilingual instruction that had been drafted by the Carter administration. And the states may follow suit. Already, the Illinois Board of Education has recommended that school districts have more flexibility in how they manage bilingual instruction; the Board also proposed abolishing a state law requiring that the history and culture of minority language students be taught in the schools. If the '*Lau* remedies', which mandate that school districts with limited English speaking students provide bilingual educational programs, are repealed or watered down, or if states adopt Illinois' proposed course of action, litigation is likely. Advocates may build upon the Supreme Court's *Lau*[18] decision, which interprets a federal regulation subsequently embraced by Congress seeking to turn it into a constitutional holding. Concerning blacks, the initial and most substantial beneficiaries of legalization, and perhaps women as well, the likely future is much the same. The less that Washington does politically, the more the courts will be asked to do judicially; and this new wave of legalization seems particularly likely when federal policy aims at cutting back entitlements previously secured by legislation.

Nor will the new legalization be confined to the federal courts. One of the less familiar aspects of judicialization in American life has been the increasing prominence of state courts, particularly in such places as New Jersey, California, and New York.[19] While the performance of state courts varies widely, many of these institutions have acted to fill in the lacunae left by the perceived unresponsiveness of the Supreme Court and, more recently, Congress.

The campaign to create more equitable state school financing systems affords the clearest illustration of this invigoration of state courts. The Nixon administration proposed to tie federal education support to states' willingness to reform their finance plans, but this idea died for lack of congressional support. And in *San Antonio Independent School District v. Rodriguez*,[20] the Supreme Court upheld the constitutionality of state school finance laws which allocate resources on the basis of local property wealth; 'chaotic and unjust,' Justice Stewart termed such statutes, even while voting to affirm them.

School finance reform did not die with *Rodriguez*; instead, attention reverted to the state level. Though school finance had been a failed target of political reform for many years — wealthy districts had banded together to defeat reform attempts — the advocates returned to the state capitals with renewed vigor. And they have been successful: since 1970, more than half of the states have narrowed the gap in the amount of money spent on rich and poor districts, relying on state funds to aid school districts unable to raise sufficient funds on their own. Some of these efforts were wholly political in character, as more reformist (and fully reapportioned) legislatures responded to equity-premised claims. But the politics of school finance has been powerfully abetted by state courts. In a number of states, the highest court rejected the existing finance scheme on state constitutional grounds. The New Jersey Supreme Court, for instance, declared that the prevailing plan did not represent a 'thorough and efficient system' of education, as required by that state's constitution.[21]

Legal challenges to state school finance laws have been varied, successes mixed. In Arkansas, Colorado, Connecticut, Maryland and New Jersey, as well as in California, courts have found that a state's finance of education according to local property wealth is unconstitutional.[22] In New York, by contrast, the Court of Appeals rejected the claim that the state had a constitutional obligation to take into account the higher non-education expenditures of urban areas, their 'municipal overburden,' in allocating school aid.[23] Even where the state courts did not directly force a particular reform, the threat of a lawsuit has remained in the wings, and this has altered the political complexion of the issue.

Similar forays into the state courts can be anticipated in other domains, when and if the New Federalism is fully implemented. The willingness of at least some state courts to intervene changes the political complexion of the issue, and undermines the capacity of state and local political agencies to act with the freedom imagined by the designers of the New Federalism.

IV

The impact of the New Federalism on legalization of educational policy depends, of course, on how the courts *actually* react. All we can manage is guesswork and prediction. A more modest judicial role than that described here is also conceivable. Federal judges have been reluctant to extend the social reforms initiated in the 1960s and 1970s: Supreme Court justices have backed away from the broad view of equal protection that held sway during the Warren era; and for their part, some lower court judges have come to appreciate the difficulties of court-mandated institutional reform. A reticent judiciary will not be so inclined as to further reshape decision-making in education as their pioneering predecessors.

Nor is it absolutely certain that the federal courts will have complete freedom to make this choice for themselves. More than thirty bills were introduced last term in Congress, each aimed at restricting the power of the district courts. Education has been at the center of this campaign, with conservatives taking aim at busing and school prayer. Other bills proposed the popular election of federal judges.

The political fate of such restrictive legislation is uncertain, its constitutional fate even more so. To the extent that the authority of the federal judiciary is diminished, other actors in thier interwined system, including the state courts, can be expected to pick up some of the legal slack.

Factors external to the bench will also influence the role of the courts in an era of diminished federal legislative responsibility. The courts are passive institutions, depending upon others to initiate suits; they cannot seek out new policy worlds to conquer. The main education reform suits of the past were filed largely by public interest law firms and government-funded legal service offices, not the private bar. The reduced level of foundation aid to public interest law firms, which depended heavily on foundation support, coupled with continued efforts to terminate the Legal Services Program, may make it harder to locate lawyers able and willing to bring such demanding cases. Reform litigation also depends on activist organizations such as the Pennsylvania Association for Retarded Children, which brought the first handicapped rights case, and the NAACP Legal Defense and Education Fund, responsible for the lion's share of desegregation litigation. If the New Federalism demoralizes some of these groups, or forces them to act defensively, they will be less able to litigate effectively on behalf of their constitutents. But the legal activities of some of these groups still continues. The West Virginia Education Association in 1983 sued Governor John D. Rockefeller IV to block his 4 per cent cut in public school funding and 10 per cent reduction in higher education spending.

The great era of legalization in education coincided with a time of apparent national prosperity. The courts announced rights — such as the right to appropriate education for handicapped children or (in one notorious case) the right of children who spoke 'Black English' to bilingual instruction — without attending to costs and benefits. Indeed, the very framework of rights as contrasted with a view that recognizes competing interests and preferences, makes this kind of balancing illegitimate, for rights are not supposed to carry a price tag.[24]

But fiscal realities for many states have changed markedly in the past decade. States that were rich in the 1970s are far poorer today. At the beginning of 1983, almost 40 states had adopted austerity measures to make up for an expected loss of $8 billion during that fiscal year. Since state budgets account for about half of total funding for elementary and secondary education, state education aid will inevitably be trimmed. In Ohio Governor Richard F. Celeste, for example, ordered a $190 million reduction in state education aid in order to help alleviate Ohio's $528 million deficit. Nor are localities able to pick up the slack.

A rights-oriented judicial posture is plausible when prosperity makes some inefficiency fiscally tolerable. It is even more plausible when court-ordered expenditures are undertaken to remedy absolute deprivations of rights, as when handicapped youngsters have been denied any instruction or limited-English-speaking students have been offered no special help. These circumstances — the persistence of absolute deprivations and gross discriminations in a time of plenty — pertained in the 1960s. They fueled the legalization revolution in education. The changed circumstances of the 1980s pose a different puzzle: how will the courts behave when resources are scarce, claims of rights conflict, and minimum constitutional guarantees are already in place? The answer may entail a rethinking of the meaning of affirmative, judicially-recognized rights in a welfare state straining under the weight of political and fiscal limits.

Notes

1 See generally KIRP, D.L. and YUDOF, M.G. (Eds) (1982) *Educational Policy and Law*, Berkeley, McCutchan.

2 The changed relationship between federal, state, and local education officials, germane to an assessment of what the New Federalism will bring about, is only now receiving scholarly attention. See RABE, B. and PETERSON, P. (1982) 'Educational Policy Implementation: Are Block Grant Proposals Based on Out of Date Research?' (unpublished paper). Interest group behavior in education is the focus of some of the literature, see CHUBB, J. (1982) 'Regulating Economic Opportunity,' Institute for Research on Educational Finance and Governance, Stanford University. The November 1982 issue of the *Harvard Educational Review* contains an extensive

discussion of the federal role in education. See also UZZELL, L. A. (1982) 'The federal role in education policy,' *The Wall Street Journal*, 23, December.

3 See generally KIRP, D.L. (1977) 'Law, politics, and equal opportunity — the limits of judicial involvement,' *Harvard Educational Review* 47, p. 104. REBELL, M. and BLOCK, A. (1982) *Educational Policy Making and the Courts: An Empirical Study of Judicial Activism*, Chicago, University of Chicago Press.

4 KIRP, D.L. (1982) *Just Schools: the Idea of Racial Equality in American Education*, Berkeley, University of California Press.

5 See KLUGER, R. (1976) *Simple Justice: The History of Brown v. Board of Education and Black America's Struggle for Equality*, New York, Knopf.

6 See, for example, NEAL, D. and KIRP, D.L. (1983) 'the allure of legalization reconsidered,' elsewhere in this volume.

7 *New York Times*, 19 May 1982.

8 See MICHELMAN, F. (1969) 'Foreword: On protecting the poor through the fourteenth amendment,' *Harvard Law Review* 83, p. 7 for an elaboration of a 'minimum rights' theory. And compare, *San Antonio Independent School District v. Rodriguez*, 411 US (1973) at 36–7:

> Even if it were conceded that some identifiable quantum of education is a constitutionally protected pre-requisite . . . we have no indication that the present level of educational expenditures in Texas provide an education that falls short. Whatever merit appellees' argument might have if a State's financing system occasioned an absolute denial of educational opportunities to any of its children, that argument provides no basis for finding an interference with fundamental rights where only relative differences in spending levels are involved and where . . . no charge fairly could be made that the system fails to provide each child with an opportunity to acquire basic minimal skills necessary for the enjoyment of the rights of speech and of full participation in the political process.

9 *Alcarez v. Lock*, 7 December 1982.

10 The Reagan administration has moved in related areas. The President's 1984 budget request proposed cutting $25 million from child nutrition programs. In 1982 the President also proposed merging childcare and school breakfast programs and eliminating the summer food, special milk, and nutrition education programs. Those proposals died in Congress, but administration changes such as the social security number requirement succeeded in eliminating three million children from the food program by November 1982. See *New York Times* 29 November 1982.

11 *Adams v. Richardson*, 480 F.2d. 1159 (DC Cir. 1973).

12 *Education Week*, 15 December 1982.

13 102 US 2382 (1983).

14 KIRP, D.L. (1982) 'Education,' *New Republic*, 31, March, See also, CLUNE, W.H. (1982) 'The deregulation critique of the federal role in education,' elsewhere in this volume.

15 See KIRP, D.L. and JENSEN, D. (1983) 'What does due process do?', *The Public Interest*, 73, Fall, p. 75.

16 343, F. Supp. 279 (ED.Pa., 1972).

17 See *Fialkowski v. Shapp* 405 F. Supp. 946 (1975); *Frederick L. v. Thomas*, 408 F. Supp. 832 (ED.Pa., 1977); *aff'd in part*, 612 F. 2d 84 (3rd Cir. 1979); *rev'd*, 451 US 1 (1981); *aff'd in part, rev'd in part*, 673 F. 2d 647 (1982); *Halderman v. Pennhurst, cert. denied* 102 SC. 82, 1981; *Armstrong v. Kline*, 476 F. Supp. 583 (ED.Pa. 1979); *aff'd sub. nom. Battle v. Commonwealth*, Slip Opinion (3rd Cir. 7/15/80).

18 *Lau v. Nichols*, 414 US 563 (1974). *Serrano v. Priest*, 487 P.2d. 1241 (1971).

19 See, for example, *Washakie County School District No. 1 v. Herschler*, 606 P.2d 310

(1980); *Lujan v. Colorado* No. C-73688 (1979): *Horton v. Meskill* 376 A.2d 359 (1977); *Caldwell v. State*, No. 50616 (Johnson County Dist. Ct., Kan., Aug. 30, 1972).

20 11 US 1 (1973).

21 *Robinson v. Cahill*, 303 A. 2d. 273 (1973). See also, LEHNE, R. (1978) *The Quest for justice: The Politics of School Finance Reform*, New York, Longman.

22 ELMORE, R. and MCLAUGHLIN, M. (1982) *Reform and Retrenchment: The Politics of California School Finance Reform*, Cambridge, Ballinger.

23 *Board of Education, Levittown Union Free School District v. Nyquist*, 57 NY 2d. 27 (1982).

24 See generally, DWORKIN, R. (1977) *Taking Rights Seriously*, Cambridge, Harvard University Press.

Notes on Contributors

Ann Swidler is Assistant Professor of Sociology at Stanford University.

David Tyack is Professor in the Department of History and School of Education at Stanford University.

Lawrence Friedman is the Kirkwood Professor of Law at Stanford University.

John Meyer is Professor of Sociology at Stanford University and a Professor by Courtesy in the Stanford University School of Education.

Deborah Rhode is an Associate Professor of Law at the Stanford Law School.

Donald N. Jensen is Research Associate at the Institute for Research on Educational Finance and Governance, Stanford University School of Education

Robert A. Kagan is a Professor of Political Science at the University of California, Berkeley.

William K. Muir is Professor of Political Science at U.C. Berkeley and former chairman of that department.

Eugene Bardach is a Professor of Public Policy at the Graduate School of Public Policy, U.C. Berkeley.

Paul Berman is a Professor of Public Policy at the Graduate School of Public Policy, U.C. Berkeley.

Paul Berman is a consultant who has written extensively on education policy.

Guy Benveniste is a Professor of Education at U.C. Berkeley.

Richard Elmore is a Professor of Public Policy at the University of Washington.

William H. Clune is Professor of Law at the University of Wisconsin.

Paula Fass is Associate Professor of History at U.C. Berkeley.

David Neal is on the Faculty at the University of New South Wales, Australia.

Thomas Griffin is an attorney specializing in school litigation. He was formerly the General Counsel for the Department of Education, State of California.

Doris Fine is a consultant in the fields of education and health policy. She received her PhD in education and sociology at U.C. Berkeley.

Index